Architecture and Tourism

Architecture and Tourism

Perception, Performance and Place

Edited by
D. Medina Lasansky and Brian McLaren

Oxford • New York

English edition
First published in 2004 by
Berg
Editorial offices:
1st Floor, Angel Court, 81 St Clements Street, Oxford, OX4 1AW
175 Fifth Avenue, New York, NY 10010, USA

Berg is the imprint of Oxford International Publishers Ltd.

Library of Congress Cataloging-in-Publication Data
Architecture and tourism : perception, performance and place / edited
by D. Medina Lasansky and Brian McLaren.
    p. cm.
    Includes bibliographical references and index.
    ISBN 1-85973-704-8 (cloth) — ISBN 1-85973-709-9 (pbk.)
    1. Architecture and tourism. I. Lasansky, D. Medina. II. McLaren,
Brian D., 1956–
    NA2543.T68A73 2004
    720'.1'03—dc22

                                                        2004006122

British Library Cataloguing-in-Publication Data
A catalogue record for this book is available from the British Library.

ISBN 1 85973 704 8 (hardback)
      1 85973 709 9 (paperback)

Typeset by JS Typesetting Ltd, Wellingborough, Northants.
Printed in the United Kingdom by Biddles Ltd, King's Lynn.

www.bergpublishers.com

Contents

List of Figures   vii

Notes on Contributors   xi

Foreword
Davydd J. Greenwood   xv

Introduction
D. Medina Lasansky   1

Part I Defining a Canon and a Mode of Perception

1   Reproduction, Fragmentation, and Collection: Rome and the
Origin of Souvenirs
Sarah Benson   15

2   Early Travelers in Greece and the Invention of Medieval
Architectural History
Kostis Kourelis   37

3   Performing Abroad: British Tourists in Italy and their Practices,
1840–1914
Jill Steward   53

Part II Politics of Pilgrimage

4   From Tripoli to Ghadames: Architecture and the Tourist Experience of
Local Culture in Italian Colonial Libya
Brian McLaren   75

5   A Pilgrimage to the Alcázar of Toledo: Ritual, Tourism and
Propaganda in Franco's Spain
Miriam Basilio   93

Contents

6 Authenticating Dungeons, Whitewashing Castles: The Former Sites of the Slave Trade on the Ghanaian Coast
Cheryl Finley 109

Part III Packaging Place

7 From Photographic Fragments to Architectural Illusions at the 1929 Poble Espanyol in Barcelona
Jordana Mendelson 129

8 Simulating France, Seducing the World: The Regional Center at the 1937 Paris Exposition
Deborah D. Hurtt 147

9 Tourist Geographies: Remapping Old Havana
D. Medina Lasansky 165

Part IV Performance

10 Sweetening Colonialism: A Mauritian Themed Resort
Tim Edensor and *Uma Kothan* 189

11 Doing it Right: Postwar Honeymoon Resorts in the Pocono Mountains
Barbara Penner 207

Part V The Postmodern Imagination

12 New Politics of the Spectacle: "Bilbao" and the Global Imagination
Joan Ockman 227

13 Egypt on Steroids: Luxor Las Vegas and Postmodern Orientalism
Jeffrey Cass 241

Index 265

List of Figures

1.1   Souvenirs for sale at the Colosseum, Rome. Summer 2002.
      Photograph by author.   16
1.2   Giovanni Battista Piranesi, *Veduta della vasta Fontana di Trevi*, from
      Vedute di Roma, mid-eighteenth century. By permission of the
      Division of Rare and Manuscript Collections, Cornell University
      Library, Ithaca, NY.   20
1.3   Pietro Bracci, collection of cameo casts reproducing objects and
      architecture from the Vatican Museum, c. 1775. White plaster.
      Research Library, The Getty Research Institute, Los Angeles
      (2001.M.27).   22
1.4   Pietro Martire Felini, woodcut depicting Michelangelo's *Moses* from
      San Pietro in Vincoli, reprinted from *Trattato Nuovo delle Cose
      Maravigliose Dell'Alma Città Di Roma*, Rome, 1615, p. 337. Rome,
      American Academy Library.   26
1.5   Roman workshop, collector's cabinet with eighteen views of Rome,
      last quarter of eighteenth century. Wood, bronze, and painted
      parchment. Rome, Museo di Roma.   32
2.1   Saint Nicholas in Mystras, from André Couchaud, *Choix d'églises
      byzantines en Grèce*, Paris: Didron, 1842, pl. 27, fig. 1.   45
2.2   View of Kyparissia, from William Gell *Narrative of a Journey in the
      Morea*, London: Longman, Hurst, Rees, Orme, and Brown, 1823, p. 1.   47
2.3   Gabriel Millet (second row, second from left) aboard the Troude on
      April 1893, from Georges Radet, *L'histoire et l'oevre de l'École
      française d'Athènes*, Paris: A. Fontemoing, 1901, fig. 254.   49
3.1   Postcard c.1905. Paul Hey "Tourists on the Rialto bridge", published
      by Otto Zieher, Munich. Collection of the author..   60
3.2   "Snob writing his name on the roof of Milan cathedral" (Doyle,
      1854: 56). Author's copy.   62
3.3   Postcard c. 1905. "Moonlight scene of the Forum" (advertising Rome
      and back for 10 guineas. Published by Thomas Cook). Collection of
      the author.   68
4.1   Libyan Tourism and Hotel Association, Vacation Combinations in
      Libya, travel brochure, 1937. Collection of the author.   78

4.2 Oriental dance, Arab Café, Suq al-Mushir, Tripoli, Libya, postcard,
1937. Collection of the author.   82

4.3 Florestano Di Fausto, Hotel Rumia, Jefren, Libya, 1934. The
Mitchell Wolfson Jr. Collection – Fondazione Regionale Cristoforo
Colombo, Genoa, Italy.   85

4.4 Florestano Di Fausto, Hotel Nalut, Nalut, Libya (1935), postcard,
1937. Collection of the author.   86

4.5 Florestano Di Fausto and Stefano Gatti-Casazza, Hotel
Ain-el-Fras, Ghadames (1935), postcard, 1937. Collection of the
author.   88

5.1 Postcard reproducing a view of the patio prior to 1936, from the
series *Alcázar de Toledo, 24 Vistas en Huecograbado*, Madrid: Jalón
Angel and Hauser y Manet, ca. 1939. Collection of the author.   94

5.2 Postcard reproducing a view of the patio following the siege, from the
series *Alcázar de Toledo, 24 Vistas en Huecograbado*, Madrid: Jalón
Angel and Hauser y Manet, ca. 1939. Collection of the author.   94

5.3 Fernando Álvarez de Sotomayor, Portrait of General Francisco
Franco, 1940. Collection Museo del Ejército, Madrid. Reproduced
with permission.   103

6.1 View of cannons, Cape Coast Castle, Ghana, 1999. Photograph by
author.   112

6.2 Plaque of remembrance and wreath, Elmina Castle, Ghana,
1999. Photograph by author.   117

6.3 Reenactment, Cape Coast Castle, Ghana, 1999. Photograph by
author.   122

7.1 Bird's eye view of the Poble Espanyol. Courtesy of the Arxiu Històric
del Col.legi d'Arquitectes de Catalunya.   130

7.2 Photograph taken by Francesc Folguera and Ramón Reventós of the
Utebo Bell Tower in Zaragoza, Aragaon. Fons Plandiura LP-26-45.
Courtesy of the Photographic Archive of the Arxiu Històric de la
Cuitat de Barcelona. Photographed by Jordi Calafell.   136

7.3 Photograph of the Poble Espanyol in construction, with the
reconstruction of the Utebo Bell Tower visible in the background.
Courtesy of the Photographic Archive of the Arxiu Històric de la
Cuitat de Barcelona.   137

7.4 Women and pony rides in the main plaza of the Poble Espanyol.
Courtesy of the Arxiu Històric del Col.legi d'Arquitectes de
Catalunya.   138

8.1 Regional Center, aerial view. *Album Officiel*, Paris: La Photolith,
1937.   148

8.2   Regional Center, master plan. *Rapport Général*, vol 8, Pl. 3,
      Paris: Imprimerie Nationale, 1938–1940.   152
8.3   Regional Center, Alsace Pavilion. Postcard, 1937. Collection of the
      author.   154
8.4   Regional Center, Flandre-Artois Pavilion. *L'Architecture, Centre
      Régional*, Paris: Alexis Sinjon, 1937.   155
9.1   Tourists seated on the steps of the Habana Capitol, 2002, negative
      (left) and the reworked print (right). Collection of the author.   166
9.2   Habanaguanex brochure advertising the historic hotels operated
      by the Office of the Historian, Habana, c. 2002.   175
9.3   Plaza Vieja, Habana. The restored fountain is visible behind the
      fence.   180
10.1 Painting of Creole Plantation Landscape, lobby of Sugar Beach
      Resort, Mauritius. Photograph by Tim Edensor, 2002.   191
10.2 Themed performance on the steps of the Manor House, Sugar
      Beach Resort, Mauritius. Photograph by Uma Kothari, 2002.   193
11.1 Promotional material for Honeymoon Haven, 1967. Collection of
      the author.   210
11.2 Pocono Gardens Lodge advertisement, *Bride's Magazine*, Spring
      1965, p. 244.   215
11.3 Cove Haven advertisement, *Bride's Magazine*, April/May 1966,
      p. 181.   216
11.4 Honeymooners at Honeymoon Haven, 1967. Collection of the
      author.   217
12.1 Frank Gehry, Guggenheim Museum, Bilbao.   228
12.2 Cover, *New York Times Magazine*, with story on the Guggenheim
      Bilbao by Herbert Muschamp, September 7, 1997. © *The New
      York Times*. Reproduced by permission.   232
13.1 Luxor Las Vegas, 1996. Courtesy of Luxor Las Vegas.   242
13.2 Talking camels at entrance to Giza Galleria, Luxor Las Vegas,
      2002. Photograph by author.   249
13.3 Series of columns at Pharaoh's Pheast Buffet, Luxor Las
      Vegas. Photograph by author.   256
13.4 Lobby mural behind registration desk, Luxor Las Vegas,
      2002. Photograph by author.   258

Contributors

Miriam Basilio is Curatorial Assistant in the Department of Drawings, The Museum of Modern Art, New York. She gained her doctorate in the History of Art from the Institute of Fine Arts, New York University, in 2002. Her chapter is drawn from part of her Ph.D. dissertation, *Re-Inventing Spain: Images of the Nation in Painting and Propaganda, 1936–1943*.

Sarah Benson has recently been Visiting Assistant Professor of the History of Art at Cornell University. Her contribution to this volume stems from a publication she is preparing on representations of Rome in prephotographic mass media. She is currently researching the role of printed images and optical instruments in cultural exchanges between the courts of Siam and Europe.

Jeffrey Cass is Associate Provost and Associate Professor of English at Texas A & M International University. He has published several essays on the work of nineteenth-century women writers, including Maria Edgeworth, Elizabeth Gaskell, Mary Shelley, and Charlotte Brontë, as well as a variety of articles on popular culture. At present, he is writing a book on Orientalist representations in the fiction of Romantic and Victorian women writers.

Tim Edensor teaches cultural studies at Staffordshire University. The author of *Tourists at the Taj* (Routledge, 1998) and *National Identity, Popular Culture and Everyday Life* (Berg, 2002), he is currently working on a book and a Web site concerning British industrial ruins. Tim has written widely on tourism as well as contributing articles and chapters about walking, football, Scottishness, automobilities and ruralities.

Cheryl Finley is a Visiting Assistant Professor in the Africana Studies Department at Cornell University as well as an art critic, columnist and curator specializing in photography, African American art, cultural heritage tourism and the politics of memorialization. Her publications include *From Swing to Soul: An Illustrated History of African American Popular Music from 1930 to 1960* (Elliott & Clark, 1994) and *Imaging African Art: Documentation and Transformation* (Yale Art Gallery, 2000).

Contributors

Davydd J. Greenwood is the Goldwin Smith Professor of Anthropology and Director of the Institute for European Studies at Cornell University. His major publications include *Unrewarding Wealth: Commercialization and the Collapse of Agriculture in a Spanish Basque Town* (Cambridge University Press, 1976) and *Introduction to Action Research: Social Research for Social Change*, co-authored with Morten Levin (Sage, 1998). His interest in tourism arose from the direct confrontation in Ondarribia (Spain) between tourism development and the agricultural and fishing economies.

Deborah Hurtt is Visiting Assistant Professor of Art History at the University of Oregon. She has published an article, "Conciliation and Controversy: Regionalist Architecture at the 1937 Paris Exposition," in the *Proceedings of the Genius Loci International Symposia: Architecture between Regional Identity and Globalization* (2002). A recent Fellow at the Camargo Foundation in Cassis, France, she is completing her doctoral dissertation, *A Watershed of Rivalries: Regionalist Architecture at the 1937 Paris Exposition*, in the Department of Architectural History at the University of Virginia.

Uma Kothari is a senior lecturer in the Institute for Development Policy and Management at the University of Manchester, UK. She teaches in postgraduate programs in Development Studies and carries out research into the relationship between colonialism and international development, labor migration, and gender and industrialization.

Kostis Kourelis is an archaeologist and architectural historian with field expertise in Greece, Italy and Tunisia. He received a Master's degree in architecture and a Ph.D. in archaeology at the University of Pennsylvania. He currently teaches art history at Clemson University. He co-authored *Houses of the Morea: Vernacular Architecture in the Northwestern Peloponnese 1205–1955* (Melissa Publishing House, Athens, 2003). His chapter in this volume is part of a larger study on the settlements of the medieval Mediterranean.

Medina Lasansky teaches the history of architecture and urbanism at Cornell University. Her research focuses on the intersection of politics, popular culture, and the built environment. She is the author of *The Renaissance Perfected: Architecture, Spectacle, and Tourism in Fascist Italy* (Penn State University Press, 2004) as well as essays on topics ranging from the pink plastic lawn flamingo to the Venetian in Las Vegas. Her interest in tourism stems from an ongoing study of the way in which popular conceptions of the Renaissance resonate with scholarly constructions of the period.

Contributors

Brian McLaren is an assistant professor in the Department of Architecture at the University of Washington, where he teaches architectural history, theory and design. He has presented his research at numerous academic conferences, including the Society of Architectural Historians and the College Art Association. His research on tourism in Italian colonial Libya is being published by the University of Washington Press in a series entitled "Studies in Modernity and National Identity."

Jordana Mendelson is an assistant professor of modern European art and the history of photography at the University of Illinois, Urbana-Champaign. In addition to numerous articles and exhibitions on Spanish art and culture, she was guest editor for a special issue on "From Albums to the Academy: Postcards and Art History" for *Visual Resources* (2001). Her book *Documenting Spain: Artists, Exhibition Culture and the Modern Nation, 1929–1939* is forthcoming.

Joan Ockman teaches history and theory of architecture in the Graduate School of Architecture, Planning and Preservation at Columbia University, where she also directs the Temple Hoyne Buell Center for the Study of American Architecture. She recently organized a major conference and exhibition at Columbia entitled "Architourism: Architecture as a Destination for Tourism," now in preparation as a book. She is the editor of the award-winning volume *Architecture Culture 1943–1968: A Documentary Anthology* (Rizzoli, 1993).

Barbara Penner is a lecturer in architectural history and theory at the Bartlett School of Architecture, University College London. Her recent doctoral dissertation, *Alone at Last: Honeymooning in Nineteenth-century America*, at the London Consortium in England, explores the intersections between public space, architecture and private lives. With Jane Rendell and Iain Borden, she has co-edited *Gender Space Architecture* (Routledge, 2000).

Jill Steward teaches cultural history at Northumbria University in Newcastle upon Tyne and is a member of the European Urban Culture Group. Recent publications deal with the history of tourism in Central Europe and the growth of spa culture. Her chapter in this volume is related to her current interest in the relationship between the emergence of the travel press and formation of social and cultural identities.

Foreword

Davydd J. Greenwood

The humanistic and social scientific study of tourism has an intriguing history. The largest peacetime movement of human beings in human history and a leisure time activity of the vast majority of academics, tourism, until recently, received relatively little analytical attention compared with the rivers of academic ink spilled over other phenomena of more modest scale. Tourism operators, related business ventures, and consulting firms, generated a significant literature on how to structure and profit from tourism activities, but usefully critical and analytical perspectives have appeared only slowly.

As someone who was an early contributor to the social science literature on this subject (Greenwood 1972, 1977), three decades ago I was fascinated by the inattention to a phenomenon that seemed to be overwhelming Europe. It was perhaps the first time I noticed the ability of so many social scientists to ignore practices that dominate the world scene while giving meticulous attention to subjects that only they and their immediate circle of colleagues could possibly care about.

While the dissociation between the research agendas of the social sciences and the humanities and the strongest concerns of society at large has itself been revealed as an historical and political product (Furner 1975; Ross, 1991), tourism research has had a harder time coming into its own because as academics we are ourselves inveterate tourists and prefer to be "off duty" when enjoying our leisure by traveling to see monuments or historical locations and to enjoy good food and beautiful landscapes. Whatever the cause, despite a variety of interesting efforts (Smith 1977, 1989; MacCannell 1976, 1999; and *The Annals of Tourism Research*), the subject of tourism only began to receive systematic critical attention in the 1990s. The current volume is part of this trend and demonstrates the riches to be found in the analytical study of tourism.

A diverse and lively group of scholars with a primarily architectural and historical focus here provides a variety of ways to problematize tourism as a set of practices to examine, compare, and critique. The chapters display a wealth of options and approaches demonstrating how rich the topic is and how the study of tourism immediately moves us beyond tourism itself and into the analysis of many broader social, historical, and artistic questions.

The authors are particularly attentive to the impact of tourism on the built environment. Precisely because tourism is such an enormous industry, which involves monuments, museums, other special purpose buildings, hotels, and the management of both urban and rural spaces, architects and planners cannot afford to be innocent of the twists and turns of the multiple logics of world tourism.

In this regard, although the present book can be read as an interesting set of monographic essays on tourism, it is also an examination of the mutual impacts of tourism and architectural and design practice. It will be particularly useful in sensitizing new generations to the complexities of the tasks they perform in the world of practice and the impossibility of realizing unmediated professional preferences.

As many of the chapters show, tourism is not a phenomenon that can be controlled by professionals. Tourism always stands within the cultural and economic politics of its environments and the historical development of the tastes and habits of the ever-increasing numbers of tourists. At the end of the day, the preferences of the tourists and how they are changing must be understood and this requires sustained social and cultural analysis. Expressed more directly still, tourism is a co-creation of tourists, entrepreneurs, and designers, and this threesome needs to be understood together.

The readers of this work will delight in the diversity of cases and materials the editors and authors have brought together. The range is enormous, from historical monuments and ruins to contemporary tourist constructions, the world of souvenirs, managed tourist experiences, and completely artificial environments with historico-cultural references. There are chapters dealing with the historical genesis of tourism tastes and practices, the search for "places" of cultural power, and the development of ways of touring and recounting. Others focus on the links between tourism and colonialism and tourism and war memorials. Still others reveal the highly dynamic impact of tourism in creating "cultural" sites or refashioning sites to create particular ways of seeing as in the Poble Espanyol of Barcelona and the Paris Exposition of 1937. There are also chapters dealing with the highly intentional creation of the kinds of simulated cultural experiences that are by now quite familiar to tourists.

The multiplictity of perspectives and types of tourism locations and experiences is a great strength of this book. Each chapter rewards a close reading and the quality and diversity of the scholarship the editors have brought together is excellent, and the editors have taken on the additional job of giving the collection a coherence of focus that can serve as an invitation. Through a broad array of intriguing cases, the editors try to pique the interest of readers to the point that they too join the process of analyzing tourism as a phenomenon and as a set of culturally generative practices.

The predominant focus is on the built environment but it is by no means the sole focus. The behaviors and practices that give significance to tourism processes and the effective monumentality of places – souvenir collecting, image creation, the "capture" of places through reification, mythologization, are dealt with extensively. The editors and the authors are also cognizant, as anyone must be, of the intrinsic historicity of the world of "cultural" tourism with its emphasis on ruins, monumentality, *emblemata*, the "sacredness" of certain spaces. The essays that engage in comparisons of the past and present give wonderful examples of the complexity of cultural/historical referentiality and reflexivity in tourism activities.

Many of the essays reveal the multiple ways tourism attempts to commoditize locations and items through fragmentation and reification. The world of engravings, photos, and souvenirs is a part of this process in which the tourist is permitted to imagine that s/he has captured and taken home a "piece" of history, much in the way an explorer brings home artifacts and proofs of her experience. This is a particularly important and complicated dimension of large-scale tourism because it involves the reconciliation of seemingly contradictory elements in a capitalist world system.

Monuments and history were not built for consumption in the sense of converting them into commodities and carrying them away. However, commodification in tourism has long involved a variety of reifications of objects that "prove" that an act of presence has taken place, an act that enhances the status of the tourist once back at home. The book as a whole makes a good case that cultural tourism depends on more than just creating experiences of places. These experiences have to be bought and sold and also reified in photos and souvenirs. Without these materials, the "proof" tourists require would involve dismantling the location they visit in the very act of visiting it. As a consequence, the apparently trivial souvenir market and flashing cameras can be understood as an essential element in the sustainability of touristic practices.

A number of the chapters show how the cultural and historical processes of tourism have been divorced from the past in the form of the creation of intentional tourist attractions. At this margin, the difference between historical authenticity and contemporary entertainment venues/theme parks becomes hard to define. Cases like the preservation of the Alcázar of Toledo with its grim Civil War history, the conversion of slave dungeons into tourist attractions in Ghana, and the presentation of indigenous culture in Libya are riveting. The old honeymoon resorts of the Poconos or the refashioning of old Havana to meet current demands reveal much both about the imaginings of architects and planners about the character of tourism demand and something about the images tourists carry away with them from such "managed" experiences.

The past is still key to the ability of contemporary tourist environments to attract, but now in a very different way from the past. The distinction between entertainment venues and historicity itself becomes difficult to maintain. Little seems to stand in the way of a Mauritian themed resort, if it lasts long enough and attracts enough visitors, or Disneyworld, for that matter, becoming historical sites to revere like Notre Dame Cathedral; it might be only a matter of time.

Thus, the chapters trouble the long-held commonsense distinction between culturally "authentic" locations and "staged" cultural experiences, following the evocative and highly productive insights of Dean MacCannell (1976, 1999) and Edmund Carpenter (1973). Perhaps this issue has bothered anthropologists and historians dealing with tourism the most because we have tended to rely on the notion of "authenticity" as a kind of unmediated cultural value. We, and I include myself (Greenwood 1977, 1989), have criticized what we take to be "falsifications" of the "authentic" as some kind of betrayal of our notions that the past is "value-full" while the present is culturally valueless.

The authors and editors of this collection have moved beyond that kind of crude dichotomization and offer us a more dynamic and troubling view of the multiple forms of cultural productivity involved in contemporary tourism. In this regard, their perspective embodies the more nuanced and challenging notions in a constructivist framework and links closely to the complex polemics over authenticity, not just in tourist cultures, but in issues of ethnic and national identities (for example, Hobsbawm and Ranger 1992; Clifton 1996; Santiago-Irizarry 2001). Perhaps this also helps us understand why academics are so uncomfortable with this subject because we routinely anchor our own sense of value in an appreciation of the past as somehow both more real and superior to the present and future.

The chapters provide much to think about. The remarkable success of the Guggenheim in Bilbao cries out for explanation, if architects aspire to similar successes. Is it the sheer brilliance of the building and the genius of the architect, the bedraggled urban location, or something else what has made this museum such a world event? Is the Luxor Casino a success architecturally or just a monumental cash register? Why does the selective eye choose some elements of Rome for attention and discard others as valueless? How would we even approach such questions with intellectual rigor? In this regard, the book challenges social and cultural analysts to make higher demands on themselves when it comes to tourism. Thus the book must be understood as a tract in favor of a broader approach to tourism, one anchored in the linkages between the complexities of the built environment, the cultural systems of the people who use the environment, the complexities of what counts as "historical" and monumental, and the diverse and divergent schemes we bring to our appreciation of the past, present, and future.

Given the number of innovations and challenges the editors and authors provide, this book reminds me of a group of spelunkers exploring a magnificent and little-known cave. Each flashes a bright beam of light on some feature of the cave and shows us things that give us much to think about. No single contribution is a

complete picture and additional elements of the cultural/historical world of ι
can and should be added. The cumulative effect of the chapters is, however, ιο give
the reader a sense of the scope and cultural importance of tourism and the scale of
the task ahead if we are to begin to grapple with it more effectively both within and
beyond architectural education and practice. In this regard, the book is
simultaneously a rich source of knowledge and experience and a successful call to
the job ahead of us.

As part of the job ahead, it is clear that scholars will need to increase their
efforts in distinguishing between types of tourism. Tourists who seek out historical
sites and monuments and who revel in their awe over the past are but a small
portion of the total array of tourists. A much greater magnitude of economic
activity is generated by resort and theme-park tourism carried out in entirely new
and purposefully artificial environments. We know intuitively that such modern
tourist sites are different from the ruins of Rome, but how and why and to what end
do we make the distinctions? And how should architects be trained to deal with
them? Between all of the examples cited in this volume there are distinctions that
matter. What are they, how do we make them, and how do and should these
differences affect our analytical strategies?

Tourism studies are also strongly pervaded by a variety of moral judgements
that do not turn out to be easy to manage. The goodness of the past turns out to be
based on a very complex process of fragmentation, distinction, and cultural
construction that makes the past intelligible in some kind of contrastive relationship (positive or negative) with the present. Why do we believe that a visit to a
"real" historical site (whose reality the authors show to be a construction as well)
is somehow culturally deeper than a day at a resort built to imitate a Mayan
pyramid? Is mass tourism less "cultural" than elite tourism or is it just a matter of
the class prejudices of those of us who write about these differences? Is our own
personal desire as off duty scholars to take our kids to the Magic Kingdom some
kind of embarrassing sign of a lack of "class" from which we must flee? Is this why
we have remained aloof from a critical analysis of tourism?

Physical mobility also needs more attention. Part of the origin of contemporary
tourism in the "Grand Tour" centered on its direct association to social class. Only
people of means had the resources to transport themselves from place to place at
will, suspending the daily process of making a living in favor of leisure, travel, and
observation. Now mass tourism through mass transportation has made the "classi-
ness" of tourism much more complex. Running around in this messy world are
notions that cruise-ship tourism is for lower class people than a visit to Mont San
Michel, that staying at a bed and breakfast is "classier" than staying at a Best
Western, even at a major historical site, and so on. Class and tourism are inextricably intertwined and the world of the built environment necessarily embraces all
of these dimensions. But how to embrace this self-consciously and use these

understandings to promote good architectural practices and more satisfactory experiences for both travelers and residents still remains problematic.

No one can complete this book without being impressed and excited by both the accomplishments of this group of scholars and the promises of the field they are opening up to us.

References

Carpenter, Edmund (1973) *Oh, What a Blow that Phantom Gave Me!* New York: Henry Holt & Company.

Clifton, James (1996) *The Invented Indian: Cultural Fictions and Government Politics*, New Brunswick NJ: Transaction Publishers.

Furner, Mary (1975) *Advocacy and Objectivity: A Crisis in the Professionalization of American Social Science*, Lexington: University of Kentucky Press.

Greenwood, Davydd (1972) "Tourism as an Agent of Change: a Spanish Basque Case", *Ethnology*, 11(1): 80–91.

Greenwood, Davydd (1977) "Culture by the Pound: An Anthropological Perspective on Tourism", in V. Smith (ed.), *Hosts and Guests: The Anthropology of Tourism*, Philadelphia: University of Pennsylvania Press, pp. 129–38.

Greenwood, Davydd (1989) "Culture by the Pound: An Anthropological Perspective on Tourism", in V. Smith (ed.), *Hosts and Guests: The Anthropology of Tourism*, second edition, revised, Philadelphia: University of Pennsylvania Press.

Hobsbawm, Eric and Terrence Ranger (1992) *The Invention of Tradition*, Cambridge: Cambridge University Press.

MacCannell, Dean (1976) *The Tourist: A New Theory of the Leisure Class*, New York: Schocken Books.

MacCannell, Dean (1999) *The Tourist: A New Theory of the Leisure Class*, Berkeley: University of California Press.

Ross, Dorothy (1991) *The Origin of American Social Science*, Cambridge: Cambridge University Press.

Santiago-Irizarry, Vilma (2001) *Medicalizing Ethnicity: The Construction of Latino Identity in Psychiatric Settings*, Ithaca: Cornell University Press.

Smith, Valene (ed.) (1977) *Hosts and Guests: The Anthropology of Tourism*, Philadelphia: University of Pennsylvania Press.

Smith, Valene (ed.) (1989) *Hosts and Guests: The Anthropology of Tourism*, second edition, revised, Philadelphia: University of Pennsylvania Press.

Introduction
D. Medina Lasansky

Today, tourism is among the world's largest industries. Millions of tourists traipse around the globe, visiting sites, taking photographs, reading guidebooks, straining to listen to tour guides and purchasing postcards and souvenirs. The past two centuries have witnessed an increase in the commodification of tourist sites across the world. Everything from historic monuments to exotic holiday destinations have been redesigned and packaged for mass consumption via various venues of mass media, scholarship and popular myth. As a result, the histories of specific structures, spaces and sites have been reconceptualized. Some have been preserved and celebrated, whereas others are left to decay. In this process of amplification and suppression, buildings, cities and entire countries have been remapped by tourism initiatives to serve political, cultural, economic and scholarly goals.

Considering these profound transformations, this book examines the reciprocal relationship between the modern practice of tourism and the built environment. The two have been inseparable since the first pilgrims descended upon Rome. Drawing upon case studies in Cuba, Ghana, Greece, France, Italy, Libya, Mauritius, Spain and the US and spanning from the Renaissance to today, this book will explore touristic experience, representation and meaning of place within distinct cultural contexts. From the former sites of the slave trade on the Ghanaian coast to the urban renewal of Old Havana, from the honeymoon resorts in the Poconos to the postmodern spectacle of Bilbao, from the world's fairs of the 1930s to the colonialist encounters in Italian Libya, the essays provide provocative insights into the practice of tourism and the conception of place. Chapters will show how photography, film and souvenirs have been deployed to help mediate and mythologize specific sites. They will also explore how tourist itineraries, behavior and literature are institutionalized for popular consumption in order to support larger cultural objectives. The contributors to this volume understand tourism as both a process through which sites are experienced and a cultural force that has shaped and interpreted them. Tourism is simultaneously a cultural product and producer of culture – an important catalyst in a complex and nuanced process of cultural exchange that is centered in the experience of the built environment.

The sociologist Dean MacCannell was among the first to make inroads into the study of tourism with his 1973 article on staged authenticity and seminal book three years later (MacCannell 1976). As a result of his groundbreaking research

MacCannell provided the foundation for what has since emerged as a field of study led by scholars from the disciplines of anthropology, cultural geography, cultural studies, economics, political science and sociology as well as pioneering journals such as *The Annals of Tourism Research.* These scholars have contributed to the development of a language for discussing tourism. Judith Adler (1989) introduced us to the origins of sightseeing – or the visualization of the travel experience which is dependent upon eyewitness observation. Political scientist Dennis Judd coined the useful phrase "tourist bubble" to describe the way in which cities have constructed clean, safe and attractive self-contained environments in which to entertain (Judd and Fainstein 1999). Gregory Ashworth and J. E. Tunbridge (1990) identified the practice of "heritage tourism" to explain the use of history as a key component in constructing a marketable image for cities. Borrowing from Michel Foucault's notion of the gaze, the sociologist John Urry (2002) has argued that the processes by which the tourist gaze is constructed, reinforced, and authorized is culturally specific. More recently, Claudia Bell and John Lyall (2002) invented the idea of the "accelerated sublime" to identify a genre of extreme tourist experiences ranging from bungee jumping to propelling.

Contemporary artists have also undertaken compelling studies of tourism. Between 1987 and 1994, Magnum photographer Martin Parr (1995) photographed tourists at tourist sites. He artfully captured the prescribed ways in which tourists interact with sites; pretending to hold up the Leaning Tower of Pisa, mesmerized by the audio tour at the Pantheon (see cover photo), riding gondolas through canals in Venice. As such, his photographs provide an intelligent critique of tourist performance. As art critic and activist Lucy Lippard (1999) has noted, the artist, like tourism itself, teaches people how to see. In her study of tourism, art and place Lippard led the reader on a trip across the US, from coastal Maine to Los Angeles, pointedly questioning the production and perception of sites on what she termed "the beaten path." She extolled contemporary artists such as Zig Jackson and Coco Fusco whose work prompts the spectator to self consciously question practices of tourist consumption.

As Mark Neumann (1999: 11) has noted, tourist sites are discursive spaces that involve planners, politicians, preservationists, artists, entrepreneurs and tourists. The discourses of these various groups in turn "frame and tame" sites for tourism, laying out "a culturally created spectacle" that can be consumed and experienced in different ways by different people. It is this very complexity that is so compelling. As Tim Edensor (1998: 3) pointed out in his provocative study, *Tourists at the Taj*, "tourism cannot be typified by one type of motivation, societal function or social condition. Rather, it consists of a range of practices and epistemologies which emerge out of particular cultural locations." In his study of the ways in which tourists both make sense of the Taj Mahal and perform on site, Edensor demonstrates that multiple and often competing narratives can be sustained within any single locus. Like Neumann, he reintroduces a sense of agency to touristic practice – overlooking the frequent derision that is applied by those who dismiss the tourist as a blind consumer or innocent victim of commodified, homogenized and globalized culture.

In the process of interviewing and photographing people on site, both Neumann and Edensor situate the history of their respective sites (the Grand Canyon in Neumann's case) within the context of their contemporary use. Integral to an understanding of any given site, monument, or event, is an understanding of how its meaning and use has changed over time. Tourism encourages scholars to ask the diachronic questions. Do contemporary tourists to Rome, for example, continue to seek out the same monuments that their predecessors did centuries before. If so, how has the purpose and meaning of their visit changed over time? Have their activities on site been modified? Is the mode of perception any different? Several of the chapters in this volume pursue such avenues of inquiry and in so doing begin to lay the groundwork for a more complete understanding of the history and meaning of these sites. From this, a more complicated history of architecture will emerge – one that is fluid and continuous as well as diachronic and interdisciplinary.

It has been suggested by architect and theorist Aldo Rossi (1982) among others, that architecture is simultaneously a site, event and sign. It is both the structure in the traditional sense of the word, as well as the way in which that structure is deployed. Inherent to this definition is the process of mediation. In this collection of essays, buildings and spaces are understood as a set of activities, products and attitudes that complement and complete both the design and meaning of specific sites. Architecture is thought of as a process of reception, representation, use, spectacularization and commodification as meaning is mediated by the rhetorical strategies of diverse media and performance. If, as Marc Augè suggested during a presentation at the Architourism conference at Columbia University in 2002, it is the travel agents and advertisers that play the most important role in constructing popular perceptions about destinations, then the concept of the architect needs to be expanded to include a greater array of "designers." The concept of architectural materials also need to be broadened to include propaganda, policy and print. The essays in this volume do just that. Despite being a book that is about architecture, few architects are mentioned. Rather than focusing on the role of the architect, these essays will show how photography, film and souvenirs have been deployed to help mediate and mythologize specific sites – thereby blurring the boundaries between so-called "high" and "low" culture.

This idea of mediation is in fact nothing new. Tourism and its related materials and strategies have roots that date to the Renaissance, if not before. After all, it was Piranesi, in the seventeenth century, who helped mythologize the popular image of Rome by using his printed views to construct a shared pan-European understanding of the city. The forced perspective, unattainable viewpoints and aggrandized sense of ancient ruins that were exploited in his engravings success-fully renarrated the image of Rome for a disparate audience (Cooper 1999). As Piranesi's oeuvre makes clear, there is a nuanced relationship between the con-struction of an architectural image, the actual site, its history and the way in which it is consumed. The essays collected in this volume will develop this notion in distinct and provocative ways. By focusing on ideas of process and function rather than the iconography of the fetishized object, the study of tourism thus provides for the reconceptualization of architectural space.

As we have seen in this cursory summary of the field, the studies that have explored tourism and questions of architecture and urban space have for the most part been undertaken outside the discipline of architectural history. While the anthropologists, sociologists and political scientists have been dealing with the issue of tourism for several decades, those interested in architectural history have all but ignored it. Only recently have architectural historians begun to assess the role played by tourism in the history of the built environment. Annabel Jane Wharton's (2001) study on the Hilton hotels and their role in disseminating an image of American culture during the Cold War is one such example. This very volume emanates from a session on the topic held in 2002 at the annual meeting of the College Art Association in Philadelphia. It was at this event, that a group of young scholars (Finley, Hurtt, Kourelis, Mendelson, and Penner) convened to present their work. In each case tourism was a central, rather than a tangential element, to the story told. A symposium organized the following fall by Joan Ockman at Columbia University's Buell Center for the Study of American Archi-tecture expanded the parameters of the dialogue. By situating architectural histori-ans and architects at the center of an interdisciplinary discussion of "Architourism: Architecture as a Destination for Tourism," Ockman's symposium provided the opportunity to explore themes recurrent in tourism practices. Thus, it is important to note that while the present volume is an attempt to address the apparent lacuna in the history of architecture concerning the relationship between tourism and built space, it is simultaneously a part of a rich body of emerging contemporary scholar-ship examining this connection (see also Coleman and Crang 2002 and Crouch and Lübbren 2003).

Defining a Canon and a Mode of Perception

The first three chapters in this volume explore the paradigms of tourist practice within the framework of particular canons and itineraries. All three address the importance of the on-site visit – and the idea of either reporting home about what was seen through drawings, travel accounts, and purchased souvenirs. In this process, tourists emerge as discoverers, their records and purchased souvenirs as proof of their experience and their itineraries as a guide for subsequent tourists. As we shall see, these rhetorical strategies provided discursive paradigms that remain in effect today. Invariably all three chapters point out how the study of tourism complicates the practice of architectural history. Considering that the discipline of art and architectural history and the practice of tourism both have their roots in the bourgeois culture of the nineteenth century, it becomes clear that the historian must now question to what extent his or her scholarly canon of monuments, modes of perception, and discourse are products of tourism. As will become clear, scholarly and tourist topographies overlap and feed off of one another – thereby raising interesting questions regarding the interdependence of scholarship and the practice of tourism.

The first chapter tackles the consummate tourist destination of Rome. In this, Benson charts the mass mediation of the city's image by analysing tourist souvenirs dating from the Renaissance to today. She unveils the logics of reproduction, fragmentation and collection that are inherent to the souvenir as a means of determining how Roman souvenirs have helped standardize a collective set of memories for those who had never been to the city and a familiar topography for those who had. Prints, guidebooks and other material artifacts not only codified a canon of architectural sites, but they helped condition tourist expectations and perception. In her nuanced reading, Benson interprets the souvenir as a site of negotiation between myth and reality, local and global patrimony. In many ways Rome provides the benchmark for other cities. As one of the most mediated sites, its tourism rhetoric has been continually finessed and widely imitated over the course of centuries. Benson shows that almost every aspect of the tourism industry and experience can find its roots in Early Modern Rome.

Kourelis, in turn, analyses the corpus of published accounts of nineteenth-century visitors to the Peloponnese. In the process of visiting ancient archeological sites, these travelers encountered an unexpected array of medieval sites. Given the recent interest in the Middle Ages in their native lands, such sites were of particular fascination. As Kourelis convincingly argues, their travel writing reveals the invention of a visual and literary vocabulary to describe the sites that in turn laid the foundation for medieval architectural history as we know it today. In so doing, Kourelis provocatively demonstrates that there is a reciprocal relationship between the academic study of monuments and the phenomenon of tourism.

In the third chapter, Steward explores the ways in which Italian sites were imaged, perceived and experienced by British tourists during the nineteenth and early twentieth centuries. For the new social groups (the middle classes, women and entire families) traveling during this period, travel was as much a process of self-discovery as it was of site discovery. As Steward shows, tourism provided the means by which to construct and maintain bourgeois social identities. Drawing

upon published letters, travelogues and guidebooks, she shows how tourist practices were unofficially regulated by a series of behavioral codes. Tourists busily
sketched, took photographs and wrote home as a process of self-edification. The
genre of the guidebook proved to be important in this process of acculturation –
helping travelers plan itineraries and scripting them on how to look when on site.
Etiquette books that identified the perils of travel were also important, particularly
for the increasing number of single women travelers. Together the widely circulated images, personal narratives and guides established a familiar place – and as
Steward argues, therein lay the success of the longstanding love affair with Italy.

Politics of Pilgrimage

In case studies of Franco's Spain, the Italian colony of Libya, and coastal Ghana,
Basilio, McLaren and Finley each explore the way in which tourism has been used
as a tool to strengthen a sense of cultural identity within a highly politicized
context. Basilio and McLaren tackle the relationship between Fascism and tourism,
and Finley addresses the contemporary politics of African American roots tourism.
In each case tourism provides the means to rewrite and reclaim the past.

Basilio's essay shows how the Toledo Alcazár became a highly charged symbol
during the Franco regime. As the site of an important siege during the Spanish
revolution, the structure was declared a national monument in 1937. It was heavily
publicized and featured on the new *Rutas de Guerra*, or war itineraries. As she
elucidates, the Alcazár played an important role in the Fascist retelling of history.
By celebrating the site (formerly associated with the Catholic Kings Charles V and
Phillip II as well as Alfonso VI, the eleventh-century king who conquered Toledo
from the Muslims) the Fascist leaders were able to draw a parallel between the
Spanish empire and the new political order. More precisely, by celebrating the
Civil War martyrs who died on site, Franco and his followers were able to establish
a modern corollary with the country's earlier Christian crusaders. By transforming
the Alcazár into a modern pilgrimage destination, the regime was able to recast
tourism as a form of sanctified patriotism.

McLaren analyses the tourist development of Libya during the latter part of the
1930s. Of particular importance to the tourism experience during this period was
an itinerary that led from Tripoli south to Ghadames on the edge of the Sahara, an
itinerary that provided a coordinated system of travel and accommodation. Drawing upon contemporary scientific research into Libyan culture and the presentation
of this same culture in tourist literature, McLaren's chapter examines the role
played by the architecture of this system in creating a seamless tourist experience.
As he shows successfully, through a metonymic relationship with their historical
settings, tourist facilities served as ethnographic museums where the Libyans and

their culture could be experienced outside of the passage of time. Ultimately, the tourism development of Libya served as an instrument of cultural politics for the Italian fascist empire.

Finley, in turn, tackles the racial politics of heritage tourism and preservation today. She studies the adaptive reuse of the castles and forts of coastal Ghana. As former centers of the slave trade between Africa and the Americas, the sites are highly charged. She shows how the restoration of these sites and their subsequent transformation into tourist destinations has been a part of a conscientious project to reclaim history. She suggests that it is the controversial nature of their history that has propelled these structures to become alluring destinations within a global tourism market, specifically for African American tourists – who seek to relive the experience of their ancestors' enslavement. Not surprisingly, the sites are heavily dependent upon on-site interactive role-playing activities – designed to recreate the experience of those who were enslaved. As such they are important devices of memory making for a tourist clientele that is eager to connect with its African roots.

Packaging Place

Several studies explore the way in which architecture has been deployed to cultivate a sense of shared civic, regional, or national patrimony. In case studies of Spain, France and Cuba, Mendelson, Hurtt and Lasansky demonstrate how new identities are constructed for these sites by visualizing a distinct architectural character. In each case, the final product results from a conflation of existing and imagined sites – reconstituted into a new whole that is presented to the public through various mass-media strategies.

Mendelson takes the case of the Poble Espanyol, a village of structures representing the different regions of Spain, constructed for the 1929 International Exposition in Barcelona. With the hope of creating the image of a unified nation and defining Spain as a viable tourist attraction for Spanish and foreign travelers alike, the Spanish dictator General Miguel Primo de Rivera commissioned the architects Ramón Reventós and Francesc Folguera to create an utopic town that was a collage of traditional vernacular architecture from the entire country. As Mendelson shows, photography was central to this process. If Mendelson's study shows how the image of a nation was constructed by creating the image of a unified whole, Hurtt's analysis of the Regional Center, built for the 1937 Paris International Exhibition, shows the opposite. With the support of the Touring Club of France, the center was designed to spawn touristic interest in the provinces during a period of economic depression. For the sake of the exhibition the country was divided into seventeen regions – each of which was identified by a unique architectural form. In the end, a small village, comprised of these representative structures, was built at the Regional Center. Through this popular venue the public was encouraged to become familiar with the new France. The center was successful as the mythical regional constructs continue to define the regions of France today. Both sites provide an utopic collage of regional architectural forms. And it was through visiting them that the public was encouraged to become familiar with ideal native topographies – whether Spanish or French. In each case the ultimate goal was to seduce people to travel as architectural tourism served as a vehicle by which the government could efficiently and effectively unify a disperse population.

Lasansky in turn studies the way in which Old Havana has been re-mapped. Under the direction of the city historian Eusebio Leal, Habana Vieja has been gutted, restored and packaged for tourism. Thanks to Leal's initiatives and the authority granted him by Fidel Castro, architecture has emerged as the single most important element in the city's transformation from a decaying, overcrowded and congested center to an attractive historic center complete with museums, sumptuous hotels, shopping districts, fine restaurants and attractive pedestrian zones. Developing an attractive historic center is the leading technique of economic development in many cities today (Ashworth and Tunbridge 1990: 262). In this regard, Havana is no different. As a part of his urban preservation program, Leal has launched a glossy journal, published a series of heavily illustrated books and produced several documentary films. The construction of such a mediascape is a common feature of urban development projects, but Havana's case is unique. The city has applied the techniques familiar to Western capitalist economies to underwrite a series of socialist projects. In other words, tourism is used as a means of supporting healthcare, education, and housing for the local population.

Performance Enclaves

As sociologist Henri Lefebvre (1991) has noted, monuments are bodily lived experiences. The chapter by Edensor and Kothari, as well as that by Penner, make this eminently clear. Both essays deal with themed resort destinations that function as theaters for tourist performance. As Edensor and Kothari demonstrate in their study of the popular Sugar Beach resort on the island of Mauritius, the resort functions as a stage set – complete with managers, choreographers and directors that collaborate to design an environment in which the foreign and exotic have been successfully domesticated. This so-called "smooth space" is designed to contain and occupy tourists – encouraging them to follow certain performative role-playing conventions. Yet, as the authors convincingly argue, this space is not a dystopian environment that simply creates a collage of colonial stereotypes. Rather, it is a complex place that has re-scripted the past – marshalling architectural space and specific materialities to create an "authenticity of affect" (rather than an authenticity of historical accuracy). The attention to textures, temperatures, atmospheres, smells, sounds and tastes ultimately creates a very sensual understanding of place that is anything but dystopic. As such it is assuredly authentic. As Edensor (1998: 6) himself has noted, accounts of tourism often fail to investigate how tourists feel and understand on site. This study nicely compensates for such oversight.

Penner has also written the story of the senses back into the discourse of architecture. In a study that explores the intersection of popular culture, commercial entrepreneurialism, and sex, she analyses the peculiarly American phenomenon of honeymoon resorts. She argues that the heart-shaped bath tubs, mirrored ceilings and dramatic lighting found at honeymoon sites in the Pocono mountains of Eastern Pennsylvania create an environment of sexual fantasy that has become integral to the construction and maintenance of a hegemonic idea of romance. Honeymoon tourism dates to the mid-nineteenth century, but Penner shows how the landscape of intimacy has, since the 1960s, become increasingly defined by the commercial interests of resorts such as Cove Haven. She shows how the image of desire constructed in the popular press has been reinforced by the resort architecture so as to set the stage for choreographed intimacy to unfold. In the process of her study Penner shows how the discourse of architecture takes place outside the professional journals – on television, in the pages of bridal magazines, and in the full-color spreads of *Playboy* – and demonstrates what we can learn from these venues. Like the Mauritius resort, the honeymoon sites are places that are to be understood with the body. With her attention to the satin sheets, lush textiles and bubble baths, Penner draws attention to the sensual and tactile nature of architecture. Like Edensor and Kothari, Penner confirms that there is still something auratic about architectural experience.

The Postmodern Imagination

Jeff Cass and Joan Ockman discuss sites that are wonderful examples of the postmodern spectacle; the Luxor Casino in Las Vegas and the Guggenheim Museum in Bilbao. The success of these sites is largely indebted to mass media, but they are not mass produced. These buildings are irreproducible events that must be experienced to be understood. They are rooted in the cultural specificity of their respective sites and, as such, decry any sense of a globalized homogeneity.

Cass proves that we can still lean from Las Vegas. The strip that Venturi Scott Brown, and Izenour (1972) analysed in their celebrated study is now long gone, but it has been replaced by one that is equally compelling. As Cass shows in his study of the Luxor casino and hotel complex, the new Las Vegas is one of heightened distinctions designed to entice a more diverse audience. The past has been select- ively reconstructed for those seeking useful pleasures – or edutainment. The tourist in turn is encouraged to become an intrepid explorer – investigating the archeo- logical ruins that lie beneath the desert floor, the replica of King Tutankhamen's tomb and the authenticated antiquities on sale in the gift shop. The porosity of boundaries between fiction and reality creates an ambiguity that forces tourists into the role of amateur archaeologists sleuthing through contested spaces. As the cultural geographer J. B. Jackson (1980: 91, 98) has argued, such environments represent a new type of monument as well as a new way of interpreting and presenting history. And yet they have deep roots. As we have seen in the case of nineteenth-century Greece, archeological and tourist discovery are once again intertwined in Las Vegas.

It is appropriate that the volume concludes with an essay on the Guggenheim Bilbao, a building that has become emblematic of a new kind of tourism. While architecture has been a destination of tourists for centuries (and the case of Rome confirms this), Bilbao embodies a new kind of architourism that focuses on modern architecture. As a recent feature in the *New York Times* reported, this is the latest tourism trend complete with specialized tour companies and tour guides (June 2002). Not surprisingly, a recent edition of *Let's Go Spain* features an image of the Guggenheim Museum on its cover. As Ockman demonstrates the context and reception of any built work goes well beyond its actual form. Nowhere is this more evident than in the case of Bilbao where the building has been mediated by the popular press – ranging from architecture critic Herbert Muschamp's public declaration of the structure as "a miracle" on the cover of the *New York Times Magazine* to the frequent television commercials in which the museum figures as the chic high-style backdrop. The frequently seen images of the museum show the glimmering new structure blossoming at the end of a city street – a celebration of urban rebirth. These images deceptively belie the site's physical, economic and cultural complexity. Indeed, as Ockman reveals, Bilbao subverts the narrative of global homogenization.

Bilbao, like the other sites discussed in this volume, represents distinct cases of cultural production and consumption that draw upon private and public construc- tions of place. They reveal the means by which the viewer has been conditioned to perceive – to see and interpret. By making visible the various cultural mechanisms that are responsible for constructing the image, myth and meaning of individual buildings, specific sites, entire cities and countries, the essays place the topic of architectural tourism within the broader context of architectural historiography as well as contemporary politics, culture and socio-economics. As we will see, the study of tourism allows the intangible to become tangible, the invisible visible, and the boundaries of the discipline porous enough to include things that are not seen but tasted, heard, smelled and touched. Ultimately each of the chapters will encourage us to reflect upon the built environment, its construction and mediation. We would like to suggest that these essays provide new paradigms for the understanding and examination of architecture, architectural history, and attitudes towards both. The implications of this research extends beyond the scope of the case studies presented in this volume as the chapters raise as many questions as they answer.

Acknowledgements

The authors would like to thank the anonymous reviewers of the manuscript for their feedback as well as the gracious editorial assistance of Kathleen May at Berg Publishers.

References

Adler, Judith (1989), "Origins of Sightseeing", *Annals of Tourism Research*, 16(1): 7–29.

Ashworth, G. J., and Tunbridge, J. E. (1990), *The Tourist-Historic City*, London: Belhaven Press.

Bell, Claudia and Lyall, John (2002), *The Accelerated Sublime. Landscape, Tourism, and Identity*, London and Westport CT: Praeger.

Coleman, Simon and Crang, Mike (eds) (2002), *Tourism: Between Place and Performance*, New York: Berghahn Books.

Cooper, Tarnya (1999), "Forgetting Rome and the voice of Piranesi's 'Speaking Ruins'", in Forty, Adrian and Kuchler, Susanne (eds), *The Art of Forgetting*, Oxford and New York: Berg.

Crouch, David and Lübbren, Nina (eds) (2003), *Visual Culture and Tourism*, Oxford and New York: Berg.

Edensor, Tim (1998), *Tourists at the Taj. Performance and Meaning at a Symbolic Site,* London and New York: Routledge.

Jackson, J. B. (1980), *The Necessity for Ruins*, Amherst: University of Massachusetts.

Judd, Dennis R. and Fainstein, Susan S. (eds) (1999), "Constructing the Tourist Bubble", in Judd, Dennis R. and Fainstein, Susan S. (eds), *The Tourist City*, New Haven and London: Yale University Press.

Lefebvre, Henri (1991), *The Production of Space*, London: Blackwell Publishers.

Lippard, Lucy (1999), *On the Beaten Track: Tourism, Art and Place*, New York: The New Press.

MacCannell, Dean (1973), "Staged authenticity: arrangements of social space in tourist settings", American Sociological Review, 79: 589–603.

—— (1976, 1999 reprint), *The Tourist: A New Theory of the Leisure Class*, Berkeley: University of California Press.

Neumann, Mark (1999), *On the Rim. Looking for the Grand Canyon*, Minneapolis and London: University of Minnesota Press, 1999.

Parr, Martin (1995), *Small World A Global Photographic Project, 1987–1994*, Heaton Moor: Dewi Lewis Publishing.

Rojek, Chris and Urry, John (1997), *Touring Cultures. Transformations of Travel and Theory*, London: Routledge.

Rossi, Aldo (1982), *Architecture of the City*, translated by Diane Ghirardo and Joan Ockman, Cambridge MA: MIT Press.

Urry, John (1990, 2002 reprint), *The Tourist Gaze: Leisure and Travel in Contemporary Societies*, London: Sage.

Venturi, R., Scott Brown, D. and Izenour, S. (1972), *Learning From Las Vegas,* Cambridge MA: MIT Press.

Wharton, Annabel Jane (2001), *Building the Cold War. Hilton International Hotels and Modern Architecture*, Chicago and London: University of Chicago Press.

Part I
Defining a Canon and a Mode of Perception

–1–

Reproduction, Fragmentation, and Collection: Rome and the Origin of Souvenirs

Sarah Benson

The Colosseum, whose very name suggests the monumentality of ancient artifacts, becomes an ashtray (Figure 1.1). Michelangelo's *Pietà* serves nicely as a paperweight. The Etruscan she-wolf, whose transfer from the Lateran to the Capitoline Hill by Pope Sixtus IV in 1471 asserted papal dominance over Rome's civic government, can be pocketed and relocated anew without meaning anything of the kind. Vistas of the city expand not across the horizon but across the 4 inches of a standard postcard. Itineraries unfold, even before they can be experienced, within the imperative pages of guidebooks. Conversion of one's own image into souvenir format is prompted and foreshadowed by a pyramid of Kodak film. Tiny Trevi Fountains, scaled to be backdrops for goldfish, do scant justice to the eighteenth-century original, which is barely contained by its piazza in central Rome. This microcosm is for sale at the many souvenir stalls that flourish around Roman tourist sites today. Such an assortment of Roman cultural achievement writ small can seem delightful, or tasteless and impious, but in any case frivolous. It is not at souvenir stalls that serious scholarship on Roman art and history is carried out. The topography of this tabletop, however, has much to tell us of the ways that Roman monuments and Roman history have been made available for study and inspection for the past 500 years.

It was about 500 years ago that an array of replicas of Roman art and architecture first assumed an important role in shaping the canon of Roman monuments known to scholars and tourists today. This is because new technologies for the reproduction of printed images (woodcuts and engravings pulled from mechanical presses), and to a more limited extent the casting of bronze or plaster objects, made the broad dissemination of facsimiles of Roman monuments possible for the first time. This chapter will focus on the sixteenth to eighteenth centuries, a period that I will refer to as Early Modern, when both the canon of monuments and modes of representing them were largely set. These Early Modern images and objects – both in two- and three-dimensions – functioned as what we would now call "souvenirs" and shared a set of characteristics inherent to their media and representational conventions and to their use by those who purchased or contemplated them.[1]

Figure 1.1 Souvenirs for sale at the Colosseum, Rome. Summer 2002. Photograph by author.

These souvenirs were mass-produced. Centuries before the Industrial Revolution, the objects that we will discuss here could, at least theoretically, be issued in unlimited and identical batches. Any one viewer could assume that an unlimited number of other people (in other words, an early mass public) had access to the same visual experience. The souvenir, furthermore, as its name makes clear, stands in a special relationship to memory. The kind of memory these souvenirs embody is not interior and personal but outward and collective. The production and consumption of souvenirs functioned to provide prefabricated, standardized memories of Rome even to those who never set foot within the city walls. As an enabler of collective memory, the souvenir is also a collected object. Souvenirs, above all, are reproductions; they translate the objects that they represent both in scale and in format. The translated monument becomes portable and can be – even should be – dislocated from its original urban context as a stage in the process of generating knowledge.

The souvenir, therefore, is not just a byproduct of modern leisure culture. It is an epistemological tool; it has affected which monuments we know and just as importantly how we experience and study them. This we can best see by tracing the origins of souvenirs to Early Modern Rome. This period saw a symbiotic development of Rome as a cultural destination and the development of souvenir genres and formats in general. I will argue that the particular case of Rome and its souvenirs can serve as a model for studying souvenir development in other places and times while also showing how, in the particular historical context of sixteenth- to eighteenth-century Europe, souvenirs of Rome fit into a pattern of the rising prominence of vision in gathering, recording, and disseminating knowledge that took place across a wide variety of disciplines. Through a series of analyses of Roman souvenirs, this essay will explore the workings of three important areas in which the subject matter of souvenirs interacts with their means of production and their use by viewers. These points of intersection are reproduction, fragmentation, and collection.

Reproduction: Relics, Ruins, and the Portable City

Rome is the paradigmatic tourist city. Its tradition of tourism dates back to the Middle Ages, when the aspiration of European Christians was to make the pilgrimage to this holiest of cities, the seat of their Church. In the Renaissance and Baroque periods, the city's double patrimony of ancient ruins and new monuments presented instead a cultural attraction to artists, architects, antiquarians (early archaeologists), historians, and the first nobles to set out on the Grand Tour from points north. Rome's transition from pilgrimage to tourist destination was in part a conscious one. By the sixteenth century, the temporal power of the papacy was at a low, and the success of Protestant Reform had undercut Rome's importance as capital of Christendom. A succession of popes undertook to refashion their city as a cultural capital (Krautheimer 1985), a mission in which they were abetted by the first visual mass medium: the printed image. Its development in the fifteenth century corresponds chronologically with this shift in Rome's role on a European stage and with an increasing interest in the monuments of Rome's ancient past on the part of scholars and dilettantes. The establishment of printing workshops within the city produced images of the Roman cityscape, its monuments, and its antique collections that were disseminated across Europe. In hindsight, this publicity campaign seems to have been quite effective. It defined a canon of Roman monuments that persists today, while also establishing Rome as a historical site of global importance. Indeed, one lingering effect of Rome's early souvenir industry is the grandiose and often-repeated claim that "This country holds 70 percent of the recognized works of art in the world," as the author of a recent memoir and accolade of life in Rome enthused (Epstein 2000: 245). The key here is the recognizability of works of art, for this is the legacy of the souvenirs that canonized Rome's monuments from the sixteenth century on. Whatever the percentage of great art to be found in Rome, thanks to the souvenir, the greatest percentage of Rome's great art is found outside Rome, albeit in duplicate form. From the sixteenth to eighteenth centuries, Rome was almost certainly the most represented city in Europe, and therefore also the most mediated.

The form that duplicate monuments took in the Early Modern period included primarily plaster casts and small bronze replicas of ancient sculptures and printed and painted views of ancient and contemporary art and architecture. Among the first to make a selection of ancient Roman monuments widely available was Sebastiano Serlio, whose *Third Book* (1540) on architecture included plans, sections, elevations, and views of ancient structures in crisp black-and-white woodcuts. Antoine Lafréry, a Frenchman who immigrated to Rome in the early sixteenth century, published printed maps and views of ancient and modern Rome. Illustrated guidebooks, also published from the mid-sixteenth century on, collected Roman art and architecture in small handy volumes. Michelangelo's statue of *Moses*, as we will see later, developed its reputation in this context (Figure 1.4).

By the eighteenth century, such replicas were so widely dispersed that Europeans of the upper and mercantile classes grew up amongst Roman souvenirs. This was the experience of Johann Wolfgang von Goethe, who indicated both the range of Roman souvenirs and their power to shape shared memories when he compared the actual cityscape to "everything long familiar to me in paintings and drawings, copperplates and woodcuts, in plaster and cork" (Goethe 1994: 104). Despite the inclusion of cork models and oil paintings among the Roman souvenirs in the Goethe household, the major work of broadcasting Roman monuments was done by mass-produced souvenirs. It was these, by dint of their easy reproducibility and general affordability, that brought Rome to the rest of Europe and to the world (on the Early Modern market for prints see Bury 1985; Landau and Parshall 1994; Robinson 1981; on casts of Roman antiques see Haskell and Penny 1981).

Before looking more closely at Early Modern souvenirs, it will be helpful to understand their relationship to earlier, medieval, representations of Rome. Reproducibility, a defining characteristic of the souvenir in general, has particular importance in the development of souvenirs of Rome. Reproducible souvenirs put in their first appearance by the twelfth century, in the form of cast metal badges that pilgrims brought home from holy sites. Impressed onto the surfaces of the badges were attributes of the saint to whom a shrine was dedicated or schematic representations of saints themselves. Such simplified signs allowed the badge to proclaim its provenance after the pilgrim returned home, proof of the successful completion of a sacred journey. This was a primary purpose of the pilgrim badge, but it was also an ersatz, a stand in for more precious objects that could not be taken away from the shrine. The ultimate source of the souvenir is, in the context of European travel, the holy relic. The conversion of singular relics into reproducible commodities provided a precedent for a similar conversion of Roman art and architecture as interest in antiquities grew in the fifteenth and sixteenth centuries. Nor did the canon of ancient architecture and sculpture emerge out of nowhere.

Medieval descriptions of Rome, the most influential of which was the *Mirabilia Urbis Romae* ("Marvels of the City of Rome," composed around 1140), had already singled out, among other monuments, the Colosseum and Pantheon, the Vatican Obelisk, the Column of Trajan, and the equestrian statue of Marcus Aurelius, all still prominent in Rome and its souvenirs. The Early Modern period inherited these two traditions – textual guides to Rome that could be reproduced exactly but in limited numbers and without visual aids, and reproducible but visually crude pilgrim badges. In joining these two with new technologies for the exact reproduction of images, the Early Modern souvenir was born.

Souvenir prints and casts demonstrate that reproducibility, a mere material convenience, in fact had important epistemological, rhetorical, and social consequences. One epistemological consequence is that mechanically reproduced souvenirs came to be associated with the authentic presentation of the cityscape. This was authenticity in the eye of the beholder, based upon expectations and previous exposure to other souvenir images. In his famous essay "The Work of Art in the Age of Mechanical Reproduction," Walter Benjamin defined authenticity as unique to original works of art. I would propose that souvenir images furnish a competing authenticity by mediating our experience of monuments (Benjamin 1935, 1968). The authenticity of an original monument is, in a sense, built on a framework of the reproductions that have established its reputation. In some cases a less accurate image might seem more authentic, as in the case of Giovanni Battista Piranesi's eighteenth-century etchings. Modern postcards of Rome still struggle to capture the views presented in his prints. His viewing angles elude the modern cameraman, however, because Piranesi's images are part documentary record and part collage (Campbell 1990: 14). The *Veduta della vasta Fontana di Trevi* (*View of the Vast Trevi Fountain*, Figure 1.2) shows the latest urban monument (the fountain was completed only in 1762) in an ensemble with the church of Santi Vicenzo e Anastasio and a cluster of ruins along the lower left-hand border. Because of the cramped nature of this square, there is no spot from which one can see both fountain and church façade in their entirety. As for the ruins, these are a complete fabrication on Piranesi's part. The view is not just an optimization but also an invention.

Why then would Piranesi's views have been considered authentic? The simplest answer is that repeatability bred familiarity. Many people who saw souvenir prints had never been to Rome and so based their expectations entirely on these representations. Piranesi meets longstanding expectations by alluding to a triple canon of ancient, contemporary, and sacred Roman patrimony. Since the time of Lafréry, these three had been the focus of Roman souvenir imagery, if not always within the same view. Eighteenth-century viewers would have been further encouraged to see this image as authentic by the inclusion of model tourists within the view (Cooper 1999), who offer by proxy a first-hand visual experience. Like the monuments, the

Figure 1.2 Giovanni Battista Piranesi, *Veduta della vasta Fontana di Trevi*, from *Vedute di Roma*, mid-eighteenth century. By permission of the Division of Rare and Manuscript Collections, Cornell University Library, Ithaca, NY.

inhabitants of his cityscape are of different types. Only the wealthy figures, however, seem to pay proper attention to their surroundings (Benson 2002). The actual viewers of the print might very well not belong to this privileged class. Sold singly rather than in bound volumes, Piranesi's prints would have been affordable for the middle classes, and the displays outside of prints shops were a free source of public visual entertainment in an era before television and film. Yet no matter who or where we are, Piranesi not only transports us to Rome but also allows us to identify with the elegant model spectators, treating us to a first-hand view of Rome through their eyes. We also then engage in a tourist masquerade, assuming the social position of the elegant traveler.

Piranesi also claims authority through his handling of the medium. He combines different kinds of lines in this view, corresponding to the different types of monument. The newly completed fountain is described with a strict linearity that, since the publication of Serlio's sixteenth-century treatise on architecture, was the norm for expository images. It is a kind of line that is native to the print medium, both woodcuts and engravings. Not only were prints the most common format for informational images, but the steadiness of hand required to execute engravings lent itself best to straight lines. Piranesi renders the imaginary ruins in a different linear style, comprising what read as hasty squiggles. He is able to do this because he is working in etching, a technique not of engraving directly into a copper plate but of drawing with a stylus on a waxy ground. The plate is then dipped in acid, which eats away the metal exposed by the stylus. By using this kind of line, which seems to have been dashed off hurriedly, as if on site, Piranesi exploits the ability of a repeatable medium to give the impression of first-hand observation. The look of the print becomes a kind of collage, as though both an etching and engraving, the first technique suggesting standardization and comprehensibility, the second immediacy. The representational conventions used by printmakers functioned rhetorically to declare their own authenticity. The mechanically produced look suggested the accuracy of knowledge recorded and copied by machines; repeatability was becoming the test of truth claims.

Format, therefore, is important to the statements made by souvenirs. In the case of Piranesi, this includes a visual vocabulary developed for translating archeological remains into reproducible linear models. Roman antiquities themselves suggested other souvenir formats that are peculiar to that city. In the late eighteenth century, tourists to Rome could purchase volumes of cameo casts that reproduced famous works of art and architecture. An opening from one such set, by the workshop of Pietro Bracci, reproduces highlights from the Vatican collections, including the celebrated *Laocoön*, at lower left (Figure 1.3). Cameos were an ancient art form that were highly prized and avidly collected by Early Modern connoisseurs and dilettantes. Bracci makes his souvenir images of Rome doubly precious by rendering them as cameos. Reproduction was always an act of translation, just as in these hybrids. Not all translations were valued equally, however. Sometimes it was the ability to capture the detail and complexity of the model that was sought, as in Piranesi's images. Curiously, the cameo is very poor for this purpose and yet was a favored form of translation. This is because in this case it is the matrix, the cameo format, as much its contents that is being reproduced. Bracci has found to a way to manufacture fresh antiquities.

The social implications of souvenir reproduction are made explicit by the English artist William Hogarth (1753) in a polemical and pedagogical tract titled *The Analysis of Beauty: Written with a View of Fixing the Fluctuating Ideas of Taste.* Two plates folded into the book illustrate the aesthetic principles of the artist. The first of these includes as prime exemplars of good design a canon of ancient sculptures that had been familiar to European audiences already for one or two centuries: the *Belvedere Torso* (discovered before 1432), the *Laocoön* group (discovered 1506), the *Apollo Belvedere* (discovered before 1509) the *Belvedere Antinous* (discovered 1543), the *Farnese Hercules* (discovered by 1556), and the *Venus de' Medici* (discovered 1638). Hogarth's mission, or at least so he tells us, was a vulgarizing one. The essay is addressed to those who are daunted by "pompous terms" and "marvelous collections" and for "ladies as well as gentlemen,"

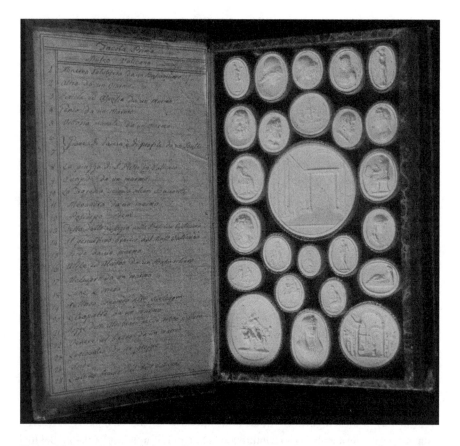

Figure 1.3 Pietro Bracci, collection of cameo casts reproducing objects and architecture from the Vatican Museum, c. 1775. White plaster. Research Library, The Getty Research Institute, Los Angeles (2001.M.27).

whereas Hogarth expresses grave doubts about painters and connoisseurs as judges of beauty (Hogarth 1753: 3).

This enterprise is not as radical as Hogarth would make it seem. Even as Hogarth seeks to overturn a contemporary crisis in taste, he acknowledges that ancient works are better known than modern ones (Hogarth 1753: 64, 66; Haskell and Penny 1981: 80). He implies the ubiquity of souvenir images of ancient sculpture when he apologizes for the cursory nature of his illustration. He assumes his readers to have these canonical sculptures either in their mind's eye or before them as reproductions. Hogarth's reliance on previous reproductions is also demonstrated by the plate itself, in which the ancient statues appear reversed. This effect was more likely to occur when printmakers copied other prints than when they worked from originals, either because they had lost track of the correct orientation or because fidelity to the model was less of an issue at this remove. The very reason, therefore, that he is able to use a virtual collection of Roman sculptures as the basis of his thesis is that these had long since been vulgarized in souvenir replicas. Ownership of an original ancient work might be a rare mark of privilege, but copies of these same monuments were already in the hands of the middle classes, primarily as inexpensive prints that could be pasted into journals or on walls or that came as illustrations in inexpensive guide books.

If anything, the creation of a canon of Roman art shows the influence of a low-budget mechanical medium on the tastes of the upper classes; the circulation of inexpensive replicas shaped the desires and directed the collecting practices of the wealthy. Historians of antiquarianism and tourism to Rome have tended to characterize the appreciation for Roman monuments as an upper-class phenomenon, which became available to a wider public only in the era of train and automobile travel. If we focus only on those who made the journey to Rome or who could afford to collect original works of art, then we are indeed dealing with an exclusive club. In the eighteenth century, we speak not of mass tourism but of the Grand Tour, a journey undertaken by people of means (usually young men) in order to complete their education. The primary destination was Italy, and within Italy, Rome, where exposure to ancient art was presumed to round out the aesthetic and ethical judgments of the youthful mind.

Souvenirs, however, were more portable than people. It was to take centuries before technologies of rapid and mass transportation caught up with the technology for the mass production of images. By the time they did, souvenirs had established how the new middle-class arrivals, long familiar with replicas, were to experience Rome and Italy. E. M. Forster satirized the experience of early mass tourism to Italy in his novel *A Room with a View*. An expatriate Anglican minister, Mr. Eager, tells the young heroine, Lucy: "We residents sometimes pity you poor tourists not a little – handed about like a parcel of goods from Venice to Florence, Florence to Rome, living herded together in pensions or hotels, quite unconscious of anything that is outside Baedeker, their one anxiety to get 'done' or 'through' and go on somewhere else" (Forster 1908; 1993: 64). The portability of the modern tourist, who rushes through a country as though it were a checklist, was foreshadowed by souvenirs. The Baedeker guide that exasperates Mr. Eager was but the latest incarnation of sixteenth- and seventeenth-century printed guidebooks, like that of Pietro Martire Felini (1610, 1615). Felini's pocket-sized guide, like others in this genre, was published not in Latin but in a modern language (in this case Italian). Both its small format and use of the vernacular increased its accessibility, while the content established itineraries and prompted recognition through carefully framed illustrations that set monuments apart from the cityscape or architectural settings (Figure 1.4). We have souvenirs to thank or blame as well for the tenacity of the checklist itself; they established Roman monuments, both ancient and

Early Modern, as the first universally shared, mass-produced visual culture of Europe.

This period from the sixteenth century to the eighteenth both established souvenir formats and set the canon that holds to this day. Admittedly, many of the works of art that were central to Early Modern ideas of taste have ceased to be universally known, even among visitors to Rome. It can no longer be taken for granted, as it could in Hogarth's day, that any literate audience would recognize the *Laocoön* or *Apollo Belvedere*. Yet although the period of greatest urban growth in Rome has been that from the late nineteenth century to today, almost nothing has been added to the canon. Souvenir Rome ceases to expand after the eighteenth century, with the inauguration of the Trevi Fountain. The absence of modernist architecture from current souvenir offerings may be political, because these were generally Fascist projects, and the social and political reasons for the absence of modern Rome from the souvenir market are doubtless complex. The point I wish to underscore is simply that there is little souvenir mediation of nineteenth- and twentieth-century Rome. Modern tourists to Rome will have to cope with buses, subways, Vespas, and cellphones, but the Rome they can take away in postcards, snow globes, statuettes, or charm bracelets, and probably the one they have come to experience, is still that of Piranesi.

Or is it? The representational tradition to which Piranesi belongs was important not only for establishing a canon of monuments and a set of ideal vantage points from which to view them. By visualizing Rome, Early Modern souvenirs helped to establish the importance of vision itself to pre-Enlightenment epistemology. Despite the apparent similarity of Early Modern to modern souvenirs in terms of which monuments they represent, their original connection to Early Modern intellectual discourses has been all but lost to us. In her essay "Origins of Sightseeing," Judith Adler argues that the emphasis on seeing came late to the practice of tourism. The original educational function of the Grand Tour privileged discourse over vision, which might be faulty in the untrained. She then follows, in precisely the period we are considering, an increasing emphasis on sight in texts associated with Italian travel, which she links to an "overarching scientific ideology" (Adler 1989: 24). The aim of this scientific approach was the cataloging of all the works of nature and of artifice through observation. Roman souvenirs should not be overlooked as important players in this project. The visual record shows a strong interest in examining contemporary and historical Roman monuments from at least the sixteenth century. The mode in which these circulated, as reproducible images, set Early Modern standards of authenticity and reliability for visual information and opened up visual investigation to a broad social spectrum.

Fragmentation: *Moses* Misplaced and the *Torso* Disemboweled

The forms and formats of souvenirs might well have developed differently had not their primary object of representation been Roman monuments. Likewise, Rome would not have become the most important tourist destination for Early Modern Europe and a taste for things Roman would not have been the mark of aesthetic discernment without the aid of the souvenir industry. The creation of a monument, therefore, is something that happens off site as much as on site. It is not architects alone who built Roman monuments but the makers of souvenir casts and prints as well.

Consider in this light the case of the tomb of Pope Julius II (r. 1503–13), which was installed in the church of San Pietro in Vincoli in the 1540s. A tomb is by its very intent and nature a monument. This was certainly the intent of Julius himself. This Renaissance pope was the patron of Michelangelo's Sistine Chapel ceiling frescos, and he had foreseen for himself an oversized burial chapel to be designed again by Michelangelo and erected in the crossing of Saint Peter's basilica in the Vatican. The plan never came to fruition, as the presence of Julius's much-abbreviated cenotaph in San Pietro in Vincoli attests. As though to redress this wrong, from the sixteenth century on, souvenirs have worked to eradicate the structure of tomb and church. If San Pietro in Vincoli takes up any space at all in the itineraries of tourists, the imaginations of Rome's inhabitants, or in the indices of art-historical treatises, it is primarily as the location of Michelangelo's *Moses* – or rather, as the original location. The *Moses* figure, unlike the tomb of which it is part and the church in which it is housed, exists in countless reproductions as an isolated statue. He appears thus in the editions of the *Cose Maravigliose dell'Alma Città di Roma* (*Marvels of the Holy City of Rome*), as in the volume published by Felini in 1610 (Figure 1.4). Giovanni Paolo Panini's eighteenth-century painting, now in the Louvre, of an ideal collection of the monuments of modern Rome is one of many other Renaissance and Baroque representations to picture the *Moses* this way. This pattern of isolation and decontextualization of the *Moses*, established in Early Modern souvenir imagery, survives in their modern descendents. *Moses* remains one of the stock plastic figurines for sale at Roman souvenir stalls. Many modern guidebooks continue to use the *Moses* to illustrate their entry on this church. This is true for the image-centric *Eyewitness Travel Guides*, which one sees in use everywhere in Rome today, as well as for the text-heavy *Blue Guide* (*Eyewitness Guides* 1993, 2000: 4, 170; Macadam 1998: 203).

A more peculiar use of the *Moses* is as the cover illustration for art historian George Hersey's *High Renaissance Art in St. Peter's and the Vatican*. Although physically *Moses* is across town, the book cover maps him onto a plan of Saint Peter's basilica. The reader is thereby invited to consider the statue in the context of Renaissance artistic production at the Vatican complex. This is not an erroneous

Figure 1.4 Pietro Martire Felini, woodcut depicting Michelangelo's *Moses* from San Pietro in Vincoli, reprinted from *Trattato Nuovo delle Cose Maravigliose Dell'Alma Città Di Roma*, Rome, 1615, p. 337. Rome, American Library.

context. There are numerous historical and art-historical reasons for including the *Moses* in a work on St. Peter's, the site for which he was originally destined. For art historians San Pietro in Vincoli is primarily the site of disappointment; Michelangelo never completed what would have been a masterwork, and poor Julius's effigy wound up in the wrong St. Peter's. Nevertheless the choice of *Moses* as a cover emblem suggests the sway of several centuries of souvenir reproduction that have severed *Moses* from his architectural context. The *Moses* statue has come, via the synecdoche of souvenirs, to stand for the whole tomb of which it is a part, for San Pietro in Vincoli as a whole, or instead Saint Peter's in the Vatican, and even for the entire corpus of Italian High Renaissance art. From the moment of the arrival of *Moses*, San Pietro in Vincoli was subsumed under the visual importance of this statue, which came to substitute for it in visual memory. When the tomb of Julius II was placed in San Pietro in Vincoli, the church became a monument to High Renaissance art, and the *Moses* statue became a souvenir of a monument that never was.

These effects of reproductions of the *Moses* show how souvenirs can function as selective templates. But this we have already acknowledged in our discussion of the role of souvenirs in the creation of a canon. By reducing Rome to a series of decontextualized monuments, however, souvenir reproductions helped to develop another type of visualization in the Early Modern period: fragmentation. Isolating monuments from the city could lead to misinterpretation, but it could also lead to reassessment and reconstruction. This is precisely what Hersey does. He must first take the *Moses* out of its current context in order to reconstruct the early stages of the planning of the monument. Historical reconstruction of this kind developed in Rome in tandem with souvenir production. Many of the prints that Lafréry published for travelers in the sixteenth century were reconstructions of ancient sites (such as the massive bath complex of Diocletian or the pagan temples in the Roman Forum). We do not today regard these attempts as scientifically accurate, but they do show an antiquarian and lay interest in using physical remains to reassemble the monuments of a past moment.

This project of seeing in and learning from fragments was particularly Roman, since it was Roman antiquity that first engaged Europeans in the reconstruction of a past culture through a study of its tangible and visible remains. Fragments of ancient art and architecture were the subjects to be reproduced in souvenirs, creating a neat fit of the effect of souvenir formats (fragmentation of Rome into topographically decontextualized monuments) to content (the monuments of ancient Rome were already decontextualized chronologically). Because the first monuments to be reproduced as souvenirs were fragments anyway, it made sense to treat them as such. It was in fact taking them out of their modern context that allowed for speculation about what their original ancient contexts might have been. The fragmentation enacted by all souvenirs – the way in which they remove monuments from a cohesive urban environment – had in the case of Rome a particular relationship both to the type of monument being represented and the way that such monuments were studied by architects and early antiquarians. This fragmentary mode of representation, which stands in an almost organic relation-ship to the study of ancient remains, was transferred to the representation and study of modern monuments as well. Felini's illustration of the *Moses* (Figure 1.4), in fact, occurs in a section of the guidebook on ancient statues; the modern sculpture is inserted into a representational format developed for printing replicas of ancient sculpture and sculptural fragments.

While Roman souvenirs function as fragments of the larger urban context, there is a marked tendency for representing fragments within them as well, even when this is seemingly inappropriate. Let's look again at the gratuitous fragments in Piranesi's view of the Trevi Fountain (Figure 1.2). As we have seen, these functioned in part as a marker of antiquity, allowing Piranesi to include all branches of the Roman canon – ancient, Early Modern, and sacred – within a single view. But it is also important that Piranesi summons up antiquity via fragments, rather than through some whole monument transplanted to this spot. To contemporary viewers familiar with Piranesi's other etchings, these ruins would have suggested the building blocks that the artist so often used in his reconstructions. In a volume on the *Antichità Romane* (*Antiquities of Rome*), for example, Piranesi combines a view of the contemporary state of the Ponte Fabricio, Rome's oldest standing bridge, with a reconstruction of the original appearance of the structure. The view of the bridge extends under the Tiber River, where heaps of rubble, much like that in Figure 1.2, have amassed. The unwieldy rubble, through Piranesi's industry, is sorted and restored to the bridge in the reconstructed view below. Because in the Trevi view, however, there is no one ancient monument that yielded the remains, we are instead to read the ancient fragments as being an inspiration for the construction of the modern city.

The study of ancient Roman art and architecture was almost never an end in itself in the Renaissance and Baroque. Hogarth's strategy in his *Analysis of Beauty* is to glean knowledge from ancient art by breaking the models down into their component parts. Across the torso of the Belvedere Antinous, Hogarth has inscribed a dotted line that runs from shoulder to shoulder and neck to abdomen in order to show the serpentine axis of the figure, the source of its grace. Framing the plate are further schemata of good and bad design, distilled from his examples. Hogarth starts with complete statues and dissects them into fragments so that we can see how they work and adopt them as models. The seeing in fragments encouraged by souvenirs led, then, in two directions: into a past that could be reconstructed and a future in which new monuments would be built on the principles delineated and isolated from ancient fragments.

The logic of the fragment carried over into other Early Modern disciplines that were likewise forming visual standards and conventions. The illustrations of the first major printed illustrated treatise on human anatomy – Andreas Vesalius's *De humani corporis fabrica*, published in 1543 – are a case in point. The classical poses adopted by flayed bodies and human skeletons in this work have often been remarked (for example by Harcourt 1987). One explanation is that the familiarity and decorum of ancient sculpture helped to defuse the horror of dissection, still a new and contested medical practice. Already familiar at this time, as in the time of Hogarth, was the *Belvedere Torso*, from which, in a Vesalian image, the inner viscera of male anatomy pour forth (Vesalius 1543: 372). In this woodcut, ribs and flesh spring back from the abdomen to provide a view of the carefully itemized organs. By contrast, the breaks where the arms and legs are missing are treated as stone surfaces, as if to reassure the viewer that this is just marble after all. Exposing the fragmented body as a sculptural fragment is more than comforting, however. Vesalius invokes and reverses the antiquarian strategy of reconstruction from fragments. Rhetorically the disemboweled *Torso* seeks to persuade squeamish sixteenth-century viewers that just as with the ancient remains they know from souvenirs, the body needs to be reduced to its component parts in order to be understood. Seeing in fragments is a way of isolating and making sense of complex visual data, something that was a necessity in the case of Roman ruins themselves, but that became a method in other branches of learning. Vesalius links the empirical authority of the body to the visual authority of ancient remains, which were becoming recognized as sources of knowledge.

Collection: Rome as "The World's Sole Cabinet"

Souvenir prints and casts were among the first mass-market commodities. David Landau and Peter Parshall have already made this point about Renaissance prints: "Prints were an early form of 'found object', a medium that required marketing and was thus inherently inclined to induce the phenomenon of collecting" (Landau and Parshall 1994: 64). The very livelihood of print publishers or makers of casts depended on establishing repeat business with a large customer base. The publishing venture of Lafréry shows us an early moment in the establishment of the print collecting habit. The prints released in this series between the 1540s and 1570s were sold unbound, and it was up to the discretion of the purchaser to choose among them. The Lafréry enterprise catered to an emerging culture of sixteenth-century print collectors with a taste for images of antiquities. Collections of prints and casts had the twofold benefit of being both standardized (because the same reproductions were owned by hundreds or thousands of people) and customizable (because reproductions removed the objects that they represented from their original contexts and put them in the hands of people who could categorize and sort them in a variety of ways). This joining of the mass-produced and the personalized was another way in which souvenirs, and the knowledge about Rome that they embodied, could be validated by the expertise of the individual collector.

Already the connections between collecting and knowing in the Early Modern period have been explored by scholars (see for example Hooper Greenhill 1992, Chapters 4 and 5). Collecting was a trendy pastime of the well to do, but its purpose was always more than a pursuit of leisure and aesthetic pleasure. In 1565, Samuel van Quicchelberg, who had organized the library and art collections of the Duke of Bavaria, published a program for an encyclopedic collection of objects and images (Quicchelberg 1565; Hajós 1958; Robinson 1981, xxxi–xxxiii; Findlen 1994, 108–10, 112, 132). Quicchelberg advised his readers to invest in engravings, which were to be placed under headings of Biblical and mythological subjects, ornament, scientific and technical pursuits from natural history to geography, topography, architecture, and depictions of contemporary mores. As the scope of Quicchelberg's collection makes clear, the collector's goal was the creation of a visual encyclopedia of the world through amassing examples of its natural and man-made objects. The overlap of the natural and the fabricated reminds us that we are in a time before a strict split between scientific and artistic modes of study or viewing. Instead, all branches of knowledge could be studied and assembled simultaneously because all were investigated through the same faculty: vision. Of primary importance was not what was studied but how this study was undertaken. Quicchelberg's focus on engravings also demonstrates an endorsement of the simulacrum. Replicas and representations were essential props in the Early Modern encyclopedic project of cataloging knowledge through observation.

Souvenirs of Rome participate in the cognitive approach that paired collecting with mastering a body of knowledge. Without replicated souvenir images, Johann Winckelmann would not have developed his chronologies of ancient sculptural styles. He became a leading authority on ancient art before he ever went to Rome (Haskell and Penny 1981: 100). Winkelmann's access to mass-produced images is also a reminder again of the social consequences of collecting via souvenir. Born outside of Italy and into a working-class family – his father was a shoemaker – he nevertheless became part of an international interpretive community interested in generating knowledge about the history of ancient art. Owning a virtual collection was enough to gain entry into this circle of people in multiple locations who were looking at and discoursing about identical images. Acknowledging the importance of souvenir copies to scholarship, a portrait of 1768 by Anton van Maron (Weimar, Kunstsammlungen) shows Winkelmann working from a print or drawing of an ancient sculpture of Antinous, even though he had access to the original in the collection of his patron.

The souvenirs that we have seen so far envision and encourage practices of collecting in a variety of ways. Pietro Bracci's cameo casts offer a ready-made collection, a canon in a box. From the point of view of the transmission of information, the downside of the cameo format is that the medium of the originals is unclear. Thus the handwritten checklist, on the left-hand side of the opening, tells us which are busts, which marble sculptures, which paintings, and which are in fact views of the Vatican Museum. Although the medium necessitated some loss of fidelity, the miniaturization made up for the pictorial simplicity it demanded by allowing several images to be seen at once. This hand-held Vatican Museum offers an encyclopedic view to whoever opens the box. We can think of almost any of Piranesi's works in the same way. Many of his etchings, especially those in the *Antichità Romane*, picture fictive collections in which fragments of building materials, sarcophagi, and limbs parted from statues are artfully displayed on tiers of shelves. This kind of collection explicitly invites the viewer to classify, catalog, and reconstruct. Even Piranesi's views can be thought of as collections rather than distortions of the urban environment. Where he departs from a literal depiction of topography, as in his image of the Trevi Fountain, he does so in order to increase the informational content of an image. He squeezes fountain, church, and ruins into a single image to make them simultaneously available for contemplation. Hogarth does the same in the *Analysis of Beauty*. Instead of making use of multiple illustrations, he opts to juxtapose his models and his visual analysis of them on a single sheet. Although in the introduction he had reassured his readers that he wanted nothing to do with "marvelous collections," that is exactly what he recreates on the page. The work of cataloging, dissecting, and comparing within this fictive collection has already been done by Hogarth.

Another kind of souvenir that encouraged habits of collecting is the item of furniture sometimes called a cabinet of curiosities (Figure 1.5). These were produced for foreign visitors in Rome and Florence (Gonzalez-Palacios and Röttgen 1982: 96–7). The example seen here is both a customizable receptacle, waiting to be filled with its owner's curios, and a ready-made collection of Roman vistas. The city splintered into a series of views is the city that had been serially reproduced for the previous 300 years. The images themselves, this time painted by hand, are still the children of mass production, for they are the canonical views of Rome that had been standardized by printed images like those of Piranesi. The luxury cabinet thus reenacts the mass-produced way of seeing and knowing Rome. The central view of St. Peter's borrows a device from Piranesi, scenically representing the square from a hill that did not exist on site. The shape of the cabinet recalls more monumental architectural works, pointing to the microcosm-macrocosm relationship between the miniature views of Rome and the encyclopedic knowledge of the city that these represented. The collecting of cityscapes afforded by this cabinet is less about classifying Rome than remembering it, however. Tourists to Rome, from the time of Felini to that of Forster and Baedecker, remembered the city first and saw it second. Prefabricated and collective souvenir memory preceded individual experience. The display cabinet is a monument to this kind of tourist memory. Like the *Moses* statue, the cabinet functions by synecdoche, alluding to and assembling the totality of Rome out of isolated views. Souvenirs train tourists to see and remember Rome itself this way, as a container or cabinet of precious monuments.

Figure 1.5 Roman workshop, collector's cabinet with eighteen views of Rome, last quarter of eighteenth century. Wood, bronze, and painted parchment. Rome, Museo di Roma.

The seventeenth-century English traveler John Evelyn had in fact described Rome as the "World's sole cabinet" in his diaries. By cabinet Evelyn could have meant the type of large-scale collectors' cabinets organized by Quicchelberg, entire rooms outfitted with drawers and display cases. Or he might have meant (the distinction is not clear in English) a small-scale storehouse for prints and precious objects like the one we have been discussing. By mimicking large-scale architecture, the cabinet also assumed another function of the Early Modern cityscape, as a place of memory. The relation of the cabinet to memory, and tourist memory in particular, is more than just evocative. Souvenirs of Rome participated explicitly in Early Modern understandings of the workings of memory.

The "art of memory" or "artificial memory" (*artificiosa memoria*) was known to medieval philosophers through the works of the classical rhetoricians Cicero and Quintilian. In his *Institutio Oratoria*, which would have been familiar to educated Renaissance and Baroque viewers, Quintilian coached his readers in the development of the faculty of memory (XI, ii, 18–21; 1922: 221–223). He proposed an architectonic and topographical method in which the individual was to conjure up a mental map of a house or cityscape to serve as the container for memory. When any series of things was to be memorized, one should simply translate each fact into a striking image and entrust it to the guardianship of a single building, room, sculpture, or other feature of the mental landscape. Early Modern students of this technique were trained to conceive of memorizing as a practice of collecting and of architectural or city vistas as the proper containers for memory collections. The inclusion among Bracci's cameo casts of two views of the architecture of the Vatican Museums is a nod to this practice, providing a memory container along with the contents.

According to the model provided by Quintilian, memory is a practice of collecting, but it is not a *collective* practice. His tradition of mnemotechnics had always defined memory as a visual faculty, but the images used to train the artificial memory had of necessity been private. Quintilian described memory as solipsistic, the hoardings of an individual mind. In the sixteenth century, humanist scholars like Giulio Camillo and Jesuit missionaries like Matteo Ricci had still imagined that the individual human mind, trained in the arts of memory, would preserve and spread the teachings of the ancients and of the Christian Church (Bolzoni 1995; Spence 1985). Camillo had actually erected what he called a memory theater, an architectural container for cataloging all knowledge. The architecture of little cabinets like the one in Figure 1.5 alluded to descriptions of large-scale memory theaters like Camillo's (on curiosity cabinets see Findlen 1994; Terpak 2001). The advent of printing rendered obsolete the feats of memory that had been necessary for the acquisition and transmission of knowledge in oral and manuscript cultures (Eisenstein 1979). As for reproducible souvenirs, they too had a decisive effect on memory. In the age of mass production, collective visual memories could be sold, prepackaged to vast publics. Through the circulation of souvenirs, Rome itself came to be conceived of as both a city of memory and as a collectors' cabinet.

Conclusion

In his book *The Tourist*, Dean MacCannell uses tourism as a point of entry into the ethnography of modern culture. Souvenirs, the material artifacts of tourism, can perform a similar function for Early Modern epistemology. The souvenir is not an isolated case of the merchandising of representations of one place (Rome) or of a few discrete types of knowledge (topographical, architectural, antiquarian). Through making repeatability a standard of authenticity, fragmenting the cityscape into comprehensible components, and collecting these components under an interpretive gaze, souvenirs helped to secure a pre-eminent role for vision in all scientific fields. One of the major projects of twentieth-century philosophy concerned an exploration of knowledge and its boundaries in the Early Modern period, from the sixteenth century to the Enlightenment. Michel Foucault defined a sixteenth-century *episteme* that was encyclopedic and based on establishing similitudes (Foucault 1966). Martin Heidegger outlined a metaphysics of modernity that distinguished our scientific age as an age in which we come to know the world as a picture: "The world picture does not change from an earlier medieval one into a modern one, but rather the fact that the world becomes a picture at all is what distinguishes the essence of the modern age" (Heidegger 1977: 130). Though the causes that lead to a culture's development of a new *episteme* are highly complex, Heidegger's "Age of the World Picture," an age of science that is also an age that equates looking with knowing, came into being in part through the agency of the souvenir and its logics.

Emanating from a Roman context, furthermore, Early Modern souvenirs generated many of the specific forms and functions that are now characteristic of souvenirs in general. Their replication of ancient remains, religious relics and shrines, and Renaissance and Baroque monuments were instrumental to the development of the scholarly and touristic interest in cultural patrimony. Their current status as kitsch alerts us to an important change between the functions of early souvenirs and the ones we can bring back from Rome today. The logic of the souvenir, which created and fulfilled demands for repeatability, collectability, and portability remained the dominant model of knowing Rome and knowing in general through much of the eighteenth and even nineteenth centuries, when it began to be supplanted by modern disciplinary boundaries, which set souvenirs apart as objects of leisure not science. Today's souvenirs repeat in the latest materials the older visions of reproduction, fragmentation, and collection, while no longer having a primary role to play in gathering and communicating data about Rome. The visual cues that they give us, however, continue to define a tourist vision of Rome that is Early Modern in character, both in its canon and in its mode of viewing. As relics of or throwbacks to the first information age, modern souvenirs are also mementoes, it turns out, of an earlier generation of souvenirs.

Notes

1. The use of the term "souvenir" for "a token of remembrance; something . . . which reminds one of some person, place, or event; a keepsake" dates to the late eighteenth century, and its use to describe objects intentionally manufactured as memorabilia is common only from the end of the nineteenth (*Oxford English Dictionary*, second edition, *s.v.* "souvenir").

References

Adler, J. (1989), "Origins of Sightseeing", *Annals of Tourism Research*, 16: 7–29.

Benjamin, W. (1935, 1968). "The Work of Art in the Age of Mechanical Reproduction", in *Illuminations: Essays and Reflections*, translated by H. Arendt, New York: Schocken Books.

Benson, S. (2002), "Une capitale culturelle européenne à l'époque moderne. la colline du Capitole et la politique du patrimoine", in Charle, C. and Roche, D. (eds), *Capitales culturelles, capitales symboliques: Paris et les expériences européennes, XVIIIe–XXe siècles*, Paris: Publications de la Sorbonne.

Bolzoni, L. (1995), *Le stanze della memoria. Modelli letterari e iconografici nell'età della stampa*, Turin: Einaudi.

Bury, M. (1985), "The Taste for Prints in Italy to c.1600", *Print Quarterly* 2: 12–26.

Campbell, M. (1990), "Introduction" to *Piranesi: Rome Recorded*, New York and Rome: American Academy in Rome.

Cooper, T. (1999), "Forgetting Rome and the Voice of Piranesi's 'Speaking Ruins'", in Forty, A. and Küchler, S. (eds), *The Art of Forgetting*, Oxford and New York: Berg.

Eisenstein, E. L. (1979), *The Printing Press as an Agent of Change*, 2 vols, Cambridge: Cambridge University Press.

Epstein, A. (2000), *As the Romans Do: The Delights, Dramas, and Daily Diversions of Life in the Eternal City*, New York: William Morrow.

Eyewitness Guides: Rome (1993, 2000), London and New York: Dorling Kindersley.

Felini, P. M. (1610, 1615), *Trattato Nuovo delle Cose Maravigliose Dell'Alma Città Di Roma*, Rome: Bartolomeo Zannetti.

Findlen, P. (1994), *Possessing Nature: Museums, Collecting, and Scientific Culture in Early Modern Italy*, Berkeley: University of California Press.

Forster, E. M. (1908, 1993), *A Room With a View*, New York: The Modern Library.

Foucault, M. (1966), *Les mots et les choses. Une archéologie des sciences humaines*, Paris, Gallimard.

Goethe, J. W. von, (1786–88, 1994) *The Italian Journey*, translated by R. Heitner, Princeton: Princeton University Press.

Gonzalez-Palacios, A. and Röttgen, S. (eds) (1982), *The Art of Mosaics: Selections from the Gilbert Collection*, translated by T. Hall, Los Angeles: Los Angeles County Museum of Art.

Hajós, E. M. (1958), "The Concept of an Engravings Collection in the Year 1565: Quicchelberg, *Inscriptiones vel Tituli Theatri Amplissimi*", *The Art Bulletin*, 40: 151–6.

Harcourt, G. (1987), "Andreas Vesalius and the Anatomy of Antique Sculpture", *Representations*, 17: 28–61.

Haskell, F. and Penny, N. (1981), *Taste and the Antique: The Lure of Classical Sculpture, 1500–1900*, New Haven: Yale University Press.

Heidegger, M. (1977), "The Age of the World Picture", in *The Question Concerning Technology and Other Essays*, translated by W. Lovitt, New York: Harper Torchbooks. This essay originally appeared in 1952 in the volume *Holzwege*, Frankfurt: Vittorio Klostermann.

Hersey, G. (1993), *High Renaissance Art in St. Peter's and the Vatican: An Interpretive Guide*, Chicago: University of Chicago Press.

Hogarth, W. (1753), *Analysis of Beauty: Written with a View of Fixing the Fluctuating Ideas of Taste*, London: J. Reeves.

Hooper-Greenhill, E. (1992), *Museums and the Shaping of Knowledge*, London: Routledge.

Krautheimer, R. (1985), *The Rome of Alexander VII, 1655–1667*, Princeton: Princeton University Press.

Landau, D. and Parshall, P. (1994), *The Renaissance Print, 1470–1550*, New Haven: Yale University Press.

Macadam, A. (1998), *Blue Guide: Rome*, sixth edition, London: A&C Black.

MacCannell, D. (1976, 1999), *The Tourist: A New Theory of the Leisure Class*, New York: Schocken Books; Berkeley: University of California Press.

Quicchelberg, S. von. (1565), *Inscriptiones vel tituli theatri amplissimi*, Munich: Ex officina Adami Berg Typographi.

Quintilian, *Institutio Oratoria* (1922, 1968), translated by H. E. Butler, London: Heinemann.

Robinson, W. W. (1981), "'This Passions for Prints': Collecting and Connoisseurship in Northern Europe During the Seventeenth Century", in C. S. Ackley (ed.), *Printmaking in the Age of Rembrandt*, Boston: Museum of Fine Arts.

Spence, J. D. (1985), *The Memory Palace of Matteo Ricci*, Harmondsworth: Penguin Books.

Terpak, F. (2001), "Wunderkammern and Wunderkabinette", in Stafford, B. and Terpak, F. *Devices of Wonder: From the World in a Box to Images on a Screen*, Los Angeles: Getty Research Institute.

Vesalius, A. (1543), *De humani corporis fabrica libri septem*, Basle: Ex officina Ioannis Oporini.

–2–

Early Travelers in Greece and the Invention of Medieval Architectural History
Kostis Kourelis

Introduction

Travel to Greece in the tourist forms that we recognize today began in the nine-teenth century with the creation of a modern nation state. Before this time, Greek landscapes such as Arcadia were fabricated not on the basis of experience but on the basis of ancient sources reconstructed by the Western imagination. Although we have evidence of limited travel to Greece as early as the twelfth century, the country was not easily accessible to academic audiences until the middle of the nineteenth century. Hence the birth of the neoclassical movement in the eighteenth century and the scientific study of Greek antiquities occurred outside Greece within the geographical confines of the Italian Grand Tour. Winckelmann and Goethe, the greatest advocates of Hellas, never set foot on Greek soil. Heinrich Wilhelm Tischbein's famous 1787 portrait of Goethe shows the poet reclining in Campagna while yearning for a distant Arcadia. Goethe manifested this wishful conflation between real Italy and imaginary Greece in the frontispiece of his *Italian Journeys* that reads 'I, too in Arcadia' (1993: 9). Winckelmann wrote the first history of classical Greek art from the distance based on works accessible to him in Rome in 1764. After the 1821 War of Independence, Philhellenes could sud-denly witness Greek antiquities directly, no longer filtered through the Italian lens. Independence from the Ottoman Empire ushered Greece into the tourist itinerary and facilitated a type of cultural colonization where European travelers exacted a new Greek experience.

From one point of view, travel to Greece can be seen as a territorial extension of the Grand Tour whose intellectual foundations lay in the previous century. Nineteenth-century travel, however, brought forth new ideologies wholly different from those of Winckelmann and Goethe. World-scale imperialism, industrializa-tion, the rise of the middle class and new philosophical movements established mass tourism, a phenomenon with its own social practices and intellectual para-digms. Travel occurred more frequently, it was accessible to a wider social class, and it was disseminated by a literary genre of great popular appeal. Unlike the aristocratic dilettantes of the Grand Tour, the travelers of the nineteenth century refashioned the past to fit the socio-economic and cultural environment of modernity. As postclassical periods emerged in European scholarly focus, the itinerary of the traveler also shifted to include monuments that the eighteenth-century traveler had ignored. Medieval architecture, thus, entered into the tourist mode of cultural appropriation and played a prominent role in negotiating between viewer and viewed, antiquity and the Middle Ages, the East and the West.

In the process of describing the medieval monuments of Greece, nineteenth-century tourists, to whom I shall refer to as the "early travelers," invented a new chapter of architectural history. From a documentary point of view, these travelers' accounts contain invaluable information about the form and condition of monuments as they found them in the nineteenth century. Their descriptions are first person testimonies about buildings that have since undergone decay or alteration. In some cases they have entirely disappeared. Early traveler accounts are often the only surviving archeological record. This paper is based on the analysis of 284 travelogs initially exploited for their factual information (Kourelis 2003). What are considered here, however, are not the recorded facts but the fictions produced by this first and most literary generation of tourists in the process of describing the monuments of medieval Greece.

Traveling East

Pilgrims, antiquarians, spies, generals and thieves have intermittently visited Greece from the twelfth century to the present and have left written records of their experience. Nevertheless, travelers in the nineteenth century were the first to experience history in a way that could be explicitly communicated to a large reading audience through books of popular appeal. These early tourists flocked to the Greek countryside in search of monuments and the inspiration by which to explain those monuments to their readers. First-person travelogs, amply illustrated with engravings, were the nineteenth-century product of a financial collaboration between tourism and the publishing industry. The early travelers thus represent both a tourist phenomenon and a literary genre. While travelers arrived from every corner of Europe, most came from Britain and France. They recorded their impressions of local customs, the landscape, architecture and the arts (Tolias 1993: 110). In London, Paris and Berlin, thousands of volumes were published in order to satisfy a vast middle-class readership. The most recent count of travel publications on Greece and Turkey includes no fewer than 3,000 volumes (Funke and Gehrke 1995–7). The sheer number of surviving editions testifies both to a wide authorship and the popularity of the genre.

A statistical analysis of all travel literature dealing with the northwestern Peloponnese, a select case study, shows a preponderance of publication between 1780 and 1930 with highest concentrations in the middle to late nineteenth century. Specifically, 75 per cent of all travelogs were published between 1800 and 1900, which stands in stark contrast to the preceding and subsequent centuries.[1] Furthermore, trends within the genre's lifetime can be correlated with historical events that affected the rate of travel. For example, peaks in publication occurred with the installment of King Otto in 1832 and with the construction of railroads in 1885. Alternatively, decline in publication occurred during the Crimean War (1853–56). The First World War (1914–18) brought an end to the genre, although this is not to say that writing about Greece ceased. On the contrary, new categories of academic literature were invented in the early twentieth century that drew upon the traditions of the early travelers' narratives. The first scholarly publication on medieval architecture in Greece, Gabriel Millet's *Greek School of Byzantine Architecture* (1916), transferred the travel genre to an official academic domain while retaining all of its methods and assumptions.

The early travelers were a diverse group of amateurs and professionals, comprising diplomats, military men, doctors, architects and artists, or simply adventurous socialites. These "travelers in tweed," as characterized by Robert Eisner (1991), were prominent in the European public conscience and not immune to journalistic ridicule. For instance, one of Gustave Dorée's illustrations for Edmond About's *King of the Mountain* (1881) caricatures a couple of early travelers ambushed by thieves. The man and woman are dressed in aristocratic clothes, and ride on horseback while the mountain thieves gather on foot below. The French couple sneers down at the thieves who scramble to collect the coins they have thrown on the ground. About's illustrated novel was based upon his journey to Greece, an account of which he published separately (About 1891). Both About's novel and travelog were extremely popular with Second Empire French audiences – one of his most enthusiastic readers being Napoleon III.

The public visibility of the early travelers can be shown by another illustration dating from 1860. In this case the anonymous caricaturist depicts three visitors to Athens, two women and one man, riding on donkeys led by local guides. The contrast between their formal European clothing and the peasant environment was intended to ridicule the travelers, especially the central figure who represents the director of *Le Figaro* (Tsigakou 1981: 68). Despite the wide dissemination of such representations of nineteenth-century travel, ascertaining the scope of the genre's audience and reconstructing the habits of its readership remain difficult. Travelogs served an ambiguous double function: as literary entertainment, on the one hand, and as actual field guides for the travel enthusiast, on the other.

By the second half of the nineteenth century, the traveling audience had grown large enough to warrant the institutional establishment of tourism as it survives in the twenty-first century. The first package cruise to Greece was organized in 1833 and Thomas Cook, the first travel agency, established an Athens branch in 1880. Thomas and Frank Cook advertised their new services with a photographic self-portrait in which they sport *phoustanelas*, the traditional Greek dress (Swinglehurst 1982: 145). In 1885, Greece became further accessible by land, when French engineers built the Corinth canal and the first railway line linking the Peloponnese with the major capitals of Europe (Magocsi 1993: 90–1).

The railway served similar important functions in France. By 1837, the French railway had linked Paris with its countryside and made convenient both domestic tourism and the scientific investigation of Gothic churches. The first activities of the French Historical Monuments Service were picnic excursions to the Parisian suburbs (Bergdoll 1994: 123–4). The railway also linked Paris with distant Europe and facilitated the study of other medieval, especially oriental cultures. Victor Hugo, whose novel *The Hunchback of Notre Dame* (1832) made the Middle Ages an object of mass appeal, saw in the railway the potential to create a visionary European Community. Greece's link with Europe via locomotive took place at precisely the moment that a shared medieval identity was brought into focus.

Representing Greece

It is important to recognize the extent to which nineteenth-century tourists inherited the modes of representation that student *pensionnaires* in Rome and Grand Tourists had established in the eighteenth century. The British Society of the Dilettanti, founded in 1732, had provided the forum of studying ancient art and architecture. In the second half of the eighteenth century, such institutions and their publications formalized the discipline of architectural history. James Stuart's and Nicholas Revett's *Antiquities of Athens* (1762–94), Richard Chandler's *Ionian Antiquities* (1797–1821), Robert Wood's *Ruins of Palmyra* (1753) and *Balbec* (1757) established the canonical principals of documenting ancient architecture. Excavations in Herculaneum in 1709 and the discovery of Pompeii in 1763 further established the methodology of archeological excavations (Parslow 1995). The modes of rational and scientific representation appropriate for the study of ancient architecture were extended into the study of an ever-growing number of sites in Greece. The site of Olympia for example, newly discovered in 1829, was extensively documented by orthographic drawings. The site was published by the German Archeological Institute with rich folios, plans, sections, details, elevations and reconstruction drawings (Curtius and Adler 1892). Such modes of scientific representation became commonplace to the study of ancient architecture.

Although often physically present at or near ancient sites, medieval churches, monasteries, mosques, castles and villages were still considered unworthy of archeological attention in the eighteenth century. Such buildings were seen as stylistically decadent, vaguely Islamic and hence uncivilized. The ethnic biases were compounded by the invention of the term *opera saracinesca* to describe medieval stone construction in Italy; the term continues to be used today despite the recognition that it has nothing to do with the Saracen Arabs (Paris 2000: 91). In Greece, the Middle Ages were considered indistinguishable from the Ottoman environment as directly observed through the early decades of the twentieth century (in Macedonia and Thrace, for example, the Ottoman Empire fell in 1913). Not only were medieval structures ignored by archaeologists and scholars but in many instances they were also actually destroyed – particularly if they encroached on ancient remains. Olympia is one such example. In 1875, Wilhelm Dörpfeld removed an extensive Byzantine settlement found over the ruins of the sanctuary of Zeus in order to liberate the ancient temple. Documentation of the complex survives only because fragments of ancient sculpture were incorporated in the medieval masonry (Treu 1897: 136). Given such widespread academic disdain for medieval monuments, the early travelers inherited no discursive tradition through which to understand, let alone describe, a thousand years of postantique architectural production spanning the Byzantine, Frankish, Venetian and Ottoman periods.

The site of Olympia further illustrates the conflict between a pre-existing *pensionnaires* tradition, represented by Dörpfeld's excavation, and the flocking of tourists that gathered around the site. Two female travelers, Edith Payne and Isabel Armstrong, published their discontent with the excavated mess they confronted in 1893. They found solace in the rational plan of the excavator:

> In spite of the beauty of the situation, this first view of Olympia almost strikes terror to the heart. The vastness of ruins, the terrible destruction that has been bared to sight, involuntarily the question arises – Can order ever be evolved out of this chaos of huge fragments? In point of fact, to any one who will sit down calmly to the study of the splendid map by Dr. Dörpfeld, the plan of Olympia is wonderfully easy to make out. (Armstrong 1893: 28–9)

Conflicts between a previously idyllic site and the trappings of the tourist industry emerged when the approach to Olympia was further assisted by the railroad. The train brought an increase in the number of tourists that had to be accommodated in a new hotel:

> Olympia, dominated by a *fin-de-siècle* hotel, Anno Domini nineteen hundred, triumphant over the centuries Before Christ! Hideous conception, a sacrilege sufficient to call down the thunder of Zeus. Olympia with turnstiles and police, a second Pompeii. But to this it must come, or else how will those thousands of glittering fragments be preserved from the omnivorous tourist? With the railway at its gates, the hotel on its hills, and the globe-trotter descending from above, the last days of Olympia are at hand. To all lovers of art,

to all lovers of nature, to all lovers of religion, I would say, Come, ere it be too late, and
see the pathetic past in its fit setting of silence and of solitude. (Armstrong 1893: 35)

Armstrong's account, thus, shows at a very early date the incompatibility
between the spheres of archeological science (Dörpfeld's plan), idyllic fantasy
(Goethe's Arcadia) and tourist infrastructure (the *fin-de-siècle* hotel).

Olympia was famous for its ancient games, revived in 1896 as the modern
Olympics. Academics like Dörpfeld and adventurous tourists visited the site in
order to see the ancient ruins. As a result, any postclassical remains that interfered
with the experience of antiquity were destroyed. Outside official archeological
sites such as Olympia, however, medieval buildings were spared. They made up a
visual landscape that the early travelers, unlike academics, sought to reproduce.
Engravings depicting postclassical monuments began to illustrate early traveler
publications. A close investigation of the nineteenth-century travelog genre reveals
the sudden invention of a vocabulary to describe, in word and image, architectural
monuments and landscapes from periods that had not existed in the historical space
of the Western imagination. In visualizing monuments such as Saint Andrew in
Patras (Tsigakou and Dollinger 1995: 110–11) or the Venetian Gates of Nauplion
(Kasimate 2000: 557, 560), the early travelers abandoned the orthographic modes
of representation typical to the academic study of antiquity for a looser, perspectival, scenographic and psychological point of view. Without the constraints of an
archeological tradition, the early travelers produced documents to be consumed by
a large audience with a taste for the unusual, the adventurous, the sublime and the
oriental. The philosophical ammunition for this new audience was furnished by the
newly grafted paradigms of Romantic Historicism, which posited cultural conflict
and dialectical confrontation as the basis of historical processes (Meinecke 1972).
It is important to recognize that the drawings and writings of the early travelers
embody the Romantic spirit while also containing the kernel of medieval architectural history. Our current notions of style, national schools, influence
and developmental progress originated in the extra-academic sphere of tourist
consumption.

How did the early travelers to Greece represent medieval monuments? Not
surprisingly, their initial impulse shows great reluctance. Joseph Woods (1828: vol.
2, pp. 269–79), a typical traveler, writes about Corinth, "The early antiquities of
this place are so interesting and the Christian ones of so little importance, that I find
it requires a considerable effort to turn my attention at all towards them." But after
the initial hesitation, travelers did make the effort. Woods proceeds to describe the
parts of a Byzantine church, an artifact he had never seen before. Although he gets
the physical description right, he fails in the interpretation: "These Greek churches,
like the ancient temples, must have been for the priests, and not for the people." In
trying to explain Byzantine monuments, the early travelers placed them whenever

possible in dialog with the more familiar ancient ones. Two examples from 1827 and 1829 illustrate typical visual strategies in representing antique and postantique buildings in Corinth. In Karl Krazeisen's drawing, medieval accretions intercede between the traveler/viewer and the prized Temple of Apollo (Kasimate 2000: 557). In Karl Wilhelm von Heideck's drawing of the same subject, rather than the drawing of medieval masonry the folkloric depiction of modern Greeks addresses the viewer's desire to connect with a fragmentary ancient ruin (Kasimate 2000: 560–1). The two drawings of Corinth illustrate the travelers' conflation of medieval and contemporary Greece. In its philosophical articulations, the aesthetics of Romanticism had already equated architectural ruins with the customs of country people. The early travelers were reenacting Friedrich Schiller's Romantic sentiments of the *Naïve and Sentimental*:

> There are moments in our life when we accord to nature in plants, minerals, animals, landscapes, as well as to human nature in children, in the customs of country people and of the primitive world, a sort of love and touching respect . . . Every sensitive person who is not wholly lacking in feeling experiences this when he wanders in the open air, when he lives in the country or lingers among the monuments of ancient times. (Schiller 1981: 21)

Postclassical Greeks and their postclassical buildings were, like children and country primitives, construed as equal and continuous parts of a larger ethnographic project.

Despite their shared Christian backgrounds, the early European travelers saw the Orthodox and its religious buildings as something "other." Woods' comment on the inaccessibility of Greek churches to parishioners reveals utter ignorance of local religion. Eastern Christianity was seen as mystical and obscure and, therefore, it had to be represented in fitting fashion. An Orthodox church seemed more akin to a Muslim mosque than its Catholic or Protestant counterpart. Peter von Hess drew the Perivleptos Monastery in Mystras as if springing out of the natural landscape (Kasimate 2000: 565–6). Philippe Le Bas (1888: pl. 16) depicted the Convent of Marina Maritsa in Santomeri as an oasis within a barren desert. For the early travelers, Byzantine churches were curiosities organically connected to the incomprehensible customs of Eastern peoples whose artistic production was dominated by decoration. The travelers thus initiated a tradition of privileging churches as the exclusive vessel of Orthodox culture, and as direct visual representations of its mystical beliefs. Sorting out differences between buildings could be done primarily by studying architectural ornament, such as the polychrome masonry of Daphni Monastery drawn by Christian Hansen (Jorgensen and Porphyrios 1987: 30), or the dogtooth frieze of Saints Demetrios and Georgios in Eleia, drawn by Le Bas (1888: pl. 17). For the first time, the travelers' drawings and textual descriptions exposed a wider European audience to a body of material that could be conveniently used in emerging academic debates over the origins of Western medieval art. Although not fully coherent and singular as a voice, the discourse of the early travelers prepared the ground for the academic consideration of the Orient.

Academic Discourses

Western medieval architecture came under systematic study at exactly the same moment that the European tourist discovered Greece. The French architect Eugène-Emmanuel Viollet-le-Duc and writer Hugo and British architects Augustus Charles Pugin and John Ruskin, established the academic foundations for the discipline of medieval architectural history in the middle of the nineteenth century. In an attempt to understand the origins of Gothic, European scholars turned their attention to indigenous pre-Gothic monuments for which, in 1818, they invented the term *style Roman*, "second Roman style," or, as we use it today, "the Romanesque" (De Caumont 1870: 162, 174). At the same time, historians turned their attention to the monuments of an older Christian East. As early as the 1830s, Stephane Niquet (1834) attributed the origin of Gothic to an ultimate French resolution between two competing aesthetic forces, the "Latin style" and the "Byzantine style." Seventeen years later, Félix de Verneihl (1851) revived the thesis that Romanesque architecture in France was a direct descendent of Byzantine architecture, causing intense debate in contemporary artistic circles. As the East was summoned to explain the formation of art in the West, medieval culture was burdened with geographic and temporal binaries. Henceforth, art and architecture in Greece could not escape the perceived struggle of time between antiquity and the Gothic, the struggle of culture between Islam and Europe, and the struggle of religion between rational Catholicism and mystical Orthodoxy.

In addition to the contributions made by the early travelers to historical narrative, there is no doubt that contemporary architectural taste was shaped by their publications. André Couchaud's (1842) folio of Greek churches, for example, was read by a young generation of Beaux-Arts architects, Félix-Jacques Duban, Henri Labrouste, Louis Duc and Léon Vaudoyer, whose tastes diverged from strict neoclassicism (Figure 2.1). The *neo-grècs*, as this group self-fashioned itself, appropriated medieval Greek monuments, which they only knew through drawings, as paradigms for a new Romantic architecture of impurity, fusion and conflict (Van Zanten 1987). Byzantium, however it was understood in 1852, triumphed as architectural model in Vaudoyer's design of Marseilles Cathedral (Bergdoll 1994: 231–74). Two years later, the Danish Christian and Theophilus Hansen brought this Byzantinizing style back to Greece with the design of the Athens Eye Clinic

Figure 2.1 Saint Nicholas in Mystras, from André Couchaud, *Choix d'églises byzantines en Grèce*, Paris: Didron, 1842, pl. 27, fig. 1.

(Philippides 1984: 91–3). Through the circuitous machinations of tourist literature, the same Byzantine style that had been exported to Western Europe was re-imported back to Greece via Marseilles. As such, the early travelers and their architectural descriptions formed a crucial link in Europe's appropriation of post-classical, 'neo-Greek' culture.

The travelers played a significant role in yet another set of historical negotiations – that of the rediscovery of a European crusader heritage. In the nineteenth century the crusades furnished an obvious precedent for Europe's colonial presence in the eastern Mediterranean. Crusader historiography came into being at the time when Europe needed it most. The Morea – medieval Arcadia – was central to the writing of crusader history because of its Latin occupation between 1204 and 1430. Historical studies of the Frankish period in the Peloponnese began in 1825 prompted that same year by the discovery of the *Chronicle of the Morea*, which narrates the heroic confrontations between Franks and Byzantines (Buchon 1825). The exploration of the crusades through textual documents, however, was not sufficient at a time of exploding tourism. Medieval accounts required direct empirical contact with monuments. Jean-Alexandre Buchon, the *Chronicle*'s first editor, recognized this well enough to supplement the medieval source with the publication of his travels in the Peloponnese (Buchon 1843). Charting territories off the beaten neoclassical track, Buchon introduced a new category of crusader landmarks to be visited by patriotic French tourists. In the dedication to his patron, the Duchess of Orleans, Buchon writes, "My journey to Greece had a goal entirely historic and entirely national" (Buchon 1843: v). Thus, Buchon the traveler signaled the emergence of a new French identity predicated on the consumption of crusader monuments in a wider colonial environment.

The *Chronicle of the Morea* contains little information about ecclesiastical architecture. Dramatic adventures between Latins and Greeks took place in a continuous siege of castles. Perched on remote hilltops, sites like Mystras conjured vivid images of medieval heroism equal only to that of ancient mythology (Bory de Saint-Vincent 1835: pl. 30). In Buchon's (1843: 474) travelog we read, "the kings of Homer were, in effect, the grand Frankish barons of the Peloponnese." Despite its diachronic contradiction, this proposition was widely echoed throughout travel literature. And from there it entered high literature, namely in the third act of the second book of *Faust* where an aging Goethe (1984) dramatized the wedding between his Faust and Helena in the Frankish castle of Mystras. We know from a prose sketch dated to 1816 that Goethe had originally intended for the wedding to take place in Faust's palace on the Rhein. John Schmitt (1904: lviii–lxvi) points out that Goethe's decision to move the dramatic location from Germany to Greece occurred in 1825, in exactly the year of Buchon's publication of the *Chronicle*. Indeed, the ultimate resolution of Europe's Gothic and Hellenic genius could not have been possible without the visual and textual records that Peloponnesian tourism brought about. In the travelers' engravings of Greek villages such as Kardomyle, distant views accentuate natural impenetrability, while armed figures negotiate below (Bory de Saint-Vincent 1835: pl. 22). The traveler/viewer enters a heroic landscape and reclaims fantastic monuments of military might.

Heroics outweighed specificity as two drawings of Kyparissia from 1823 and 1831 demonstrate (Gell 1823: 79. Bory de Saint-Vincent 1835: pl. 14) (Figure 2.2). The slight variation in the representation of its architectural elements as seen, for example, in round versus square towers, illustrates disinterest in the realistic portrayal of the fortifications or the careful recording of architectural details. Homeric kings and crusader barons may have been presented as equals in heroism, but the study of their monuments was governed by entirely different methods and intellectual traditions. The ancient temples were studied objectively through state plans, sections and elevations, whereas the medieval castles were represented subjectively through scenic perspective views. The study of Peloponnesean castles seems to have never recovered from this Romantic vision. Today they are used for theatrical performance, entertainment and spectacle rather than scientific archeological investigation. The site of ancient Olympia, for example, is tightly controlled by archeological guards, strict time schedules and admission tickets. In contrast, the acropolis of medieval Kyparissia is open to the public, it houses a café, bar

Figure 2.2 View of Kyparissia, from William Gell *Narrative of a Journey in the Morea*, London: Longman, Hurst, Rees, Orme, and Brown, 1823, p. 1.

and open-air theater bustling with activity during the summer tourist season. The early travelers' visual vocabulary continues to reign over Greece's self-presentation. An engraving of Karytaina, for example, decorates the 5,000-drachma bill, designed in 1984, and serves as an image of national pride. Ironically enough, this very bill was superseded in 2002 by the adoption of a pan-European currency whose twenty-Euro denomination also exploits medieval iconography in the form of idealized Gothic windows.

Despite the discovery of Byzantine architecture by the *neo-grèc* architects, the interest in medieval Greek architecture by the academic community of architects and architectural historians remained limited through the course of the nineteenth century. James Ferguson (1907: vol. 1, p. 460) gives the following evaluation in his standard English language history of architecture published in 1907 (second edition):

> For Greece proper we are dependent almost wholly on Couchaud and Blouet [travelers]. So far as their illustrations go they suggest that there are no churches of such dimensions as would ensure dignity, nor are any so beautiful in outline or detail as to make us regret much that we do not know more about them.

Serious academic study of Greek medieval architecture had to await architectural historian Gabriel Millet. His pioneering *Greek School of Byzantine Architecture* (1916), formalized a cultural struggle between Hellenism and the Orient, and it placed Greece within the sphere of the latter. According to Millet, the oriental influence originated in Armenia and passed Greece *en route* to its ultimate destination, the Romanesque shores of southern France. In other words, Millet recycled earlier Francocentric notions of Byzantine architecture by Niquet and de Verneilh. His patriotism was celebrated by his contemporaries: "The four campaigns of Gabriel Millet in Mystras, on the glorious fortress of Villehardouin, promises us a book which interests our curiosity no less that our patriotism" (Radet 1901: 292).

The notion of an oriental Greek School was ultimately constructed in order to explain the birth of French Gothic. Its genesis took place in 1893 when Millet and other French academes embarked from Marseilles on a maiden voyage to Greece. As both tourists and proto-scholars, they tracked in reverse the journey of Europe's oriental influence. A photograph taken on the ship commemorates Millet's journey (Figure 2.3). This generic snapshot marks the shift from tourism to scholarship as the early travelers were institutionalized in foreign schools of archeology in Athens (Radet 1901: fig. 254).[2] The traveling group portrait is complimented by another Millet photograph that shows the tourist-scholars at work in medieval Monemvasia picnicking in the ruins of Saint Sophia (Radet 1901: fig. 230).[3] Millet in general and these photos in particular document the subtle shift from travel literature to academic authority, from drawing to photography, from fiction to fact. *The Greek School of Byzantine Architecture* established the principles of Byzantine archeology as a photographic endeavor. The publication is illustrated with almost 100 photographs, a third of which were executed by the author.[4] Photographs not shot by Millet are carefully credited. Each photographer was thus honored with authorship and academic expertise. Lampakis, Ermakov, Laurent, Bals, Ebersolt, Le Tourneau, Tafrali, Cacoulis and Poulitsas were the first to photograph Byzantine churches in Greece and by default became the country's first architectural historians.

Conclusion

Positioned outside the tight reigns of academicism that governed the study of antiquity, the early travelers of the nineteenth century constructed a loose discourse on medieval architecture. Unfettered by stringent requirements for evidentiary proof, they used the paradigm of Romantic Historicism, according to which monuments equaled the symbolic expression of different peoples and the struggles between them. The Peloponnese offered no shortage of historical confrontations. Nineteenth-century travelogs answered Europe's need to comprehend an expanding historical and geographic field. By explaining the origins of the Gothic in relation to Byzantine architecture, the early travelers brought the East to the West. At the same time they brought the West to the East by reclaiming the monuments of the crusades. Armies of tourists flocked to Greece in the nineteenth century to be

Figure 2.3 Gabriel Millet (second row, second from left) aboard the Troude on April 1893, from Georges Radet, *L'histoire et l'oevre de l'École française d'Athènes*, Paris: A. Fontemoing, 1901, fig. 254.

followed by armies of scholars in the twentieth century. A study of the visual and narrative strategies of the early travelers thus reveals a fossilized tourism buried in the objective practices of contemporary academic discourse.

Notes

1. The statistical data come specifically from the case study of the northwestern Peloponnese (the modern provinces of Achaia and Eleia). The best collection of early traveler publications is housed in the Gennadios Library in the American School of Classical Studies at Athens (Weber 1952, 1953). The following

percentages reflect the distribution of publications according to century based on a sum of 248 travelogs dealing with the northwestern Peloponnese: Twelfth century 0 per cent, thirteenth century 0 per cent, fourteenth century 1 per cent, fifteenth century 0 per cent, sixteenth century 3 per cent, seventeenth century 4 per cent, eighteenth century 7 per cent, nineteenth century 75 per cent, twentieth century 10 per cent.

2. The photograph is dated April 1893, aboard the *Troude*. The figures shown are Louis Couve, Eustache, Chamonard, Millet, Bourguet, Ardaillon, De Ridder, Sortais, Carré and Canuet.

3. The photograph is dated May 1896 and credited to Gabriel Millet. The figures shown are Chesnay, Liris, Emmanuel Kapitzini and Jean Negroponte.

4. Millet 34 per cent, Lampakis and Ermakov 20 per cent each, Laurent 10 per cent, the Hautes études collection 6 per cent, and Bals, Ebersolt, Le Tourneau, Tafrali, Cacoulis and Poulitsas 1–3 per cent each.

References

About, E. (1881), *Le roi des montagnes*, Paris: Hachette.

—— (1891), *Grèce contemporaine*, Paris: Hachette.

Armstrong, I. (1893), *Two Roving Englishwomen in Greece*, London: S. Low, Marston.

Bergdoll, B. (1994), *Léon Vaudoyer. Historicism in the Age of Industry*. New York: Architectural History Foundation; Cambridge, MA: MIT Press.

Bory de Saint-Vincent, J. B. G. M. (1835), *Expédition scientifique de Morée. Atlas (1831–1835)*, Paris: F. G. Levrault.

Buchon, J.-A. (1825), *Chronique de la conquête de Constantinople et de l'éstablissement des Français en Morée*, Paris: Verdière.

—— (1843), *La Grèce continentale et la Morée. Voyage, séjour et études historiques en 1840 et 1841*, Paris: C. Gosselin.

Caumont, A. de (1870), *Abécédaire ou rudiment d'archéologie*, 5th edition, Caen: F. Le Blanc-Hardel.

Chandler, R. (1797–1821), *Antiquities of Ionia*, 2 vols, London: The Society of Dilettanti.

Couchaud, A. (1842), *Choix d'églises byzantines en Gréce*, Paris: Didron.

Curtius, E. and Adler, F. (1892), *Olympia*, vol. 1, "Tafelband," Berlin: A. Asher & Co.

Eisner, R. (1991), *Travelers to an Antique Land. The History and Literature of Travel to Greece*, Ann Arbor: University of Michigan Press.

Ferguson, J. (1907), *A History of Architecture in All Countries*, 2 vols, New York: Dodd, Mead & Co.

Funke, P. and Gehrke, H.-J. (1995–7), *Hellas. Datenbank der nachantiken Reisenberichte über Griechenland bis zum Mitte des 20. Jahrhunderts*, computer software, *Hellas für Windows, Version 1.05*, Copyright Michael Tieke for HILAND, Munster and Freiburg.

Gell, W. (1823), *Narrative of a Journey in the Morea*, London: Longman, Hurst, Rees, Orme & Brown.

Goethe, J. W. (1984), *Faust I and II*, edited and translated by Stuart Atkins, Goethe Edition, vol. 2, Cambridge MA: Suhrkamp/Insel Publishers Boston.

—— (1993), *Italienische Reise*, edited by Michel, Christoph and Dewitz, Hans Georg, Sämtliche Werke, vol. 15.1, Frankfurt: Deutscher Klassiker Verlag.

Hugo, V. (1832), *Notre-Dame de Paris*, Paris: C. Marpon and E. Flammarion.

Jorgensen L. B. and Porphyrios, D. (eds) (1987), *Neoclassical Architecture in Copenhagen and Athens*, Architectural Design Profile, no. 66, London and New York: St. Martin's Press.

Kasimate, M. Z. (ed.) (2000), *Athena-Monacho. Techne kai politismos ste nea Ellada*, Athens: National Gallery.

Kourelis, K. (2003), *Monuments of Rural Archaeology. Medieval Settlements in the Northwestern Peloponnese*, Ph.D. dissertation, University of Pennsylvania.

Le Bas, P. (1888), *Voyage Archéologique en Grèce et en Asie Mineure,* ed. Salomon Reinach, Paris: Firmin-Didot.

Magocsi, P. R. (1993), *Historical Atlas of East Central Europe*, A History of East Central Europe, vol. 1, Seattle and London: University of Washington Press.

Meinecke, F. (1972), *Historism. The Rise of a New Historical Outlook*, translated by J. E. Anderson, London: Herder & Herder.

Millet, G. (1916), *L'École grecque dans l'architecture Byzantine*, Paris: E. Leroux.

Niquet, S. (1834), "Exposition et discussion générale des doctrines historiques. De l'architecture en France au Moyen-Age. Premier article: Style byzantine, style Lombard," *Journal de l'Institut historique*, 1: 65–73.

Paris, R. (ed.) (2000), *Via Appia. The Tomb of Cecilia Metella and the Castrum Caetani*, Milan: Electa.

Parslow, C. C. (1995), *Rediscovering Antiquity. Karl Weber and the Excavation of Herculaneum, Pompeii, and Stabiae*, Cambridge, New York and Melbourne: Cambridge University Press.

Philippides, D. (1984), *Neoellenike architektonike. Architektonike theoria kai praxe (1830–1980) san antanaklase ton epilogon tes neollenikes koultouras*, Athens: Melissa Books.

Radet, G. (1901), *L'histoire et l'oevre de l'École française d'Athènes*, Paris: A. Fontemoing.

Schiller, F. (1981), *On the Naïve and Sentimental in Literature*, translated by Helen Watanabe-O'Kelly, Manchester: Carcanet New Press.

Schmitt, J. (1904), *The Chronicle of the Morea. A History in Political Verse, Relating the Establishment of Feudalism in Greece by the Franks in the Thirteenth Century*, London: Methuen & Co.

Stuart J. and Revett, N. (1762–94), *The Antiquities of Athens*, 3 vols, London: John Haberkorn.

Swinglehurst, E. (1982), *Cook's Tours. The Story of Popular Travel*, Poole, Dorset: Blandford Press.

Tolias, G. (ed.) (1993), *Travellers to the Mani 15th–19th Century. An Exhibition of Historical Material*, Gytheio: Historiko Ethnologiko Mouseio Manes.

Treu, G. (1897), *Olympia* v. 3, *Die Bildwerke von Olympia in Stein und Thur*, Berlin: A. Asher & Co.

Tsigakou, F.-M. (1981), *The Rediscovery of Greece. Travellers and Painters in the Romantic Era*, London: Thames & Hudson.

Tsigakou, F.-N. and Dollinger, A. S. (1995), *Glanz der Ruisen. Die Wiederentdeckung Griechenlands in Gemälden des 19. Jahrhunderts ans den Beständen des Banaki Museums, Athen, und des Rheinischen Landesmuseums Bonn.* Cologne: Rheinland-Verlag.

van Zanten, D. (1987), *Designing Paris. The Architecture of Duban, Labrouste, Duc and Vaudoyer*, Cambridge MA: MIT Press.

Verneilh, F. de (1851), *De l'Architecture Byzantine en France*, Paris: Victor Didron.

Weber, S. H. (1952), *Voyages and Travels in the Near East Made during the XIX Century*, Catalogues of the Gennadius Library, vol. 1, Princeton: American School of Classical Studies at Athens.

—— (1953), *Voyages and Travels in Greece, the Near East and Adjacent Regions Made Previous to the Year 1801*, Catalogues of the Gennadius Library, vol. 2, Princeton: American School of Classical Studies at Athens.

Wood, R. (1753), *Ruins of Palmyra. Otherwise Tedmor in the Desert*, London, s.n.

—— (1757), *Ruins of Balbec. Otherwise Heliopolis in Closyria*, London, s.n.

Woods, J. (1828), *Letters of an Architect, from France, Italy, and Greece*, 2 vols, London: John & Arthur Arch.

–3–

Performing Abroad: British Tourists in Italy and their Practices, 1840–1914*
Jill Steward

. . . Italy is the goal: and that, after Italy, you will understand everything else by the light of what you have learned in the "cities of the soul" – Venice, Rome and Florence . . . Italy is the key by which you may unlock the secret of Europe. (Grant Allen 1901: 33–4)[1]

The relationship between British tourists and Italian architecture is both complex and longstanding. To the British the architectural monuments of Italy represented classical civilization, early Christianity and Renaissance art and culture while its more recent churches and palaces stood for Catholicism and political decay, its landscapes and people represented sun and sensuality. In the 1840s these perceptions still provided the general framework of expectation with which tourists set out, but in the later decades of the nineteenth century the arrival of new types of travelers with different social and cultural backgrounds led to changes in the practices of cultural tourism accompanied by new forms of tourist experience.

This chapter focuses on the behavior of British tourists traveling in Italy as it was manifested in practices that were both expressive and constitutive of different forms of social and cultural identity. For this purpose it is helpful to think of tourism as an art of performance and a cultural practice of movement (Adler 1989a: 1368; Hetherington 1998: 117; Edensor 1998: 61–8), inflected by boundaries of social class, gender and nationality (Leask 2002: 4). Generations of Britons toured Italy's historic cities, their ruins and monuments, churches and cultural artefacts, galleries and museums, streets and places of entertainment seeking various forms of cultural education and individual satisfaction. The particular ways in which individuals interacted with the different environments in which they found themselves and enacted the role of tourist were deeply influenced by their own individual social and cultural histories and shaped by the legacy of the habitus

---

*An earlier version of parts of this chapter appeared in *Journeys: an International Journal of Travel and Travel Writing*, 2000; vol. 1, issues 1/2.

from which they derived their distinctive modes of feeling and thinking (Bourdieu 1978: 170–2).

As performance, tourism constitutes a way of "world-making" or "self-fashioning" (Goodman 1978 cited in Adler 1989: 1368). A great deal has been written about traditional modes of travel and associated narratives that bestow a particular form of identity upon the traveler (Todorov 1998). As travelers, tourists also have created their own distinctive tropes as they move through space, from one place to another, adopting corporeal and discursive strategies using the equivalent of classic aesthetic devices in the construction of the narratives through which they register their travels and evoke their realities for the audiences implied by the metaphor (Adler 1989: 1382–3). For the British tourist, "Italy" was a distinctive "world" the configurations of which functioned as a regulatory influence on the way its constitutive parts were perceived and performed (Chard 1996). Equally influential on tourist narratives was the way that particular places were imaged, perceived and directly experienced, an event that had to be registered through the acquisition of souvenirs and the sending of letters, sketches, photographs and postcards to others. This suggests that tourist practices are further regulated by "explicitly articulated standards of performance" associated with particular audiences. As audiences change, so do standards (Adler 1989: 1378) and performances (Schlechner 1981: 16) while particular styles of the latter offer a means through which individuals are able to express their perceptions of their situations and modes of being (Chaney 1993: 4).

"Ours is a nation of travelers," observed the English poet Samuel Rogers (cited in Murray 1859: x) whose poem *Italy* was much beloved by tourists, notably Lord Byron, whose own works did much to shape nineteenth-century tourist behavior. In 1800 British travel to Italy was still dominated by aristocratic Grand Tourists with a growing middle-class presence (Towner 1985). By the 1830s the traditional Grand Tour was dead although the British dominated the main tourist centers until the 1870s when they were outnumbered by Americans and Germans. By 1900 modern Italy was very different to that of the past but it continued to exercise its hold over the British who regarded it as "the ideal venue for a summer holiday" (Sladen 1912: xix) while the modern travel industry and relatively cheap package tours began to make it accessible to new social groups. Changes in the social profile of British tourists were accompanied by cultural changes as the conventions evolved by a highly educated and leisured body of tourists were adapted to the needs of different types of travelers from different social and cultural backgrounds.

In the 1840s the average tour to Italy lasted for four to six months instead of the former two years or more (Towner 1996: 132). Steamships across the Channel and on major rivers like the Rhine and the Danube, improvements in roads, particularly over the Alps (thanks to Napoleon), and the construction and extension of the railways made the journey easier and more comfortable and began the compression of time and space that was to radically change the experience of travel. Viaducts, railway bridges and tunnels changed the face of the landscape, notably the view of Venice from the mainland, which Ruskin complained now resembled "as nearly as possible as Liverpool at the end of the dockyard wall" (1845 cited in Quill 2000: 31) rather than "a ghost upon the sands of the sea" (Ruskin 1858: vol. 1, 1).

The great bulk of British tourists continued to follow the same spatial patterns as the aristocratic Grand Tourists of the past, modified to accommodate the modern taste for sublime and romantic scenery of the kind particularly associated with the Rhine valley and the Alps. Itineraries were adapted to include Rhineland castles and brief tours of Switzerland. The romantic interest in the medieval world attracted tourists to new places of interest like Padua, Pisa and Arezzo, and the influential art critic John Ruskin to Venice. Despite the British distaste for Baroque architecture, particularly that of Rome, the city was still the ultimate destination for most tourists who wished to visit the architectural sites and monuments they associated with the history of their own culture and its origins in the classical and Christian past and the Renaissance. Tourists of the past looked at the overgrown ruins of the Colosseum and the Forum in Rome, the decaying villas of Tivoli, the Pantheon and the Arch of Constantine seeing them in the melancholy relics of a destroyed civilization. Looking back on his immediate predecessors James Sully reflected on the way that they had come to value these relics more for their aesthetic properties and literary associations, finding in the "imperfect beauty in broken arch, column and entablature, and in the great overgrown masses of crumbling masonry" (Sully 1912: 79) ample material upon which to project their own reflections and fantasies.

The Taylor family exemplified the new kind of middle-class family party now embarking on the tour and that often included women. In the autumn of 1839 they travelled from Geneva to Genoa, crossing the Alps before they became impassable, boarded a ship for Leghorn from whence they travelled to Florence, via Pisa. They wintered in Rome, staying for Carnival and Easter, then moving on to Naples they returned to Florence in late Spring, via the Apennines, and then on to Venice, Verona and Padua and back to Geneva, via the Simplon Pass. Excursions included trips to the "antique" ruins around Rome and Naples, as well as to Herculaneum, Pompeii, Vesuvius and the Greek temple at Paestum (Towner 1996: 117) and a stormy sea voyage to Amalfi. The daughter of a musician, Catherine Taylor approached the role of tourist with an earnestness typical of the new urban middle classes who were anxious to distinguish themselves from their aristocratic and gentrified predecessors and less genteel contemporaries.

The way that the new tourists conceived their role determined the way they approached the practice of sightseeing. The more serious engaged in preparatory reading and took with them portmanteaus of instructive works on Italian history, art and antiquities. Once abroad the registering of the journey in letters and journals was mandatory. A foreign "tour" for a middle-class family like the Taylors was not something to be undertaken lightly and, in a culture in which writing was regarded as a primary form of communication, individuals were expected to justify the expense of the trip by recording their experiences in journals and letters for the benefit of family and friends at home. Journal writing was a routine activity for cultivated women. Harriet Martineau's advice to traveling journalists *How to Observe* was based on ethnographic and utilitarian principles and advocated the recording of daily impressions as the basis for more generalized and truthful observations that would benefit others (1838: 234–6).

Moreover, in an increasingly mobile and complex domestic society, the publication of reworked travel letters and journals had a positional use for their authors, particularly women like Catherine Taylor, in that they generated a wider audience before whom the demonstration of cultivation and competence as a tourist was a means of establishing the author's credentials as a member of the "genteel" and "cultivated classes" and its associated literary culture. Travel writing also constituted a space in which the usual hierarchical distinctions of gender were not as strictly applied as with the novel (Frawley 1994). Catherine Taylor's (1840–1: vol. 1, p. 260) published *Letters* contained detailed accounts of buildings she visited and were written ostensibly to educate her younger sister whom she warned against an "overly quick and imaginative response" in sightseeing because "the formation of opinions can only rest upon the exercise of the powers of the mind properly disciplined by study and reflection." Such publications, like other forms of travel literature, positioned their female readers as potential tourists, showing them to engage with the role and making the adventure of foreign travel seem relatively normal. This function was particularly evident in the travel pages of the Samuel Beeton's magazine *Queen*, which, in its early days, was aimed at middle-class women and offered a question-and-answer service and a letters column that dispensed sensible advice to lady travelers.

One of the strongest determinants of tourist behavior was a "sense of place." This was almost overwhelming in the case of Italy where tourists came looking for a familiar but imaginary world that sometimes proved as elusive and insubstantial as the towers of Venice seen through the shifting haze of the lagoon. The architectural canon focused their attention on the pagan and Christian past rather than the present. The majority of British tourists regarded Catholicism with fear and antipathy. They also held stereotyped views of foreigners and their alien manners and mores (Chard 1996) and invariably disregarded Harriet Martineau's (1838) injunction to avoid pre-conceived ideas and judgments. The widespread circulation of stereotyped descriptions and pictorial representations of contributed to the imageability of this "classic ground" (Lynch 1960: 9–10).[2] Medieval urban landscapes, classical ruins and architectural sites and monuments, domes and spires featured as key landmarks in the private inscapes of the weary travelers who, nearing their destination, were suddenly thrilled by a glimpse of a familiar dome or spire. Approaching Rome across the dreary Campagna in 1846 the actress Fanny Kemble was suddenly aware that against:

> the clear azure of the sky, a huge shadowy cupola suddenly rose up . . . the great vision rose higher and higher as we drove under its mighty mass; and as we turned within the Porta da Cavallegheri and stopped again at the barrier, St Peter's stood over against us, towering into the violet-coloured sky, and it was real, – and I really saw it, I knew the huge pillars of the noble arcade, and the pale ghost-like shining of the moonlit fountains through the colonnades, I was in Rome and it was the Rome of my imagination. (Butler 1847: 116)

Many tourists self-consciously saw particular places through the eyes of others. Catherine Taylor allowed Goethe, her favored literary companion, to represent her feelings on arrival:

> I now see all the dreams of my youth come alive, I am now seeing for real the first engravings I can remember (my father had views of Rome hanging in an antechamber) and everything I have for so long known in paintings and drawings, engravings and woodcuts, plaster and cork, now stands before me in one piece, wherever I go I find an acquaintance in a new world, it is all just as I imagined it and all new . . . . (cited in Taylor 1840–1: 115)

Not everything was as expected. Kemble had not anticipated the chasm-like "dark, dismal stinking streets" of Rome "through which we now rattled." The miseries of inadequate accommodation, bad smells, inclement weather, ill health and undesirable company were often just as memorable as the pleasures and disappointments associated with mandatory sights such as the Colosseum by moonlight (Birchall, 1985: 27). In places with no sidewalks the Wilson sisters only ventured out when the weather was good because the mud would ruin their skirts (Wilson 1987). Other experiences might include unfortunate encounters at the *table d'hôte* or on the promenade, lost luggage, wayward *vetturini* and *gondolieri* and sore feet. Most tourists used hotels on their arrival, then took apartments in neighbourhoods frequented by compatriots such as the Lungarno in Florence or the Piazza di Spagna in Rome where the artists' models congregating on the 'great, wide, beautiful steps' created a picturesque if slightly disturbing scene (Butler 1847: vol. I, 132).

English noses recognized the "smell of the Continent" that hung about so many hotels and streets. At the end of the century Florence was reputed to be one of Europe's filthiest cities where it was common practice to urinate on street walls (Leavitt 2002: 33). Bad smells were also associated with miasma, fever and death (Woodward, 2002: 26). The sounds of a place were as distinctive as its smell. The noise of Naples contrasted with the silence of Genoa's grass-grown streets, which Taylor preferred to the "busy streets and noisy multitudes of Leghorn." The silence of Venice was particularly striking while the sound of tourist laughter disrupted the awesome experience of the Colosseum at night. Places were also characterized by the pattern of the life flowing through their streets for while:

> The crowd in London is uniform and intelligible, it is a double line in quick motion – it is the crowd of business, The crowd of Naples consists of a general tide rolling up and down, and in the middle of this tide a hundred eddies of men; here you are swept by the current there you are wheeled around by the vortex. (Taylor 1840, 2: 50–7)

Sightseeing is usually regarded as one of the constitutive acts of tourism: but what to see and how to see it? It was here that the weight of the many distinguished and literate tourists of the past bore increasingly heavily on those of the present. The original author of Murray's *Handbook to Northern Italy*, Francis Palgrave, thankfully remarked that the necessity of being useful to his readers saved him from "the pursuit of that originality of a tourist which consists in omitting to omit great works because they have been noticed by others, and in crying up some object which has been deservedly passed over" (Murray 1869: ix). The management of sightseeing was both expressive and constitutive of social and cultural identity and an important determinant of individual style. An extreme example of the latter was revealed in William Beckford's *Italy* (1834), a belated publication of his suppressed Grand Tour memoir *Dreams, Waking Thoughts and Incidents* (1783) in which his youthful and romantic sensibility found a "gothic" experience in an Italian inn where broken pavings and newly strewn earth intimated "something horrid was concealed beneath" (Beckford 1834: 227–8) more evocative than the architectural wonders of Rome.

More conventional nineteenth-century tourists were anxious to see the accredited and unmissable sights, helpfully identified in the first of the relatively modern guides Marianna Starke's *Letters* (1815) embellished with exclamation marks and commentary. Starke's list of what to see adhered closely to the traditional architectural canon listed in such scholarly works as Eustace (1813) and Hoare (1819) and was focused on the ruins of the "classical south," Renaissance churches and palaces and expeditions to sites of Greek and Roman antiquities. John Ruskin's highly influential *Stones of Venice* (1851–3) and its passionate defence of the Gothic placed the Byzantine and medieval architecture of that city firmly on the tourist map. It was not until the next century that the beauty of Italy's Baroque churches began to be appreciated fully by more than a handful of art historians because most tourists and their guidebooks continued to view the Baroque as "degenerated Renaissance." (Baekeder 1900: lxxiv). As Edith Wharton (1928: 188) remarked of Rome, "for centuries it has been the fashion to look only on a city which has almost disappeared, and to close the eyes to one which is alive and actual."

Tourists faced with a mountain of luggage and a plethora of monuments were relieved to find help at hand in the form of John Murray's Italian *Handbooks*, first published in 1842 and which divided the country into three zones. Of the 13 British tour-guides to Italy published in the 1820s (Buzard 2001: 69–70) only Starke's popular and much revised guide was approved by the younger John Murray who described it as "a work of real utility" because it contained much practical information gathered on the spot." Notebook in hand, Murray planned to ease the path of travelers by systematically studying the needs and habits of fellow tourists and ordering and arranging his facts in the most convenient way. On arrival in a place he set out to:

> find out what was really worth seeing there, to make a selection of such objects, and to tell how best to see them . . . and not bewildering my readers by describing all that *might* be seen and using the most condensed and singular style in description of special objects. I made it my aim to point out things peculiar to the spot, or which might be seen better elsewhere. (Murray, cited in Smiles 1891: 462)

His labors provided his readers with lists of hotels, shops and small portable maps. Tourists accompanied by Murray could no longer claim like Goethe (1999: 138) that "everything was my own direct responsibility" thereby reinforcing the inclination of some travelers to use the word "tourist" pejoratively as a means of pointing to the social and cultural inferiority of others (Buzard 1993: 96–7). Most tourists however, found that Murray's *Handbooks* made it easier to plan routes and sightseeing itineraries, organize travel arrangements and, above all, to save time.

The prescriptive and regulative authority that Murray, Baedeker and later guides such as Augustus Hare came to exercise over tourist behavior has often been commented on for their injunctions became key agents in the acculturation process as did their itineraries. In his 1908 novel *A Room with a View*, E. M. Forster, for example, made much of poor Lucy Honeychurch's discomfort when she found herself in Florence's Santa Croce without her trusty Baedeker. Guidebook commentaries promoted and reinforced particular ways of seeing people and places. Read in front of the actual buildings, guidebooks appeared as "scripts" controlling what and how they were seen (Figure 3.1). The successive fashions for picturesque, sublime and romantic views left their mark on sightseeing conventions and generated many stereotyped and repetitive observations as tourists dutifully recorded their critical judgments on architecture in the appropriate language, often paying more attention to the view than the buildings themselves. Historical and literary associations allowed greater scope for imaginative response and required less artistic expertise and were actively encouraged by some guidebooks such

Figure 3.1 Postcard c.1905. Paul Hey "Tourists on the Rialto bridge," published by Otto Zieher, Munich. Collection of the author.

Augustus Hare's *Walks in Rome* (1871) based extensively on quotations from popular authors. Emily Birchall, honeymooning in Italy in 1873, vividly describes her sight of what, thanks to Macaulay's *Lays of Ancient Rome* (1842), was for her a sight "that I longed to see, more perhaps than anything else in Rome," as beneath her she spotted the remains of an old bridge she instinctively knew was the one where "brave Horatius stood alone." Leaning down she saw the basements of the piers:

> I look up and across the "broad floods" to the "further shore." I gaze on the yellow river, as tawny then as now, my feet are on the very spot where 'now he feels the bottom', now on dry earth he stands and the grand heroism of twenty four hundred years ago seems clear and real before my eyes. (Birchall 1985: 39)

Birchall belonged to the category of well educated middle-class tourists for whom recreational tourism remained a metaphorical vehicle of social and spiritual improvement and who assiduously followed Murray's (1858: xv) advice "to ascend some tower or eminence" in search of a "commanding view" for, as the author of "Off for the holidays" in the *Cornhill Magazine* announced "Mere rest is not true recreation" (Clayden 1867: 320). As attitudes to leisure became more relaxed, holiday travel began to be accepted as a legitimate means of recuperation from work. Among new tourists traveling abroad were a number of the new urban types mocked by humorists of the period and highly visible to their fellow Britons for, as William Thackeray (1866: 34) commented, "We carry our nation everywhere with us; and we are in our island wherever we go . . . always separated from the people in the midst of who we are." Kept aloof from their hosts by their lack of language skills and suspicious and superior attitudes to foreigners, the British were also acutely aware of social and cultural distinctions. The new tourists were also often isolated from the resident expatriate communities in Florence and Rome by their lack of formal introductions and social difference.

Some of the social types now traveling were represented in Richard Doyle's (1854) popular *The Foreign Tour*, a sketchbook-narrative relating the adventures of new suburban types engaged in a "middle-class tour." It shows them dutifully, if uncomprehendingly, studying architecture in Milan, where they are besieged by beggars and compatriots behave disgracefully in a church and a "snob" is spotted carving his name on the cathedral roof (Figure 3.2). In Verona they are harassed by the Austrians then occupying northern Italy (much to the disgust of the British). In Venice they quote Byron, take refreshment in St. Mark's Square and view the palaces of the Grand Canal from a gondola. Despite the best efforts of Murray and the humorists of the British press to spread awareness of the "tourist code," displays of snobbery, chauvinism and "ungentlemanly behavior" of the kind depicted by Doyle continued to distress "respectable" British tourists who were

A SNOB THEY SAW WRITING HIS NAME UPON ROOF OF
MILAN CATHEDRAL.

Figure 3.2 "Snob writing his name on the roof of Milan cathedral" (Doyle, 1854: 56). Author's copy.

extremely sensitive to the bad behavior of others for, as Frances Trollope (1842: 271–2) remarked, it was the few who created an image for the many and "the best of us cannot act as balance weight against the worst."

Doyle's kind of humour spotlights the self-consciousness liable to afflict inexperienced tourists. His sketches subjected them to the same kind of rhetorical framing and distancing devices as their guidebooks applied to the sights, providing a guide to the informal codes and conventions regulating tourist behavior. Not all treatments were so sympathetic for growing numbers of visitors led to complaints in the British press of the "herds," "flocks" and "droves" to be found in places like Florence. Displays of contempt evinced by the word "tourist" revealed the resentment felt by particular social groups at the invasion of the social and geographical spaces such as the Roman *Corso*, which they regarded as their own. Charles Lever (1865: 230–3) was particularly irritated by Thomas Cook's "excursionists," disparaging their dress, manners and deportment and the presence of females in the party. In a defensive interview Cook pointed out that though socially diverse, his customers for Italy all travelled "as if impressed with the notion that they are engaged in fulfilling the wishes of a lifetime, in a pleasant duty never to be repeated" and are "full of discussion among themselves, proving that they are all thoroughly well up with the subject. Many of them carry books of reference with them, and nearly all take notes" (cited in Wilson 1951: 311–12).

Elizabeth Tuckett recalled an encounter with a party of the infamous "excursionists" at a communal *table d'hôte* in Florence. The daughter of a clergyman, she adopts a superior view, observing that the "oddest thing is that Mr Cook himself cannot speak a word of any language but his own" (Tuckett 1866: 182). Her "letters home" frame the respectability of her own performance, distancing it from that of her fellow tourists, even as she subjects them to the same kind of critical scrutiny she applied to the sights. It was not the mixed social composition of the group or noisy arrival in the middle of the night that aroused her disapproval, but the uncomfortable, compressed and cut-price nature of the trip itself that, by ignoring established connections between season and place, endangered the health of participants. Nor was there sufficient time for the kind of reflective viewing of the city in which Tuckett was herself engaged, using George Eliot's 1862 medieval novel *Romola* as "an idealised Murray; just as the city in its turn is a daily illustration for the book" (Tuckett 1866: 105, 152).

The galleries and museums of Florence, the *Corso* and piazza, provided Tuckett with plentiful opportunities for "people-watching." Like most tourists she was acutely aware of other tourists, particular her own compatriots and she comments primly on the "utterly unprincipled . . . utterly bad" nature of some English people and distinguishes different sets, "fast, literary, fashionable, the high, low church, the sociable, the exclusive and the Americans" who were given to amateur theatricals (Tuckett 1866: 182). Tourists who travelled to keep up with their own social set used the promenades and public places such as theatres and hotel dining rooms as arenas for displays of conspicuous consumption through which they attempted to distinguish themselves from others (Richards 1990), thereby incurring the disapproval of those like Tuckett who adhered to codes of gentility in which respect for civic position, knowledge and taste were preeminent. At home, nineteenth-century Britons were skilled in detecting the signs of social standing, respectability and individual character in the physiognomy, facial expressions, gestures, style of dress, manners and deportment of their fellows (Cowling 1989). Letters to *Queen* indicate readers worried that unknown foreign territory was likely to generate situations requiring close scrutiny of the manners and behavior of themselves and others. Unfamiliar surroundings could provoke anxiety and acute self-consciousness, "particularly as the know-how of the habitus suddenly ceased to be able to modulate unforeseen events" (Edensor 1998).

Social difficulties of the kind associated with the congested urban spaces of home could be replicated by encounters with strangers in the new stations and the public rooms of hotels, in *trattoria*, tea rooms and cafés, in twisty narrow streets and stairwells and in gloomy old crypts and churches and in situations of enforced sociability such as the *table d'hôte*. Within the tourist community sociability was structured by many of the same codes of civility and the rules of etiquette that prevailed at home such as the calling card system which enabled members of different social and cultural networks, particularly women, to negotiate the shifting boundaries of social life and to protect the exclusivity of their social circles (Curtin 1985). Books of etiquette identified the perils of travel. Hotels were regarded as particularly dangerous places where "you are always exposed to the inspection and to the remarks of strangers" and categorized "according to the polish or coarseness of your manner" and "whispers are always overheard and glances always observed" (Anon. 1879: 26, 37).

The rise in tourist numbers was linked to industrialization and urbanization in Britain, increasing the attraction of environments perceived as untouched by the ugliness of modern life. For Taylor, one of the attractions of Italy was the "absence of smoke, the clear deep sky of deep azure . . . the thin pure atmosphere" (1840–1: 260). However, five years later the shock of seeing gas lamps along the Grand Canal impelled Ruskin to write of "the modern work that has set up its plague spot everywhere – the moment you begin to feel some gas pipe business forces itself upon the eye, until you are thrust into the 19th century" (cited in Quill 2000: 32). By the last quarter of the century unification and modernization were changing many of Italy's urban centers, especially the new capital of Rome "which is at once the great storehouse of Italy's monuments, and her modern capital, the center of her stirring life" but where "The full collision of the noisy present with silenced past is experienced" (Sully 1912: 74).

The effect of tourism on the built environment was increasingly apparent in the construction of building types such as stations, grand hotels, pump rooms for the drinking of mineral water, shopping facilities, museums and other places of entertainment. Modernity in the form of electric light, gas works in the Circus

Maximus, factories and tenements on the Campagna (Symons 1907: 56), trams, pavements and traffic impacted on the historic urban landscapes so highly valued by the tourists of the past and, until now, unchanged for decades. Visitors wrapped up in the contemplation of the architectural relics of the past were rudely recalled to the present-day world of the "noisy modern capital, to its hotels, to its photograph shops, and the rest" by the sight of the "personally conducted crowds" (Sully 1912: 82) for whose benefit Renaissance villas and palaces were demolished to make way for ugly new hotels and apartment blocks, and the masses of crumbling Roman masonry once beloved by poets and artists were stripped of vegetation by archeologists in the name of conservation. Reflective tourists like Arthur Symons wondered gloomily whether the Romans had lost their artistic sense. He complained bitterly of the devastation wrought by the building of the monument to Victor Emanuel, of the proposed destruction of part of the Castel San Angelo to make way for more traffic and of "the latest bevy of Cook's tourists sitting down to dinner on the exact spot where the gardens of Sallust had delighted the Romans for nearly the whole of the Christian era" (Symons 1907: 57).

In the early summer Americans greatly outnumbered the European travelers, among them many Germans, who "if apt to be a little loud in their manners are now probably the most studious and methodical of the new visitors." They were easily distinguished by their dress from "the English tourist with his rather too easy gait and set of the hat," and "the tall, straight, black-robed American, who has never mixed his languages and preserves a sublime, self-possession in the midst of a world unrealised" (Sully 1912: 64). Women were increasingly visible among the British tourists for as *Etiquette for Ladies* remarked "the ladies go everywhere now-a-days" (Anon c.1880: 179), possibly with a copy of *Hints to Lady Travellers* in their luggage. It became relatively common to see them in Italy traveling unescorted by male relatives (Cunningham 1990: 290; Pemble 1987: 77), indicating the continuing role that places like Florence played in British life. Here the influence of change was less visible than in Rome, its English *pensions* and teashops appearing as an extension of home, albeit one where, as elsewhere in Italy, greater social and sexual freedoms were possible for those who desired them.

Ordinary tourists were easily identified by their equipment of binoculars, sketchbooks and cameras. At home, sketching was a long-established practice, widely regarded as a valuable adjunct to the journal. Many tourists belonged to sketching circles, which, like essay clubs, were particularly popular in the 1860s and 1870s. For middle- and upper-class women sketching was still an important accomplishment (Bermingham 1993; Cherry 1993: 131–3, 169), licensing "discreet" scrutiny of the environment and its inhabitants. Occasionally the sketches were thought good enough for the author to seek publication. Photography soon provided another way of acquiring mementos, usually in the form of *cartes de visite* as well as views. Particularly important and distinctive were the high quality photographic reproductions of architectural subjects emanating from the studios of the Fratelli Alinari (Conti in Zevi 1978: 17–18). Treated as "monuments" separated from their urban context, they were valued by many experts interested in architecture, including Ruskin, and helped to extend appreciation of less well-known buildings. Tourists were able to buy prints from the Alinari shops, together with entire photographic albums and, later on, heavily illustrated guides. Sometimes new work was also commissioned.

In the 1880s Italy drew a new generation of students who longed to see its historic buildings and cultural artifacts for themselves. Canon Barnett organized an educational trip to Florence with the Toynbee Travelers, members of a philanthropic educational settlement in the East End of London, an enterprise now made feasible by improvements in the working hours, salaries and wages of the adult students for whom it catered. Revealing the influence of Ruskin, the publisher J. M. Dent, who was a member of the party, noted that:

> I can never make anyone understand what the revelation of this wondrous old world meant to me. Here was a city built before industrialism had destroyed the spirit of beauty, where man lived by something other than money-making, luxury and power. A city of flowers indeed, and a city beautified by men's handicraft. (Dent 1928: 52)

Dent later included the *Story of Venice* (1905) by his fellow student Thomas Okey in his *Medieval Towns* series, intended as educational guides. The series situated buildings and monuments in their historical context and was a further tribute to the value that the British continued to place on an Italian education.

The writer Vernon Lee, a member of the residential expatriate community in Florence, was among those called upon to lecture to the party. She believed that for true tourists an act of imaginative anticipation preceded the experience of the actual sight. "Honour the tourist; he walks in a halo of romance," she wrote, unlike those for whom travel was simply an extension of their normal mode of existence in some "metropolitan suburb" or those mysterious "dwellers in obscure pensions; curious beings who migrate without seeing any change of landscape and people but only change of fare" (Lee 1894: 311). Her avowed willingness to be "jostled in alpine valleys and Venetian canals by any number of vociferous tourists, for the sake of the one, schoolmistress, or clerk, or artisan, or curate, who may by this means have reached at last . . . the St Brandan's Isle of his or her longings" (Lee 1894: 307) was not shared by others. Stung by criticism of the proposed visit, Canon Barnett made every effort to educate his students in the tourist code with "one of his inimitable addresses on unselfishness in travel" with the result that as the party crossed the Alps they "huddled together . . . everybody being too unselfish to look out of the windows in case another's view should be intercepted" (Barnett 1919: vol. I, 359).

In the last decades of the century the desire to be different and to be published encouraged would-be authors to find novel ways of traveling. The journalist Hilaire Belloc walked to Rome along the old pilgrimage route while Ruskin's image of the railway traveller as "a living parcel" struck a chord with supporters of the bicycle such as journalist Elizabeth Robins Pennell, who with her husband Joseph, toured Italy's medieval towns on tricycles, reporting on the experience for *Harper's*. The journalist Douglas Sladen, one of the new breed of professional travel writers, wrote of the way that the new Italy:

> has golf and fox-hunting beside the tombs of the Appian Way, and a brilliant café at the very foot of the new Capitol while the great military roads of the Peninsula echo all day long with the whirr of the swift Darracq or the mountain-climbing F.I.A.T. For Italy . . . is the happy hunting ground of the Automobilist. (Sladen 1912: 4)

Authors with more literary aspirations were haunted by romantic attitudes to travel but found it increasingly difficult to demonstrate the originality of their performance. Acutely aware of the social meanings of style and place, impressionistic essays of the kind written by Vernon Lee or Arthur Symons exemplified the mode of "the writer as embodied sensorium" (Clifford 1997: 53), a phrase that neatly describes the narrative devices of the telling detail, casual erudition and self-reflexive allusion through which they tried to distinguish themselves from the less perceptive or gifted.

Reading communities, like tourists were differentiated by social class and gender. Popular writing, including the representation of tourist experiences in fictional form continued to be socially prescriptive: different styles of performance were useful for indicating social, cultural and national differences. British stereotypes of Americans abroad were particularly popular as a means of highlighting "correct" English or European behavior, or for making fun of it. Most protagonists of the romantic novels aimed at the rapidly growing numbers of young working women and set abroad continued to be upper class, although some were not. The promotional magazine *Travel,* published by the travel agent Henry Lunn, included a short story by L. T. Meade, a tale of a "lady-like" young woman on a trip to Rome, which gave clear guidance about what to expect on such a trip. Her performance as a tourist led to romance and a job as a travel writer (Meade 1898–99: 571–7). Tales of this kind gave clear guidance as to what to expect and indicated the opening up of a potential market of yet more travelers who would be drawn southwards by Italian sun and culture (Steward 1998).

The rapidity with which communication by postcard ceased to be regarded as "vulgar," and became almost universal practice (Figure 3.3), is a clear example of the way that changing standards interacted with styles of performance. In 1900 the artist G. R. Sims complained that "there is barely room for you to write your

MOONLIGHT SCENE OF THE FORUM (COOK'S TEN GUINEA ROME TOURS)

Figure 3.3 Postcard c. 1905 "Moonlight scene of the Forum" (advertising Rome and back for 10 guineas, published by Thomas Cook). Collection of the author.

name . . . they are utterly destructive of style, and give absolutely no play to the emotions" (cited in Carline 1971: 57). Seven years later many shared the relief of the journalist James Douglas:

> Many a man in the epistolary age could not face the terrors of the Grand Tour, for he knew that he would be obliged to spend most of his time describing what he saw or ought to have seen . . . he was forced to tear himself from the scenery in order to write laborious descriptions of it to his friends at home. Now he merely buys a picture postcard at each station, scribbles on it a few words in pencil, and posts it. This enhances the pleasures of travel. (Douglas 1907, cited in Staff 1978: 79)

Conclusion

At the outbreak of the First World War the British love affair with Italy was unabated although its nature was very different from that of the 1840s. Changes in modes of travel and attitudes to Italian culture contributed to the mapping out of the complex network of social distinctions and snobberies comprising British society, many of which were exemplified in E. M. Forster's *Room with a View* (1908). The different styles of tourist performance manifested by the successive generations passing through the Piazza Vecchio or along the Roman Corso represented the shifting boundaries of British social life as well as changes in the habitus and personal aspirations of individual travelers and the social and cultural networks to which they belonged. As an art of performance, the practices of nineteenth-century cultural tourism as they were viewed by their different audiences, at home and abroad, contributed to the network of social distinctions constituting British social life. They evoked not so much the realities of the geographical spaces through which particular tourists passed, as the social and cultural spaces left behind and to which they returned.

Notes

1. Allen wrote a series of historical guides to Europe's leading cultural centers in which the itineraries were organized according to his own particular theory of historical and cultural evolution (Steward, 2004).
2. Lynch's imageable city (he cites Venice as an example) is one that is "(apparent, legible or visible) . . . it invites the eye and ear to greater attention and participation . . . such a city would be one that could be apprehended over time as pattern of high continuity with many distinctive parts interconnected. The perceptive and familiar observer could absorb new and sensuous impacts without disruption of his basic images image, and each new image would touch on many previous elements" (Lynch 1960: 10).

References

Adler, J. (1989a), "Travel as Performed Art", *American Journal of Sociology*, 84: 1366–91.

Allen, G. (1901), *The European Tour*, New York: Dodd, Mead.

Anon. (1879), *How to Travel, or, Etiquette of Ship, Rail, Coach and Saddle*, London: Ward, Lock, Tyler.

Anon. (c.1880), *Etiquette for Ladies: a Complete Guide the Table, the Toilette, and the Ball-room with Hints on Courtship, Music and Manners*, London: Ward, Lock.

Baedeker, K. (1900), *Italy: Handbook for Travellers*, 13th revised edition, Leipzig: K. Baedeker.

Bailey, P. (1978), *Victorian England: Rational Recreation and the Contest for Control, 1830–1865*, London: Routledge & Kegan Paul.

Barnett, H. (1918), *Canon Barnett, His Life, Work and Friends*, London: John Murray.

Beckford, W. (1834), *Italy: with Sketches of Spain and Portugal*, vol. 1, London: Richard Bentley.

Bermingham, A. (1993), "The Aesthetics of Ignorance: the Accomplished Woman in the Culture of Connoisseurship", *Oxford Art Journal*, 16(2): 1–20.

Birchall, E. (1985), *Wedding Tour: January–June 1873*, edited by D. Verey, New York: St. Martin's Press.

Bourdieu, P. (1978). *Distinction: a Social Critique of Taste*, Routledge & Kegan Paul: London.

Butler, Mrs. (*neé* Kemble, F.) (1847), *A Year of Consolation*, 2 vols, London: Edward Mason.

Buzard, J. (1993), *The Beaten Track: European Tourism and the Ways to Culture, 1800–1918*, Oxford: Clarendon Press.

Buzard, J. (2001), "The Grand Tour and after – 1840", in Hulme, P. and Youngs, T. (eds), *The Cambridge Companion to Travel Writing*, Cambridge: Cambridge University, pp. 37–52.

Carline, R. (1971), *Pictures in the Post: the Story of the Picture Postcard and its Place in the History of Popular Art*, London: Gordon Fraser.

Chaney, D. (1993), *Fictions of Collective Life*, London: Routledge.

Chard, C. (1996), "Crossing Boundaries and Exceeding Limits: Destablization, Tourism and the Sublime", in Chard, C. and Langdon, H. (eds), *Transports: Travel, Pleasure and Imaginative Geography, 1600–1830*, New Haven and London: Yale University, pp. 117–49.

Cherry, D. (1993), *Painting Women, Victorian Women Artists*, London/New York: Routledge.

Clayden, P. (1867), "Off for the Holidays: the Rationale of Recreation", *Cornhill Magazine*, 16: 315–22.

Clifford, J. (1997), *Routes: Travel and Translation in the Late Twentieth Century*, Cambridge MA: Harvard.

Conti, A. (1978), "The Photographic Documentation of Nineteenth-century Art", in Zevi, F. (ed.), *Alinari, Photographers of Florence*, Florence: Alinari Edizioni/ Idea Editions in association with the Arts Council of Scotland, pp 17–19.

Cowling, M. (1989), *The Artist as Anthropologist: The Representation of Types and Characters in Victorian Society*, Cambridge: Cambridge University Press.

Cunningham, H. (1990), "Leisure and Culture", in Thompson, F.M.L. (ed.), *The Cambridge Social History of Britain 1750–1950* (II), People and their Environment, Cambridge: Cambridge University Press.

Curtin, M. (1985), "A Question of Manners: Status and Gender in Etiquette and Courtesy", in *Journal of Modern History*, 57: 395–423.

Davidson, L. Campbell (1889), *Hints to Lady Traveller at Home and Abroad*, London: Iliffe.

Dent, J. M. (1928), *The Memoirs of J. M. Dent*, London: J. M. Dent.

Doyle, R. (1854), *The Foreign Tour of Messrs. Brown, Jones and Robinson in Belgium, Germany, Switzerland and Italy*, London: Bradbury & Evans.

Edensor, T. (1998), *Tourists at the Taj*, London/New York: Routledge.

Eustace, J. C. (1813), *Classical Tour through Italy*, 2 vols, London: J. Mawson.

Frawley, M. (1994), *A Wider Range: Travel Writing by Women in Victorian England*, Rutherford. N. J.: Fairleigh Dickinson.

Goodman, N. (1978), *Ways of World-making*, Indianpolis/Ind: Hachett.

Goethe, J. M. (1999), *The Flight to Italy: Diary and Selected Letters,* translated by T. J. Reed, Oxford: Oxford University.

Hare, A. (1871), *Walks in Rome*, 2 vols, London: Strahan.

Hetherington, K. (1998), *Expressions of Identity: Space, Performance and Politics*, London: Sage.

Hoare, Sir R. (1819), *A Classical Tour through Italy and Sicily,* London: J. Newman.

Hoare, R. (1819), *A Classical Tour through Italy and Sicily, tending to illustrate some of the Districts which have not been described by Mr. Eustace in his Classical Tour*, London: Lawson

Leask, N. (2002), *Curiosity and the Aesthetics of Travel Writing 1770–1840; From an Antique Land*, Oxford: Oxford University.

Leavitt, D. (2002), *Florence: a Delicate Case*, London: Bloomsbury.

Lee, V. (1894), "On Modern Travelling", *Macmillan's Magazine*, 69: 306–11.

Lever, C. (1865), *Blackwood's Magazine*, 97, February: 230–33.

Lynch, K. (1960), *The Image of the City*, Cambridge MA: Technology/Harvard University.

Martineau, H. (1838), *How to Observe, Morals and Manner,* London: C. Knight.

Meade, L. T. (1898/99), "A Lover of the Beautiful", *Travel*, 3, May–April: 571–77.

Murray, J, III (1858), *A Handbook for Travellers on the Continent*, 11th edition, London: John Murray.

Murray, J, III (1869), *Handbook for Travellers in Northern Italy*, 11th edition, orig. by Sir Francis Palgrave. London: John Murray.

Okey, T. (1905), *The Story of Venice* (Medieval Towns Series), London: J. M. Dent.

Pemble, J. (1987), *The Mediterranean Passion: Victorians and Edwardians in the South*, Oxford: Oxford University Press.

Quill, S. (2000), *Ruskin's Venice: the Stones Revisited*, Aldershot: Ashgate.

Richards, T. (1990), *The Commodity Culture of Victorian England: Advertising and Spectacle, 1851–1914*, London: Verso.

Ruskin, J. (1858), *The Stones of Venice*, second edition, 3 vols, London: Smith Elder.
—— (1903), "The Seven Lamps of Architecture", in Cook, E. T. and Wedderburn, A. (eds), *The Collected Works of John Ruskin,* London: George Allen.
Schlechner, R. (1981), *Between Theatre and Anthropology,* Philadelphia: University of Pennsylvania.
Sketchley, A. (G. Rose) (1870), *Out for a Holiday with Cook's Excursion through Switzerland and Italy*, London: George Routledge.
Sladen, D. (1912), *How to See Italy by Rail,* London: Kegan Paul, Trench, Trübner.
Smiles, S. (1891), *A Publisher and his Friends: Memoir and Correspondence of the late John Murray*, London: John Murray.
Staff, F. (1978), *The Picture Postcard and its History*, London: Lutterworth.
Starke, M. (1815), *Letters from Italy*, second revised edition, London: G. and S. Robinson.
Steward, J. (1998), "The 'Travel Romance' and the Emergence of the Female Tourist", *Studies in Travel Writing*, 2: 85–105.
—— (2004), "Grant Allen and the Business of Travel", in Greenslade, W. and Rodgers, T. (eds), *Fin de-Siècle Politics*, Basingstoke: Ashgate.
Sully, J. (1912), *Italian Travel Sketches*, London: Constable.
Symons. A. (1907), *Cities of Italy*, London: J. M. Dent.
Taylor, C. (1840–1), *Letters from Italy to a Younger Sister*, London: John Murray.
Thackeray, W. M. [Mr. M. A. Titmarsh] (1866), *The Kickleburys on the Rhine*, London: Smith Elder.
Titmarsh, M-A. [W. Thackeray] (1866), *The Kickleburys on the Rhine*, second edition, London: Smith Elder.
Todorov, T. (1996), "The Journey and its Narratives", in Chard, C. and Langdon, H. (eds), *Transports: Travel, Pleasure and Imaginative Geography, 1600–1830*, New Haven and London: Yale University, pp. 287–98.
Towner, J. (1985), "The Grand Tour: a Key Phase in the History of Tourism", *Annals of Tourism Research*, 12(3): 297–333.
—— (1996), *An Historical Geography of Recreation and Tourism in the Western World: 1540–1940,* Chichester: John Wiley.
Trollope, F. (1842), *A Visit to Italy*, 2 vols, London: Richard Bentley.
Tuckett, E. (1866), *Beaten Tracks: or Pen and Pencil Sketches in Italy*, London: Longman, Green.
Wharton, E. (1905, 1928), *Italian Backgrounds*, London: Macmillan.
Wilson, M. (1951), "Travel and Holidays", in Young, G. M. (ed.), *Early Victorian England* 1830–1865, London, Oxford University Press, pp. 288–313.
Wilson, M. (1987), *A European Journal: Two Sisters Abroad in 1847*, edited by J. Simpson, London: Bloomsbury.
Woodward, C. (2002), *In Ruins*, London: Vintage.
Zevi, F. (ed.) (1978), *Alinari: Photographers of Florence 1852–1920,* Florence: Alinari/Idea/Scottish Arts Council.

Part II
Politics of Pilgrimage

–4–

From Tripoli to Ghadames: Architecture and the Tourist Experience of Local Culture in Italian Colonial Libya

Brian McLaren

On 30 May 1925, just one month before he would resign his post as governor of the Tripolitanian region of Libya to join the Ministry of Finance under Fascist dictator Benito Mussolini, Giuseppe Volpi returned to Tripoli from an automobile *raid* that had taken him to the oasis of Ghadames and back in a total of ten travel days. Volpi, who was Governor from 1921 to 1925, was accompanied on this rather dangerous motorized journey by his wife and daughter, as well as an entourage of four guests that included General Rodolfo Graziani and his wife (Volpi 1925). Although he participated in this expedition as a tourist, this was the same General Graziani who had presided over Volpi's reconquest of Tripolitania – a process that culminated just over one year earlier with a series of military exercises that recaptured this oasis settlement on the edge of the Sahara (Del Boca 1991: 36–7). The participation of Graziani in this event is no coincidence. With only seven passengers on board, this caravan was comprised of twelve officers guiding four vehicles and one equipment truck – something that gave it the appearance of a military exercise rather than a tourist excursion.

Although the conjunction of tourism and military control found in the automobile *raid* was only a temporary stage in the development of the tourist system, this mode of travel reflects a distinguishing feature of the tourist experience in Libya during the period of Italian colonialism (1911–43). The presentation of even the most authentic forms of indigenous culture was almost always filtered through the means and mechanisms of the modern metropole, thereby producing a liminal state in which the identities of East and West, indigenous and metropolitan, were fused into a single, but highly contested, reality. The central argument of this chapter is that the tourist experience in Libya existed in a space of interaction where the modernization of the colony and the preservation of its indigenous culture were negotiated. To be a tourist was to be simultaneously framed by the mechanisms of modern metropolitan culture – including the systems of transportation and accommodation as well as hierarchies of political and social control – and removed from them – escaping the moral and cultural boundaries of the West in favor of an experience of difference.

However, in Libya the presentation of local culture in the tourist architecture was more than a form of "staged authenticity" that Dean MacCannell (1999: 99) argues self-consciously presents the inner workings of a given tourist environment, thereby providing an experience that is purported to be free of all artifice. Given that the Italian colonial authorities were presenting Libyan culture and not their own, this tourist system instead offered a staging of cultural difference. It was a political gesture – a reification of the Italian colonial policy that called for the incorporation of the native into the modern. This approach can be seen as distinct from the "civilizing mission" of the French whose colonial order, Patricia Morton (2000: 6) argues, sought to maintain a strict segregation of Europeans from the natives. Beginning with the Governorship of Volpi, the official policy was to incorporate Libya into metropolitan Italy at the same time as preserving the customs and practices of the local populations. This second strategy led to initiatives that included a relatively systematic program of preserving Muslim religious sites (Bartoccini 1926: 350–52). Such programs were part of a so-called "indigenous politics" whose aim was to simultaneously disarm dissent by gestures of reconciliation and place the culture of the Libyans under the strictest form of regulation.

Tourism and Modernization

> The tourist organization of Libya is strictly tied to the rebirth and development of the colony. With the indigenous populations subdued and large groups of Italian farmers introduced into the agricultural zones – that is to say, with the conclusive phase of the colonial arrangement being reached – the problem of tourist organization was born and namely, the necessity to bring the colonial environment in line with a tone and a level of civilization capable of establishing active currents of life with the outside, because these same propelling elements of civilization and wealth flow back [to the colony]. (Brunelli 1937: 1)

The modernization program of the Italian colonial authorities in Libya was to a great extent a necessary precondition for the creation of a tourist system. In fact, along with the reoccupation of land, the creation of an agricultural economy and the construction of a suitable image to mark the Italian presence, the development of a tourist system was one of the four main components of the program of rebirth of Tripolitania under Volpi (Talamona 1992: 69). It was in this context that tourism was presented as an integral part of the politics of transportation and communication – systems that were referred to as a: "new source of well-being and of activity for the colony." (Queirolo 1925: 260).

Although the initial tourist development of Libya began during the mid-1920s, an organized tourist system was not possible until an extensive infrastructure of roads and public services was completed during the governorship of Italo Balbo (1934–40). The connection between the new infrastructure and the tourist system was the subject of a 1936 article published in the Italian Touring Club (TCI) journal *Le Vie d'Italia*. This essay dealt with the new transportation arteries that connected Tripoli with the towns of Garian, Jefren, Nalut and the oasis of Ghadames. Though lamenting the loss of the "romantic aspect" of travel, this paved highway system was described as: "the most beautiful way of tourist penetration in our Mediterranean colony" (Loschi 1936: 529).

The most important initiative that the Balbo administration pursued for the creation of a well-ordered tourist system was the foundation of a centralized authority for the control of all related activities. This stage was reached with the formation of the Libyan Tourism and Hotel Association (ETAL) in May of 1935. After more than a year of working with the existing organizations, Balbo decided to create a single group that could preside over and participate in all areas of the tourist economy (Vicari 1942: 955–75). This association provided the services of a travel agency, organizing itineraries involving all forms of travel. It acted as a tour operator, supplying car and motor coach transportation throughout this region. The ETAL was also responsible for the management of the eighteen hotels that belonged to the colonial government and the municipality – including the most prominent hotels in Tripoli, Benghazi and the Libyan interior – and the supervision of a network of entertainment facilities that included a theater and casino. Finally, this group handled its own publicity campaigns, producing brochures, guide books, and postcards and organizing displays at exhibitions and fairs in Italy and abroad (Figure 4.1). This combination of activities and resources not only facilitated the provision of an inclusive package of services; it allowed the ETAL to conduct these activities with a unity of purpose that, it was argued: "without exaggeration can be called totalitarian" (ETAL 1938: 1).

One of the key components of the tourist system was the means by which the experience of modernity was constructed for the Italian and foreign visitor. The first of these was through the organization of a series of activities that effectively transported the metropolitan context to the shores of Libya. One such venue was the Arena at Sharah al-Shatt – an outdoor facility that could seat up to 2,000 people. This building was used for a festival of Italian and foreign films that ran between July and October each year and attracted some 60,000 visitors (Vicari 1942: 971). In addition to such cultural events, it was used for boxing matches and outdoor shooting competitions, both of which were held at an international level. The Theater in the Uaddan Hotel and Casino in Tripoli provided a similar experience of the metropole in the colony. Notably, the Libyan Tourism and Hotel Association brought in actors and musicians from Italy to provide forms of

ENTE TURISTICO ED ALBERGHIERO
DELLA LIBIA

COMBINAZIONI DI SOGGIORNO
IN
LIBIA
A PREZZI SPECIALI (TUTTO COMPRESO)

Figure 4.1 Libyan Tourism and Hotel Association, Vacation Combinations in Libya, travel brochure, 1937. Collection of the author.

entertainment that principally appealed to a highly cultured Western audience. During the 1938/9 tourist season this program included inviting nine different drama companies and sponsoring four orchestral concerts (Vicari 1942: 971). The metropolitan aspirations of this facility are particularly evident in the architectural expression of the interior. Designed by the architect Florestano di Fausto in conjunction with Stefano Gatti-Casazza, this space provided an opulent but conventional context for these performances – a space that would have seemed just as appropriate in the streets of Milan as it was in Tripoli.

The experience of the metropole was not limited to such entertainment facilities. It was quite literally suffused throughout the tourist system, which attempted to provide a network of amenities that met the expectations of the Italian and foreign traveler. These services included the motor coaches that were used for travel into the pre-Saharan regions of Libya, which were described as representing: "the best automobile technology that has been realized" (ETAL 1939: 60). From a practical standpoint, these vehicles were well insulated against the sun and equipped with a small bar and bathroom facilities. They also provided for a level of personal luxury, furnishing each passenger with a separate seat that reclined and swiveled, and had individual tables and radios. In contrast with the adventurous experience of the much earlier automobile *raid*, these "spacious, comfortable and luminous" motor coaches rendered the difficult realities of travel invisible (ETAL 1938b: 5).

The explicitly stated goal of creating an experience of the metropole in the colony also extended to the network of hotels. This system was seen to have the same level of service in centers of secondary tourist importance as they did in the major cities of Tripoli and Benghazi. In fact, all of the hotels provided at least first- or second-class accommodation, all had modern bathroom facilities, and almost all offered the option of three meals with a room. The importance of these amenities was certainly not lost on the ETAL, which in a news release stated: "to find a bathroom for each room and hot and cold running water 750 kilometers from the heart of Africa is undoubtedly a very pleasurable surprise" (ETAL n.d.: 2).

The application of a Western standard of comfort in Libya was not without political implications. Colonial travel during the latter 1930s was closely tied to the government policy that aimed to modernize this region in order to incorporate it into the larger Italy – an aspiration that came to fruition in January of 1939 when Libya became the nineteenth region of Italy (Del Boca 1991: 279–80). The tourist system was a projection of these same standards onto the colonial context, and as such it offered an experience that was continuous with metropolitan Italy. In a sense, tourism in Libya during the Balbo era was a kind of propelling mechanism for the modernization program that was official colonial policy. By participating in this modernizing and colonizing program, the creation of an efficient system of travel and accommodation provided a means for escaping the colony for the comfort of the metropole.

Staging the Indigenous

For its Oriental, indigenous and primitive fascination, Tripolitania has preeminence over all of the regions of the African Mediterranean, being less profoundly penetrated by the cosmopolitanism that radiates from the cities of Egypt, Tunisia, Algeria and Morocco. The Arab, devoted to traditions, lives in his psychological and social climate, without mystifications and contaminations. Moreover, the faith that the Italians inspire in the natives allows us to experience their way of life. (Bertarelli 1929: 269)

The experience of local culture through the tourist system in Libya was increasingly determined by an influential body of scholarly study. In fact, the difference between organized travel and scientific research was somewhat blurred – something that is expressed in a compelling way in the book *Da Leptis Magna a Gadames*. This publication recounts Raffaele Calzini's visit to Libya including his participation in an automobile *raid*. In so doing, it offers a carefully written examination of the indigenous populations like the Tuareghs, who are described as: "the most fierce and bellicose population of the African world" (Calzini 1926: 202). Like the early writings of Italian anthropologists, this book provides what was believed to be an objective examination of the indigenous body, which in this case is fully integrated with the experience of colonial travel.

The discourse on the study and representation of indigenous culture had a great influence on the evolution of the tourist experience in Libya. The research conducted during the 1930s was one of the most important sources of information on local culture, and it disseminated this information directly or infiltrated tourist related publications like guide books and brochures. Moreover, the objects of attention of this research – the human and material culture of Libya – was the same culture that the tourist audience was seeking to experience. Accordingly, the activities that these fields of research undertook were often directly grafted into tourist related representations – such as the identification and classification of different racial groups within the local populations (Bertarelli 1929: 218–29). The assumptions underlying these disciplines – the presumed organic relationship between so-called primitive societies and their cultural artifacts – and even their scientific method – that these cultures should be viewed in a manner that is undisturbed by modern influences – also became determining factors for the tourist experience.

Not only did the research expedition offer a model for structuring tourist experience in the colonies, in some cases tourism so thoroughly assumed the procedures of scholarly fields like anthropology that it became a form of analogous research. An example of this phenomenon can be found in the 1935 "National Excursion" by the TCI to the Fezzan in the southwestern desert region of Libya. One of the significant aspects of this excursion, which visited the oases of Suknah, Brach, Sabha and Marzuq, is that it followed an itinerary that was almost identical to that of the 1933 research mission led by Lidio Cipriani and Antonio Mordini. Equally important to the connection between scientific study and tourism is the fact that the results of this expedition were published in *Le Vie d'Italia* in September of 1933 (Cipriani 1933: 679–91). In looking at the subsequent report of the National Excursion, it is quite apparent that not only was this tourist itinerary inspired by and following the route of a research mission, it was clearly organized according to the same logic and showed the same kind of "systematic and patient inquiry" (Bonardi 1935: 485–96).

The scientific means of representation of native culture also informed the creation of a number of tourist environments that were owned and operated by the Libyan Tourism and Hotel Association. One of the most compelling of these settings was the so-called Arab Café designed by the architect Di Fausto, which was located in the artisanal quarter at the Suq al-Mushir. This larger project was one of the most important restoration works carried out during the Balbo administration due to its location within the nineteenth century covered market just inside the walls of the old city of Tripoli. The work of Di Fausto included remaking the city gate alongside the castle and restructuring one of the sixteenth century Spanish bastions (Bucciante 1937: 10–11). This facility was equally significant for its close connection with the government-sponsored reorganization of the indigenous craft industries of Libya. It accommodated the new facilities for the Muslim School of Arts and Crafts, which required a combination of classrooms and workshops and some small shops for the sale of goods.

As part of this larger facility, the Arab Café presented native performances in a setting that one commentator argued: "fully reproduces the suggestive local environment" (Vicari 1942: 971). The project is a carefully studied reinterpretation of the local forms, expressed through a restrained and simplified architectural vocabulary. The sense of authenticity of the space was reinforced through the use of decorative tiles produced in the adjacent school that reenacted traditional forms and patterns. The interest in creating an authentic experience for the tourists extended to the indigenous performances, which included the eroticism of "traditional" oriental dance – where Arab women were clad in thin layers of revealing clothing (Figure 4.2).

This tourist experience was assembled according to the same eminent logic that pervaded the Italian intervention in Libyan culture. From the time of the foundation of the Government Office of Indigenous Applied Arts in January of 1925, the improvement of the production of local craftsmen – who were seen to be practicing an "unclear and impure" interpretation of Arab art – was tied to their education in techniques that better corresponded with what Italian scholars argued was authentic to the region (Quadrotta 1937: 1–37). In a similar manner, in response to a perceived lack of qualified local musicians and dancers to work in the Arab Café, the ETAL created a music school to train the Libyans. It would thus seem that in the tourist system, indigenous culture was not presented so much as it was represented according to the demands of the modern tourist and the politics of colonial rule.

While the appeal of the indigenous culture of Libya was in its exotic qualities – in its difference – it is also clear that this presentation had to conform to a contemporary "scientific" understanding. The preservation discourse related to the creation of authentic tourist environments and the rational logic with which the indigenous events were planned and staged, underscores the fact that the apparent

Figure 4.2 Oriental dance, Arab Café, Suq al-Mushir, Tripoli, Libya, postcard, 1937. Collection of the author.

opposition between the modern and the indigenous has every appearance of being false. The preservation and presentation of local culture in Libya was itself modern – conceived according to the modern demands of tourism, and presented through means that, despite their appearance, were modern. In this sense it can be argued that in the context of the tourist system in Libya, the indigenous was also modern.

From Tripoli to Ghadames

> In the distance we see the triangle marking the meeting of the borders of Libya, Tunisia and Algeria. Is this the symbolic expression of a no man's land? No, because still invisible, magically protected by the mobile barrier of the dunes, Ghadames awaits in the gleaming oasis of the day, glowing red at night and the deep violet shadow of the evening. It is the gateway to the Sahara, the magic sentinel of the desert, the prophetic citadel of dreams. (ETAL 1938b: 53–4)

The route from Tripoli to Ghadames had been understood, at least from the time of the Governorship of Volpi, as one of the most desirable and characteristic tourist experiences in Libya. To a great extent this interest was linked to the fact that Ghadames had been a crucial stopping point along the caravan routes that linked the Sudan to Tripoli and the Mediterranean. This fascination was then fueled by a combination of literary speculation and reportage that reached a mass audience, and scientific exploration and research that informed and influenced these various representations. In the first case, the image of Ghadames, and of the interior of Libya, was constructed in literary discourse as a mysterious and timeless repository of the most primitive origins of Libyan culture. One such publication is Angelo Piccioli's *La Porta magica del Sahara*, which was widely disseminated in Italy and eventually translated into German and English. In this publication, the author offers the following poetic description of the experience of the oasis: "everywhere around us, and also within us, a marvelous silence – a silence as transparent as the water . . . The impression [of Ghadames] is of beauty and a fleeting ancient harmony" (Piccioli 1931).

Such literary representations were parallel to and supported by a considerable body of research (Del Boca 1991: 271–78). The most significant of these studies was produced by Emilio Scarin, a professor from the University of Florence who published *L'Insediamento umano nella Libia occidentale* in 1940. A culmination of the work he presented at the first Congress of Colonial Studies of 1931, this book provides detailed documentation of the relationship between the forms of housing, the physical and environmental landscape and the patterns of living of the indigenous settlements in western Libya (Scarin 1931: 24–39). It is interesting to note that the objects of greatest interest to researchers like Scarin, like the Berber castle in Nalut and the oasis of Ghadames, were also important elements of the tourist itinerary.

The representation of the indigenous culture of the Libyan interior occurred parallel to the tourist development, which began after the conquest by Governor Volpi. The subsequent military control of the region coincided with a program of improvement of the road network under the governorships of Emilio De Bono (1925–8) and Pietro Badoglio (1929–33). These improvements were quickly followed by the initiation of bi-monthly transportation service between Tripoli and Ghadames in January of 1929. The tourist experience of this itinerary was greatly enhanced with the construction of the first hotel in Ghadames in November 1931, at which time travel in this region was available to a wider audience (Bertarelli 1929: 321). During the governorship of Italo Balbo, the construction of the hotels in Jefren and Nalut and the substantial renovation of the hotel in Ghadames were undertaken. Notably, these projects were executed with the most scrupulous attention to a historic fabric that was at the same time being restored by the municipality (Bucciante 1937: 15–16). By late 1935, this route took on the status of a coordinated tourist system. Not only had all of these hotels been completed but weekly excursions to Ghadames had been initiated using Saharan motor coaches, a journey that involved two travel days in each direction (Vicari 1942: 968–70). Under the direction of the Libyan Tourism and Hotel Association and with the support of the building program of the Balbo administration, the itinerary to

Ghadames combined a modern transportation system with a tourist infrastructure that was intended to harmonize with the local environment.

The pre-Saharan hotels in Jefren, Nalut and Ghadames, each designed by the architect Di Fausto, were an integral part of a continuous tourist experience. The importance of this travel route to the identity of tourism in Libya was evidenced in the publication *Itinerario Tripoli-Gadames* – whose cover conveys an evocative image of its final destination. The experience was characterized as providing an efficient and comfortable means of travel supported by hotels which, in addition to being carefully contextualized to their site and the local architecture, provided: "the most comfortable hospitality" (ETAL 1938b: 29). It is also clear from this book that the journey could provide insights into the traditional architecture of this region – such as the so-called troglodyte houses of the Gharyan and Jabal regions – and the history, customs and practices of its Arab and Berber populations – thus imparting views that were taken from contemporary research (Scarin 1940: 144–59). By the means of this representation, the itinerary to Ghadames was a curious hybrid of a modern tourist excursion and a scientific expedition.

A Pre-Saharan Regionalism

> Like the hotel in Jefren, that in Nalut enjoys a stupendous panorama not only towards the primitive Berber town, dominated by the arduous extravagant mass of the castle, but to the subordinate landscape, to that prodigious precipitate of cliffs between the crevices of valleys and the profound chasms of the wadis, that slope to the plain in a flooding outburst. (ETAL 1938b: 41)

The first hotel along the route from Tripoli to Ghadames, the Hotel Rumia in Jefren, was named for a legendary natural spring that existed in the adjacent valley. The hotel was located on the ruins of an existing fortress from the period of Ottoman rule, acting as a simple horizontal block set in relation to the remains of the existing structure. In this sense, the form of the hotel was generated out of a careful reading of the site. Its battered walls and blank stucco surfaces established a dialectical relationship to the remaining bastion and the horizontal plateau on which it was located (Figure 4.3). However, its profile can be understood as a more than just a response to similar qualities in the site and the surrounding landscape. The Hotel Rumia was a physical manifestation of the view for which it became a self-conscious framing device.

Although the hotel in Jefren does not directly reflect the local forms of the Berber settlements, it is a product of the same processes that produced these kinds of indigenous constructions. In this regard, Di Fausto was extremely attentive to the harsh climate of this region, to which he responded with a largely solid exterior wall and the discreet use of loggias and arched recesses. Equally well considered

Figure 4.3 Florestano Di Fausto, Hotel Rumia, Jefren, Libya, 1934. The Mitchell Wolfson Jr. Collection – Fondazione Regionale Cristoforo Colombo, Genoa, Italy.

in relation to climatic exigencies were the various window openings, which used a combination of shutters and screening devices. The interior of the project, which was executed in conjunction with the architect Gatti-Casazza, was similarly derived from its context. It employed rich materials and patterns that recreated the sense of intimacy and repose often found in the domestic architecture of the region. Finally, and perhaps most importantly the Hotel Rumia provided all of the conveniences that might be expected of a modern tourist facility. Although it was an extremely modest size, with only fifteen guest rooms, the hotel contained a restaurant and bar and provided private baths with each room (Vicari 1942: 966).

In the design of the Hotel Nalut, Di Fausto adopted a similar site strategy, where a low horizontal building was located on the edge of a large plain, with the restaurant and guest rooms overlooking an immense valley. However, in this case the project directly faced this surrounding landscape and the Berber town, which by proximity and view alone established a powerful connection. This link is particularly well conveyed in the publicity photographs – the strong horizontal profile of the building and its simple rectangular massing appearing superimposed with that of the abandoned Berber castle. What these images also communicate is that this relationship is one of opposition, the white smooth surfaces of the hotel acting as a dramatic counterpoint to the ruinous state of the indigenous settlements.

Figure 4.4 Florestano Di Fausto, Hotel Nalut, Nalut, Libya (1935), postcard, 1937. Collection of the author.

The relationship between the Hotel Nalut and the town is most compellingly conveyed in two postcards that were part of a series that the Libyan Tourism and Hotel Association issued to document this travel itinerary. These images suggest a strong connection between the buttressed base of the hotel and the tapered forms of the local constructions (Figure 4.4). They also communicate the unqualified modernity of the building. This effect is the result of the strong horizontal line of the roof, which was designed to provide shade for a series of recessed spaces in front of the guest rooms. The detailed development of this facade, which included the careful design of its openings, make it quite clear that this tourist facility was conceived according to the view of a landscape that: "seems to have existed uninhabited for millennia" (Brunelli 1937: 3). Although like the Hotel Rumia in Jefren this project was unquestionably a response to the demands of the foreign traveler this was not its most important role within the tourist experience. Through the various relationships that it established with its site, from the conscious framing of views, to direct references to its forms, the Hotel Nalut became a kind of instrument through which the context could be presented and represented to the traveler.

A final relationship between the Hotel Nalut and the adjacent town can be found in its representation in the publication *Itinerario Tripoli-Gadames*, where the discussion of its facilities is accompanied by a historical and ethnographic description of the people. This publication is an indication of the intersection of the tourist discourse with contemporary studies in which this region and the Berber populations were important subjects. It is also quite apparent that, in this presentation, an analogy is being made between their "heroic resistance" against the Ottoman invaders and the rugged forms of the ancient castle, which was referred to as: "a sort of petrified myth" (ETAL 1938b: 36). Through reenacting these indigenous forms, this tourist project was participating in a contemporary ethnographic discourse – its stark and primitive qualities suggesting the stern resistance of the Berbers and the perceived timeless quality of their culture.

While the pre-Saharan hotels in Jefren and Nalut share a site specificity with, and a common reference to, the native architecture of this region, one of the most critical aspects of these two designs is that they are almost exactly identical. This repetition even extends beyond their forms to the relationships that each of them established with their respective contexts. Their use of local forms was thus general, not specific. While the modernity of these hotels can certainly be found in the amenities that they provided to the tourist audience, it can be argued that the most modern aspect of these two projects was in their repetition – in the creation of a regional identity through a fixed vocabulary of forms that could be applied on any number of sites.

An Architectural Oasis

> . . . the hotel in Ghadames, like that in Jefren and Nalut – constructed . . . according to the most modern rules of technique and of art – [also] constitutes the synthesis of the essential characteristics of the landscape – an anticipation of the traveler who does not know the city and the oasis, its delights, its enchantment of colors, its profound effects on the spirit. (ETAL 1938b: 56)

The final hotel along this itinerary was the Hotel Ain el-Fras in Ghadames, which was named after the celebrated natural spring that provided water to this oasis settlement. The project by Di Fausto and Gatti Casazza was a renovation of the original hotel. It was able to provide first-class accommodation with a restaurant and bar and fifteen rooms, each with a private bath (Bucciante 1937: 7). As with the previous pre-Saharan hotels, the Hotel Ain-el-Fras responds quite directly to the formal language of the indigenous town, which in this case is a complex labyrinth of narrow passages, covered courtyards and terraces shaped by dense walled structures. Forming one edge of a large piazza in front of one of the main gates of the old city, this project establishes a metonymic relationship to its luxuriant setting. The connection between the building and its context is particularly well expressed in the central portico, where columns shaped like the trunks of palm trees mingle with those of its own verdant landscape (ETAL 1938b: 56).

Figure 4.5 Florestano Di Fausto and Stefano Gatti-Casazza, Hotel Ain-el-Fras, Ghadames (1935), postcard, 1937. Collection of the author.

This literal incorporation of an element of landscape into architecture is an indication of the fact that with the Hotel Ain el-Fras, the means of appropriation of local references was more direct than in the hotels in Jefren and Nalut. When looking more closely at the arcaded wings that flank the central body of this building, there is an unmistakable relationship between this element and the detailed articulation of openings in the so-called Piazza of the Mulberry (Figure 4.5). The mimetic relationship between the building and the town can also seen in the interior spaces of the hotel, whose timber ceilings, rich wall coverings and minimal use of furnishings was intended to suggest the characteristic experience of the domestic architecture.

Through the direct incorporation of indigenous forms in this tourist facility, Di Fausto created a continuous relationship between the building and its context. However, such a faithful representation of native forms is something that, for the tourist, would have blurred the distinction between the hotel and its historical setting. The use of local forms in this project was not merely a way of better contextualizing this work of tourist architecture. The hotel was an integral part of a self-conscious staging of the image and the patterns of living of Ghadames that a tourist could comfortably experience. In fact, to experience the indigenous architecture and culture of the oasis of Ghadames, it may no longer have been necessary to see the actual town. The attempt to simulate the indigenous culture through architecture was enhanced by the fact that the entire hotel staff were dressed in local costume (Vicari 1942: 966).

The hotel in Ghadames by Di Fausto represents a crisis in the status of architecture, and in its relationship to its context. While the intention was to create a regional expression within a contemporary architecture, the implications of the project are quite different. The Hotel Ain el-Fras so closely imitates the identity of the traditional forms of the town of Ghadames that it challenges the conventionally understood distinction between historic restoration and new construction. However, rather than consider this a fundamentally antimodern approach to architecture, when looking at this project it is quite clear that it is the opposite. The hotel in Ghadames is the logical outcome of the modern tourist demand for historical authenticity. It is related to, and a product of, contemporary scientific research into the form and the culture of the Berber people. In so carefully reenacting the forms of the town, the Hotel Ain el-Fras was both a tourist facility and an ethnographic museum, where the Libyan people and their culture could be experienced outside of the passage of time.

Conclusion

Looking carefully, and in retrospect, at the tourist experience in Libya during the period of Italian colonization one can detect a set of preoccupations that continue to inform the design of tourist environments today. These themes include a predilection for authentic experiences, an emphasis on the preservation of the historical context, and even a tendency to invent these same experiences and contexts to feed the demands of the modern tourist, whose thirst for new sensations seem to never be satiated. In this sense, the tourist system in Libya was a precursor to the consciously preserved tourist sites generated by the mass tourist movement of recent decades. It also seems quite appropriate to see such tourist settings as veritable museums, that is, as descendents of carefully staged events like the presentation of European colonies in nineteenth and twentieth century World's Fairs and Exhibitions (Çelik 1992).

Such a consciously orchestrated tourist environment is related to a broader discourse on the preservation and presentation of local culture, but during the latter part of the 1930s the intersection between scientific research and tourist environments had some quite distinct political implications. With the passing of the "Provisions of the defense of the Italian race" in November of 1938 the same views that informed anthropological research on Libyan culture were being mobilized to justify a politics of empire. A number of noted scholars like Lidio Cipriani, who was a professor at the University of Florence and Director of the National Museum of Anthropology and Ethnography, participated in the journal *Difesa della Razza*, whose mission was to theorize a racial science that would support Fascist imperial politics (Cipriani 1938: 18–20). It is therefore imperative that the experience of "the native" in the tourist system be viewed in relation to the racially motivated political discourses that were already infused into modern scientific practices – discourses that viewed Libyan culture as the inevitable product of an essentially backward people. Seen in this context, the presentation of indigenous culture in the tourist architecture of Libya was more than just a precursor to contemporary tourist environments. By directly reenacting the forms of the local building traditions for the benefit of Western tourists, it was an affirmation of a politics of exclusion and racial purification.

References

Bartoccini, Renato (1926), "Gli edifici di interesse storico, artistico ed archeologico di Tripoli e dintorni", in *La rinascità della Tripolitania. Memorie e studi sui quattro anni di governo del Conte Giuseppe Volpi di Misurata*, Milan: Casa Editrice A. Mondadori.

Béguin, François (1983), *Arabisances. Décor architectural et tracé urbain en Afrique du Nord, 1830–1950*, Paris: Dunod.

Bertarelli, L. V. (1929), *Guida d'Italia del TCI. Possedimenti e Colonie*, Milan: Touring Club Italiano.

Bonardi, Carlo (1935), "Col touring nel Fezzan", *Le Vie d'Italia*, 41(7): 485–96.

Brunelli, Claudio (1937), "Ospitalità e turismo in Libia", in *Viaggio del Duce in Libia per l'inaugurazione della litoranea. Anno XV. Orientamenti e note ad uso dei giornalisti*, Rome: Stabilmento Tipografico "Il Lavoro Fascista".

Bucciante, G. (1937), "Lo sviluppo edilizio della Libia", in *Viaggio del Duce in Libia per l'inaugurazione della litoranea. Anno XV. Orientamenti e note ad uso dei giornalisti*, Rome: Stabilmento Tipografico "Il Lavoro Fascista".

Calzini, Raffaele (1926), *Da Leptis Magna a Gadames*, Milan: Fratelli Treves Editori.

Çelik, Zeynep (1992), *Displaying the Orient. Architecture of Islam at Nineteenth-Century World's Fairs*, Berkeley CA: University of California Press.

Cipriani, Lidio (1933), "Una missione scientifica italiana nel Fezzan", *Le Vie d'Italia*, 39 (9): 679–691.

—— (1938), "Razzismo Coloniale", *Difesa della Razza*, 1(2): 18–20.

De Agostini, Giovanni (1938), *La Libia Turistica*, Milan: Prof. G. De Agostini.

Del Boca, Angelo (1991), *Gli italiani in Libia. Dal fascismo a Gheddafi*, Rome: Giuseppe Laterza & Figli.

—— (1992), *L'Africa nella coscienza degli Italiani: miti, memorie, errori, sconfitte*, Rome: Giuseppe Laterza & Figli.

ETAL (1938), *Annual Report of the Ente Turistico ed Alberghiero della Libia*, Historic Archive of the Ministry of Foreign Affairs – Documents of the Ministry of Italy in Africa (ASMAE–MAI. 4–29).

—— (1938b), *Itinerario Tripoli-Gadames*, Milan: Tipo-Litografia Turati Lombardi.

—— (1939), *Tripoli e dintorni*, Milan: Tipo-Litografia Turati Lombardi.

—— (n.d.), "Realizzazioni fasciste. Gli sviluppi del turismo libico", ASMAE–MAI.5–5.

Loschi, M.A. (1936), "L'autostrada del deserto libico", *Le Vie d'Italia*, 42(8): 529–37.

MacCannell, Dean (1999), *The Tourist: A New Theory of the Leisure Class*, Berkeley, CA: University of California Press.

Morton, Patricia A. (2000), *Hybrid Modernities: Architecture and Representation at the 1931 Colonial Exposition, Paris*, Cambridge MA: The MIT Press.

Paloscia, Franco (1994), *Storia del turismo nell'economia italiana*, Città di Castello: Editore Petruzzi.

Piccioli, Angelo (1931), *La porta magica del Sahara*, Tripoli: Libreria Edit. Minerva.

—— (1933), *La nuova Italia d'oltremare*, Milan: A Mondadori Editore.

Quadrotta, Guglielmo (1937), "Appunti sull'artigianato libico", in *Viaggio del Duce in Libia per l'inaugurazione della litoranea. Anno XV. Orientamenti e note ad uso dei giornalisti*, Rome: Stabilmento Tipografico "Il Lavoro Fascista".

Queirolo, Ernesto (1925), "La politica delle comunicazioni", in *La rinascità della Tripolitania. Memorie e studi sui quattro anni di governo del Conte Giuseppe Volpi di Misurata*, Milan: Casa Editrice A. Mondadori.

Scarin, Emilio (1931), "Tipi indigeni di insediamento umano e loro distribuzione nella Tripolitania settentrionale", in *Atti del Primo Congresso di Studi Coloniali. Firenze, 8–12 April 1931*, Volume 4, Florence: Sicc B. Seeber.

—— (1940), *L'Insediamento umano nella Libia occidentale*, Verona: A. Mondadori.

Segrè, Claudio (1974), *Fourth Shore: The Italian Colonization of Libya*, Chicago: The University of Chicago Press.

—— (1987), *Italo Balbo. A Fascist Life*, Berkeley CA: University of California Press.

Talamona, Marida (1992), "Libya: An Architectural Workshop", *Rassegna*, 51: 62–79.

Tomasello, Giovanna (1984), *La letteratura coloniale italiana dalle avanguardie al fascismo*, Palermo: Sellerio Editore.

Vicari, Eros (1942), "L'Ente turistico ed alberghiero della Libia (ETAL)", *Gli Annali dell'Africa Italiana*, 5(4): 955–75.

Volpi, Giuseppe (1925), "Telegram to Ministry of the Colonies, May 31", ASMAE–MAI 3–154, Raid automobilistico.

Vota, Giuseppe (ed.) (1954), *I sessant'anni del Touring Club Italiano, 1894–1954*, Milan: Touring Club Italiano.

Wright, Gwendolyn (1991), *The Politics of Design in French Colonial Urbanism*, Chicago: University of Chicago Press.

Wright, John (1969), *Libya*, London: Ernest Benn Limited.

–5–

A Pilgrimage to the Alcázar of Toledo: Ritual, Tourism and Propaganda in Franco's Spain
Miriam Basilio

Introduction

On 18 July 1936 a group of right-wing generals launched a military uprising aiming to topple the democratically elected left-wing coalition government that led the Spanish Republic. This was the beginning of the Spanish Civil War – a war that would last until 1939 and would result in Spain's physical devastation and the rise of General Francisco Franco, who would govern the country until his death in 1975 (Figure 5.1). One of the war's major battles was the siege of the Alcázar, a sixteenth-century palace-fortress in the historic city of Toledo. It had been the site of a royal residence since the reign of Alfonso VI, who captured Toledo from the Muslims in 1085. In the sixteenth century, King Charles V and his son Philip II rebuilt the fortified palace. Beginning in the mid-nineteenth century, the Alcázar housed the Infantry Academy and a museum of arms, further linking it to the military history of Spain (Reig Tapia 1999: 149–88).

During the siege of the Alcázar, the rebels barricaded themselves in as Republican attacks destroyed much of the building (Figure 5.2). Sixty-eight days later, on 27 September 1936, over one thousand soldiers, civil guards, volunteers, students and civilians loyal to the generals arrived to end the siege. Their successful takeover was a major propaganda coup for their cause (Brothers 1997: 58, 60, 62–4). Pivotal to their publicity campaign was the alleged martyrdom of Luís Moscardó, son of the site's commander, Colonel José Moscardó. The facts surrounding the death are a subject for debate even today, but the version of events Franco's supporters celebrated presents the colonel as the epitome of heroism, willing to sacrifice his own son for the rebel cause (Reig Tapia 1999: 163–85). In this account, a Republican official telephoned the colonel to offer freedom for his son, whom the Republicans were holding hostage in Toledo, in exchange for surrendering the Alcázar. He advised his son to die a heroic death in the name of God and Spain. In the recorded reenactment that could be heard until recently in Colonel Moscardó's office at the Alcázar, the father's parting advice to his son was: "Offer your soul up to God, cry out 'Long Live Spain!' and die like a patriot." The

Alcázar de Toledo. *Patio antes del Asedio.*

Figure 5.1 Postcard reproducing a view of the patio prior to 1936, from the series *Alcázar de Toledo, 24 Vistas en Huecograbado*, Madrid: Jalón Angel and Hauser y Manet, ca. 1939. Collection of the author.

Alcázar de Toledo. *Patio después del Asedio.*

Figure 5.2 Postcard reproducing a view of the patio following the siege, from the series *Alcázar de Toledo, 24 Vistas en Huecograbado*, Madrid: Jalón Angel and Hauser y Manet, ca. 1939. Collection of the author.

colonel, who was given 10 minutes to consider this, is said to have immediately refused and heard the mortal gunshots through the receiver. There are many versions of the telephone conversation, conflicting dates, as well as questions about the identities of the Republican officials who made the call. In fact, even apologists for the rebels' cause admit that the young Moscardó was killed sometime in August. Historians now believe Luis Moscardó was one of a group of people killed in reprisal for aerial bombardments of Toledo by Franco's forces, 10 days after the telephone call. (Reig Tapia 1999: 165, 179–181).

Following the Republicans' defeat, the Alcázar became central to the new regime's mythic retelling of history. It was promoted as a tourist destination – a site of memory that linked Spanish military and imperial history with Franco's Civil War victory. The rhetoric of *Hispanidad* and the desire to inculcate patriotism in the masses led to experimentation with exhibition formats that fused ceremonial ritual and historic simulation. At the same time, the hagiographic literature of the siege and the imperial iconography of the Alcázar's ruined courtyard were widely disseminated, thereby lending a sacred aura to the site. Photography, printed media and film were used to promote the Alcázar as a tourist destination, while Catholic devotional conventions were mined to combine tourist travel with religious pilgrimage. A war museum and site of memory dedicated to Franco's military victory were created that perpetuated the dictator's version of events long after his death in 1975 and well into the transition to democracy in Spain.

Site of Memory: The Alcázar as Patriotic Tourist Destination

During the war, Franco launched a propaganda campaign that promoted the ruins of the Alcázar as a patriotic tourist destination. This was made possible by Franco's appointment as Head of State of the provisional government, the Junta Técnica de Estado (Technical State Junta) in Burgos on 1 October 1936. By late January 1938 Franco's government maintained a national propaganda office that included departments for publications, visual arts, film, theatre, music, and propaganda at the fronts. (Payne 1989: 280–2; 292–3) Franco and his Falangist (members of the Spanish Fascist Party) political supporters used nationalist rhetoric of *Hispanidad* to legitimize the dictatorship by appealing to Spain's past as an imperial power and defender of Catholicism (González Calleja and Limón Nevado 1988). They deliberately fostered parallels between the new regime and Spain's past including the period of unification under the Catholic monarchs, Ferdinand (r. 1479–1516) and Isabelle (r. 1479–1504), and the consolidation of the empire during the reigns of Charles V (r. 1517–56) and Philip II (r. 1556–98). In addition, they and others, including influential Catholic clerics such as Cardinal Isidro Gomá, portrayed the uprising at the Alcázar as a contemporary *cruzada* or crusade against communism undertaken to defend Spain's Catholic roots. The desire to promote the new regime's version of history to a wide audience influenced the initial conservation of the ruins and shaped the content of the museum built to commemorate the siege.

Franco's interest in promoting the Alcázar as a site of memory exemplifies his promotion of patriotic tourism in general. In a speech given on 18 April 1937 announcing the unification of supporters of the uprising, Franco recognized the importance of establishing monuments throughout Spain to commemorate the war. "[T]o honor your heroic sacrifices," he declared, "we will erect stelae and monuments at the battle grounds where the light of weapons' fire shone and the blood of heroes ran . . . so that passers-by and travelers may stop one day before the glorious stones and remember the heroic forgers of this great Spanish Fatherland" (Franco 1937: 29). His personal interest in the Alcázar in particular is evidenced in, among other things, his numerous visits to the site and his financial contribution to the construction of a Crypt for the defenders of the Alcázar (Anon. 1959: n.p.). More importantly, as Spanish art historian Angel Llorente Hernández (1992: 1867–71) has noted, Franco himself was consulted about proposed alterations to the site.

Foreshadowing the development of the Alcázar as a patriotic tourist destination is a proposal for a Museum of the National Revolution published by Falangist poet and writer Federico de Urrutia in 1937, shortly after the siege (Urrutia 1937: 4). Urrutia argued that a public display of the history of the military uprising, which he called a *Guerra Santa* or Holy War, was necessary both to educate future generations about Franco's "crusade" and to preserve the memory of individual heroism, which might otherwise be limited to private commemoration. He cited examples of the types of materials that should be preserved: "'blue shirts' [Falange party militia uniform] bloodied by anonymous heroes, Carlist 'red berets' of the first re-conquerors [supporters of the pretender to the throne Don Carlos], enemy trophies, documents, irrefutable evidence of the enemy's infamous and sinister aims, decorated flags and memories of the difficult times" (Urrutia 1937: 4). He concluded by proposing a museum consisting of a series of galleries devoted to "martyrs," "heroes" and "trophies;" a *Sagrario de los Caidos* (Chapel of the Fallen); and a *Claustro de la Fe* (Cloister of the Faith).

The development of the Alcázar itself as a patriotic tourist destination proceeded rapidly. Development began immediately after the siege's end, when the government organized group visits to the ruins. On 19 February 1937, Franco's government declared the Alcázar a national monument (Ministerio de Educación y Ciencia 1975: n.p.) and shortly thereafter established a museum of the siege christened the *Museo de Recuerdos del Alcázar de Toledo* (Museum of Mementos of Toledo's Alcazar) (Reig Tapia 1999: 154). That same year, it appointed a conservator, Mariano López de Ayala, Conde de Peremoro, who remained at this post until sometime in 1940, when a *Patronato* (Board) was formed. Eduardo Lagarde was the *conservador artístico* (artistic restorer) responsible for the cleanup and early installations (Anon. 1959: n.p.). By 1940, there were official guides for the site, admission fees began to be charged, and additional income was earned through the sale of tourist materials such as audiotapes reenacting the telephone call between Colonel Moscardó and his son in twelve languages (Anon. 1959: n.p.). In October of that year, the colonel himself led an unidentified visitor through the museum. At that time, the museum included the ruins of the courtyard, the infirmary-chapel, the provisional cemetery and the office. This last space contained portraits of father and son, copies of the dialogue between them, an album with images of the site, and other "relics" of the siege. Finally, to underscore the international recognition of this event, the *Exposición de Material de Guerra Tomado al Enemígo* (Exhibition of War Trophies Taken from the Enemy) that was held in San Sebastián in 1938, devoted one area to the commemoration of the rebel struggle at the Alcázar.

In addition to the establishment of the commemorative museum, equally integral to the development of the Alcázar as a patriotic tourist destination was the June 1938 announcement by Ramón Serrano Suñer, then Franco's Minister of the Interior, (which included the propaganda office), that the Alcázar would be incorporated into the *Rutas de Guerra* (War Routes). The *Rutas de Guerra* were guided luxury bus tours organized by Franco's Ministry of Tourism that provided participants with the opportunity to view landmarks in "the epic of the reconquest of Spain" (Anon. 1938a: 20–1). There were four routes, each lasting nine days and with capacity for up to thirty travelers. Scheduled for departure every two days from the French–Spanish border, the tours were promoted through illustrated brochures, magazine articles and in travel agencies. (Anon. 1938b: 18–19) The first route spanned northern cities (Bilbao, San Sebastián, Santander and Oviedo), all of which had fallen to Franco's forces by October 1937. The second traversed the province of Aragón, including Teruel, the site of a failed Republican offensive, which was taken in February 1938. The fourth included the cities of Granada and Seville in the southern region of Andalucía, which were taken by Franco in the initial stages of the uprising.

The third route included Madrid, Segovia, Avila, El Escorial, Toledo's Alcázar and Brunete, where in July 1937, the Republicans launched a failed offensive that led to one of the war's most deadly battles (Jackson 1976: 344–6). One of the brochures that promoted the *Rutas* drew a parallel between its "pious pilgrimages" and earlier battle sites such as Waterloo or Verdun while at the same time promoting the first-class lodgings, recreational and sports activities that were made available to tourists. The illustrations of this publication underscored the strange conjunction of conventional tourism and warfare in the *Rutas* by featuring picturesque scenes of beaches, mountains, cathedrals and villages along with wartime scenes of trench warfare, prisoners held captive and women enthusiastically greeting members of Franco's army. The Spanish *Rutas* were not an isolated case, however, as similar battleground tourism developed in other areas of Europe, especially after the First World War (Mosse 1990: 152–6).

In the rhetoric common in writing about the siege during this period, historical parallels were drawn between the defense of the Alcázar – and by extension the war against the Republic itself – and other periods in Spain's imperial history (Payne 1999: 333). One guidebook advised visitors that "Aquí todo es Historia" ("Here, everything is History") (Otamendi 1938: 8). Another called on tourists to draw parallels between past instances of Spanish heroism in battle and the siege of the Alcázar: "Traveler, you who arrive . . . with the aim of satisfying your curiosity at the ruins of the glorious Alcázar, before entering think of the drama that took place here . . . and let the spiritual overcome the material as the sentimental part of you prevails." It continued: "Remember that it was here that the future of Spain and of humanity as a whole were decided" (Peremoro 1938: 7, 11). One of the official histories of the site – written by Franco's official biographer and Minister of Foreign Affairs – called the Alcázar "the incarnation of Spain's power at its peak" (Arrarás and Jordana 1937: 14). Among the specific periods invoked were the *Reconquista* or Christian conquest of Spain from the Muslims, and the height of Spain imperial power. At the Alcázar, the evidentiary quality of objects associated with the siege would elicit visitors' emotions, contribute to the coalescence of a sense of collective "conscience" and transform visitors into witnesses of the dramatic historic events.

Tourism as Religious Devotion

The conscious decision to leave the site in a ruined state following the siege, the orchestrated display of objects, as well as the extensive imagery and hagiographic literature about its recent history, served to authenticate the government's interpretation of what happened at the Alcázar. Integral to this effort were appeals to visitors' and readers' emotions in a manner that followed Catholic visual and textual conventions. This emotional appeal fostered a sense of awe in the face of the martyrs' heroic deeds. Indeed, the *gloriosas ruinas* (glorious ruins) of the Alcázar, as they were referred to in the contemporary press, as well as objects associated with the siege, were presented not only as documentary evidence of the justness of Franco's cause, but as religious relics. The rebels' version of events was promoted in a manner strikingly similar to the promotion of a Catholic saint's shrine built to mark the location of a miracle or apparition. As such, patriotic tourism became a mode of religious devotion.

Guidebooks, illustrated pamphlets and postcards of the siege were available to assist visitors and readers in this process. A 1938 article by Miner Otamendi published in *La Voz de España* (Otamendi 1938: 8), gave a description of the

Alcázar, already converted to a museum, which reads like an account of a saint's gruesome martyrdom in Counter-Reformation era devotional literature. Otamendi's graphic descriptions of a mine that "smelled of heroic flesh," vividly recreated the sights, smells and sounds of the Alcázar. The article continued: "Those blackish blood stains that run down the wall to the floor and clean – not sully – the stairway, tell us about all of the incredible and real heroic deeds" (Otamendi 1938: 8). The building itself was described as riddled with *heridas* (wounds) and filled with *reliquias* (relics) associated with the siege. Readers, and by extension visitors to the site, were advised to enter with an attitude of *recogimiento* (reverence). Visitors could see areas where women and children had taken shelter from artillery fire, the ruined courtyard, and the office where the telephone call to Colonel Moscardó took place. On display were a variety of "relics," including the two telephones, loaves of black bread produced during the siege and bombs. Otamendi noted: "Everything is Providential in this Ark of the Covenant, the Alcázar" (Otamendi 1938: 8).

Accounts such as these suggested that a visit to the site was an unmediated experience. The objects and setting were to act as an aid to memory, much as the narratives and images in Catholic devotional manuals on lives of the saints or visits to sites linked to miracles would have done (Freedberg 1989). Indeed, such devotional rhetoric is explicit in the section of the official guidebook that presented the office where the telephone call between the colonel and his son took place. As the guide notes, "Here you have the setting. Here you have the characters. Here you have the telephones and their cords. Those of you fortunate enough to visit this room remove your hats in front of the hero and offer up a prayer to the Fallen One" (Peremoro 1938: 14). Nearby, the *Sala de los Caídos* (Hall of the Fallen) contained a wall with a large cross and photographs of those who died within the Alcázar during the siege (Peremoro 1938: 35). Throughout the Alcázar, the martyrs to Franco's cause were presented as contemporary Catholic heroes.

Supplementing the countless propagandistic articles and books on the Alcázar were stories of the "miraculous" events that allegedly took place during the siege (Anon. 1937: 8–10). These included the survival of an image of the Virgin Mary that was then venerated in a makeshift chapel, the success of medical operations held in an improvised infirmary without basic supplies and the appearance of wheat to feed the besieged population. These stories gave the objects displayed a miraculous aura and invested the experience of viewing them with the authority of divine revelation. This was in keeping with Franco's self-presentation as a providential leader and modern crusader, sent to save Catholic Spain from secular and Republican ideologies.

An article entitled "Entre las ruinas del Alcázar," published on the first anniversary of the Franco's troops' occupation of the site, gave a typical "eyewitness" account of a visit to the ruins rendered as a religious experience. It stated: "And I fell to my knees before the Imperial Alcazar! . . . I was rendered ecstatic, immobile by the perfect deed" (Talavera 1937: 16–19). The writer Agustín de Foxá proposed a similar view of the Alcázar, opposing the artifice and picturesque character of traditional museums to the spiritual and persuasive possibilities offered by "pilgrimages" to the war's ruins. In so doing, he linked "relics" like the artworks and liturgical objects that survived anticlerical vandalism during the war to the ruins and portrayed the war itself as an agent of national spiritual regeneration: "It's a lie that Spain lies in ruins; never has Toledo been more whole . . . Because we have known suffering, we already understand the beauty of ruins" (Foxá 1937, n.p.).

This kind of visceral museum experience contrasted with the conventional presentation of objects in glass cases. It was especially exploited at the Alcázar while the site was still in its ruined state (through the mid-1950s). Visitors could move through a space where recent events had taken place and imagine themselves facing enemy artillery or surviving under dire conditions in the fortress's subterranean areas. This was an experience familiar to Spaniards who had actually survived the war, or to foreign tourists sympathetic to Franco's cause. The visit offered an illusion of immediacy months and years after the war's conclusion.

The emphasis on the preserving the authenticity of the Alcázar is evident in an article written by the painter José María Sert published in *El Diario Vasco* in 1938. Sert argued that the ruins should not be reconstructed. He referred to Toledo as a *milagrosa estampa* (miraculous print), likened it to Reims Cathedral and argued that the ruins' beauty and horror should be left intact. At the same time he proposed that the ruins be tidied up and that areas filled with rubble turned into a garden with laurel trees. He also suggested that the architect Pedro Muguruza build a new chapel on the grounds dedicated to Franco (Sert 1938: n.p.). Muguruza was then head of the *Servicio de Recuperación del Patrimonio Artístico* (SERPAN), the government agency charged with the conservation of the national architectural and artistic patrimony. Sert proposed that the chapel should have a ceiling draped with the Spanish flag that would also line the walls. Allegorical murals should decorate the chapel. These scenes should depict the themes of Faith, Hope and Charity accompanied by Spanish saints and alongside figures representing Spain's martyrs – all set within a Crucifixion scene. Had Sert's proposal for a chapel been realized, it would have been the culmination of the propagandistic use of Catholic devotion to interpret the tourist experience of visiting the site.

The architect Muguruza along with Vicente Machimbarrena, Director of the School of Engineering, however, both responded negatively to Sert's proposal. In a series of rebuttals published in *El Diario Vasco*. The former argued that the preservation of Spanish cultural patrimony called for a centralized plan that would view each city as a "total organism" (Muguruza 1938: n.p.). Such a plan, organized according to "a corporative structure . . . based on genuinely Spanish roots at its essence," would not allow for individual proposals such as Sert's. Muguruza (1937: n.p.) referred to the works of art and architecture under SERPAN's jurisdiction as "that sorrowful Way of the Cross that is our artistic patrimony, destroyed in the Red Republican-controlled zone." Machimbarrena (1938: n.p.) argued that the ruins' power to appeal to viewers' emotions meant that they should be left unchanged, save for removal of dangerous rubble. The site would thus be appropriate for the many who would undertake the *sagrada peregrinación* (sacred pilgrimage) after the war.

Representing the Alcázar

Images greatly aided the promotion of the Alcázar as a patriotic tourist destination whose experience was akin to religious devotion. Illustrated articles were printed in the widely circulated illustrated dailies and weeklies. Numerous histories, illustrated pamphlets, biographies and "eyewitness" accounts were published in Spain and abroad. Postcards featured before and after photographs that heightened the impact of the building's ruined appearance. And the siege inspired paintings and prints as well as the 1940 film *Sin Novedad en el Alcázar/L'assedio dell'Alcazar* (Gubern 1986: 83, 86–8). These images contributed to the promotion of the site by Franco's propagandists.

The majority of images of the Alcázar featured its central courtyard, as evidenced by illustrations in books, press articles, postcards and portraits. The courtyard, whose construction during the reign of Charles V and his son Philip II led many to regard it as an architectural embodiment of the Spanish nation and its imperial tradition. Moreover, the courtyard was linked figuratively to the monarch, as a copy of Leone Leoni's sculpture *Charles V and the Fury* (1551–3, Madrid, Museo del Prado) stood at its center. This statue had fallen after an artillery attack during the siege. But by 1938, on Franco's orders, the statue was put back on its pedestal (Peremoro 1938: 19). An inscription attributed to Charles V underscored the symbolic importance of this act. The inscription stated: "If my horse and standard should fall in battle, raise these before tending to me" (Arrarás and Jordana 1937: 16).

Photographs of the sculpture amid the rubble at the center of the courtyard were reproduced in postcards, newspapers and book covers, thereby commemorating the destructive events of the siege. The numerous books and articles glorifying the site, however, stressed that despite the attacks on the Alcázar, Spain's traditions prevailed – just as the statue of Charles V survived unharmed. In this way, the new regime's propagandists attempted to link the military and imperial tradition represented by the statute with Franco's leadership of the victorious uprising against the Republic.

Indeed, because of its architectural pedigree as a military fortress, the Alcázar fit perfectly within the new regime's efforts to foster historical parallels that legitimized Franco, who was presented as the political offspring of Charles V. The caption of a photograph of the courtyard reproduced in Arrarás and Jordana's official history of the siege is typical of such interpretations: "Isn't it symbolic and surprising that the pedestal survives intact as does the statue, so that the Cesar recuperates his position and majesty?" (Arrarás and Jordana 1937: 249). An illustration by Domingo Villadomat for *Laureados de España* (1940) exemplifies this fusion of the image of the courtyard with the providential interpretations of the siege (Bonilla and Villadomat 1939). This lavish book commemorated the recipients of a prestigious military medal, the *Cruz Laureada de San Fernando*, for their service during the war. Set in the ruined courtyard with the statue of Charles V, the illustration represents a female captive and her child consoled by the Virgin of the Alcázar as holy protector and empathetic mother.

In addition to its presence in popular imagery, the site of the Alcázar enjoyed a significant place in official painting and literature. As María de Cardona argued in an untitled 1939 article, "The sublime episode at the Alcázar could appear in the background of paintings, as was done by Old Masters in Crucifixion and Road to Calvary scenes" (Cardona 1939: n.p). For example, in Fernando Álvarez de Sotomayor's 1940 equestrian portrait, Franco is shown astride a white horse, a modern military crusader, victorious amidst the ruins of the courtyard (Figure 5.3). In the composition, and pose, Sotomayor's painting recalls the famous equestrian portrait of *Charles V at Muhlberg* by Titian (1548, Prado Museum, Madrid), furthering the historic parallels between Franco and the king. The fact that Franco commissioned this state portrait for display at the Pazo de Meiras, his country home in La Coruña (Galicia), further underscores the importance Franco bestowed upon the Alcázar.

Many artists and writers portrayed Colonel Moscardó's sacrifice of his son as a spiritual act that linked Spain's past and present. They repeatedly compared him to the thirteenth-century Christian conqueror of Tarifa, Guzmán el Bueno, who sacrificed his own son rather than surrender his besieged city (Peremoro 1938: 8; Anon. 1939: n.p.; Martínez Leal 1937: 45; Barrachina 1998: 196). Franco himself shared these views. In a speech he gave at the Alcázar on 28 September 1939, he compared the colonel to El Cid (Rodrigo Díaz de Vivar), the conqueror of Valencia in 1094, stating: "And thus our history takes place within these ancient stones that were raised by Alfonso VI and that had as their first Captain Ruiz Díaz del Vivar, el Cid of Spain, first commander of this fortress. And here two notable figures are united." He continued: "The first is the most glorious of medieval times, el Cid Campeador, the most recent is the most symbolic of our times, Colonel Moscardó, the latest commander of this fortress, who proving wrong the enemies of our glories, proves that the race of the Guzmans has not died out . . . History repeats itself . . . But when attempts are made to erase history, a new history is written; when the glory of these stones is attacked, a greater one arises from its ruins" (Barrachina 1998: 278).

Figure 5.3 Fernando Álvarez de Sotomayor, Portrait of General Francisco Franco, 1940. Collection Museo del Ejército, Madrid. Reproduced with permission.

One of the most well-known paintings featuring Colonel Moscardó is Juan Francés y Mexias's official portrait painted between 1939 and 1941 for the Sala de Laureados at Madrid's Museo del Ejército (Museum of the Army) – a room filled with portraits of recipients of the *Cruz Laureada de San Fernando*. In this image, the colonel is majestically seated with a view of the courtyard's ruins as a theatrical backdrop. The choice of the courtyard as the backdrop for the colonel's first portrait commissioned after the Civil War testifies to the key role of the Alcázar as an embodiment of the regime's ideals.

Finally, in the reenactment of the entry of rebel troops into the Alcázar, which took place two days after the end of the siege, Franco himself was given a central role. The staged photograph of the general "occupying" the site was the most widely disseminated portrayal of the end of the event. Its prevalence gradually fostered the false impression that Franco himself had led the troops that ended the siege on 27 September 1936 (Reig Tapia 1999: 156). This event was choreographed to cement the image of the siege as a key military victory under Franco's leadership. Sometime after the occupation of Toledo, and before the war's end, a sculptural bust of the general was placed at the center of one of the colonnades facing the patio, forming an axis that connected it spatially and symbolically to the sculpture of Charles V. Historians have argued that Franco's decision to divert troops from attacking a then-unprepared Republican Madrid prolonged the war because the time spent capturing Toledo gave the besieged capital time to organize its defense. Notwithstanding such criticism, historians, notably Paul Preston (1994: 174–5), agree that in choosing to focus on "liberating" the Alcázar, Franco won a battle on the propaganda front that rallied supporters of the uprising – within Spain and abroad – to champion his leadership. A speech read over the radio by José María Pemán on the day after the end of the siege sums up the importance of the Alcázar in the new regime's rewriting of history: "Your Alcazar has been the great propaganda office of this war. You have spoken with actions and facts . . . with an air of History and Romance, easily understood by all" (Arrarás and Jordana de Pozas 1937: 309).

Conclusion

By 1957, the Alcázar was rebuilt to recreate its prewar appearance. It became a branch of the Madrid's Military Museum and thus housed various collections devoted to all periods of Spanish military history. Despite its function as a national military museum, elements of its use as a tourist destination devoted to Franco's regime persisted until very recently. Countless plaques dedicated to the memory of those who died in the siege lined the museum's walls and those called "defenders" of the Alcázar are still buried in the crypt. The most recent Alcázar installation included a series of spaces devoted to the history of the siege, including a replica of Colonel Moscardó's office, in which the famous telephone conversation was re-enacted in several languages. Visitors could enter the basement areas where the infirmary was housed and where women and children slept. Another room displayed newspapers printed within the Alcázar, artillery casings and other mementoes. These war-related installations probably dated from the mid-1950s and were for many a disturbing "time capsule" of Franco-era propaganda that most visitors to the site could still recall vividly. Periodically, particularly during the anniversaries of the uprising and conclusion of the war, a flurry of press articles was published expressing outrage that such an anachronistic installation remained on view in a democratic Spain. For supporters of Franco's regime and veterans who fought on the side of the rebels, of course, the site is regarded as a memorial to their ideals. As of this writing, the Alcázar is being renovated in order to accommodate its new function as the site of Spain's Military Museum, incorporating both the original collections and those to be brought from Madrid, which include weapons, uniforms, medals, military trophies, paintings and documents (Europa Press 2003). It remains to be seen whether the areas linked to the Alcázar will remain part of the new museum, and if so, how the war period materials and rooms will be interpreted.

The powerful combination of commemoration, tourism and religious pilgrimage staged at the Alcázar of Toledo and its persistence after the end of the dictatorship will pose a challenge for those now attempting to design a new museum at the site. The Alcázar became preeminent among civil war sites of memory for the new regime. The royal fortress – linked to Spain's aegis as a Catholic, imperial power – was a place where history seemed to repeat itself through the actions of Colonel Moscardó and General Franco. Tourists, both local and foreign, could visit a battleground that represented Franco's vision of a victorious Catholic, traditional, militaristic Spain, while paying their respects to those who died and struggled to save lives there. It is also a reminder that such politically charged historic sites are susceptible to appropriation by regimes seeking legitimization, and vulnerable to transformation for the purposes of tourist promotion.

Acknowledgements

I would like to thank Medina Lasansky and Brian McLaren for inviting me to contribute to this volume and for their helpful editorial suggestions. This essay is dedicated to the memory of my grandfather, Vicente Basilio Bellver, who fought to defend the Spanish Republic. I am grateful to Karina Marotta, formerly of the Museo del Ejército, for granting me access to unpublished documents, paintings and posters in the collection of this museum. This essay is based in part on sections of my doctoral dissertation, *Re-Inventing Spain: Images of the Nation in Painting and Propaganda, 1936–1943*, Institute of Fine Arts, New York University (May 2002).

References

Anon. (1937), "Casta de heroes. El General Moscardó visto por su hija", in *Fotos*, 4, 13 March: 8–10.

—— (1938a), "España abre al turismo las rutas de guerra", in *Orientación Española*, 15 July: 20–1.

—— (1938b), "Turistas extranjeros por la ruta de guerra del norte", in *Orientación Española*, 1 September: 18–19.

—— (1939), *El Alcázar*, Bilbao: Editora Nacional.

—— (1959), "Patronato de las Ruinas del Alcázar, October 20, 1959", in Víctor Martínez Simancas Papers, Madrid, Museo del Ejército Archive.

Arrarás, J. and Jordana de Pozas, L. (1937), *El Sitio del Alcázar de Toledo con una introducción del Padre Pérez de Urbel y el Diario de Operaciones del Coronel Moscardó*, Zaragoza: Editora "Heraldo de Aragón".

Barrachina, M. (1998), *Propagande et culture dans l'Espagne franquiste, 1936–1945*, Grenoble, Université Stendhal.

Bonilla, F. and Villadomat, D. (1939), *Laureados de España*, Madrid: Ediciones Fermina Bonilla.

Brothers, C. (1997), *War and Photography. A Cultural History*, London: Routledge.

Cardona, M. de (1939), untitled article in *El Alcázar*, 3 May: n.p.

Di Febo, G. (1988), *La Santa de la Raza. Teresa de Avila: Un Culto Barroco en la España franquista, 1937–1962*, Barcelona: Icaria.

Europa Press (2003), "Anuncio de la Ministra Pilar del Castillo. Madrid no acogerá ninguna instalación del Museo del Ejército. Será trasladado integramente al Alcázar de Toledo", in *El Mundo*, 31 January: [n.p.].

Foxá, A. de (1937), "Arquitectura hermosa de las ruinas", in *Vértice*, 1, April: n.p.

Franco, F. (1937), *Palabras de Franco,* Bilbao: Editora Nacional.

Freedberg, D. (1989), *The Power of Images: Studies in the History and Theory of Response,* Chicago: University of Chicago Press.

González Calleja, E. and Limón Nevado, F. (1988), *La Hispanidad como instrumento de Combate: Raza e imperio en la prensa franquista durante la guerra civil española*, Madrid: Consejo Superior de Investigaciones Científicas, Centro de Estudios Historicos.

Gubern, R. (1986), *1936–1939: La guerra de España en la pantalla*, Madrid: Filmoteca Española.

Jackson, G. (1976), *La República española y la Guerra Civil,* Barcelona: Critica, Grupo Editorial Grijalbo.

Llorente Hernández, A. (1992), *Arte e ideología en la España de la postguerra, 1939–1951*, Ph.D. dissertation, Madrid, Universidad Complutense.

Machimbarrena, V. (1938) "Al márgen de unas declaraciones del pintor José María Sert", in *El Diario Vasco,* 1 November 1938: n.p.

Martínez Leal, C. (1937), *El Asedio del Alcázar de Toledo. Memorias de un testígo*, Toledo: Editorial Católica Toledana.

Ministerio de Educación y Ciencia (1975), "Boletín Oficial del Estado 23, Art. 3, Decreto 22 February 19, 1937", in *Inventario del Patrimonio Artístico y arqueológico de España*, Madrid: Ministerio de Educación y Ciencia.

Mosse, G. L. (1990), *Fallen Soldiers: Re-Shaping the Memory of the World Wars,* New York: Oxford University Press.

Muguruza, P. (1938), [Letter published in] *El Diario Vasco*, 2 November, n.p.

Otamendi, M. (1938), "En el escenario del más alto heroísmo. Como está actualmente el Alcázar de Toledo", in *La Voz de España*, 20 July 1938: 8.

Payne, S. G. (1989) *Fascism in Spain, 1923–1977*, Madison: University of Wisconsin Press.

Peremoro, C. de (1938), *Alcázar de Toledo: Pinceladas. Recuerdos de sus gloriosas ruinas y de su gesta grandiosa durante los meses de Julio, Agosto y Septiembre de 1936*, Toledo: Ed. Católica Toledana.

Preston, P. (1994), *Franco: A Biography*, New York: HarperCollins.

Reig Tapia, A. (1999), *Memoria de la Guerra Civil: los mitos de la tribu*, Madrid: Alianza Editorial.

Sert, J. M. (1938), "José María Sert, el gran pintor, habla de nuestros monumentos destruídos", in *El Diario Vasco*, 29 October 1938: cover, n.p.

Talavera, M. (1937), "Entre las ruinas gloriosas del Alcázar. Gran reportaje en el aniversario de una Gesta sin par", in *Fotos*, 31, 25 September: 16–19.

Urrutia, F. de (1937), "Por un Museo de la Revolución Nacional", *ABC*, 1 August: 4.

–6–

Authenticating Dungeons, Whitewashing Castles: The Former Sites of the Slave Trade on the Ghanaian Coast
Cheryl Finley

For centuries, the castles and forts of coastal Ghana have been important sites of African- European contact and centers of cultural exchange. Built between 1482 and 1784 by rival European nations, these rare examples of late medieval, fortified architecture in sub-Saharan Africa are remembered today for their fundamental role in facilitating the notorious trans-Atlantic slave trade. In all, there are some sixty remaining structures in varying condition and used to differing extents along Ghana's coast. The rocky and treacherous promontories of this region provided defense from enemies approaching by land and sea and furnished the materials with which to build structures that would withstand centuries of human suffering. Indeed, the paradoxical combination of the shocking history of these manmade sites, the natural beauty of the seashore and the monumental grandeur of the architecture has produced the most popular tourist attractions in contemporary Ghana. Even the novelist Richard Wright, was taken by the hypnotizing beauty of Elmina Castle when he visited half a century ago:

> Towers rise two hundred feet in the air. What spacious dreams! What august faith! How elegantly laid-out the castle is! What bold plunging lines! What, yes, taste . . . (Wright 1995: 384)

According to the Ghana Museums and Monuments Board, there are only three structures designated as castles among the sixty colonial fortified structures that remain on Ghana's coast: Elmina, initially built by the Portuguese in 1482, Cape Coast, erected by the Swedish in 1653, and Christiansborg, built by the Danish in 1661 at Osu in what is now the capital city of Accra. Of the three, Cape Coast and Elmina are the most popular with present-day tourists. These two castles are located about a 3 hour bus or car ride from Accra in the Central Region of Ghana. Part of their popularity is due to their location, less than 10 miles from one another along the coastal road that connects the towns that grew up around them, also named Cape Coast and Elmina. These towns host a number of other tourist amenities that have sprung up over the past 10 to 15 years, including small hotels and bed-and-breakfast establishments. Of particular note are the world-class Best Western Berjaya Elmina Beach Resort, a resort called the Coconut Grove, and One Africa – a small establishment with nicely appointed bungalows, catering primarily to roots tourists.[1] Travelers often take part in walking tours of the towns, focusing on architectural and local interests as well as visiting the vibrant and colorful crafts and fishing markets. Another popular attraction less than an hour away is Kakum National Park, a protected rainforest that was restructured to include a breathtaking canopy walkway in 1995 as part of a campaign to promote tourism in Ghana's Central Region by UNESCO, the International Commission on Monuments (ICOM) and the Slave Routes Project.

Over the past 300 years, Elmina and Cape Coast have been classified as castles for their style of architecture, massive size and multiplicity of function (Anquandah 1999: 10–11). Distinguished from the more numerous, but smaller forts, the castles have a large perimeter, a more intricate complex of connecting structures, and the facilities to house a great number of people. The enormous scale of these structures is particularly evident in the way the space inside of the walls was designated and utilized as if to comprise a small town unto itself. The upper floors were designed as living quarters for the European traders, governors, officers and colonial officials. Trading halls and sales rooms generally were located on the second level, but on the opposite side of the complex from the living quarters of the upper management. The separate men's and women's dungeons were built at ground level or in some cases below ground with only a glimpse of light through small openings intended for air circulation. They still emit the stench of human excrement, bodily fluids, suffering and death. The smallest of the prison cells set aside for the condemned were marked overhead with a skull and cross bones. Even the dark spaces that housed ammunitions, cannon balls and gun powder still have a toxic odor. In addition to these spaces of incarceration and warfare, each castle included a church and a school as well as various courtyards, terraces and lookout towers.

Some of the smaller forts, such as Fort St. Jago in Elmina (1660s – Dutch) and Fort William (1820s – British) in Cape Coast, served primarily to defend the castles and surrounding towns in which they were situated. Located atop hills adjacent to the castles, and with the ability to track enemies that might attack by land or by sea, these structures apparently were never intended to hold enslaved Africans. Several other forts of comparable or slightly larger size, however, served the double purposes of providing defense and acting as slave dungeons. Examples of these include Fort St. Sebastian at Shama (1520s – Portuguese), Fort Metal Cross at Dixcove (1692 – British), Fort Gross-Friedrichsburg at Princestown (1683 – Brandenburg), and Fort Apollonia at Beyin (1768 – Britain), which had separate holding cells for men and women either above or below ground.[2]

This chapter considers a range of controversial issues that arise when monuments fraught with such multifaceted historical and cultural meaning become the objects of global tourism. It questions the complexities of memory and identity politics at play amongst tourists, museum officials and local inhabitants who frequent the castles and dungeons of Cape Coast and Elmina. It argues that practices of remembrance at these sites are necessarily politicized along racial, ethnic, class and gender lines, evidenced by the ways individuals and groups *perform* memory in the physical space of the monuments. These performances of memory, enacted primarily by roots tourists and tourist industry workers, actively create novel forms of ritual and artistic practice that engage photography (tourist, documentary, fashion and art), film (narrative and documentary) historical reenactment, and altar building (ephemeral and permanent). Panafest, the biennial Pan African Festival of Performing Arts, which was instituted in 1992, is one of the notable venues that opened up a space for many of these innovative performances to flourish. Even the choice of making places like Cape Coast and Elmina annual sites of pilgrimage, one of the hallmarks of roots tourist activity, can be counted as a symbolic act of performing memory.

This essay considers just whose history and what memory is presented and interpreted at these sites. Most African Americans and black people from the diaspora stress that the history of the slave trade, made tangible by the presence of the dungeons beneath the castles, should be the focal point. In contrast, many Ghanaians feel that the long, rich history and multiple uses of the sites should take precedence. Others still concentrate on the aesthetic quality and architectural splendor of the white washed buildings against the dramatic seascape (Figure 6.1).

The concept of memory employed here is intricately tied to a textured understanding of authenticity, which is seen to operate at these sites on at least three levels. First, using the theoretical work of Dean MacCannell (1999) on staged authenticity in tourist settings, the specific structure of the tourist experience at the castles of Cape Coast and Elmina in Ghana is examined. Second, a notion of perceived individual authenticity is explored through the claims made by tourists themselves as they interact with one another in the tourist setting. Third, the initiatives that tourists take in order to validate their experiences – from taking pictures to buying souvenirs to writing notes – are discussed as authenticating actions.

This chapter also questions the validity of certain architectural and interpretive changes to Cape Coast and Elmina made in the name of facilitating tourism at these sites. I would like to suggest that the authentic moment that is being offered to the tourist is the memory of the enslaved Africans that left the dungeons centuries ago: the now absent black bodies that become part of the allure of these monuments. It is a perplexing problem that some recent visitors to the castles have passionately vocalized. As one African American tourist demanded, "Don't turn our memories

Figure 6.1 View of cannons, Cape Coast Castle, Ghana, 1999. Photograph by author.

into a tourist attraction." (visitor comment books, Cape Coast Castle). Finally, it is argued that in the current age of global tourism, memory itself becomes a commodity – a thing to be bought, sold, and traded.

"Roots" Tourism

Sankofa is an Akan word meaning, "one must return to the past in order to move forward."[3] One of the early, notable African American tourists to visit Elmina was Richard Wright, who traveled to the Gold Coast (present-day Ghana) in 1953 to observe Kwame Nkrumah's rise to power as the first black leader of an African state on the brink of freedom from colonial rule.[4] The book that Wright published chronicling his return to the motherland, entitled *Black Power*, inspired a generation of African American intellectuals and artists in the 1960s, including the art historian Sylvia Ardyn Boone, the poet Maya Angelou, the illustrator Tom Feelings and the philosopher and scholar W. E. B. du Bois, to make pilgrimages to Cape Coast, Elmina and other sites in Ghana imbued with cultural and ancestral significance (Wright 1954). For them, Ghana represented not only a symbolic homeland in Africa, but also a space of freedom and they hoped to emulate in the United States some of the political advances that it had won for black people.[5]

John Lennon and Malcolm Foley have discussed the importance of pilgrimage as an organizing principle for groups that have survived, yet are still coping with the impact of significant death and upheaval:

> Several commentators view pilgrimage as one of the earliest forms of tourism. This pilgrimage is often (but not only) associated with the death of individuals or groups, mainly in circumstances which are associated with the violent and the untimely. Equally, these deaths tend to have a religious or ideological significance which transcends the event itself to provide meaning to a group of people. Generally, it has been those who attribute significance to the events who have comprised the pilgrims, who have visited either the site of the deed or the site of the burial or both. (Lennon and Foley 2000: 3)

Both Cape Coast and Elmina share the double meaning of "the site of the deed" (the transatlantic slave trade) and "the site of the burial" (the dungeons where many died), and so take on the significance of memorial for those who are the descendants of survivors. In 1972, UNESCO accorded the castles of Cape Coast and Elmina with the designation World Heritage Monument, recognizing that "there are some parts of heritage which are of such outstanding value to the world as a whole that their protection, conservation and transmission to future generations is a matter not just for any one nation but for the international community as a whole" (Anquandah 1999: 8). Since that time, the first wave of African American tourists began making pilgrimages to these sites to make sense of their past. Inspired initially by the social and political advances won by the Black Arts and Black Power Movements of the late 1960s and early 1970s, and subsequently by Alex Haley's (1976) popular novel *Roots*, which premiered as a television mini-series in 1977, a steady and regular flow of African American tourists has been participating in, if not shaping, a particular type of tourism that has at its center the need to seek and pay homage to an authentic cultural heritage.

This brand of tourism has been called *roots* tourism, as many of its practitioners seek a return to an ancestral homeland often made visible by the idea or racial memory of Africa as a place of familial origin in the transatlantic slave trade. But beyond the mere sight of Africa as a symbolic motherland, the physical and imposing sites of Cape Coast and Elmina are claimed by roots tourists as tangible and necessary memorials, some of the very few places where material evidence of the legacy of slavery still stands before their eyes and is available to be touched, walked through, and experienced with all of their senses and with the movement of their bodies through time and space. Cape Coast and Elmina are profound examples of Pierre Nora's influential and useful term, *lieux des memoire*, or sites of memory, "where memory crystallizes and secrets itself" (Nora 1989: 9) They are also places where different performances of authenticity validate the tourist experience – performances that are mediated by various forms of memory.

Memory serves a central function in roots tourism. Like heritage it is somewhat of an intangible commodity and a social construction that mediates individuals' experiences, actions and expectations. It is offered to the tourist for consumption and it is the thing that tourists themselves enact and perform in order to authenticate and make meaningful their experiences at the sites. Memory also shapes the expectations of roots tourists, guiding their hopes for some sort of connection with their ancestral past. It is the thing that lures them to places like Cape Coast and Elmina, offering the memory of their ancestors and the symbolic *and* real representation of the physical monuments as the places from which they came to be part of a diaspora. Memory thus functions in the creation of a shared racial historical consciousness that roots tourists use to make sense of their past, to sift through the historical elements – the trauma and the triumph – tied to the lived experience of modern racial formation. At the destinations of roots tourists, like the monuments of Cape Coast and Elmina, the concept of memory is active and fluid as in the performative, human function of *re-membering* that is, putting back together, restoring the body, making whole the body politic. As a bodily practice, memory performed at these sites serves a temporal spatial function by incorporating the awareness of sight, sound, smell, touch and taste to experience fully the spatial arrangement of the memorial.

Authenticities of Tourism

The experience of the authentic is central to the allure of tourism as an industry. Bound up in representations of reality and truth, notions of authenticity are proffered by the actuality of the tourist setting and the actions of the tourists themselves. When choosing a vacation destination, the average tourist goes in search of the authentic "native" experience, the authentic white sand beach, or the authentic ancient ruins. Cape Coast and Elmina can be seen as neatly combining these popular notions of authenticity into one package. Dean MacCannell (1999: 105) has suggested some useful ways for understanding the structure of tourist activity as a social performance evocative of the desire for "authentic experiences, perceptions and insights." In his seminal book, *The Tourist: A New Theory of the Leisure Class*, MacCannell set about theorizing the ways in which the quest for authenticity is a guiding principal of the tourist experience, especially as those tourists negotiate built environments. According to this argument, the tourist setting is divided into front and back regions: "the front is the meeting place of hosts and guests or customers and service persons, and the back is the place where members of the home team retire between performances to relax and to prepare" (MacCannell 1999: 92). In other words, the front region is the space that is presented to the public, as in a stage where actors perform, and the back region is the space hidden behind stage, where actors' secrets or special effects might be revealed. These zones are structured by architectural arrangements and the touristic activity that takes place within them. MacCannell further suggests that:

> ... for the study of tourist settings, *front* and *back* be treated as ideal poles of a con-
> tinuum, poles linked by a series of front regions decorated to appear as back regions, and
> back regions set up to accommodate outsiders ... The quest for authenticity is marked
> off in stages in the passage from front to back. Movement from stage to stage corre-
> sponds to growing touristic understanding.

But with monuments such as Cape Coast and Elmina and the advent of cultural heritage and roots tourism, it may be necessary to abandon the strictly delineated front and back regions. Perhaps now, the time is ripe to consider another space that MacCannell (1999: 99) alluded to, the "staged back region," which he suggested at the time of his writing in 1976 to be "a kind of living museum for which we have no analytical terms." The concept of this staged back region may allow for the introduction of a sort of conceptual or liminal space that is the result of the production of heritage as a tourist export and commodity (Kirschenblatt-Gimblett 1998: 149–76; Walsh 1992: 116–47). Such a space offers another layer of analysis that addresses the specificity of monuments and the phenomenon of sites billed for heritage and roots tourism. In places such as these – which are highly charged *lieux de memoire* – front and back activity tends to collapse. Indeed, the entire site of the monument can be thought of as a back region punctuated by the appearance of a front region, this type of layering reflected in the ways that tourists negotiate their movements. For example, at both Cape Coast and Elmina, museum officials in charge of interpreting the sites have indicated the points of interest with bold signs in black and white lettering, such as "Condemned Cell," "Male Dungeon," "Female Dungeon," "Palaver Hall," "Bastion," and "Door of No Return." These clearly marked signs validate different points of interest in such a way as to lend authenticity to them, to mark them as different theaters within the tourist setting. The act of naming specific rooms and the larger places of architectural, historical and cultural interest serves an authenticating function, reinforced by the actions of the tourists *and* the guides – the actors, the performers who lend authenticity to each room or stage of the monument (Figure 6.2).[6]

In an effort to represent – to show "this is how it really was" – the principal highlights of the castle tours perform an authenticating function by focusing on the historical points of pain and suffering or strength and resistance. Thus, visitors learn from the tour guides that the condemned cell, a small room marked by a blackened, barred door and the sign of a skull and cross bones, was where those sentenced to death were left in solitary confinement to perish. At both castles, the condemned cell was located in open view off of the central courtyard so as to emphasize the public nature of the punishment, and to act as a deterrent and an example to potential offenders. The governor's apartment, the residence of the official in charge of the castle, was situated on the upper floors with optimal views for the surveillance of the inner castle activity, and the exterior landscape of the sea and the village. At Elmina, the governor's quarters were located above a courtyard around which dungeons for enslaved women were arranged. The tragic story of how many of the women were raped and subjected to physical and mental violence by the nearby governor is often recounted by the tour guide, who points out how the architectural arrangement of the rooms, and their proximity to one another, facilitated such patterns of abuse. Apparently, the governor could observe (and choose from) the women in the dungeons from a balcony off his quarters that overlooked the courtyard. The dungeons reserved for enslaved men were the largest, darkest and most cavernous spaces. Their massive size in relation to the smaller female dungeons reflected the ratios of men to women that were sent away in slave ships to work on plantations in the new world. At any given time, the dungeons could hold more than 1,000 captives. At Cape Coast, the three male dungeons were carved into the coarse, rocky coastline, each with vaulted ceilings and only two or three small air holes, which also offered occasional glimpses of light. In one of these dungeons, iron links remain fastened tight to the cobblestone floors as reminders of how enslaved men were chained together by shackles. The unmistakable smell of human excrement and bodily fluids is a constant reminder

Figure 6.2 Plaque of remembrance and wreath, Elmina Castle, Ghana, 1999. Photograph by author.

of the death and destruction that took place there. In sharp contrast, the presence of places of worship, of Portuguese, Anglican and Dutch churches, within the same castle walls that housed dungeons remains a source of confusion for tourists – adding another layer to the experience of the authentic.[7]

Authentic Tourists?

The thousands of tourists who visit the castles and forts of Ghana each year make bold claims for a form of perceived *individual* authenticity based on an inherent need to validate their reasons for being there. Such claims attempt to establish who has the right to be there, who is the most authentic tourist, or put plainly, who is entitled to mourn in the space of the dungeons. Made from the standpoint of heritage, race, gender and national origin, these personal claims are often articulated at the monuments through competing performances of authenticity. An example of this is the guided tour for which individuals congregate at random in the courtyard. Each tour guide takes a group of about twenty people, who are usually racially and ethnically diverse and of different ages and nationalities. However, on occasion, some members of the tours complain that they are made to feel uncomfortable, if not unwelcome, by other members of the group. The comments of a tourist who distinguished himself as a white American from Connecticut described his uneasy experience of the hour-long tour of Elmina Castle:

> Very impressive castle. Tour was very good. Great views toward the city, beach and ocean. One concern – a man during the tour was distracting and I felt offended by his anti-white sentiments, as he kept saying, "white people this . . ." I couldn't understand exactly, but he should respect other people more who are trying to follow the tour guide. Overall, I enjoyed my visit here. (Visitor comment book, Elmina Castle)

A Ghanaian member of the same tour group also denounced the racialized comments, "it should be strictly forbidden for visitors in the group to keep making offensive comments which directly or indirectly concern individuals in the group" (visitor comment books, Elmina Castle). Yet incidents such as this one are examples of the pervasive effects of raciology and the legacy of slavery on the world stage (Gilroy 2000: 12). Consequently, in addition to the public guided tours, groups of tourists traveling together from afar – usually distinguished by a particular racial, ethnic, educational, religious or social affiliation – often request their own personal tour guide to learn about specific parts of the castle, such as the churches, the dungeons or the architecture. Moreover, many organized groups of roots tourists demand that whites be barred from participating in their tour, especially when they descend into the sacred spaces of the dungeons for the first time. It is there that roots tourists seek to claim a privileged status, indeed a certain aura of authenticity. They refuse the presence of whites, citing that they do not wish to experience the pain of their ancestors with a descendant of the oppressor in their midst, so that they may find solace in the protection of the group. One African American visitor to Cape Coast suggested: "White visitors should come on different days than the black visitors" (visitor comment book, Cape Coast Castle). Comments such as these suggest a form of authenticity that concerns who is *allowed* to mourn. This raises the question of who is designated the more authentic tourist: African Americans, Europeans, or Ghanaians?

The residual effects of these performances of individual and group authenticity have ramifications that extend beyond an afternoon visit to the castles. Indeed, such performances are carried outside of the monuments into the streets, market-places and other tourist destinations.[8] But most notably, individual claims for authenticity are made visible in the architectural changes made to the monuments themselves and in related tourism initiatives. For example, the presence of roots tourists at Cape Coast and Elmina has influenced the ways in which these sites of memory have been remodeled as tourist attractions. But so too have the voices of the local Ghanaian population, European tourists, the resident African American expatriate community, the Ghana Museums and Monuments Board (GMMB), and North American museum consultants. Converging in the space of the monuments then are the contested notions of the significance of the sites, different perspectives on which histories should be most emphasized and what aspects of the monuments should be "authenticated."

At issue is even the use of the name "castle" for the monuments of Cape Coast and Elmina, which some roots tourists feel dismisses the stories of their ancestors who suffered in the dungeons. For this group, fairytale notions of European architectural grandeur associated with a popular understanding of the term "castle" seem to downplay the fact that enslaved Africans, possibly their ancestors, were held captive there. This is, however, more than a wholesale rejection of the term "castle," which is largely used for militaristic strongholds born out of the medieval period. Some roots tourists also disagree with the renovation efforts being made in the name of historic preservation. They feel that the renovations privilege high architecture and transform the castles into "make believe" places. One visitor from Jamaica plainly stated, "It is horrible to watch this dungeon being turned into a Walt Disney castle!" referring to coats of fresh white paint on the bastions, the addition of potted plants and flowers at the entrance, and the effort to clean and *paint* the inside of the dungeons. The double-edged phrase, "Stop white washing our history!" appears frequently in the visitor comment books at Cape Coast and Elmina (visitor comment book, Cape Coast Castle; Robinson 1994: 48–50).[9] Instead of the regular program of maintenance and renovation that includes whitewashing, Robinson and others feel that these monuments should be left to naturally deteriorate and fall into the sea.

Other tourists argue for renovations and additions of period furniture and artifacts that might help to activate the mostly vacant rooms and buildings that comprise the castle complexes. Even though many of the spaces are marked by the black and white signposts, they are without furniture, installations or diagrams that would suggest to visitors how they might have been utilized in the past. One visitor at Cape Coast demanded: "Please authenticate the Governor's residence to look exactly the way it was then. I think that will make the necessary contrast with the dungeons" (visitor comment book, Cape Coast Castle). In the mid-1990s, some restorations were made to the dungeons at Elmina. Metal bars were added to the arched window openings that lead out to the courtyard of the female dungeons. However, the fresh coats of *white* paint on the walls of some of the male dungeons outraged many visitors. As one person commented, "The Jews would not paint the ovens in Germany!" (visitor comment book, Cape Coast Castle) Similarly problematic was the renovation of one of the male dungeons into a gift shop, replete with merchandising shelves and walls painted with coats of fresh yellow paint. So many visitors complained about it that it was eventually dismantled and moved to an outer service area across from the castle restaurant, the presence of which has also provoked criticism.

Despite the contentious nature of interpretive changes to these sites, visitors continue to suggest the ways in which the dungeons might be authenticated. One visitor to Elmina offered the following solution, "Renovate with models of slaves, sound effects, and smells to give authenticity and real feel for what it was like for our ancestors" (visitor comment book, Elmina Castle). But would such an attempt to recreate a sensorium of the unspeakable go too far, especially when the physical architecture of the dungeons themselves is still there to be experienced? How would the curators and designers choose the models to represent the enslaved men and women, and which actors might be asked to create the sound effects? The intense heat would likely rule out the use of wax figures of the type seen in natural history exhibits, the popular international tourist attraction Madame Toussaud's Wax Museum, or the Blacks in Wax Museum in Baltimore.

One of the most significant renovations to the dungeons occurred at Cape Coast Castle. The dark and dismal space of one of the male dungeons has been transformed through the construction of an altar by the local priest to Nana Tabir, a god who is believed to inhabit the rock out of which the dungeons were carved. Decorated with flowers, candles and offerings, it operates as a sacred place where tourists are invited to make prayers to ancestors, pour libations and give monetary offerings. It is attended by a priest in white robes during opening hours. The altar to Nana Tabir – which symbolizes a story of strength and survival – was lobbied for by residents of Cape Coast. Many people find a sense of peace and solace by its presence there and others seem to emulate it by placing temporary altars in other parts of the castle complex. For many local inhabitants, it represents their ability to have a stake in the decisions being made about the appearance and function of the castles.

In general, the dungeons have been left hauntingly bare, with the exception of wreaths, poems, notes and burning candles left by visitors on a daily basis. Most tourists see this as the only authentic way for the dungeons to be represented, feeling that the emptiness of the buildings best signifies the absence of the many millions gone. Visitors regularly use the vacant dungeons to perform rituals of tribute and commemoration. Returning roots tourists, some of whom make annual pilgrimages to the monuments, often hold candlelight vigils there.

Authenticating Actions

During their visits to the castles, tourists initiate a number of authenticating actions that serve to validate their experiences there. Such actions, whether conscious or unconscious, endorse their positions as stake holders, enhance the way they experience the monuments and provide material evidence of their fleeting presence. These actions include, for example, taking photographs, participating in reenactments, leaving symbolic objects behind and purchasing souvenirs. Many tourists plan their pilgrimages to the castles during Panafest, the biennial Pan African Festival of Performing Arts, which has taken place since 1992. While there, they act as participant observers in many events, including carnival celebrations in the streets of Cape Coast, musical and dramatic performances as well as reenactments of the capture of slaves. In one of the reenactments staged by local Ghanaian actors in 1999, masks of American presidents, such as Ronald Reagan, were worn by the actors who portrayed the slave catchers. The use of these costumes boldly emphasized the history of American involvement in the slave trade with a decidedly politicized contemporary reference to continued American domination over global affairs (Figure 6.3).

Photography is the leading authenticating action among tourists. Individuals, armed with the most basic disposable camera or the most sophisticated digital technology, engage in intense and constant photographic activity that documents historical points of interest, members of their group or details of architectural or aesthetic import. At Elmina, the courtyard is a popular place of photography, where views of the Portuguese church and the surrounding dungeons can be had. The most popular point of reference for photography at Cape Coast Castle is the balustrade walkway with the angular row of cannons pointed at the dramatic sea. In fact, some visitors to the castles come only to make photographs of the architectural details. The paradox of the visitors' fascination with taking photographs at these monuments is echoed in the sentiment expressed by one tourist, "The disparity between the horrific history of the castle and the natural and physical

Figure 6.3 Reenactment, Cape Coast Castle, Ghana, 1999. Photograph by author.

beauty of the seashore is a difficult mix for the present day visitor" (visitor comment book, Cape Coast Castle). Seemingly attracted by the "physical beauty" alone, some visitors come with sophisticated view cameras, tripods and black and white film to make "art" photographs of the castles and the surrounding environment.

In 1993, the renowned African American artist Carrie Mae Weems incorporated photographs of Cape Coast and Elmina in the *Slave Coast Series*, a project that combined documentary-style photographs and text to reinterpret the *lieux de memoire* along the West African coast (Piché Jr. and Golden 1998; Cornell and Finley 2000). Her photographs, presented as diptychs and triptychs, record architectural details of the desolate slave forts and dungeons, absent of any signs of life, their mood silent, solemn, chilling, empty. Text panels, written in blood red type, reclaim the sites and infuse them with restorative narratives – *Congo, Ibo, Mandingo, Togo* recites ethnic and regional origins of enslaved Africans, while *Elmina, Cape Coast, Ile de Gorée* names the three most notorious castles and dungeons where they were held captive. Together, Weems' photographs and text panels from the *Slave Coast Series* perform a transformative and recuperative function, recasting meaning, embracing memory.

Even fashion photographers have chosen the castles as stylish backdrops for their glossy magazine work. Inspired in part by this seemingly perverse phenomenon, the noted Ethiopian filmmaker Haile Gerima wrote, directed and produced the critically acclaimed film, *Sankofa* (1993). The opening and closing scenes of the film, which establish its flashback narrative structure, were shot at Cape Coast Castle. In the beginning, a group of visitors is taken on a guided tour of the castle and dungeons. A black fashion model, who wears a blond wig (symbolizing that she has forsaken her African heritage), is being photographed by a white photographer in the courtyard adjacent to the tunnel entrance to the male dungeons. During a break from the shoot, she follows the tour group into the dungeon and is then possessed by the spirits and psychically taken back a couple of hundred years to where she finds herself in the place of those held captive in the dungeon. Unable to escape, she experiences the Middle Passage with them and ends up as a house slave on a new world plantation. The protagonist experiences all of the horrors of chattel slavery and emerges at the end of the film a changed woman. Returned to the present at Cape Coast Castle, she rejects the blond wig and what it represents and reclaims her African roots.

Photography, especially for roots tourists, serves a commemorative function, and should be recognized as a special authenticating action. The photographs taken by roots tourists are evidence of a return to the ancestral homeland, of the buildings that still stand as a reminder of the birth of the African diaspora in the trans-Atlantic slave trade. Back home, they share their photographs with family and friends as proof of having been there, of having walked through the "door of no return," the visual symbol for the initial passageway through which millions of Africans forcibly left the shores of their homeland for points unknown across the Atlantic. In fact, the "door of no return" is one of the popular, almost required sites that roots tourists choose to record on film. It is also one of the places, like the dungeons, where they choose to leave notes, poems and letters, or sing spirituals, pour libations and say prayers. Authenticating actions such as these signal the creation of novel forms of African diasporic ritual and performance. Moreover, these authenticating actions leave physical evidence of the presence of roots tourists, of their pilgrimages to the ancestral homeland. The physical evidence that they leave behind is at once ephemeral (as in the candles, wreaths, and notes that with time blow away or are removed by the castle maintenance) and lasting. Now, a marble plaque of remembrance permanently displayed at Elmina Castle bears these words carved in marble:

IN EVERLASTING MEMORY
Of the anguish of our ancestors.
May those who died rest in peace.
May those who return find their roots.
May humanity never again perpetuate
Such injustice against humanity.
We, the living, vow to uphold this.
(Plaque dedicated at Cape Coast Castle)

Acknowledgements

This chapter is based on research undertaken in Ghana in 1999 and interviews conducted with local residents, museum officials and tourists. I am particularly grateful to the following entities at Yale University for generously funding the field research for this project: the History of Art Department (Lehman Traveling Fellowship), the John F. Enders Research Fellowship, the Pew Program in Religion and American History, and the Center for the Study of Race, Inequality and Politics. I also would like to acknowledge Robert Forbes, Jacqueline Francis, Kellie Jones, Jane Kamensky, D. Medina Lasansky, and Brian McLaren for their helpful comments.

Notes

1. Cape Coast is also home to one of the country's leading academic institutions, the University of Ghana, Cape Coast.
2. Many of these forts are within 1–3 hours' drive from Cape Coast and Elmina along the coastal road, and like the castles, they also have been slated for restoration and incorporation into the tourist economy. But the controversy about some of the renovation initiatives at the forts concerns their reassignment or reinterpretation as bed and breakfast establishments.
3. Akan refers to the language, cultural and social customs shared by people in a large part of southern Ghana, especially along the coast, and extending west into neighboring Ivory Coast.
4. Nkrumah was elected the first African Prime Minister of the Gold Coast in 1952 and later became Ghana's first head of state in 1957 when it gained its independence from Britain.
5. W. E. B. du Bois migrated to Ghana in 1961 and at the invitation of Kwame Nkrumah, established permanent residency in Accra, where he died in 1963 on the eve of the historic March on Washington. His former home and burial place in Accra has been established as a museum, library and memorial. It is now a requisite place of homage for most roots tourists.
6. It is important to reiterate that a particular type of authenticating is at work in the naming of points of interest at Cape Coast and Elmina, one that puts the history of the slave trade at the center. In other words, the more recent historical uses of the castles (such as the use of Cape Coast as a prison) are not indicated by signs and rarely mentioned by tour guides.

7. These points of interest have had multiple uses over the years, such as the Portuguese church in the central courtyard at Elmina. After the castle was taken over by the Dutch and a Dutch church built, the Portuguese church was modified to be the trading halls and the officers' mess hall. The houses of worship within the castle walls also promoted Western education in the region and served as organizational centers for the efforts of Christian missionaries.

8. For example the efforts on the part of the International Commission of Monuments (ICOM) to restore colonial buildings of architectural interest in Cape Coast and Elmina led to the establishment of walking tours in these cities. These networks extended the tourist web, but also were not without comment. Perhaps not unexpectedly, some local inhabitants argued that walking tours, which emphasize Victorian-era and colonial architecture, overshadow the contributions of native inhabitants to the historical infrastructure of the city. Consequently, they have established walking tours that highlight local history and culture, such as the contributions of the fishing industry, which predates the European presence in this region.

9. The phrase, "Stop Whitewashing Our History," was popularized by the writings and activism of the influential ex-patriot African American Imahkus Vienna Robinson. She and her husband, Nana Okoko Robinson founded One Africa Productions, an activist roots tourism business that hosts reenactments in the dungeons at Cape Coast as well as operates a lodging establishment on the Cape Coast-Elmina road, from which both castles are visible.

References

Anquandah, Kwesi J. (1999), *Castles and Forts of Ghana*, Accra and Paris: Ghana Museums and Monuments Board and Atalante.

Bachelard, Gaston (1969), *The Poetics of Space*, translated from the French by Maria Jolas, Boston: Beacon Press.

Benedict, Burton (1983), *The Anthropology of World's Fairs: San Francisco's Panama Pacific International Exposition of 1915*, London and Berkeley: The Lowie Museum of Anthropology in association with Scholar Press.

Bouquet, Mary (2001), *Academic Anthropology and the Museum: Back to the Future*, New York: Berghahn Books.

Briggs, Phillip (1998), *Guide to Ghana*, Chalfont St Peter, Bucks: Bradt.

Cape Coast Castle Museum (1995), *Crossroads of People, Crossroads of Trade*, Cape Coast: The Cape Coast Castle Museum.

Cornell, Daniell and Finley, Cheryl (2000), *Imaging African Art: Documentation and Transformation*, New Haven CT: Yale University Art Gallery.

DeCorse, Christopher R. (2001), *An Archaeology of Elmina: Africans and Europeans on the Gold Coast, 1400–1900*, Washington: Smithsonian Institution Press.

Finley, Cheryl (2001), "The Door of (No) Return," *Common-place*, www.common-place.org, vol. 1, no. 4, July.

Gerima, Haile (1993), *Sankofa*, Washington DC: Mypheduh Films, 125 minutes, color.

Gilroy, Paul (2000), *Against Race: Imagining Political Culture Beyond the Color Line*, Cambridge MA: Harvard University Press.

Haley, Alex (1976), *Roots*, Garden City NY: Doubleday & Company.

Hayden, Dolores (1995), *The Power of Place: Urban Landscapes as Public History*, Cambridge MA: MIT Press.

Kirshenblatt-Gimblett, Barbara (1998), *Destination Culture: Tourism, Museums, and Heritage*, Berkeley: University of California Press.

Lennon, John and Foley, Malcolm (2000), *Dark Tourism: The Attraction of Death and Disaster*, New York: Continuum.

MacCannell, Dean (1976, 1999), *The Tourist: A New Theory of the Leisure Class*, Berkeley: University of California Press.

Nora, Pierre (1989), "Between Memory and History: *Les Lieux des Memoire*", *Representations* 26.

Piché, Jr., Thomas and Golden, Thelma (1998), *Carrie Mae Weems: Recent Work, 1992–1998*, New York: George Braziller.

Robinson, Imahkus Vienna (1994), "Is the Black Man's History Being Whitewashed?" *Uhuru*, 9: 48–50.

Simpson, Moira G. (1996), *Making Representations: Museums in the Post-Colonial Era*, London: Routledge.

Walsh, Kevin (1992), *The Representation of the Past: Museums and Heritage in the Post-modern World*, New York: Routledge.

Wright, Richard (1954, 1995), *Black Power: A Record of Reactions in a Land of Pathos,* New York: Harper Perennial.

Public Archives, Museums and Historic Sites

W. E. B. du Bois Center and Memorial, Accra, Ghana
Cape Coast Castle Museum, Cape Coast, Ghana
National Museum, Accra, Ghana
Maison des Esclaves, Dakar, Sénégal
Musée Historique de Gorée, Dakar, Sénégal
Visitor Comment Books, Cape Coast and Elmina Castles

Part III
Packaging Place

From Photographic Fragments to Architectural Illusions at the 1929 Poble Espanyol in Barcelona

Jordana Mendelson

During the mid-1920s a small group of artists and architects from Barcelona traveled across Spain photographing and sketching the nation's architecture. Their pictorial records, souvenirs of their research, formed the basis for the plans they drew up for the construction of a "typical" Spanish village to be built for the 1929 International Exposition in Barcelona (Figure 7.1). Unlike other national displays of architecture at world's fairs, either designed as a street or a conglomerate of related pavilions and attractions (for example, the "Ville de Paris" in Paris, 1900; the Irish Village in Edinburgh, 1908; a Portuguese Street in London, 1909; and the "Regional Center" in Paris, 1937), the Spanish village was built as a self-contained, functional village that would appear to tourists as an authentic representation of the nation's diverse architecture, customs and trades.

The Spanish village is the only town of its kind, built for an International Exposition, to still stand today (Greenhalgh 1994: 106). It is located at the base of Montjüic, a large hill that was converted from its original military use as a fortress and prison to an elaborate complex of gardens, gallery spaces, theaters and pavilions for the Exposition. Just diagonally below the National Palace and to the right of Mies van der Rohe's modernist German Pavilion, the Spanish village made a significant imprint upon the Exposition site. Measuring about 23,000 m² and consisting of 115 interconnected buildings, the village is enclosed within a reconstruction of the medieval walls of the Castilian town of Ávila, with just one entrance into the village that is modeled after the medieval town's towers and gates. Once inside, the Castilian exterior gives way to an architectural collage of buildings from across Spain, including examples of domestic and civic architecture from Extremadura, Galicia, Andalusia, Castile, Aragon and Catalonia. In addition to a main plaza, there are numerous other plazas, patios and narrow streets through which visitors are brought into contact with replicas of artificial stone that nonetheless aspire to authenticity in appearance and scale. Still within the district of the village but beyond the rear enclosure of its walls, visitors cross a bridge to arrive at a Romanesque monastery.

Figure 7.1 Bird's eye view of the Poble Espanyol. Courtesy of the Arxiu Històric del Col.legi d'Arquitectes de Catalunya.

All of this becomes, for both national and foreign tourists, a stage set within which to enact narratives of travel, citizenship, identification and difference. Almost cinematic in its compression of spatial and temporal differences, the Spanish village allows visitors to stroll through impossible juxtapositions and across distances of style and region effortlessly. Within minutes, a visitor passes through the entrance gate and into the main plaza, which alone brings together twenty-two examples of national architecture. Each of these architectural references is blended together by fusing their façades into an over-arching town structure. The architect's plan unified the nation's diversity by creating a space in which difference was neither shocking nor disturbing. Entertainment, surprise and ease of mobility replaced the rigors and dangers of travel and brought tourists into contact with a highly mediated (and yet seemingly transparent) reproduction of provincial Spain. Past and present visitors are guided to interpret the site as a model preindustrial town constructed in the heart of Spain's most industrialized city (Epps 2001: 172). The Spanish village is both an historical and a contemporary tourist site, it affords scholars the opportunity to think at once about the history of its production and reception as well as its relevance to current theories on architecture, tourism and ideology.

The architects' travels and their use of photography anchored the village's authenticity by creating a narrative of origins and experience that could be revisited by tourists repeatedly to create different itineraries within a town that was nonetheless shaped by that first impression of a village enclosed within its medieval, Castilian walls. At the time of its inauguration and throughout 1929–30, critics considered the village to be both an archeological mystery and an artistic reconstruction. Commentators praised the village for its truthfulness in detail and its reproduction of Spanish heritage and lifestyle, while also remarking on the serene harmony of its unified plan. Photography inscribed such a duality within the village's history; it was both fact and fiction, testimony and fantasy. Perhaps the most fascinating aspect of the transformation from architecture to photographic fragment and back again is that the village itself became the subject of uncountable photographic reproductions in postcards, posters and the press.

The dictatorship of General Miguel Primo de Rivera and the reign of King Alfonso XIII influenced the conditions and components of the Exposition's Spanish village. Yet, the village's meanings and uses were not exclusively determined by the government's or the aristocracy's policies and practices; variance as much as stricture was part of the political and linguistic ground upon which the village was built. In Castilian, the dominant language in Spain and the official discourse of the central government led by Primo de Rivera, it was known as the Pueblo Español. In Barcelona, where Catalan was the national language and had been censored by the government for its association with separatism and Catalanisme (Roig Rosich 1992: 41, 120–3, 206), it was called the Poble Espanyol. The very project of building a Spanish village in Barcelona held deep significance at a time of political instability for a dictatorship that was faced with economic and social crises. (In 1923, when Primo declared a nationwide military coup, he did so from Barcelona where he was General Captain of Catalonia.) The dictatorship had built its reputation on the promise of unifying Spain within a rhetoric that was firmly grounded in the identity, language and history of central Spain, or Castile. This was done at the expense of the country's other national identities, which included Catalonia. By building an architectural representation of Spain unified in Barcelona, Primo put forward a brand of national diversity that converted potentially volatile displays of national difference into the illusion of a controlled pluralism.

Through the tourist experience, first of the architects in Spain and later of visitors to the Poble Espanyol, origin and authenticity, fragmentation and unity, became closely associated with consumption and performance. Mechanical reproduction, which supported the village's truth value by grounding architecture in photography, was also what enabled visitors and viewers playfully to subvert the regime's political dependence on truth and authenticity. Once reproduced in the form of another photograph, film, sketch or advertisement, the International

Exposition's artificial village was transformed into an historical fact by virtue of its reproducibility. Visitors and viewers chose to participate in the Poble's fictions, but did so, I believe, with an awareness of their role in staging national heritage for both pleasure and politics. From an examination of their letters, photographs and sketches, it is clear that the artists and architects involved in the planning and construction of the Poble were aware of the village's potential dualities and played with them in the planning process and later in their comments to the press.

Touring Spain: The Photographers behind the Village

The artists and architects behind the Poble Espanyol were all Catalan with important backgrounds in the cultural history of Barcelona. The director of the group's trips was Miguel Utrillo, an art historian and cultural impresario who, despite some public debate in 1929–30, is most often considered the originator of the idea for the Poble Espanyol; one article went so far as to name Utrillo the village's "father" (Anon. 1929: 3). Francesc Folguera and Ramón Reventós were hired as architects and the visual artist Xavier Nogués was assigned, like Utrillo, as an artistic consultant to the project. Nogués also drew sketches during the group's tour through Spain and designed much of the publicity material used to promote the Poble Espanyol and the International Exposition. If Utrillo was the man behind the idea and to a large degree the instigator of many aspects of the Poble Espanyol's planning and construction, Lluís Plandiura was its overseer. As a wealthy industrialist, a prominent art collector and a member of the Exposition's artistic committee, Plandiura served as the liaison between the group and the requisites and goals of the Exposition's director, who was a personal confidant of the dictator (Miralles 1985: 104).

Together from 1926 to 1928, Utrillo, Nogués, Reventós and Folguera undertook several trips across Spain. Utrillo suggested purchasing a 1920s version of a station wagon to make their travels more economical, reliable and flexible (Utrillo 1927a). He even prepared his colleagues for their trip by compiling a list of essential equipment and personal effects that they would need while crossing the Spanish countryside (Domènech i Polo 1989: 44–5). While visiting towns to collect visual and historical documentation about the sites, Utrillo delivered lectures on Spanish art and architecture, and distributed publicity materials on the International Exposition. The most important and extensive of their trips took place from September to October 1927. The map that they submitted to Plandiura as a record of their travels demonstrates the circuit that they took across Spain. The group visited important cities, provincial centers and more distanced rural towns. Utrillo included in their itinerary both recognized monuments of historic and artistic value (designated as such by the government to form part of the national patrimony) as well as little-known or hardly documented elements from public monuments, religious buildings and domestic architecture. Utrillo divided the trip into thirty-three stages. The group left from Barcelona and went northwest across Spain to Galicia and then came down to Salamanca, through Extremadura, across Castile, over to Valencia and then back up the coast to Barcelona. At this point in the group's planning, Andalusia was not yet part of the Poble and so was left off of Utrillo's itinerary.

Folguera and Reventós became the group's photographers, with Nogués and Utrillo remarking, over and over again, in amazement the architects' prolific photographic activity. In Utrillo's letters to Plandiura he emphasized the sheer quantity of photographs being taken: "Mr. Folguera and Mr. Reventós . . . have already taken 38 photographs" (Utrillo 1927b). Nogués, whose own tasks were limited to the more traditional method of drawing sketches, praised both the speed and veracity of the photographers' work: "we have already made 104 photographs between yesterday and today of many interesting things for the village; every moment we are convinced that the photographs will make it better and that without our trip there would never have been a real village" (Nogués 1927). The group made smaller trips throughout 1928, and continued to take a camera with them. Reventós reported triumphantly in May: "We continue the photographic harvest, which threatens to be very plentiful" (Nogués 1928). By the time the Exposition opened, writers had inflated the number of photographs amassed to thousands. One article qualified their accomplishments as dizzying: "the architects go from here to there in vertiginous trips in which they go and return over highways for 20,000 kilometers with thousands of notes and photographs of the more than 600 towns and villages visited" ("L'Exposició de Barcelona 1929–1930" 1930).

Out of the notes and photographs, the architects and artists began configuring their plans for the Poble Espanyol. Reventós explained in an article published months after the Exposition's inauguration that the process of forging out of this vast quantity of documentary material a cohesive and representative group of buildings was, surprisingly, a more subjective process than might be expected. Opinion and individual choice took priority over a previously established criterion: "Things that were good were later rejected as vulgar or not so characteristic. Other things that from the first glance had been doubtfully accepted, would impose themselves with force because of their own charm. Other unpublished things with no image reproduced or spoken of in any book were chosen as the most representative and eloquent image of popular architecture" (Reventós 1929: 41–2). In the face of such vague notions of type and taste, it is ironic that the built complex to emerge from the architects' photographs was rarely challenged as authentic or accurate in representing a cross-section of Spanish architecture.

Exposition organizers, and the architects themselves, were able to rely upon the legend of the photographs (and their indexical status as transparent records of an existing site) to substantiate any claims to truth. At the same time that photography insured veracity, the subjectivity of the architects' choice and the manipulations of scale to which they subjected the buildings undermine the Poble Espanyol as an absolute record of any single agenda. In other words, the photographic fragments that formed the material out of which the village was imagined irritate the possibility for it to operate solely within one artistic or national (Spanish or Catalan) archive of types. In their photographs, the architects focused squarely on isolated architectural elements – technical aspects of construction, ornamentation and town planning – or on groups of buildings and interesting views. Any figures that do appear in the photographs are generally caught offguard, pushing the relation between architecture, ethnicity and politics out of the frame. Sometimes traces of figures are registered near the edges of the frame; rarely are they the center of attention. The figures in the photographs are most often blurred, awkwardly cropped or seemingly oblivious to the photographer's lens.

The Poble Espanyol as Origin and Mass Spectacle

The photographs taken for the Poble Espanyol supported the Exposition organizers' goal of creating a mass spectacle. The technique that had helped the architects mediate their experiences with Spain's architecture and fragment it into recombinable pieces, was the same tool that promoters, the press and the public used to fuse those elements back together. Not only did photography give to the village its documentary foundation, it also allowed other visual arts to gain a similar status in testifying to its legitimacy. As the geographer and folklorist Francisco Carreras y Candi wrote in his article about the Poble Espanyol in 1929, "[The village's] success will increase if one day we see, painted in some art exhibition, 'A corner of the Pueblo Español of Barcelona'." In other words, the only authentication needed to guarantee the artistic (and ideological) cohesion of the village would be for it to become the subject of another artist's rendition.

The transformation of the Utebo Bell Tower from Zaragoza in Aragon from *in situ* monument to a fundamental architectural element within the Poble Espanyol provides a typical example of the role of photography in forming the basis for the planners' architectural collage. In the photograph of the Tower taken by Reventós and Folguera, the structure is isolated (Figure 7. 2). The Tower stands alone in a tightly cropped image. In the Poble Espanyol, however, the scale of the Tower was brought into relation with the other elements of the village to insure a prescripted view for visitors, who could see the Tower from multiple viewpoints within the Poble. From one entrypoint, the Tower stands at the end of an ascending street, filling the space between two converging lines of other buildings (Figure 7. 3). It provides a sense of focus and closure. Here the idea of a unifying composite took precedence over original scale, context, details and perspective. The photographs taken by Folguera and Reventós set into motion a process through which isolated, provincial monuments became part of an idealized architectural complex and the Poble Espanyol became the most picturesque of sites for tourists. In the poster that Nogués designed to advertise the village, he brought together the viewpoint and impressive scale of the Tower as captured by the architects' photograph with a depiction of a typical scene that emphasized the Tower's placement within the village. Both aspects of the Poble's mechanisms for communicating believability to its visitors were brought together by Nogués in this poster: a reference to the original photograph taken by the architects and the representation of the Tower as a part of a new reference point for civic activities and performances.

In order for the village to be a viable creation, its spaces had to be activated by the participation of visitors in activities and scenes that were considered typical. Several cafés were opened, among them was the Café del Pueblo Español in the Plaça Mayor, or main plaza. The original menu from the Café features a drawing of a view from the terrace into the plaza. After consuming Spanish fare like Valencian *horchata* and Andalusian sherry visitors could stroll down the Poble's streets to find regionally produced crafts, like the ceramic stalls set up in sections devoted to Zamora, Catalonia and Castile. By entering a diorama at the far end of the main plaza, visitors were able to recreate the architects' tour through Spain. Behind the façades of the various regional buildings along the main plaza, one could work one's way through typical scenes and practices; the diorama offered an easy representation of that experience for visitors without the potential shifts in trajectory that a walking tour through the village might entail. As with a trip by train or automobile, the dioramas emphasized destinations, both geographic and historical, instead of the journey. The blur that represented the distance between places and peoples was eliminated, as it was in the village's cinematic compression of difference. In the process, the Poble itself appeared to defy mediation and become, like the diorama contained within its walls, a transparent reproduction of the travel experience. As one writer commented, "In the Spanish village, turning a corner is like traveling many kilometers" (Gribau 1929: 21).

The organizers had accomplished their goal: to naturalize what would have otherwise been considered impossible juxtapositions of different styles and geographic locations by imbuing the Poble Espanyol with all of the characteristics of a typical, functioning town, complete with imported performers and craftsmen from nearly all of Spain's regions. M. Aguilar, writing in the widely distributed national magazine *La Ilustración Ibero-Americana*, exclaimed to his readers: "This is more than an Exhibition, it's a nation" (Aguilar 1929: 44). The presence of local products and festivals was an integral part of the typical villages constructed at world's fairs beginning in the late nineteenth century. In the case of the Poble Espanyol, the trade of tradition and heritage was established between Spanish rural

Figure 7.2 Photograph taken by Francesc Folguera and Ramón Reventós of the Utebo Bell Tower in Zaragoza, Aragaon. Fons Plandiura LP-26-45. Courtesy of the Photographic Archive of the Arxiu Històric de la Cuitat de Barcelona. Photographed by Jordi Calafell.

Figure 7.3 Photograph of the Poble Espanyol in construction, with the reconstruction of the Utebo Bell Tower visible in the background. Courtesy of the Photographic Archive of the Arxiu Històric de la Cuitat de Barcelona.

types and the nation's urban population and foreign visitors. Like the exotic streets and neighborhoods created at other world fairs, here too, difference was diffused and assimilated through a multiplicity of events and products. For the nationalist rhetoric of the dictatorship to succeed, the diversity of Spain's regions had to be contextualized within a broader picture of entertaining pluralism.

The performance of authenticity was carefully staged to bring parcels of Spanish customs into the village's precinct. Regional festivals were regularly celebrated and featured in local and national newspapers. Bullfights were also held in an *ad hoc* ring built in the center of the main plaza; evening parties, open markets, and numerous official ceremonies were staged in the same plaza (Planes 1929: 2). Pony rides were given in the main plaza, and women dressed in regional costume took souvenir photographs of visitors (Figure 7. 4). In the act of having their picture taken, visitors became part of the village's history and, in turn, enacted a ritual of citizenship. Artifice and authenticity were put into dialogue. Postcards of the Poble were purchased and kept as souvenirs or sent away to friends and family. These familiarly sized photographs offered any tourist the opportunity to keep a record of their experiences at the Poble Espanyol. The photographic souvenir made their experience real and converted the village into a part of each visitor's personal history. The new visitors, in effect, reenacted the architects'

Figure 7.4 Women and pony rides in the main plaza of the Poble Espanyol. Courtesy of the Arxiu Històric del Col.legi d'Arquitectes de Catalunya.

journey through Spain not only by walking the Poble's streets and participating in its fairs, but also by taking photographs and having themselves photographed in the village.

John Gillis's observation on memory and identity in relation to national acts of commemoration clarifies how the space of the Poble Espanyol and its representations involved the visitor/viewer directly in the act of remaking history: "If the conflicts of the present seemed intractable, the past offered a screen on which desires for unity and continuity, that is, identity, could be projected" (Gillis 1994: 9). That the city's troubled recent past was on the public's mind is evidenced by writers' comments of both before and after the Exposition's inauguration. For example, an editorial in the forty-ninth number of *Mirador* in 1930 explained that the Poble Espanyol "served to erase the memory of the recent past, so catastrophic." Through the intervention of the architects' plan and the photographer's postcards, the visitor/viewer was encouraged to manufacture and relive a dreamlike, phantasmagoric childhood far away from political conflict (*España en sus exposiciones* 1931: 18). The Poble was constructed as and perceived by many writers as a site of collective memory for the Spanish people. One commentator praised the Poble for embodying a universal past: "This is the Spanish village, an evocation of the past of each and every one of us (Carranza 1929: 24)." Another bridged collective memory to personal nostalgia: "The national visitor encounters his corner, his little street, that reminds him of the beloved corner of Spain where he was born" (*Barcelona 1929–1930* 1930).

The Case of Andalusia

During the same year that the International Exposition in Barcelona was inaugurated, Primo de Rivera and King Alfonso XIII opened another major fair in Seville, the Ibero-American Exposition. The Expositions marked the government's political and economic ambitions at home and abroad. As one writer remarked, "Seville has been Spain's mirror in Iberian-America, and Barcelona the reflection of our European spirit" (*España en sus exposiciones* 1931); together they were the most important propaganda events to be held during the dictator's regime. While the Seville Exposition began under Primo's rule, the Barcelona Exposition had a longer history. It had originally been scheduled to open in 1917, but was postponed because of the outbreak of the First World War. Spain had been neutral throughout the war and had benefited artistically and economically while other countries experienced extreme human and material loss. When Primo came to power in 1923, he enthusiastically resurrected the idea for the Exposition as an opportunity to promote Spain as the harbinger of peace, prosperity and industry in postwar Europe.

In returning to the Exposition as a device to promote his own government's aspirations, Primo appropriated and subverted an idea that had originally emerged among Barcelona's business and civic leaders. What had been imagined as a means to foster the city's growth following the staging of the 1888 International Exposition in Barcelona, and supported by the Catalan government, was now placed at the service of the dictatorship's central government in Madrid. Primo combined the Barcelona Exposition's emphasis on technology and pan-European solidarity with the Ibero-American Exposition's promotion of Spain as the center of a postcolonial alliance within the Hispanic world by featuring regional and pan-American pavilions (Braojos Garrido 1992). Having faced defeats in Cuba, Morocco and the Philippines, the Seville Exposition took on a compensatory role for a government whose primary difficulties still resided in the nation's inability to come to terms with its colonial loses. In short, the Expositions served a dual role: to bring international attention to Spain and to promote an image of national stability, unity and growth both to foreign and domestic audiences. In trying to achieve these goals, it was critically important that the image of a nation unified be present in all of the government's projects and actions for the Expositions, including the Poble Espanyol.

Part of the strategy for persuading visitors of the transformative potential of these Expositions was to publicize them as dreamscapes. Magazines like the

Ilustración Ibero-Americana featured color photographs of Carles Buïgas's invent-
ive and technologically advanced light displays and syncopated fountains in front
of the National Palace at the Barcelona Exposition. Visitors' imaginations were
filled with visions of Barcelona as a techno-color fantasy and of Seville as the
reenactment of colonial dreams resurrected in the present. Advertisers for the
Barcelona Exposition asked readers of one Valencian magazine the question:
"¿Sueño o Realidad?," dream or reality? The answer provided by promoters
encouraged readers to believe that the Exposition made dreams a reality. For every
Spaniard, the ads seemed to suggest, the Exposition offered an opportunity to
become part of a national fantasy. Had the public agreed to the government's
suggestion that they convert their dreams into reality by participating in the
Exposition's illusions of national harmony, Primo might have succeeded in fore-
stalling the real problems facing Spain during the late-1920s. Instead, behind the
bright lights and government propaganda was a nation on the verge of historic
changes. Fears about Spain's political future leaked into the international press.
One flyer published by the Spanish travel bureau in London in March 1929
attempted a campaign of counter-propaganda. With a declarative title that proclaimed "No Revolution in Spain," the flyer sought to turn the tables on rumors of
government instability and popular revolution. The "alarmist reports" that the
poster sought to counter were not unfounded. As the editors of *D'Ací i d'Allà*
explained to its readers in July 1930: "it is curious that this [Barcelona Inter-
national] Exhibition, which was to have been a kind of armistice for the dictatorship, that would allow it to spend a year in tranquillity, has lasted half a year longer
than the dictatorial government."

   If the Expositions failed to guard against the government's defeat, they did
accomplish another of Primo's goals, which was to publicize the modernity of
Spain's tourist industry. In 1928, the Patronato Nacional de Turismo was founded
by Royal Decree to assist in promoting the Expositions abroad and to foster travel
within Spain (Ferreras 1973: 26–7). As part of its charge, the Patronato established
offices throughout Europe. Understanding that the Expositions would bring
visitors, the government tried to correct the image of Spain as a backward and
difficult place to travel by emphasizing its newly constructed highways and the
availability of comfortable facilities. Despite the government's efforts, critics
continued to complain about the poor condition of the nation's roads and the
dangers of tourism within Spain ("Hay que Evitar el 'sabotage' del turismo español"
1929, "Acerca del turismo" 1929). The Poble Espanyol offered an ideal solution
to real travel since in Barcelona foreigners could experience the whole of Spain in
the passage of a few hours strolling around the village's plazas and streets. Ironically, whereas travel increasingly required the assistance of trains and automobiles,
in the Spanish village the inventions of modernity were carefully eliminated from
sight. Ceramic plaques at the entrance clearly indicated that automobiles were not

allowed. The imposing reconstructed walls of Ávila delineated the space within from outside the Poble. For visitors to the Exposition, the Poble represented an ideal topography cordoned off from the troubles and technologies of urban life.

Numerous maps of the Poble were published at the time of the Exposition. One distributed by the department store El Siglo provided a bird's eye view with a key to help visitors identify different sites, shops and monuments. Having the Poble mapped out for visitors also allowed them to see and understand the site as a comprehensive display of Spain's areas and traditions. Designed to be enclosed within a walled circumference, the architects created a space that appeared flawless in its unification of all of Spain. However, that unity, which was witnessed by visitors and is apparent in the shape and design of the village's plan, was one that was insisted upon by the central government. In this, the architects had the input of King Alfonso XIII. The King made his own views on Spanish nationalism known to the group through his insistence upon the inclusion of an area dedicated to Andalusia at the Poble. Originally, the Exposition organizers had refrained from including Andalusia, claiming that it would draw attention away from Seville's own Exposition ("Idea del Barrio Andaluz," AHCB, LP25–9). The King's insistence to the contrary must have been motivated in part by the Exposition's newly defined goals. The elimination of Spain's most typical and picturesque region would have broken the appearance of completeness and integrity that the Spanish village, both in the Exposition and in reality, relied upon for political stability.

In the architects' plans for the village, the newly added section dedicated to Andalusia was highlighted in red. Rather than modeling the buildings after monumental examples of Spain's southern architecture, especially the Alhambra, as had been done at previous world's fairs (Bueno Fidel 1987: 25–63), the architects chose to reproduce what they described as the spirit of the *pueblo*. This meant focusing on the built environment and trying to capture what was at once recognizable but not stereotypical about Spain's most admired, yet according to the architects misunderstood areas of the country. For Reventós and Folguera, it was more important to create the atmosphere of southern Spain than to include citations to specific buildings that visitors to Spain might experience when they traveled to the Seville Exposition or had already seen illustrated in travel accounts or reconstructed at previous world's fairs. The Andalusian neighborhood consisted of primarily domestic architecture, narrow thoroughfares and open patios. In the sketches that the architects submitted with their plan, and despite their desire to depart from foreign stereotypes, they inhabited the neighborhood's streets with figures and scenarios of Andalusia's southern charm, which included costumed couples and romantic interludes along the neighborhood's streets. In addition, the architects and organizers planned taverns within the neighborhood where Flamenco was regularly performed. Rather than being an apparent afterthought or appendage to the architects' plan, Andalusia became a main attraction for visitors to the Poble Espanyol and occupied a significant portion of the Poble's total area. The Calle de Arcos, which was one of two streets within the section, was probably one of the most widely photographed and publicized of the village's features.

Taking into consideration that Andalusia had become Spain in the minds of many foreigners, its absence from the Poble Espanyol would have shattered any illusion of national unity. Its absence would have also disappointed tourists who, after all were invited to tour the Poble Espanyol in order to gain a complete picture of Spain's architecture and traditions. Despite the architects' desire to side-step stereotype in favor of the popular traditions of Spanish architecture, visitors no doubt found in the Andalusian neighborhood the closest image they had already constructed about Spain confirmed for them in three-dimensions.

Alternative Readings?

Given the modifications to the plan for the Poble Espanyol, the popularity of the Andalusian neighborhood and the apparent success with which the Poble's architecture and attractions were received, it might appear as if the government's illusion was complete. Had, in fact, the distinct identities of Spain's nationalities been completely absorbed into a unifying program in support of the government's nationalist ideology? Was Spain successfully grafted onto Barcelona? Had Catalonia in turn relinquished its authority over the production of this typical village? According to reports from the period, the government's illusion was both upheld and suggestively undermined. Of the commentaries, Jaume Passarell's 1929 article in the Barcelona magazine *Mirador* was the most succinct: "Finally . . . they have given us the grace to transplant onto Montjuïc a Spanish village, that is a Catalan translation of the real thing" (Passarell 1929: 2). Passarell seems to acknowledge here the agency of the Catalan group to translate, though perhaps not transform, the central government's view of Spanish nationality. This differs from other writers, who betrayed in their comments an acknowledgement of the Poble's dual origins. Perhaps the greatest evidence of this was an article published in the Exposition's *Diario Oficial* titled "The Best Village in Spain" in which Francisco Higuero Bazaga asserted that "From Catalonia, that simple and generous land . . . has emerged the idea and the general execution of the Pueblo Español." He went on to state in the very next paragraph that "Everything in this silent village has a mystic and dreamy stamp of exclusively Spanish manufacture" (Higuero Bazaga 1929: 19). Thus, rather than symbolizing a break with predictatorship ideas, the Poble Espanyol represented for many a continuation of certain aspects of earlier ideologies now modified by the exigencies of the dictatorship and put in the service of entertainment, consumption and, of course, a different national politics.

In describing the processes through which visitors came to identify with the Poble Espanyol as an operative space for the enactment of national ideals, I do not want to imply by this that visitors naively or uniformly participated in the government's project to create a surrogate nation with the unchallenged cooperation of architects, artists, national visitors, critics and foreign tourists. In fact, I want to suggest the opposite. In a newsreel taken in 1929 of the female photographers employed in the Poble Espanyol, it is the smirk on the faces of the women dressed in regional costume that most calls my attention. Knowing that they are being filmed, they pose while taking photographs of visitors. In an article from 1929, a reporter recreated their photographic activities: "There they are, in the intersections and in the picturesque little plazas, waiting for the visitor, a few beautiful girls; they wear the characteristic costumes of each region; they justify well, in the foreigner's eyes, the fame that our women have for being pretty and beautiful, charming and discrete. They offer a photograph. A 'snap shot'" (Centeno 1929: n.p.). The reporter described for readers the tipping habits of the female photographers' clients. The task of making commemorative souvenirs was fundamentally tied to an economic reality for the women taking the photographs. Commerce and exchange motivate the relationship between tourism and authenticity.

Photography became the broker for these relationships by first providing the means through which authenticity was established from the beginning of the architects' plans, and second by offering visitors the opportunity to partake in the recreation of the Poble Espanyol through their role as subjects being photographed. Behind the female photographers, the newsreel captures a performance of the *Sardana*. Here, the Catalan national dance finds expression, not in the first plane but in the background. I can't help but see in this newsreel a lesson about the potential heterogeneity that existed all along in the Poble Espanyol. Despite the dictator's desire to regulate the design and promotion of Barcelona's Poble Espanyol, one finds instances of the village's fragmentary illusions made visible to the public.

There are other ways that architectural fragments and illusions circulated concurrently in the press. Rather than providing a fracture-proof image of Spain unified and centralized under the careful watch of the Madrid-based government, I would argue that some of Barcelona's "separateness" may have found its way into the Poble. With a cast of Catalan artists, architects and patrons it would have been hard for the project not to coincide, at least in part, with Catalonia's own national ambitions. While the government was spinning stories about the ideal village, publicity materials for the Poble Espanyol promoted fragmentation and multiplicity as another option for consumption. Sheets of Xavier Nogués's stamps of the Poble supplied repetition as a possible response to claims of authenticity. Similarly, the *Ilustración Ibero-Americana* published a cutout of the Poble in April 1930; children could build (and un-build) their own paper version of the Utebo Tower. The fact that the village had been built out of photographic records collected by the architects finds its moment of disclosure in a child's game. Rather than being a seamless illusion, these publicity materials reveal that the Poble Espanyol was a well-crafted construction. Instead of the fable of unification, it may have been the possibility of difference that ultimately led to the village's great success and its unexpected survival into the present, long after the fall of Primo's dictatorship.

Today, the Poble Espanyol is still one of Barcelona's greatest tourist attractions. Billed as "la ciutat dels artesans," the city of craftsmen, it is populated by local artisans, commercial vendors and small private and public enterprises. By night, the Poble is transformed into a popular entertainment spot, with several disco-theques nestled behind the village's façades. Despite these attempts to modernize the village's attractions and update its relevance for tourists, visitors can still be found shopping the stores of the Andalusian neighborhood to purchase brightly colored Flamenco outfits. In the village's main plaza, groups of young Catalan dancers still perform the *Sardana*.

Acknowledgements

I would like to thank D. Medina Lasanksy and Brian McLaren for their invitation to present a version of this paper at the College Art Association Conference in 2002. They have been supportive and critical interlocutors in the transformation of that paper into this chapter. The research and writing of this material was funded by the U.S. Department of Education, a Fulbright Award, a grant from the Program for Cultural Cooperation between Spain's Ministry of Culture, Education and Sport and North American Universities, a Mrs. Giles Whiting Foundation Fellowship at Yale University, and the Research Board and the Center for Advanced Study at the University of Illinois, Urbana-Champaign. An expanded version of this chapter will appear in *Documenting Spain: Artists, Exhibition Culture, and the Modern Nation 1929–1939*, forthcoming from Penn State University Press.

References

"Acerca del turismo: Cómo ven a España los extranjeros", (1929), *Heraldo de Madrid* (5 October): 1.

Aguilar, M. (1929), "La Exposición milagrosa", *La Ilustración Ibero-Americana*, (1 December): 44.

Anon. (1929), "La paternitat del *Poble Espanyol*: La primativa idea es deua a don Ignasi Girona?", *Mirador*, 31: 3.

Assassin, S. (1992), *Séville: l'Exposition Ibéro-Américaine, 1929–1930*, Paris: Institut français d'architecture, NORMA.

"Balanç de l'Any", (1930), *Mirador*, 49: 1.

Barcelona 1929–1930. Recuerdo de la Exposicón. Anuario de la Ciudad (1930), Barcelona: Sociedad de Atracción de Forasteros,

Braojos Garrido, A. (1992), *Alfonso XIII y la Exposición Iberoamericana de Sevilla de 1929*, Seville: Secretariado de Publicaciones, Universidad de Sevilla.

Bueno Fidel, M.J. (1987), *Arquitectura y Nacionalismo (Pabellones Españoles en las Exposiciones Universales del Siglo XIX*, Málaga: Universidad de Málaga and Colegio de Arquitectos de Málaga.

Carranza, A. de (1929), "Evocación en el Pueblo Español", *Diario Oficial de la Exposición Internacional Barcelona 1929*, 22 (11 August).

Carreras y Candi, F. (1929), "El 1929 'Pueblo Español' de la Exposición de Barcelona", *Barcelona y sus Exposiciones de 1888–1929*, Barcelona: Las Noticias.

Çelik, Z. and L. Kinney (1990), "Ethnography and Exhibitionism at the Expositions Universelles", *Assemblage*: 35–59.

Centeno, F. (1929), "Una 'foto' y un rato de palique", *Diario Oficial de la Exposición Internacional Barcelona 1929*, 15: n.p.

Domènech i Polo, J. (1989), "El Pueblo Español", *El Pueblo Español*, Barcelona: Lunwerg.

Epps, B. (2001), "Modern Spaces: Building Barcelona", in Resina, J. R. (ed.), *Iberian Cities*, New York and London: Routledge.

España en sus exposiciones: Barcelona-Sevilla 1929–1930, (1931), Barcelona: Editorial de la Revista Laboratorio.

Fabre, J. (1979), "L'Exposició que no va salvar una dictadura", *L'Avenç*, 14: n.p.

Ferreras, A. (1973), *El Turisme a Catalunya del 1931 al 1936*, Barcelona: Editorial Pòrtic.

Gillis, J. R. (ed.) (1994), *Commemorations: The Politics of National Identity*, Princeton: Princeton University Press.

Grandas, M. C. (1988), *L'Exposició Internacional de Barcelona de 1929*, Barcelona: Els Llibres de la Frontera.

Greenhalgh, P. (1994), *Ephemeral Vistas: The Expositions Universelles, Great Exhibitions and World's Fairs, 1851–1939*, Manchester: Manchester University Press.

Gribau, V. (1929), "Retazos (Al modo de las greguerías de Ramón)", *Diario Oficial de la Exposición Internacional Barcelona 1929*, 25: 21.

"Hay que evitar el 'sabotage' del turismo español", (1929), *Heraldo de Madrid* (31 August): 7.

Higuero Bazaga, F. (1929), "El mejor pueblo de España", *Diario Oficial de la Exposición Internacional de Barcelona 1929*, 27: 19.

Hinsley, C. M. (1991), "The World as Marketplace: Commodification of the Exotic at the World's Columbia Exposition, Chicago 1898", in Karp, I. and Levine, S. (eds), *Exhibiting Cultures: The Poetics and Politcs of Museum Display*, Washington and London: Smithsonian Institute Press.

"Idea del Barrio Andaluz", LP25–9. Fons Plandiura, Arxiu Històric de la Ciutat, Barcelona (AHCB).

Julian González, I. (1988), *L'urbanisme a Barcelona entre dues exposicions (1888–1929)*, Barcelona: Els llibres de la Frontera.

"La clausura de l'Exposició", (1930), *Mirador*, 77: 1.

Lemus López, E. (1991), *Extremadura y América: La participación regional en la Exposición Ibero-Americana de 1929*, Merida: Editora Regional de Extremadura.

"L'Exposició de Barcelona 1929–1930", *La Publicitat*, 7 May 1930, n.p.

Marfany, L. (1990), *Aspectes del Modernisme*, Barcelona: Curial.

Mendelson, J. (1999), "From Documents to Monuments: The Representation of Spain and the Avant-garde in the 1930s", Ph.D. thesis, New Haven: Yale University.

Miralles, Francesc (1985), "L'Època de les avantguardes 1917–1970", *Història de l'Art Català*, vol. VIII, Barcelona: Edicions 62.

MYSELF [Carles Soldevila] (1929), "El què és el '*Poble* típic Espanyol'", *D'Ací i d'Allà*, número extraordinari: 43.

Nogués, X. (1927), Letter to Lluís Plandiura. LP26–32. Fons Plandiura, Arxiu Històric de la Ciutat, Barcelona (AHCB).

Nogués, X. (1928), Letter to Lluís Plandiura, 17 May. LP26–35. Fons Plandiura, Arxiu Històric de la Ciutat, Barcelona (AHCB).

Passarell, J. (1929), "En Miguel Utrillo pare del *Poble Espanyol*", *Mirador*, 21: 2.

Planes, J. M. (1929), "Nit de Revetlla a l'Exposició", *Mirador*, 22: 2.

Reventós, R. (1929), "Com s'ha fet el *Poble Espanyol*. Algunes impressions d'un que hi ha treballat", *D'Ací i d'Allà*, número extraordinari: 41–2.

Rohrer, J. and Solà Morales, I. de (eds) (1990), *Josep Puig i Cadafalch: la arquitectura entre la casa y la ciudad*, Barcelona: Fundación Caja de Pensiones and Collegi d'Arquitectes de Catalunya.

Roig Rosich, J. M. (1992), *La Dictadura de Primo de Rivera a Catalunya. Un assaig de repressió cultural*, Barcelona: Publicacions de l'Abadia de Montserrat.

Rovira, J.M. (n.d.), *Espacio sin Tiempo: El Pueblo Español de Barcelona*, unpublished manuscript.

Stewart, S. (1993), *On Longing: Narratives of the Miniature, the Gigantic, the Souvenir, the Collection*, Durham and London: Duke University Press.

Utrillo, M. (1927a), Letter to Lluís Plandiura. LP25–33. Fons Plandiura, Arxiu Històric de la Ciutat, Barcelona (AHCB).

Utrillo, M. (1927b), Letter to Lluís Plandiura, Leon, 11 September. LP26–6. Fons Plandiura, Arxiu Històric de la Ciutat, Barcelona (AHCB).

–8–

Simulating France, Seducing the World: The Regional Center at the 1937 Paris Exposition

Deborah D. Hurtt

Edmond Labbé, General Commissioner of the 1937 *Exposition Internationale des arts et des techniques dans la vie moderne* in Paris proclaimed:

> We must not forget that, in France, the cause of regionalism is linked to the cause of tourism. Those things that attract the foreigner to visit us are not only the differences among our nations but also, and perhaps primarily, our [internal] regional differences . . . The Regional Center will serve as the bait to lead Exposition visitors into the diverse provinces . . . [and] will produce [in them] the most powerful reawakening. (Labbé 1936b: 4)

To accomplish this explicit and ambitious agenda for the Regional Center, Labbé formed a Regionalist Commission and charged it with construction of the project on 10 acres immediately adjacent to the Eiffel Tower and the Champs-de-Mars, site of numerous prior expositions. Architects would build separate pavilions, representing each of France's multiple regions, arranged in a unified ensemble to form a microcosm of France (Figure 8.1). Since, as expressed in the words of one organizer, "Everything depends on and connects to the architecture," these pavilions would anchor the entire project (French National Archives [FNA] F12 12397 1935). Yet they were based on the construction of falsehoods. The Regional Center was not to be a composition of permanent monuments, but a simulacrum. Illusory stage sets would create an ambiance powerful enough to revive not only tourism, but also French regional culture and the entire national economy (FNA F12 12397 1935; Labbé 1936a: 3). As one journalist remarked, "the only thing missing will be the climate" (Dervaux 1936: 17)! Thus, in the center of Paris, the false would recover the real.

Planning for the exposition began at the onset of the Depression. Unemployment in France had doubled between 1931 and 1936 and numerous proposals made to government agencies maintained that an international exposition would provide construction jobs and create a market for French products. Similarly, since tourism had fallen by a factor of four, organizers placed it among the exposition's

Figure 8.1 Regional Center, aerial view. *Album Officiel*, Paris: La Photolith, 1937.

primary goals (Anon. 1934; Kemp 1972: 100; Labbé 1936b: 3). Facing an unprecedented response from countries that wanted to participate, Labbé conveyed the pressure France felt as host to the world in the exposition's *Bulletin Officiel*. "Surrounded by foreign displays, the French presentations must be a success." In fact, Labbé expressed that the French exhibitors had a "patriotic duty" to produce "an appearance worthy of our country" (Labbé 1936a: 4). In keeping with this mission, the organizers developed a series of specifically French exhibits that featured recent progress in such fields as aeronautics, film and radio, and also celebrated the nation's rich cultural resources in such permanent structures as the Chaillot Palace and the twin Museums of Modern Art. Yet, of all the French displays, organizers hailed the Regional Center as the exposition's "star attraction" and Labbé emphasized the unprecedented status given to the regions at a French world's fair (Labbé 1938; Hermant 1936; Labbé 1936b: 3, 4).

Labbé knew, however, that convincing the regions to participate would be a challenging task. They had complained before that international expositions favored Paris and drained their local economies (Labbé 1936b: 8). This time, promised the organizers, it would be different. Members of the French Regionalist Federation (FRF) and the Touring Club of France sat on the Regional Center's planning commission and, together, they developed a comprehensive strategy to court the regions. The exhibit would feature the often ignored and misunderstood regions as an integral element of a newly conceived nation. Instead of emphasizing

Paris, they employed such phrases as "total France" or "entire France" (Institut Français d'Architecture [IFA] Maigrot n.d.; Mihura 1937a; IFA Le Même n.d.).

Furthermore, in contrast to the 1900 exposition where the regions "only appeared as a rough sketch," the Regional Center would celebrate them with respect (IFA Maigrot n.d.). In particular, it would portray them as neither quaint nor nostalgic but as thoroughly up-to-date; they would be modern. In November 1935, Labbé had remarked that because of new developments in transportation, communication, and tourism, "the old provinces had [already] been modernized . . . [and] it was precisely this modernism" that he wanted the Regional Center to convey (FNA F12 12388 1935).

The organizers further elevated the regions by emphasizing their diversity as a vital ingredient of a unified nation (Mihura 1937b; Peer 1998: 95). Qualifying their desire to portray the regions as modern, however, they also promoted their diversity as a means to offset the uniformity commonly attributed to modernism. If modernism produced uniformity, did diversity therefore require tradition? Jules Mihura, member of the Regionalism Commission, addressed this paradox. Viewing the Regional Center as an exhibition of France's national heritage, he likened the French provinces to an extended family. Like relatives, though each province had its own distinct character and history, its particularities were "indissolubly united by an essential link."

> Does it follow that we are reduced to uniformity, [he asked]? Certainly not. The Regional Center is designed to be . . . a rich conciliation, combining all the progress achieved by new techniques and recent materials with the necessary and precious experience brought by local traditions. (Mihura 1937a)

In addition to this rhetoric about a newly valued position in the nation, the Regional Center organizers further sought to convince the regions to participate because it would bring them tangible benefits. They described how the Regional Center would show visitors the many nuances of France's unknown regions and would thereby whet their appetites for the real thing; it would seduce them to travel. The deputy chief architect, Jacques Greber, proclaimed that the Regional Center "will be the turntable for foreigners who, from Paris, will want to visit the provinces and, once there, will then receive a flavorful picture of them. It will thus serve the national agenda for tourism" (FNA F12 12397 1935; Anon. 1935; IFA Maigrot n.d.). Moreover, tourism would also bring money. One proponent argued, for example:

> This is why the provinces must organize themselves in Paris, where they must collect the tourists, must catch them, to direct them towards the provinces . . . Tourism is not limited to the discovery of hidden wonders . . . It is an industry. The provinces . . . "must be in it for the money". (Keller 1936: 2)

It became increasingly evident and problematic as the project proceeded, however, that the Regional Center organizers had constructed a centralized regionalism, a patent contradiction in terms. For the organizers were either Parisians or *originaires*, those born in the provinces but who had since moved to the capital. To the most avid regionalists, *originaires* were traitors. Nevertheless, a sufficient number of more moderate regionalists were willing to compromise with the central administration because they perceived that the potential value of the project made their participation worthwhile. Oddly, despite the energy behind these divergent views on regionalism, the very regions everyone spoke so much about did not actually exist. They were a fiction.

Since the Revolution in 1789, France had been divided into departments, administrative units designed to reinforce Parisian control. With little attention paid to geographic or cultural considerations, each was approximately the same size, small enough to be governed by a representative of the State, the prefect. The region, by contrast, was a nineteenth-century concept meant to replace the province of pre-Revolutionary France. Neither region nor province had clearly defined boundaries because they were mythical concepts that arose organically from the local folk culture, climate, and topography. Repeated efforts were made, especially during the nineteenth century, to develop a genuine local life in France independent of Paris, but the reality behind this concept took hold only gradually and, indeed, tensions between the capital and regions remain today. The word "regionalism" emerged towards the close of the century and the founding of the French Regionalist Federation (FRF) by Jean Charles-Brun in 1900 identified regionalism as a legitimate movement, one that soon acquired a wide-ranging membership (Charles-Brun 1911; Jean-Desthieux 1918; Flory 1966).

The subsequent production of several regional maps exemplifies not merely the mounting regional consciousness, but the specific desire to inscribe the regional concept more definitively into the image of France. Paul Vidal de la Blache, a member of the FRF and founder of the human geography movement, an approach to geography that explores relationships between society and the land, published a map in 1910 where he divided France into seventeen regions. Jean Charles-Brun proposed a map of twenty-five regions in 1912 and Minister of Commerce, Etienne Clémentel, also a member of the FRF, won parliamentary approval in 1919 for his proposal of sixteen economic regions that established regional Chambers of Commerce.[1] As influential as these and numerous other maps were, however, the departments still remained the nation's primary administrative unit. In common parlance, the provinces remained as well. Despite careful rhetoric that differentiated between the old province and the new region, most used the words interchangeably throughout the exposition.

Therefore, often called the Regional Center's first project – and I would add, its first simulacrum – organizers began the Regional Center with their own definition of the regions, the creation of another map of France (FNA F12 12397 1935). But regional delegates – a hybrid grouping of politicians, business leaders and presidents of local professional associations who first met at the Regional Center's major planning congress in April 1935 – contested the scheme. With little agreement as to where their boundaries lay and no consistent criteria to determine them, discussions revolved around geographic, economic, historic, as well as architectural and cultural affinities. Many focused on such elusive notions as character and basic likes and dislikes among neighbors (FNA F12 12397 1935; FNA F60 968 n.d.). Eventually, they revised the initial proposal of seventeen regions into a final map of twenty-seven, a process the congress reporter, Léandre Vaillat, likened to "topographic surgery" (FNA F12 12397 1935). A group of delegates so quarreled over how to delineate the south of France, for example, that a moderator sent them into a separate room to work out their differences. Finally they agreed to subdivide the former Pyrénées and Languedoc provinces into three regions: the Pyrénées-Atlantique, Pyrénées-Languedoc, and Languedoc-Méditerranée. The overlapping use of the provincial names attests to their tenuous compromise. Another group divided the former province of Provence into Provence-Marseille and the Côte-d'Azur, prompting a delegate to complain that, without the Côte d'Azur, Provence had been "mutilated" (Hauser 1937). All admitted that the regional map was ultimately "arbitrary" (FNA F12 12397 1935).

Nevertheless, this revised map directly shaped the Regional Center's master plan (Figure 8.2). With the architectural ensemble intended as a coherent reconstruction of French geography in three-dimensions, the maritime regions bordered the Seine to mimic their coastal locations from Normandy all the way to the Côte d'Azur. On the interior of the site, the alpine regions of Dauphiné and the Savoie stood on heavily landscaped platforms to fabricate their mountainous topography. In between, those regions that had major cities such as Alsace (Strasbourg) and Pyrénées-Languedoc (Toulouse) surrounded a central plaza to represent their urban dimension.

This fabrication of the regions in both map and master plan form reveals the first of many problems elicited by the fundamentally false nature of the Regional Center project. While regional delegates negotiated the geographical boundaries, the architects wrestled over how to represent each region architecturally. Labbé repeatedly specified that, though the Regional Center pavilions were to be traditional in the sense that they identified something recognizable about an individual region, they were not to be a copy, pastiche, or reconstitution. They were also to be modern, in the sense that they were to adapt extant local models by incorporating contemporary advances such as electricity, central heating, and new materials. They were not, however, to be "international" (IFA Le Même n.d.; FNA F12 12397 1935; IFA Le Même 1935).[2] Organizers acknowledged and delighted in the contradiction that the traditional/modern charge entailed. Satisfied that no single formula

EXPOSITION INTERNATIONALE DE 1937

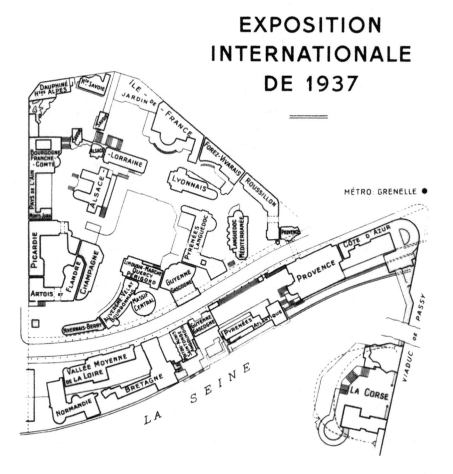

Figure 8.2 Regional Center, master plan. *Rapport Général*, vol 8, Pl. 3, Paris: Imprimerie Nationale, 1938–1940.

could resolve it, they challenged the architects to discern between traditional and modern aspects in such a way that they would achieve a just balance between the two (FNA F12 12397 1935). In the absence of precise guidelines, many called the Regional Center an architectural laboratory; the architects had been invited to experiment (Labbé 1935; IFA Maigrot 1936). Three architectural devices: style, building type and materials show how differently the architects interpreted these complex charges.

All parties grappled with the predicament that no one architectural identity existed within a region. One of the organizers, Maurice Dufrène, remarked, for example, that architectural styles, just like those of language or costume, often changed from one valley to the next (FNA F12 12397 1935). The president of the

Pryénées-Atlantique regional committee insisted that, though the region constituted two departments, it actually comprised three discernible architectural regions:
the Pays Basque, Béarn and Bigorre. Adopting the nickname, "the Three Bs," its
architects produced a single building in which the three architectural styles remained
distinct (FNA F12 12405 1936c). The Alsace pavilion, by contrast, portrayed a
consistent approach to style but its more abstract formal properties left its regional
affiliation unclear (Figure 8.3). With an exterior of white-painted simulated stucco,
rectangular in shape, and with two rear wings and a tower, it possessed a simplified
and largely symmetrical Beaux-Arts plan. A hipped roof carried three dormers that
capped three bays below. Simplified strips comprised the wide mullions and
surrounds of the oversized windows in each bay. Similarly reductive were the
darkened cornices beneath the roof line and above each window. In a clear political
statement, its architects had chosen to identify their region, whose territory
had been newly returned to France from Germany after the First World War, as
French and not German. This meant, however, that without the more familiar
image of a half-timbered facade and steeply pitched roof, the only indicator of its
Alsatian identity was its thinly applied ornamental graphics with explicit local
references.[3]

Still many other regions opted to convey their identity by emphasizing larger
architectural features over smaller ornamental detail. As demonstrated by the belfry
and shaped gables of Flandre-Artois (Figure 8.4) or the pronounced Roman arches
of Provence, however, they often did not integrate these elements into the building
mass. This raises the second subject, building type, of which massing is one
dimension. The volumes did not adhere to a recognizable functional type, such as
a church or a house, so their regional identity was more easily conveyed through
familiar but isolated elements, rather than through the mass as a whole. The
architects of the Languedoc-Mediterranean pavilion even inscribed names of
tourist destinations such as Carcassone and the Pont du Gard over its entire facade.
As much as this gesture testifies to their clear understanding of the Regional
Center's touristic agenda, the explicit nature of the advertisement accentuates the
false nature of the structures. Such a billboard-like façade certainly would not have
been found on a permanent building in the region.

The subject of building type comprises not only a recognizable volume based
on the structure's function but also the function itself or program, as expressed by
the interior. Here again, the incorporation of tourism is clear. Above an entrance to
the Flandre-Artois pavilion, a relief sculpture contained the words "art, work,
commerce, and science." Inside, its ground floor contained a display of the region's
main industries: textiles, mining, and metals; and the *brasserie* featured its local
specialty, *la belle pinte*. Social and cultural exhibits occupied its second floor.
Housed in the most recognizable architectural symbol of the region, the belfry, a
tourist office featured an electrically illuminated map and a talking film, both of

Figure 8.3 Regional Center, Alsace Pavilion. Postcard, 1937. Collection of the author.

which highlighted tourist destinations. Members of its tourist bureau, the Friends of Lille, also provided maps and information on tourist itineraries.

Finally, a building type also includes the relationship between the exterior and interior. In this exposition setting, where the relationship was characterized primarily by disjuncture, the false nature of the Regional Center structures emerges with particular clarity. When examining the Savoie pavilions, the larger chalet appeared like an integrated barn and residential structure that one would find deep in the Savoie, but its ground floor held a restaurant overlooking a large-scale diorama of Mont Blanc. The second level was entirely dedicated to displays of the region's artisanal and industrial production. Similarly, the smaller chalet resembled a mountain cabin and, though its second floor contained a small living room with an inglenook, its ground floor housed an exhibition of ski manufacturers and a series of small dioramas that illustrated the region's tourist sites. Especially with their emphasis on tourism, all the pavilions were essentially display spaces. Not surprisingly, the ambiguous word "pavilion" appeared most consistently in descriptions of the Regional Center structures because, as a vague building-type designation, it elicited no defining visual attributes other than its temporary and idealized showcase quality.

The third factor that illustrates the Regional Center's simulated architecture is the pavilions' construction in temporary – or false – materials. The use of false materials was not new to exposition pavilions and early plans for the exposition

Figure 8.4 Regional Center, Flandre-Artois Pavilion. *L'Architecture, Centre Régional*, Paris: Alexis Sinjon, 1937.

noted favorably that temporary materials encouraged experimentation, even fantasy (FNA F12 13001 n.d.). Yet regional delegates had overwhelmingly supported proposals for the Regional Center to be constructed *en dur* because they considered local materials to be fundamental to regional architecture (Couture 1935; FNA F12 12397 1935). One delegate argued, for example, that "regional architecture is distinguished not only by its lines, but by the materials of the *pays* . . . and if we build the structures of staff or plaster, many of the regions will not have any of the character of regional architecture" (FNA F12 12397 1935). In this view, regionalism assumed the real. In *Modernity and Nostalgia*, Romy Golan's alliance of the regionalist movement with the rise of realist painting in 1930s France validates this understanding (Golan 1995).

In addition to this concern for an authentic architectural treatment of the regions, many sought to construct the Regional Center in genuine materials so that it could become a permanent museum and a headquarters for the regions in Paris. They felt that the regions deserved such a representation in the capital. They argued further that a permanent museum of the regions in Paris would continue to attract foreigners and thereby provide a long-term boon to tourism (Couture 1935).

While exposition organizers initially considered the use of permanent materials for the Regional Center, mounting financial difficulties and construction delays finally led to their decision to build the pavilions in temporary form.Though they permitted real wood and some custom ornamentation by artisans in local materials, simulated stucco, brick, and stone dominated the structures. This was plainly evident in the Pyrénées-Languedoc and Flandre-Artois pavilions where rippling and seams revealed thin papier-maché-like surfaces. A mountain of false rocks connected the Corsica pavilion, placed on an island in the middle of the Seine, to a bridge above, the Pont du Passy. Many interpreted the decision to use false materials as a devaluation of the regions by the central administration who had promised to portray them with substance and dignity.

These diverse interpretations of such architectural devices as style, building type, and materials were also evident in the architects' responses to the traditional/ modern charge. Some, such as in the Alsatian pavilion, expressed modernism primarily through the abstraction of standard details, such as cornices and window surrounds, and expressed tradition through a limited but highly literal quotation of regional lore: the superficial application of the coats of arms and the name, *A la Cigogne*, for the restaurant. The adoption of a simplified Beaux-Arts composition can be viewed as both traditional and modern. By associating with the long tradition of French classicism, Alsace simultaneously distanced itself from its more localized German affiliations. At this moment in Alsatian history the choice of a more universal form was, paradoxically, a highly specific and deliberate marker of its newly politicized regional identity. While the shaped gables of the Flandre-Artois pavilion brought a traditional dimension into the building fabric, the mostly over-sized and squared windows on the facade equally incorporated a modern sensibility. Bare concrete strips that framed both the gables and windows rein-forced the modern approach. The Normandy pavilion exemplified perhaps the most integrated combination of traditional and modern elements. Possessing a steeply pitched roof with half-timbered detailing and an extensive use of (simulated) brick, pronounced glass gables dominated the entrances, and columns that supported a side balcony suggested inverted screws, an unmistakable tribute to the machine.

This range of architectural choices highlights not only the considerable freedom given to the regional architects but also the organizers' ambiguous vision and conflicting rhetoric. To what extent did they intend an authentic portrayal of the regions as they truly were in 1937 or an idealized version?

Nevertheless, through this multi-layered simulacrum of the French regions, the Regional Center's coordinating architect, Emile Maigrot, produced a coherent whole, a "France in miniature" (IFA Maigrot 1936). He placed the individual pavilions along the metaphoric Mediterranean and formed streets and plazas where visitors could stroll among neighboring pavilions as if in a city. Raised platforms and simulated rock outcroppings signaled the mountains. This total environment created the ambiance where visitors would be entranced. A description of the Regional Center entitled "La Visite de la France" (The Visit to France) read, "It is natural to think that the visitors to the Regional Center, having tasted it like an appetizer of France, will then sense the desire to see our Regions and their inhabitants, no longer, if one can say it, at the scale of Paris, but in the full magnitude of the real setting, at the scale of our Country" (IFA Le Même n.d.). In a similar vein, Paul Hermant of *Le Figaro* commented, "I can easily imagine the infatuation of the visitors. Won't it be charming to hear them say among themselves . . . 'Come, let's go see the provincials'" (Hermant 1936). Yet, as intended by its organizers, the Regional Center was a simulation of the real thing. Journalist Michel Maubourg remarked of the ensemble, "We only need the Mediterranean sun to reinforce the illusion" (Bibliothèque Historique de la Ville de Paris [BHVP] Actualités n.d.: 3).

To supplement this fantasy of architectural production, exposition organizers developed a multifaceted publicity machine that intensified after June of 1936 when a new socialist government, the Popular Front, came into power. With only one year remaining until the exposition's opening, seizing rhetorical control was one of the most effective ways it could make its mark. They formed a new Direction of Propaganda and, by declaring it a people's fair, they made tourism accessible to the masses (Ory 1987: 34, 35; Peer 1998: 37). Behind this shift lay the widespread labor strikes of May 1936 that not only brought the Popular Front to power but also resulted in specific new legislation, the 40 hour work week and paid vacations. The Popular Front thus produced an entirely new class of tourists who had never before taken a vacation (Weber 1994: 161–63). To encourage these new vacationers to visit the exposition, they organized a series of discount packages that included, for example, a half-price entry fee on Monday, soon moved to Sunday to accommodate the working-class day off. Not surprisingly some resisted these changes. Siding with the status quo, the hotel industry refused such concessions and insisted that low-cost accommodations be limited to youth. The Bourgeois could opt to visit the exposition on Friday when a doubled entry fee dissuaded the working-class presence (Peer 1998: 37).

Though the Popular Front programs opened tourism to a larger audience, mounting political turmoil and, soon, war thwarted the entire tourist industry. General attendance at the exposition was below expectations, but tourism in France did rise in 1937 (Peer 1998: 30). Perhaps more importantly, the Regional Center yielded marks of genuine regional revival. To resist the Parisian organizers' central control, the regional committees formed a union and gained membership on the Regional Center's planning commission. Two-thirds of the regional committees also registered themselves as permanent associations that would continue as organizational bodies after the exposition's close (Peer 1998: 95). Moreover, the response of visitors to the Regional Center was overwhelmingly positive. Typical of the pejorative ridicule of the regions found in Parisian texts of this and earlier periods, Michel Maubourg had expected the Regional Center to typify an "eternal parade of costumed grandmothers, the clinging to traditions that are often manifested by some pitiful masquerade . . . ." Yet his assumptions were shattered:

> This is not at all what we are finding [he wrote] . . . No, no, this time, we must say, the picturesque in no way encroaches on the serious aspects of the demonstration. There is certainly a picturesque element . . . Flandre has its belfry, Artois a beautiful facade with rounded gables, Savoie its chalet overlooking an alpine panorama (*mais oui!*) . . . But because of the intelligence and the taste that has governed the overall arrangement, the picturesque appears throughout in a very pleasant and harmonious manner. (BHVP Actualités, n.d.: 3)

In his opinion, the Regional Center was "a perfect success." He and many others argued heartily for it to remain open after the exposition was to close in November. Certainly this compelling stimulus for tourism would remain a popular site.

But representatives of the regions would have none of it. Construction delays meant that many pavilions had not opened until August, half way into the exposition's six-month season, and budget cuts had not only mandated false materials and a compromised aesthetic, but also left many regions in debt. During the planning stages Breton president, O.-L. Aubert complained that the organizers had no idea what was really going on in the regions. He also remarked that "the General Commissioner [Labbé] seems . . . to only occupy himself with those things that concern the Capital and to abandon somewhat this famous Regional Center which we have spoken so much about" (FNA F12 12401 1935b). The President of the Pyrénées-Atlantique committee expressed a similar disappointment:

> The opinion is increasing, nearly everywhere, that the Regional Center, because of its success and consequently [its] benefits for the Exposition and the city of Paris, will barely serve the regions since it is already jeopardizing them by depriving them of some of their travel support and even of their inhabitants who are lured away by the great international festival. The "mystique" that we hoped would spread and for which we have worked our hardest is emerging, however, in a way completely contrary to our publicity. (FNA F12 12405: 1936b)

Not surprisingly, many local associations insisted that the Regional Center be closed as scheduled (Peer 1998: 96). Much as Paris had tried to convince them that it would be different this time, members of the regions concluded that the Parisian promises had been a sham. The regionalism of the 1937 exposition remained centralized, controlled by Paris.

Basque architect, Henri Godbarge, predicted this soon after the initial scheme for the Regional Center had been outlined. He wrote a letter in June 1935 to Charles Letrosne, then chief architect of the exposition and an important popularizer of regionalist architecture through his widely acclaimed three-volume text of 1923–26, *Murs et toits pour les pays de chez nous*. The letter, published in the journal *Construction Moderne*, severely criticized the organizers of the Regional Center for claiming to promote an authentic regionalist architecture. Godbarge made it clear that its location in Paris would yield a counterfeit (Godbarge 1935).[4] He also maintained that the exposition's central administration had grossly misconstrued the contemporary production of regionalist architecture. They had described it as based on the copying of earlier models and called it archeological and false. They had argued that modernizing it would reclaim its authenticity. Inverting the organizers' criticisms and adding a political barb, Godbarge reasoned, "Obviously, an ardent regionalist could retort by defining, in his turn and according to his views, a false modern rationalism of Paris which, in his eyes, would be worth nothing more than foreign archeology and pure plagiarism of industrial German architecture." According to Godbarge, modernization and centralization were fundamentally different notions (Godbarge 1935: xxiv).

Instead, Godbarge explained, architects in the regions have been producing a modern and authentic regionalist architecture for over 25 years. By making something new out of the extant architecture of the provinces, they have been continuing and modifying tradition. Such adaptation does not produce copies. Rather, by retaining the buildings' essential principles and juxtaposing them "with contemporary complexities, needs, new materials, and scientific applications," they have been transposing the older models. In particular, they have built this architecture "at home, in its own milieu, within its own natural evolution, in the open air," in keeping with the specificities of a given landscape and climate. According to this view, regionalist architecture is, by definition, both modern and local (Godbarge 1935: xxvi).

Angrily protesting the arrogance of condensing regionalist architecture to fit a small site in central Paris, Godbarge viewed the organizers' conception of regionalist architecture as a grave insult. "Programs created by tourism and master planning," he wrote, had "infantalized" regionalist architecture. He remarked however, "it is no longer a child." While he conceded that support from the capital could potentially facilitate the growth of regionalist architecture, he insisted that Paris must "neither deform nor destroy it . . . It must be appreciated and understood, before it is preached to." Godbarge concluded that regional architects had a fundamental choice. They could reproduce that which was "centralized," "official," and fundamentally "*dépaysés*" [disconnected from their national or geographic identity], or they could transform the plentiful models of local tradition. His preference was clear. Since true regionalist architecture could never be found in Paris, centralization would make it neither real nor modern, only false. Above all, regionalism and an exposition were irreconcilable:

> I have always said and let me repeat: an exposition is something too artificial, especially, too superficial, too *dépaysés*, so that the pretenses that accompany it only harm the cause that we are trying to defend, which is, in this case, the aesthetic of the soil, which must derive its luster and its value from the soil itself. (Godbarge 1935: xxiii)

Regionalism was inherently real and an exposition was inherently false and Godbarge was unwilling to compromise. He protested the Regional Center from its inception and refused to participate in the project (Godbarge 1935: xxvi).

In contrast to Godbarge, art historian, Pierre du Colombier, offered a more sanguine view on the experience of falsehood. He wrote one year after the exposition had closed, "People will object that the preservation of tradition is artificial. So is every fashion. And how many things which seem natural to us were artificial to begin with" (Peer 1998: 164, 165)? According to him, falsehood was a fact of life whose reality one would soon cease to notice. Many visitors had apparently concurred.

Though the organizers had never stated that the Regional Center would be false, neither had they promised, as Godbarge had thought, that it would be real. They had promised only that it would be respectful and, when combined with tourism, that it would be persuasive enough to produce tangible results. Many rejoiced that these goals had been met, but not the regions.

Regional committees had clearly adopted the organizers' vision to link tourism and regionalism. A member of the Breton committee called their structure a "pavilion of regional propaganda" and the president of the Pyrénées-Atlantique committee requested permission to sell a brochure of the region in the pavilion's tourist section. Once the visitors leave the pavilion, he argued, "they might stray from the very goal so strongly put forth by the Regional Center, to incite the visitors to travel in France" (Hauser 1936; FNA F12 12405 1936a). The brochure was sold, however, not in the Pyrénées-Atlantique pavilion, but in the Tourism Pavilion, a structure located a substantial distance away from the Regional Center on another portion of the exposition grounds. Given the centrality of the Regional Center's tourist agenda, many regional delegates had campaigned for the Tourism Pavilion to be located within the Regional Center. This did not happen, however, and regional committees complained that it pulled resources away from the individual pavilions (Aubert n.d.; FNA F12 12405 1936d; Dubois 1987).

A promotional image for the Regional Center entitled "The Regions of France in Paris" displayed a group of costumed figures surrounding a map of France. Although their large forms portrayed these regional symbols as vital members of the nation, the small map portrayed Paris as a star with rays that shone into the regions. A nearly identical view ornamented the exposition's Tourism Pavilion. Names of the French regions adorned its prominent tower that overlooked the Seine and at its top a star extended rays to the regional names. While these images indicate that the regions remained a featured element in the French tourist agenda, Paris nevertheless remained the starting point. Evidently, the ideal of the Regional Center in Paris had become more real in the minds of exposition organizers than the actual regions themselves, the intended tourist destination; in this sense, the false had supplanted the real. It was, after all, an exposition, where matters of truth and falsehood had always occupied blurred terrain. Conflated between a microcosm of France and a laboratory, the regions' appreciable presence in Paris represented a significant gain in many respects, but one truth remained: Paris still viewed itself as the star of France. In an ironic reversal of their original objectives, perhaps the organizers had created such an effective illusion of the regions that, rather then whetting the tourists' appetites to visit the regions as they had promised, they fully satisfied them in Paris.

Notes

1. The close link between the human geography and regionalist movements particularly resonates in the French language. The words *pays* (country), *paysan* (farmer, peasant or, more literally, land-worker) and *paysage* (landscape) illustrate just how deeply the French tied their social identity to the land. This understanding is entirely inaccessible in English. Furthermore, while the French word *pays* most often means country it also refers to a smaller locality with its own geographic and historic identity. In discussions of regionalism, *pays* is frequently used in this latter sense.

2. Before the codification of the term "International Style" by Henry-Russell Hitchcock and Philip Johnson in *The International Style: Architecture Since 1922* (1932), based on the Museum of Modern Art exhibit of the same year, Europeans who opposed the work of the avant-garde frequently used the word "international" to criticize its excessive uniformity and corresponding lack of distinction between one place and another.

3. Coats of arms of Alsatian cities decorated a tree that was appliquéed to the tower and the name *A la Cigogne* announced a restaurant. The *cigogne*, stork, is a cherished and ubiquitous symbol of Alsace.
4. While Charles Letrosne began as the exposition's chief architect and Jacques Greber his assistant, Greber assumed the lead role in December 1935 after Letrosne's resignation due to illness.

References

Anon. (1934), "L'Exposition paraît naître sous de fâcheux presages", *Le Petit-Bleu* (27 July).

—— (1935), "L'Exposition de 1937: Ce que promet d'être le Centre Régional", *Le Batiment* (17 October).

—— (1936), "Paris 1937, Le Régionalisme à l'exposition des arts et techniques dans la vie moderne", *La Journée Industrielle* (12–14 April).

Aubert, O.-L. (n.d.), Exposition des arts et techniques appliqués à la vie moderne (1937), Région III (Bretagne), Rapport sur le thème général de la présentation et de l'amenagement de la "Maison de Bretagne".

BHVP. Fonds Actualités (n.d.), Maubourg, Michel. Le Centre Régional. (Newspaper article in a file entitled "Coupures Le Presse". Name and town of publication of newspaper not identified.)

Charles-Brun, Jean (1911), *Le Régionalisme*, Paris: Bloud.

Couture, J. (1935), "La Participation des provinces à l'exposition de 1937", *Construction Moderne*, 21 (24 February): i, ii, xvii.

Dervaux, Adolphe (1936), "Ce qu'est le régionalisme", *Exposition Paris 1937: Arts et techniques dans la vie moderne,* no. 2 (June): 16–18.

Dubois, Jean-Marie (1987), "Tourisme", in Lemoine, Bertrand (ed.), *Cinquantenaire de l'exposition internationale des arts et des techniques dans la vie moderne*, Paris: Institut Français d'Architecture/Paris-Musées.

Flory, Thiébaut (1966), *Le Mouvement régionaliste français.* Paris: Presses Universitaires de France.

FNA. F12 12388 (1935), Note sur les comités régionaux, leur composition, leur programme (28 November).

—— F12 12397 (1935) Speeches at the Regional Art Congress by François Carnot, Maurice Dufrène, Jacques Greber, Edmond Labbé, Charles Letrosne, Léandre Vaillat, and unidentified others (4–6 April).

—— F12 12401 (1935a), Aubert to Hiriart (14 September and 23 July).

—— F12 12401 (1935b), Unidentified newspaper clipping attached to letters of 27 December, Aubert to Labbé.

—— F12 12405 (1936a), Boissel to Petsche, President of the Regionalist Commission (2 October).

—— F12 12405 (1936b), Boissel to Petsche (29 June).

—— F12 12405 (1936c), Boissel to the Chef du Service Central du Centre Régional (28 January).

—— F12 12405 (1936d) Rousseau, to Ancelle (27 October).

—— F12 13001. Comité d'Etudes pour l'Exposition Internationale d'Art Moderne à Paris en 1937 (CEEIAMP). Programme d'une étude collective et d'un concours en vue de la réalisation d'une exposition internationale d'art moderne à Paris vers 1937.

—— F60 968. (n.d.), Note pour Monsieur Loquin, Délègue à la Présidence du Conseil, in a file entitled Centre Régional.

Godbarge, Henri (1935), "Lettre ouverte à M. Letrosne", *Construction Moderne*, 36 (9 June): xxiii–xxvi.

Golan, Romy (1995), *Modernity and Nostalgia: Art and Politics in France Between the Wars*, New Haven: Yale University Press.

Hauser, Fernand (1937), "La Provence à Paris", *Marseille-Matin* (18 August).

Hauser, Yvette (1936), "La Participation de la Bretagne à l'exposition de 1937", *Le Journal des Mairies*, 127 (2 August).

Hermant, Paul (1936), "L'Exposition: L'Important question du régionalisme", *Le Figaro* (28 May).

Hitchcock, Henry-Russell and Johnson, Philip (1932, 1966), *The International Style.* Reprint, with a forward by Henry-Russell Hitchcock; originally published as *The International Style: Architecture Since 1922*, New York: Museum of Modern Art.

IFA. Fonds Emile Maigrot (1936), Utudjian, Edouard. Les Grands ensembles de l'exposition de 1937: Le Centre Régional (1 December).

—— Fonds Emile Maigrot (n.d.), Labbé, Edmond. La Collaboration des provinces à l'Exposition de 1937.

—— Fonds Henri-Jacques Le Même (1935), Charles Letrosne and Jacques Greber. Note relative au Centre Régional (22 September).

—— Fonds Henri-Jacques Le Même, n.d., Exposition Paris 1937.

Jean-Desthieux, F. (1918), *L'Evolution régionaliste, du Félibrige au féderalisme*, Paris: Editions Bossard.

Keller, Charles A. (1936), "Ce que la province peut attendre de l'exposition", *Bulletin Officiel*, 7 (15 June): 1–2.

Kemp, Tom (1972), *The French Economy, 1913–1939: The History of a Decline*, London: Longman.

Labbé, Edmond (1935), *Le Régionalisme à l'exposition internationale*, Paris: Imprimerìe Chaix.

—— (1936a) Un Appel aux exposants. *Bulletin Officiel*, 11 (1 September): 1–4.

—— (1936b), *Le Régionalisme et l'exposition internationale de Paris 1937*. Paris: Imprimerìe Nationale.

—— (1938), *Exposition internationale des arts et techniques dans la vie moderne, Paris 1937, Rapport général*. Vol. 8. Paris: Imprimerìe Nationale.

Letrosne, Charles (1923–6), *Murs et toits pour les pays de chez nous*. 3 vols. Paris: Niestlé.

Mihura, Jules (1937a), "Ce que sera à l'exposition: Le Centre Régional", *Tribune de L'Yonne*, (4 March).

Mihura, Jules (1937b), "Vers l'organization du régionalisme", *Le Temps*, (24 November).

Ory, Pascal (1987), "Le Front Populaire et l'exposition", in Bertrand Lemoine (ed.), *Cinquantenaire de l'exposition internationale des arts et des techniques dans la vie moderne*, Paris: Institut Français d'Architecture/Paris-Musées.

Peer, Shanny (1998), *France on Display: Peasants, Provincials, and Folklore in the 1937 Paris World's Fair*, Albany: State University of New York Press.

Weber, Eugen (1994), *The Hollow Years: France in the 1930s*, New York: Norton.

–9–

Tourist Geographies: Remapping Old Havana
D. Medina Lasansky

A Souvenir

On a recent trip to Havana I sat with a friend on the steps of the capitol. The building's dome, designed in 1929 to emulate that of Washington, DC, loomed behind us. We sat motionless for a few moments as an itinerant photographer, equipped with a large mounted box camera (ingeniously assembled from the parts of several different cameras, scraps of wood, and a section of black cardboard) took our portrait. When the negative emerged we noticed that the capitol's dome was not visible within its frame (Figure 9.1). In fact, the only part of the building that could be seen was the vast staircase. Apparently the photographer's lens was not wide enough to capture both us and the building's most iconic feature. Dismayed, we mentioned to the photographer that we had hoped to have a snapshot similar to those displayed on his camera stand, that would show us sitting in front of the capitol, not on a seemingly anonymous staircase. The photographer dismissed our concern with a wave of his hand. He reached inside the camera box and withdrew another negative featuring the dome. He placed it over the upper half of our negative and within a few minutes had developed a print that combined the two images. The resulting photographic collage depicted the two of us seated on the steps of the famous *capitolio*.

We paid the photographer a dollar for the snap shot, commended him on his talents, and for a few minutes engaged in small talk about the US. We said goodbye to the photographer and hailed a bicycle taxi to pedal us across the colonial city center of Old Havana, known in Spanish as Habana Vieja. As we bounced over the numerous potholes awaiting repair, we marveled at our encounter with the photographer. The photograph he had produced, the composite of two separate images fashioned to provide the ideal souvenir, seemed to be emblematic of the regime's own ability to refashion the city of Habana Vieja into an idealized tourist destination. Like the photograph of the *capitolio*, a new image of the city has been carefully fabricated in the face of economic adversity.

Figure 9.1 Tourists seated on the steps of the Habana Capitol, 2002, negative (left) and the reworked print (right). Collection of the author.

Rescripting Urban Space

This chapter explores the ways in Habana's past has been rescripted to serve contemporary political agendas. While exploiting a city's history is common when it is a tourist destination, the case of Habana is distinct as there the techniques of capitalist tourist development have been harnessed for a socialist project. Tourism revenues are reinvested directly into the city. As such tourism has proven to be a positive regenerative force; transforming the local economy and physical infrastructure while guaranteeing a wide range of social programs.

Habana's touristic success resides as much in the physical form of the architecture as in the methods of mass mediation and dissemination of that form. The designers of maps, pamphlets and postcards, the travel agents and tour guides, scholars and historians, emerge as the true architects of the city's new image. While this is a phenomenon familiar to tourist sites throughout the world, the speed with which these designers have refashioned Habana deserves study. Unlike other heritage tourist destinations that have been developed over hundreds of years, Habana's historic center has been restored, packaged, and presented to the public within the past decade. The project has been carefully monitored by government officials who themselves simultaneously serve as planners, architects, investors, travel agents, and chroniclers. As a result, the redesigning of Habana's provides an opportunity to expose the mechanisms of the tourist system and the range of its various components.

Habana Vieja

Metropolitan Habana occupies an area of 460 square miles and sustains a population of 2.3 million. Habana Vieja is one of the city's fifteen municipalities. It is bounded by the old port area to the east and the Prado, a wide tree-lined pedestrian promenade, renovated by J. C. Nicolas Forestier between 1925 and 1930 (Lejeune 1996) to the west. The neighborhood is a densely packed 1.3 square miles containing over 3,500 buildings, some of which date to the earliest phase of Spanish colonial rule in the sixteenth century. The majority of structures were built in the eighteenth and nineteenth centuries when Habana was a thriving port – the entry point into the Caribbean and the third largest city in Latin America. An estimated 70,000 people inhabit Habana Vieja today – many living in makeshift quarters constructed within former grand colonial palaces. These alterations have converted former mansions into cramped tenement-style living conditions that provide little privacy or comfort and lack proper ventilation and lighting. Hundreds of people now live in buildings originally designed for a single family. As a result Habana Vieja is one of the most densely populated areas of the greater metropolitan region, not to mention all of Latin America (Segre 1997: 298). Clusters of electricity meters located inside building entrances provide the only readily available means of measuring urban density. Housing is at a premium – a fact confirmed by the active black market apartment exchange which takes place at the end of the Prado as well as the large number of ex-votive houses left at a shrine in the Cathedral by those hoping for the miraculous gift of better housing.

In addition to being overcrowded, much of Old Havana is in ruins. Roughly two-thirds of the buildings are in poor condition. Most have not been touched since the onset of the Revolution in 1959 – suffering the inevitable vagaries of neglect. As a result, numerous structures are on the verge of collapse. One statistic claims that there is a building collapse in the city every third day. The underground hydraulic system (hailed as a technical marvel at the 1878 World Exposition held in Paris) has not been maintained. It now leaks more water than it provides and many houses lack running water entirely.

It is no secret that the Castro regime has been more interested in developing social projects than investing in architecture. As architect Thom Mayne noted during a visit to Habana in 1997, the city suffers from a particular type of decay (Noever 1995: 24). While the built environment is in ruin, the inhabitants are healthy and social services are intact. Unlike other twentieth-century dictators who skillfully deployed new architecture in the service of politics Castro patronized relatively little new construction.[1] This lack of interest in architecture was at least in part a condemnation of the bourgeois culture associated with building that prevailed in the decades leading up to the Revolution when new construction provided the primary means to flaunt social status and wealth (Segre 1997: 302).

The extravagant villas lining Fifth Avenue in the once chic Miramar neighborhood are a testament to these materialistic values.

Castro of course rejected such ostentatious display. In a manner that was both economically efficient and politically expedient, he sought to reoccupy and reconfigure extant buildings rather than build new ones. In the process he suppressed existing programmatic associations that were seen as being in conflict with his revolutionary socialist philosophies. For example, the luxurious Presidential Palace (occupied by President Fulgencio Batista until he was overthrown in 1959) was transformed into the Museum of the Revolution. Today the museum's exhibits chronicle the victories of Fidel, Ché, and their followers within the former home of the very man the young revolutionaries overthrew. Thus, while Castro did in fact deploy architecture to support his political goals, his mode of operating – consisting of recycling existing buildings – was distinct from the architectural rhetoric employed under the previous Cuban leadership as well as distinct from dictators in other countries.

It was not until the onset of the so-called "Special Period" (the period of self-imposed austerity in effect from 1990–5) following the fall of the Soviet Union that the Castro government assumed a proactive stance towards architecture. In contrast to the previous decades of relative inactivity, the government now began to invest heavily in Habana Vieja. Through a complex project of both physical and ephemeral urban redefinition, the government began to shape a desirable tourism product and cultivate a broadbased multinational clientele. This was undertaken by renovating select areas of city's built environment which had fallen into neglect during the revolution, and packaging its colonial heritage in a manner that would appeal to a discerning audience. The project has been underway in earnest since 1993.[2] It is lauded by those in the Castro government as a way to generate income in an era of severe economic restraint incurred by the cessation of lucrative trade relationships with former Soviet and Eastern Bloc countries. It is praised by those outside of Cuba as an innovative historic preservation project.

In a process of transculturation that typifies all things Cuban, Castro's key advisors have launched an ingenious form of entrepreneurial socialism that combines capitalist process with socialist goals. Although the project is ongoing, the results are already clearly evident. Habana Vieja has become one of the most popular tourist destinations in the Caribbean.

The Office of the Historian

There is no doubt that the success with which Habana has repositioned itself as a tourist destination is largely due to the unusual character of its built environment. Despite the fragility of its buildings and urban infrastructure, in the 1990s Habana

Vieja was still one of the least altered colonial cities in Latin America. Unlike other cities, Habana Vieja had not been transformed by large-scale twentieth-century urban renewal, projects. In fact, since Castro seized power in 1959 the city's urban fabric had remained virtually untouched. Ironically it was the regime's very neglect of the city's built environment that had facilitated its survival (Duany 2000: 34).

In 1993 the government decreed that the restoration efforts would be overseen by the Office of the Historian and lent one million dollars to cover startup costs. The goal of the Office was to "rehabilitate patrimonial areas while maintaining a clear cultural and social vocation" (Rodriguéz 1999: 43). The man responsible for coordinating these efforts was, and has remained, Eusebio Leal Spengler, Habana's influential *Historiador de la ciudad*, or city historian. Leal is knowledgeable, charismatic, persuasive, and extremely dedicated. His work has garnered praise from around the world (Rodriguéz 1999: 6–7). Feature-length stories detailing his efforts have appeared in *Preservation Magazine, Newsweek*, the *New Yorker, Smithsonian, National Geographic*, and the *New York Times* among others. In the process of coordinating social and economic development in specific neighborhoods he has drawn attention to, and excited interest in, colonial architecture. By every account he has placed Habana on the tourist itinerary for the first time since the onset of the regime.

There is no doubt that Leal's achievements over the course of the past decade are truly remarkable. Under his watch the Office of the Historian has developed a master plan and systematically classified all buildings in Habana Vieja (Ochoa 2002: 82–3). Over 100 structures have been rebuilt and restored. Dozens more are in progress and an equal number have been identified as sites for future work (Rodriguéz 1999: 43). The task is costly and involved, and like any of the projects undertaken during the Castro regime, its success depends heavily upon dictatorial managing practices. Ultimately Leal, and only Leal, is responsible for the renovations of Habana Vieja. However, this does not mean that he operates alone. He oversees an office of 5,000 workers (including 130 architects and engineers), which is organized like a complex corporation with a series of separate specialized departments (Rodriguéz 1999: 13).

As director of the Office of the Historian, Leal is simultaneously the city's master planner, developer, chief architect, C.E.O, publicist, preservation officer, social service coordinator, and historian. His efforts require long-range planning as well as the sustained commitment of the thousands of individuals involved. Working with a crew of historians, planners, architects, engineers, and social demographers, Leal and his associates determine how each building will be preserved as well as how it will be reprogrammed. They evaluate whether the building should be demolished and rebuilt, or gutted. They then determine its future use – whether it should be transformed into a hotel, a museum, apartment housing, or senior citizen center, among others. The decision-making process involves a careful physical and historical analysis of the site including locating documents that describe the original character of the building. The process also involves analyzing socio-demographic data to determine what function the building would best fulfill, and which residents will be able to remain in the neighborhood once the building is converted into its new use. The goal, as Orestes del Castillo, an architect and historian who works for the Office of the Historian notes, is to sustain a living city along the lines of Paris or Rome – wherein historical sites and tourist infrastructure coexist with institutions and services for a permanent resident community (del Castillo 2002). In the end, as del Castillo suggests, Habana will avoid the malady that characterizes most historic centers – that of being transformed into a deadened city that serves tourists and tourists alone.

While historical accuracy is of relative interest to the architects and historians employed by the Office, it is not their ultimate concern. In truth, many of the buildings are restored in a manner that most preservationists and architectural historians would consider to be highly problematic. In some cases buildings are torn down and rebuilt in what is vaguely described as "colonial style." In many cases only the building façades are saved while interiors are recreated in a manner that deceptively appears to be of some age. In others cases, existing windows, doors, and, balconies are altered keeping in mind the new use to which the building will be put, rather than its historic form.

For the Office of the Historian, the buildings of colonial Habana provide a means to an end. The proceeds from their restoration help to augment the effectiveness of the city's socialist system. It is therefore difficult for those involved to assess critically the project's architectural integrity as separate from its socialist successes. They are integral and interdependent. Or, to phrase it in another way, it could be argued that however questionable the architectural renovations might be, they are "truthful" in the sense that they contribute to the city's vitality and welfare.

While Habana is in the process of being remade into an appealing destination, Leal and his colleagues are quite conscious of the fine line that exists between promoting tourism to the city while preventing its "Cancúnization." Del Castillo and others are adamant that they are trying to create a site that will be distinct from the commercialized destinations that have inundated the Mexican coast. They are also hopeful that the work undertaken in Habana Vieja will serve as an important example for other cities on the island.[3] Perhaps because of this, Leal and his colleagues are not only extremely articulate and forthcoming about current projects, but openly self reflective. They regularly discuss their goals, strategies, and concerns in public fora, at conferences and within scholarly articles. Ultimately such discursive transparency is a form of control. By establishing the perimeters for criticism and debate, the Office has cleverly defined the analysis of its own projects.

Implicit amongst Leal's many roles is that of politician. As an outspoken member of the Cuban General Assembly, he has maintained the unfailing support of Castro and his administration. Leal's office has the unique status of an autonomous urban development company. The office has complete control and eminent domain over the neighborhood of Habana Vieja. As such, it has been able to identify projects and move very quickly to develop, manage, and publicize them. It also controls the bulk of the profits (70 million dollars in 2001 alone). Eighty per cent of the proceeds from the various projects are reinvested directly in Habana Vieja (45 per cent of all profits is earmarked for future restoration projects, while 35 per cent is invested into community social services). The remaining 20 per cent is turned over to the national government to be dispersed at its discretion (Guerra 1998: 27). This arrangement is unlike that of any of the other fourteen municipalities in Habana. Money made at hotels located in the Vedado neighborhood for example, is not necessarily reinvested in the Vedado but rather placed directly into government coffers to be used according to the government's wish. In contrast, money made in Habana Vieja remains in Habana Vieja.

Like many of Castro's other revolutionary projects, the Office is self-sustaining. Leal repaid the initial one million dollar government loan in 3 years and has not received state subsidies since. As architecture critic Paul Goldberger has noted, Leal is a "New Age Cuban bureaucrat, turning capitalism to the benefit of socialism" (Goldberger 1998: 61). Not surprisingly, Leal's projects have received praise from tourists who visit Habana Vieja, the *Habaneros* who reside there, the Cuban government, as well as international organizations such as UNESCO (which designated Habana Vieja a World Heritage Site in 1982). It is widely believed that Leal has single-handedly saved Old Havana. The long list of bestowed prizes, commendations, and honorary degrees seem to confirm this (Ochoa 2002: 4–7).

Promoting the Colonial

It needs to be made explicitly clear that the city Leal has saved is that of colonial Habana. Although not everything in Habana Vieja dates to the colonial era, the period has been privileged to the exclusion of all else. As Cuban architect and preservationist Mario Coyula has lamented, the attention lavished on the city center has not reached modern Habana (McGuigan 2002: 54). The diverse architectural styles (the neoclassical, art nouveau, art deco, and modern) prevalent in neighborhoods such as the Cerro, Centro Habana, or the Vedado have been overlooked by Leal – who is the Historian of the whole city, not solely Habana Vieja. The Vedado municipality for example, is a mecca for structures dating to the 1930s, 1940s, and 1950s, including the famous Capri, Riviera, and (former) Hilton hotels. These hotels still attract foreign tourists, but they do so outside of Leal's purview. While their physical distance from the colonial quarter makes them easy to ignore, Leal's exclusive focus on the colonial is more strategic than happenstance.

As Goldberger has hypothesized, colonial architecture "is ideologically safe" (Goldberger 1998: 61). It was "created neither by the capitalist sugar barons, who made the city's great mansions in the first three decades of this century, nor by the hated Batista regime, which made the city's buildings in the fifties." Because of this the colonial is nonthreatening. It is historically remote enough so as not to engender conflict. Furthermore, the extended period of Spanish colonization (1512–1898) provides a wide variety of building types, styles, and materials ready for manipulation. The varied character of the "colonial" gives Leal tremendous freedom to recreate Habana Vieja as he wishes.

Emphasizing the colonial image allows Leal to define Habana Vieja as a city filled with interesting heritage sites and cultural events. While many of these sites existed prior to Leal's intervention, just as many did not. And all have been subjected to Leal's particular form of branding that presents them as authentically colonial. The colonial rhetoric allows Leal to recast Habana as a site of world patrimony – a move that is key to attracting an international tourist audience. As Leal notes in one of his videotaped guided tours through Old Habana (produced for Cuban television and subsequently sold to tourists on videocassette), the city is a "lost page in universal history" that is in the process of being recovered and restored. He goes on to remind the viewer that it was King Philip II of Spain who first identified Habana as "the key to the New World" (Leal 1994). And it was from the city's secure harbor that Spanish conquistadors such as Hernán Cortez launched their campaigns to conquer the land that would become Latin America. Cuba quickly emerged as the point of transit for goods being transported between Spain and the New World, became the richest island in the Caribbean and the link between the Old and New Worlds. Leal implies that the island has a strong pedigree – one that will reemerge through the aegis of global tourism.

By rooting the city in its historical past, Leal seeks to distinguish Habana from other Caribbean vacation destinations, which are typically advertised by their white sand beaches populated by bikini-clad women, recreational sports, and succulent buffet dinners. While Habana could easily capitalize on this stereotypical Caribbean image (beaches, including the Varadero coastal resort district, can be found within an easy drive of the city), it does not. Instead Leal has ensured that Habana offers something that in his eyes is of greater significance – an unimitable cultural center. In this we see how Habana has learned the lessons of Cancún – a destination that has struggled to redefine itself as a site of cultural tourism once excessive sun and sex were deemed unhealthy (Hiernaux-Nicolas 1999).

For contemporary tourists (most of whom are European – Spanish, Italian, British, French, and German) Habana provides the perfect combination of Old-World charm in an exoticized New World location. The evocative character of a colonial city (what Leal refers to as 'poetic mystery') (Leal 1994) holds tremendous appeal for those seeking an experience that is simultaneously relaxing and educational – the latest trend in cultural tourism development.

More importantly, however, by telescoping back to the colonial period, Leal has successfully rewritten history. By amplifying the city's colonial heritage he has suppressed memories of Habana's other pasts – most notably the era of capitalist gluttony and entertainment extravagance that defined the decades leading up to the revolution. In other words, while Leal seeks to revive tourist interest in Habana – he seeks to do so by constructing an image of the city that is quite distinct from that which prevailed between the 1920s and 1950s; more precisely the period of North American domination. As such, the selective reconstruction of Habana says more about the contemporary desire to eradicate this particular past than it does about the true nature of the city's past.

Erasing the Memory of the US

Cuba's antagonistic relationship with the US began at the end of the period of Spanish Colonialism in 1898. Following the removal of Spanish investment, Cuba became increasingly dependent upon its North American neighbor for economic and cultural support and quickly developed as an annex to the U.S. Companies such as Shell, Hershey, Bethlehem Steel, Procter & Gamble, Coca-Cola, and Firestone all had Cuban subsidiaries (Pérez 1999). Branches of the North American banks lined Obispo and Cuba streets – forming the so-called "little Wall Street" area of Old Havana. Hotels such as the Sevilla Biltmore (built in 1908 and expanded in 1921 by the American firm Schultze & Weaver), the Nacional (designed by New York architects McKim, Mead, & White in 1929), the Hotel Riviera with its Gold Leaf Casino (built in 1957 by Igor B. Polevitzky and Verner Johnson), and the Capri, were owned (at least in part) by US investors (the Nacional and Riviera were owned by the notorious mafia financeer Meyer Lansky whereas the Capri was owned by mobster Santo Traficante Jr.). As historian Roberto Segre has noted, during this period, Habana maintained the appearance of a busy North American City (Segre 1997: 29).

Not surprisingly Habana was a popular tourist destination during the first half of the twentieth century – heavily frequented by North Americans who made the short trip (via ferry from Key West) to visit the infamous casinos, night clubs, and *exhibiciones* (live sex shows). As has been recorded in popular culture – ranging from the tawdry portrait of the city captured by Graham Greene in his 1958 novel *Our Man In Havana* to the mob reunion portrayed in Francis Ford Coppola's film *Godfather II* – Habana was a city of bourgeois excess – a popular destination for honeymooning, gambling, drinking and prostitution. It was, as many period visitors observed, seedy and corrupt. The British author Norman Lewis captured the city's gritty character in a 1957 essay noting that the Prado was lined with cafes that advertised "HANGOVER BREAKFASTS" (Lewis 1997: 136).

From the outset of the revolution Castro sought to break with this past. His Habana assumed a very different form. Casinos were shut down and their movable goods destroyed. Foreign-owned properties were nationalized. The haunts of the elite were repossessed. Traces of city's former character of excess were carefully expunged. Today, no casinos or nightclub cabarets have survived within the neighborhood of Habana Vieja. And Leal is not interested in seeing them reemerge. The drunken excess of Prohibition period tourism has been replaced by more sedate educational activities such as the center for Early Modern Hispano-music housed in the former church of San Francisco de Paula, the recently renovated Museum of Contemporary Art, and the Museum of Rum (all of which are run by the Office of the Historian). Sex shows have gone underground – officially replaced by demonstrations of *salsa y son* (two of Cuba's musical traditions). La Floridita, Ernest Hemingway's favorite bar and one of the only establishments to survive the revolution, is now a sedate lounge where guests can order a version of Papá's favorite daiquirí. It is clear that the newly edited image of Habana Vieja focuses on the city's historical and artistic colonial culture. This is a cleaner romanticized image that boasts a wider market appeal. But more importantly, it is an image that has completely erased the era of North American domination. The city's raucous past is no longer accessible. Whether the memory of that past survives in tourists' expectations would be harder to determine. Nonetheless, there is no trace of it in Habana Vieja.

Hotels to Admire

One of the most important elements in solidifying the city's new image as a cultural hub is the chain of hotels operated by the Office of the Historian. Nine hotels have been built, ten more are projected to open within the next 2 years. The promotional literature and well-maintained Web sites used to advertise these hotels emphasize their "historic importance," "individual character," and "serene elegant atmosphere." The Habaguanex company brochure (the department in the Office of the Historian devoted to the administration of hotels and restaurants) claims that the hotels provide a "different, unique, and irrepeatable environment" (Figure 9.2). The company slogan, *hoteles para admirar* (hotels to admire), underscores this point. Loosely modeled after the Spanish *paradores* (historic buildings that have been converted by the government into luxury accommodations), the Habaguanex hotels offer old-world charm combined with modern comfort, which in this case is equated with air conditioning, room service, fax and photocopy capabilities, and international cuisine.

Figure 9.2 Habanaguanex brochure advertising the historic hotels operated by the Office of the Historian, Habana, c. 2002.

Each hotel celebrates the generic idea of colonial splendor, but they are distinct from one another. Indeed, there are few clues that suggest they belong to the same chain. The Hostal Conde de Villanueva, the former home of the Count Villanueva (an important figure in the promotion of Cuban cigars), is an intimate nine-room hotel "of authentic colonial beauty." The upscale five-star Santa Isabel occupies the famous eighteenth-century mansion built by the Count of Santovenia and is decorated in what is described as "serene Spanish style." The Hotel Telégrafo (a former grand nineteenth-century hotel once frequented by visitors such as Heinrich Schliemann) has been rebuilt. Similarly the Hotel Florida, founded in 1885, has been "reborn to once again captivate guests with its charm and architectural beauty." Like others, it is "decorated in the most genuine colonial style" (Hotel Florida Brochure 2002). The message is clear. These hotels provide the stage from which to initiate the tourist's experience of the colonial city.

In addition to celebrating their colonial character, the promotional pamphlets for these hotels underscore their prime location – in the heart of the old city, "surrounded by squares of singular attractiveness, museums, and important shopping centers" (Hostal Villanueva Brochure 2002). The courtyard of the Hostal del Tejadillo is described as a "reprieve from activities of the city." The promotional pamphlet for the Hostal El Comendador is even more precise noting that the hotel's "quiet location, soothing patios, and intimate rooms provide a perfect refuge from a hard day's sight-seeing." While references to the sites of Habana seem benign, the promotion of these hotels as refuges from an active city cleverly reinforces the image of Habana's rich cultural life. As such, the hotels help to underscore the city's new cultural geography; concert halls, ethnic restaurants, shops selling Cuban souvenirs, and museums (such as the Museum of Colonial Art, the Casa de la Obra Pía which houses seventeenth- and eighteenth-century decorative arts, or the Museum of the Maqueta which features an illuminated 32-square-meter three-dimensional model of the old city), as well as numerous sites that are still under construction. As such Habana has been recast as a city saturated with heritage sites and captivating cultural venues. A few of these sites (such as the Museum of Colonial Art) existed prior to Leal's interventions, but most (such as the Casa de la Obra Pía, the Archeological Museum, the concert halls, and ethnic restaurants) did not. And all have been overhauled under his watch. Socialist planning has been enlisted to control all aspects of the tourism experience.

The extent to which the city has been redesigned as tourist destination is most clearly evident in the map of neighborhood produced by the Office of the Historian, printed by Habaguanex and readily available at all Habaguanex hotels, gift shops, and restaurants. It is printed in shades of brown and as such is distinct from the colorful informational materials typically distributed at tourist sites. A nineteenth-century image of the city's old military square, the Plaza de Armas constitutes the background image, visually reinforcing the idea of the colonial city. Hotels, restaurants, shops, museums, and other sites of cultural interest are listed and numbered.

Like the photograph printed by the itinerant photographer, the image of Habana depicted on this map is not entirely accurate. It has been designed by the Office of the Historian to promote projects overseen by the Office. Nothing appears on the map that is not controlled by the Historian. Hotels which predate Leal's tenure as city Historian such as the Inglaterra (built in 1856 and expanded in 1891), the Sevilla Biltmore (1908), or the Plaza (1909), are not listed. The second-rate hotels that service Cubans, shops where rationed foodstuffs are distributed, and the various stores that have not yet been appropriated by the Historian, have been silently expunged from the cartographic representation of the city. At the same time there are numerous featured sites (such as Habaguanex hotels O'Farril, Saratoga, and Raquel and several museums that are in various stages of planning and construction) that do not yet exist. As such the map is an idealized projection of Habana Vieja intended for tourist consumption. It underscores the extent to which the city's tourist topography has been successfully segregated from its Cuban geography.

Tourist Geographies

As the map makes clear, Leal's idealized Habana has very little to do with the urban reality experienced by the average *Habanero*. As such, it is emblematic of the dual economy and dual culture that is sustained in Habana – a city that is comprised of distinctive, if at times overlapping geographies. One city is designed for the tourists while a second is maintained for *Habaneros*. In the end both geographies are controlled by the Office of the Historian – either through the construction of tourist sites in the first case, or through financing new housing, schools, and social services in the second. While these cities are interdependent (in that the social programming of the second city depends upon revenues raised by the tourist city), for the most part they remain culturally distinct.

This schism is exacerbated by the fact that *Habaneros* and tourists use three different currencies – the former use the Cuban peso and the latter the dollar. While the widely circulated so-called "convertible" coins (which tellingly feature images of Cuban colonial architecture) allow for easy currency exchange between pesos and dollars, in truth the two currencies are not comparable. The average salary of a university graduate is 280 pesos per month (at roughly 35 pesos to the dollar this equates to less than 10 dollars a month). Such salaries afford Cubans the ability to augment government rations with the purchase of goods at stores that accept pesos, but they preclude them from buying anything of significance at a store that accepts only dollars. In other words, the new gift shops, bars, restaurants and hotels that now line the streets of Old Havana (and accept only dollars) are prohibitively expensive for Cubans. Moreover, until recently Cubans were not allowed to frequent the bars and restaurants that were a part of the Habaguanex chain (eating instead at local cafeterías – simple settings that post their limited menus on chalkboards displayed in the doorway). In fact Cubans still remain excluded from spending the night in Habaguanex hotels (even if this was something they could afford). The Cuban government gives every newly married couple a two-night honeymoon in a first-class hotel, but those run by the Office of the Historian are off limits. Doormen function as bouncers, discretely making sure that their fellow Cubans remain outside, apologizing profusely when they mistake a tourist for a native. Ironically the hotels' amenities and colonial-themed containers serve as a form of neocolonialist exploration in a postcolonial era.

Hotels always provide the comfortable and familiar conditions of the "tourist bubble." However, in Havana, the distinction between the cultural geography of the hotel and that which lies outside, is heightened. Inside the hotel room the Habaguanex company has created an atmosphere that seeks to meet the needs of the discerning international traveler. The hotel rooms boast minibars, room service, and air conditioning. Habaguanex brand soap and shampoo is available in the bathroom and pencils and paper sit by the phone – items that are tightly rationed outside the hotel. (The state gives each Cuban one bar of soap and two pencils each month.) With the abundance of amenities available within the hotels it is easy to forget that outside Cubans are living under severe economic restraint outside. Within the rooms multilingual satellite televisions carry CNN, MTV, ESPN, and other networks. Ironically, tourists have every program at their disposal except for the two state-run Cuban television stations that are in turn the only stations available in Cuban homes.

Clearly one of Leal's goals is to edit out Cuban reality from the tourist experience. In fact, even Fidel is noticeably absent in Old Havana. The familiar patriotic slogans (*Viva Fidel!* or *Hasta La Vittoria Siempre!*) which can be found painted on the sides of buildings or incorporated into billboard propaganda elsewhere in the city are not readily available for tourist consumption in Habana Vieja. In truth, the only reminder of the revolution visible at tourist sites takes the form of Ché Guevara paraphernalia, which, in its variety of form and material – from clay ash trays to t-shirts – borders on kitsch. While Ché is a central figure of the Cuban Revolution, he is as much revered for his activism outside of Cuba (in Angola, Bolivia, and Mexico), his charisma, and gallant good looks. His presence in the tourist city is therefore happily accommodated and readily sought out. Fidel, on the other hand, is more problematic than useful. As a result his appearance is infrequent. Such self-abnegation is both insidious and clever, as it is through his absence that the tourist-city is depoliticized. And it is through such depoliticization that the true nature of the realities and hardships of contemporary Cuba remain hidden from the tourist. Once such realities are suppressed, Habana becomes inherently more appealing. This is of course similar to any tourist site where an enclavic "tourist bubble" (Judd 1999) is constructed to distance and protect the tourist. In Habana however, the contrast between what lies within the bubble and what lies without is stark.

This becomes apparent as one travels by taxi through some of the more remote neighborhoods of metropolitan Habana. On one trip a taxi driver (a former university English professor as it happened) drove a friend and myself along the so-called calzada del Cerro – miles of collonaded streets that once connected the rural *campo*, or countryside, with the city center. Lined with graceful, if derelict, single-storied neo-classical structures built at the turn-of-the-century by the city's elite as weekend retreats, these gently winding avenues are repositories of architectural splendor. The taxi driver seemed intrigued that a tourist would want to see this part of town – miles from the well-trodden terrain maintained by Leal. We in turn were surprised that these magnificent avenues were not included in Leal's purview. "So you don't bring people here often" we naively asked. "Oh yes I do" he replied, "in fact it is one of the most popular destinations for returning Cuban exiles and their children – eager to seek out their former ancestral homes." As he articulated this, it struck us that while this part of the city was a popular destination for visitors, these were not the tourists that Leal sought to cultivate.

As is the case in other cities, Havana sustains multiple forms of tourism. In Habana Vieja Leal has constructed a tourist geography for a specific clientele. His heritage tourism project does not overlap with that of the Cerro – a fact confirmed when we encountered an elderly man on the porch of a senior citizen center in the Cerro. He seemed genuinely pleased to meet us, claiming not to have seen an American in 40 years – since his days as a Black Jack dealer at the famous Tropicana casino. Indeed, he had not seen a foreigner in years. The idea that this was possible, when throngs of foreign tourists (not to mention many Americans) could be found several miles away ambling along the picturesque cobblestone streets of Habana Vieja confirmed the intense segregation of the average tourist itinerary.

The Politics of Space

In the process of mapping Habana Vieja's tourist geography, public spaces have become increasingly less accessible to the resident *Habanero*. While this often happens at sites that simultaneously serve tourists and a permanent resident population, the situation in Habana seems extreme. Thanks to the efforts of the Office of the Historian public plazas are now animated by a variety of choreographed activities. The Habaguanex company sponsors so-called *Noches en la Plaza*, or Nights in the Plaza, held in the Cathedral square. These are colonial-themed

Figure 9.3 Plaza Vieja, Habana, 2002. The restored fountain is visible behind the fence.

block parties – evenings of Cuban music and food – delivered to a captive tourist audience for a fee (an astronomical $100 on New Year's Eve 2002). Leal sees such theatrical events (including the *comparsas* or groups of costumed musicians and actors that parade "spontaneously" through the city streets and musical entertainment held at the local taverns) as proof of the city's "living" character. In truth these events are designed for tourists. Locals are excluded by both the cost of the ticket (the equivalent of a year's salary) and the barricades that are erected at the entrances to the square.

Many of the city's public arteries and other amenities have also been appropriated for exclusive tourist use. Perhaps the most overt evidence for this is the decision by the Historian to fence off the newly restored public fountain in the Plaza Vieja – the public square that is sited between the heavily trafficked tourist zone around the church of San Francesco de Asís and the impoverished working class San Isidro quarter (Figure 9.3). Access to the fountain has been restricted so as to protect its scenic character. It was argued that the fountain would be threatened by heavy use – which could be expected in a neighborhood where not everyone has easy access to running water. The fencing of the fountain represents a moment in the city where two parallel cities (that of the tourist and that of the *Habanero*) collide.

It is clear that Habana Vieja has been redesigned for foreign consumption. While Cubans can be seen strolling through the neighborhood on Sunday afternoons and some even manage to make purchases at stores that sell only in dollars, the city that is marketed to the tourists is not a "Cuban" city. In fact, public transportation to the capital city is so poor, that it would be nearly impossible for someone living in the outlying provinces to visit Habana. Furthermore, tourism is in fact illegal for the vast majority of Cubans. Thus, unlike many cities in the US and Europe, where internal tourism has been used as a catalyst for defining local and national identity, this is not the case in Habana. Instead, by providing the economic resources to maintain social projects tourism is a means to an end.

Remarkably, Habana residents do not seem antagonistic towards tourists and the sites that have been created for their pleasure. The revolutionary rhetoric of self-sacrifice, instilled in the Cuban population by Castro's regime, seems to have influenced their acceptance of the way in which tourism has reshaped their city. In fact, most Cubans applaud the efforts in Habana Vieja claiming that tourism to this neighborhood is not only the vehicle by which Castro's regime will survive, but has provided them with improved sanitation, better schools, medical clinics, and new housing for those residents that are permanently displaced by the various restoration projects. And they are right.

Tourism to Cuba now generates more income than sugar. Jobs in the tourism industry figure amongst the most sought-after professions. Enrollment at the two-year professional program at the Escuela de Altos Estudios de Hoteleria y Turismo in Habana (the School for Advanced Study in Hotel Administration and Tourism) has recently peaked at 800 students. The Ministry of Tourism (founded in 1989) is thriving and the new minister, Ibrahim Ferradaz, is an outspoken promoter of what he has termed the island's diverse culture (unique historical patrimony, natural beauty, good climate, and safety) (Ferradaz 2002: 8).

Mass Mediation

The success of this tourist project is largely due to Leal's closely managed mass media campaign. Leal launched a glossy journal (*Opus Habana*) in 1999, published a series of heavily illustrated books (*Para No Olvidar, Ciudad de la Habana, Desafío Una Utopia*), and produced several documentary films (*Andar la Habana*) as a means of both publicizing and legitimizing the restoration of Habana Vieja. The media is self-referential and self-serving. The restoration projects are documented by the books which are in turn advertised in the journal which is given away in the hotels run by the Habaguanex company – creating a dense intersecting web of publicity. A photograph of Leal (surrounded by rolled architectural drawings and engaged in serious thought), coupled with his lengthy curriculum vitae appears in many publications – underscoring the patriarchal role he assumes in relation to Habana.

In a country where new books are a rare luxury, magazines are non-existent, and two thin newspapers (the *Granma* and the youth newspaper *Rebelde*) serve the entire island, publications of the Office of the Historian are an anomaly. They are professionally designed, lush volumes, with full-color printing on each page. They are an embarassment of riches. In fact they maintain the appearance of a product more familiar to a capitalist world than the socialist one. The appearance is of course deceptive. Advertisements are nothing more than publicity by and for the various divisions of the Office of the Historian. Essay topics are chosen not for their journalistic value but for the ways in which they can promote and further the efforts of the Historian. An article on the Mercury figure perched on top of the Lonja del Comercio provides an opportunity to discuss the restoration of the Lonja itself (del Castillo 2001). Other articles feature the history of the Palacio de Armas, the tradition of colonial wrought iron work, the refounding of the Fine Arts Museum, and the contemporary art scene. It is hard to imagine the promotional publication of any other popular Caribbean destination filled with similarly well written, informed, and scholarly articles. And yet this is the case for Habana Vieja. The publications provide Leal with the opportunity to promote understanding about a variety of historical and cultural topics.

As Leal noted in the first editorial published in *Opus Habana*, the goal of the publications is to "bring life to the project of curating, restoring, and reconstructing Old Havana." And this they do. They are filled with "before and after" photographs – allowing the readers to assess the work that has been invested in this transformation. It is hard not to be impressed. The documentarist aesthetic that underscores the publications helps reinforce the notion that the city's colonial image (as reconstructed by Leal) is indeed authentic. This is confirmed in each issue of *Opus Habana* by the published testimonials of schoolchildren whose handwritten letters and colorful drawings note their genuine amazement.

The publications also ensure that Leal's efforts will not be forgotten (as the title of one book, *Para No Olvidar*, or *So as to Not Forget*, makes explicitly clear). We must, as Leal notes "safeguard the social memory of history" (Leal 1999b: 3). This is also achieved by encouraging active participation in the project. Readers are encouraged to buy "history bonds" to support the restoration work in Habana Vieja ("Don't Let History Disappear" one advertisement beseeches). Furthermore, a private subscription to *Opus Habana* entitles the reader to unlimited use of the archives of the Office of the Historian where they can consult rare books from the colonial period and a vast photo archive. Whether the reader takes advantage of this privilege is irrelevant. It is the fact that he or she has been invited to consult the archives under the pretense of encouraging research. Of course any form of true historical sleuthing would be problematic as the man (Leal) who controls the conception, construction, documentation, analysis, and interpretation of renovated Habana is also director of the city's only archive. As a result it would be difficult, if not impossible, to prove that Leal's projects were questionable in terms of historical authenticity.

While Leal claims that these publications are about and for Cuba (Leal 1999a: 3) and in the end they may be, in the short term they are intended for foreigners. Each includes advertisements promoting services that pertain only to foreign tourists and investors. They are available only at the hotels, shops, and museums run by the Historian. And all are fairly pricey. *Opus*, the least expensive of the publications costs $7. Several of the books cost as much as $50. These are not items that the average Cuban can afford. In a country where product placement is unheard of, billboard advertising is limited to revolutionary slogans, and tourist trinkets are dominated by the image of Ché, the polished media campaign to sell Habana Vieja stands out. The city center has been packaged as a series of palpable cultural/historical products – each presented as more attractive than the next – in a manner that helps the tourist navigate through the city. For a capitalist audience it is easy to take such advertising at face value and assume that it is designed to cultivate a consumer in a commercial sense. The project is more complicated than that. By promoting Habana's unique history and architecture – Leal has success-fully recast the bourgeois anti-intellectual landscape of Batista (who, as Mario Coyula has noted, "with rare exception, did not care for history") (Noever 1995: 63) into a cultural hub of noted historical importance. The mass media have been essential to this transformation process.

Revolutionary Tourism

While the rhetoric and methods of Leal's redesign of Habana Vieja might appear to be capitalist in character, ultimately it is a socialist project. The city's celebration guarantees the social welfare of its inhabitants. Like Castro's other revolutionary projects the remapping of Habana as a touristic center is comprehensive and complete – the benefits of which are identified as long range, permanent, and public (rather than immediate, transitory, and private goals indicative of a capitalist system). It is a project that is ongoing – encapsulating the socialist philosophy of continuous reform.

Habana has also been recast as the center for renewed revolutionary rhetoric of educational reform. Tourists who come to colonial Habana will leave having learned something about the city's history, its architecture, visionary leaders, and artists. They will become familiar with the ouevre of painter Wilfredo Lam and writer Alejo Carpentier (whose description of Habana as a "city of columns" is cited ad nauseum by the tour guides employed by the Office). As such the tourist will leave with an image of this Caribbean destination that is uniquely Cuban, and more precisely, distinctly *Habanero*. In this way Leal has repudiated the all-too-frequent marginalization of local culture that results in the process of tourist development

Anthony Tung has claimed that the biggest challenge facing the development of heritage destinations is to design a distinctive identity (Tung 2001). In many ways Tung has inverted the central problem. The biggest hurdle to sites today is to maintain a distinct identity while designing tourist amenities of comfort, safety, and intrigue. This has been successful undertaken in Habana. Not only has the city been packaged as distinctly *Habanera*, it has been done in a way that is distinctly Cuban. As Leal has noted, the threats of globalization will be overcome by continuing to invest in the social commitment to the community (Leal 2002).

Having spent centuries under colonial rule, the Cuban government is now successfully profiting from that period. The city's colonial past is being mined as a resource to support a new industry (that of tourism) as well as permanent social change (better housing, an enhanced water system, and so forth). In this way, the current tourism project is regenerative. As Leal himself has noted the "so-called leisure industry is recycled into social and cultural works. Children and older folk from Old Habana are taken care of directly by this system" (Leal 2002). As he is proud to point out, in one case a public library stands in front of a luxury Habanaguanex hotel (the Santa Isabel) – proof that the *Habaneros* not only gain from the proceeds of tourism, but coexist with it. As such, Habana challenges our assumptions about tourism. Similar to the case study in this volume by Edensor and Kothari, Leal's careful orchestration of the image of colonial Habana is an empowering one. Leal has demonstrated how traditional Western, capitalist tourism is put to the service of revolutionary, non-Western socialist ends.

Acknowledgements

Conversations with Orestes del Castillo, Edilzon Machado, Maria Elena Martín Zequeira, Manuel Perrera, and Eduardo Luis Rodríguez and Mary Woods aided the development of this chapter. I would additionally like to thank Paula Horrigan, Carlos Martín, John Stuart and the participants in my architecture and tourism graduate seminar for reading an earlier version of this chapter.

Notes

1. The five art schools built on the golf course of the former Habana Country Club and the austere high-rise housing blocks of East Habana, built on land owned by former Batista cronies, are the notable exceptions. See Loomis (1999).
2. Law decree #143 was passed in October 1993 awarding the authority to develop tourism and social welfare to the Office of the Historian.
3. Offices of the Historian have already been established in the colonial towns of Santiago, Camaguey, Cienfuegos, and Trinidad.

References

del Castillo, Orestes (2001), "el Retorno de Mercurio", *Opus Habana*, V, 2: 44–50.
—— (2002), interview conducted June 24, 2002.
Duany, Andres (2000), "The Future of La Habana", *Cuba Update*, VIX, (2–3): 35–6.
Ferradaz, Ibrahim (2002), "Cuba sí, como siempre", *Sol y Son*, 3: 8.
Goldberger, Paul (1998), "Bringing Back Havana", *The New Yorker*, January 26: 50–61.
Guerra, Charo (ed.) (1998), *San Isidro. La Nueva Imagen. Proyecto Social para la revitalización integral de un Barrio Habanero*, Habana: Officina del historiador de la Ciudad.
Hiernaux-Nicolas, Daniel (1999), "Cancún Bliss", in Judd, Dennis R. and Fainstein, Susan S. (eds), *The Tourist City*, New Haven: Yale University Press.
Judd, Dennis R. (1999), "Constructing the Tourist Bubble", in Judd, Dennis R. and Fainstein, Susan (eds), *The Tourist City*, New Haven: Yale University Press.
Leal Spengler, Eusebio (1994), *Andar La Habana*, videocassette, vol. 1, Habana: Oficina del Historiador.
—— (1999a), "Tributo a la Esperanza", *Opus Habana*, 3(1): 3.
—— (1999b), "Afán de Perseverar,' *Opus Habana*, 3(2): 3.
—— (2002), Key note address to Association of Collegiate Schools of Architecture, International Conference, "Architecture, Culture, and the Challenges of Globalization" held in Havana, 21–24 June.
Lejeune, Jean-François (1996), "The City as Landscape: Jean Claude Nicolas Forestier and the Great Urban Works of Havana, 1925–1930", *The Journal of Decorative and Propaganda Arts* 22. Cuba Theme issue edited by Cathy Leff.
Lewis, Norman (1997), "Havana and the Finca Vigia, 1957: Visiting Hemingway and one-fourth of James Bond", reprinted in Ryan, Alan (ed.), *The Reader's Companion to Cuba*, New York: Harcourt, Brace & Company.

Loomis, John (1999), *Revolution of Forms. Cuba's Forgotten Art Schools*, New York: Princeton Architecture Press.

McGuigan, Cathleen (2002), "Keeping the Past Alive in Havana", *Newsweek*, July 15: 52–5.

Noever, Peter (ed.) (1995), *The Havana Project: Architecture Again*, Munich and New York: Prestel.

Ochoa Alomá, Alina (2002), *Desafío de una utopía. Una estrategia integral para la gestión de salvaguarda de la habana vieja*, Habana: Officina del historiador del la Ciudad.

Pérez Jr., Louis A. (1999), *On Becoming Cuban. Identity, Nationality and Culture*, New York: The Ecco Press.

Rodriguéz Alomá, Patricia (1999), *Desafío de una utopía. Una estrategia integral para la gestión de salvaguarda de la habana vieja*, Habana: Officina del historiador del la Ciudad.

Segre, Roberto, Coyula, Mario and Scarpaci, Joseph L. (1997), *Havana. Two Faces of the Antillean Metropolis*, New York: John Wiley & Sons.

Tung, Anthony M. (2001), *Preserving the World's Great Cities. The Destruction and Renewal of the Historic Metropolis*, New York: Clarkson Potter.

Part IV
Performance

–10–

Sweetening Colonialism: A Mauritian Themed Resort

Tim Edensor and Uma Kothari

Introduction

In this chapter, we explore the production of a themed resort in Mauritius, a tropical island located off the African coast east of Madagascar, in order to discuss critically the often dystopian view that themed space is typified by a landscape full of stereotypical and ideological signifiers that guide interpretation and practice along preferred lines. By drawing on notions about the complexity of place, on tourism as performance and on the materiality of space, we question these assumptions. After providing a brief outline of tourism in Mauritius, we examine the production of the resort's major themes, before going on to look at the distinct kinds of performances and experiences that are encouraged through design, regulation and material effects. Following this, we discuss critically the limitations of existing conceptualizations of themed spaces, putting forward arguments which demand that, like other spaces, they be considered in terms of a "progressive sense of place" – (Massey 1993), that is, understood as ceaselessly constituted by the processes and flows which cross and center upon them.

Tourism in Mauritius

Over the last three decades, Mauritius has developed from a low-income, agriculturally based economy – what V. S. Naipaul (1973) called an "overcrowded barracoon" – to a middle-income diversified economy with growing industrial, financial, and tourist sectors. For most of the period, annual growth has been in the order of 5 per cent to 6 per cent, and this is reflected in a more equitable income distribution, increased life expectancy, lowered infant mortality, and a much improved infrastructure. Much of this growth has been achieved through the expansion of luxury tourism, and Mauritius continues to be a destination for tourism at the high end of the market, providing relatively expensive air travel and accommodation. Accordingly, tourist strategy ensures that package tourism predominates, and there is very little backpacking or independent travel. A growing number of resorts cluster around parts of the coastline despite worries about destruction of coral reefs and pollution. Broadly speaking, policy has been devised to keep tourists within these hotel enclaves to regulate contact between Mauritians society and tourists because of fears about cultural and social problems.

Its splendid beaches, climate and sea life mean that Mauritius has typically presented itself as a somewhat unspecific tropical paradise. Certain hotels have adopted Polynesian themes but the complex, syncretic culture of Mauritius is rarely sold – although there are vague gestures towards being a "rainbow island" – its complicated nature not being appropriate for easy branding. The spread of hotels around the island's coastline means that there is considerable competition for the primarily European (mainly French and British) tourists who come. Larger hotels may distinguish themselves from each other according to the degree of luxury and amenities they offer, but increasingly, theming serves as a strategy to differentiate the tourist product on offer. Besides Polynesian themes, fishing village, ecological and child-centered themes have emerged. The resort that we focus upon, Sugar Beach, has developed a theme based upon colonialism in a Mauritian context.

Sugar Beach – Details of Design and Organization

Sugar Beach Resort is situated in extensive grounds close to the lively public beach of Flic-en-Flac on the west of the island, away from the greatest concentration of resorts and hotels in the north. All buildings have been constructed in Mauritian colonial style, a distinct, Creole plantation-domain architectural form visible across the island, which is captured in a painting hung in the hotel lobby (Figure 10.1). Extensive research by the resort designers has ensured that great attention to architectural detail and furnishings extends throughout the enclave. Sugar Beach has 238 rooms, can accommodate over 500 guests, and employs about 520 staff.

Like many similar beach resorts, especially those based outside the West, Sugar Beach erects clear boundaries from the surrounding locale. The commanding single entrance, with its gates, security barrier and imposing, sweeping drive through an immaculately maintained lawn acts to distinguish it from the less kempt surrounding land and buildings. The walk or drive up to the reception area offers a symbolic passage from one realm to another, a sensation consolidated by walking through the lobby to the broad stairway leading down to the heart of the resort, where the visitor may behold a verdant expanse containing lawns, palm trees, pools, bars, promenade and colonial-style buildings. The large reception area from which the stairway leads is designed in the form of a sugar mill and is furnished with colonial furniture and other accoutrements. Behind the reception area is a

Figure 10.1 Painting of Creole Plantation Landscape, lobby of Sugar Beach Resort, Mauritius. Photograph by Tim Edensor, 2002.

scene-setting tapestry (made in Madagascar) depicting a tropical paradise seemingly on the point of "discovery" and the aforementioned painting of a "typical" Mauritian colonial house.

The colonial buildings are painted in white, and are wooden and colonnaded, with verandas. The largest building – housing the most luxurious accommodation – is the manor house, with its imposing staircase and large entrance hall, replete with exhibition cases and paintings. The smaller accommodation blocks, constructed in the same style, are named after most of the twenty or so sugar estates that operated during colonial times, and continue to be managed almost exclusively by the white Franco-Mauritian families who have owned them for centuries. This was, for us, immediately jarring in that the wealth gained through colonial exploitation of slaves and indentured workers forms the basis upon which these large plantations continue to produce sugar. Accordingly, the colonial theme, although intended to connote a nostalgic colonialism, still resonates with a contemporary sugar production based on the colonial pattern which remains imprinted upon Mauritius in these powerful establishments. According to the manager, the names of these still existing plantations – for instance, Belle-Vue, Mon-Tresor and Savannah – possess "romantic" and "poetic" allusions that reinforce strong historical continuities.

At this juncture, we need to further contextualize the discussion. Mauritius remains still very much a monoculture as a result of the climate's suitability for sugar production, extensive since the mid-eighteenth century, with some 90 per cent of arable land used for this crop, producing 25 per cent of Mauritian export earnings. Imported by the French to work on the plantations were large numbers of slaves from Mozambique, Tanzania and Madagascar, the ancestors of the Creole population of Mauritius, accounting for roughly 30 per cent of the population. Indians compose over 60 per cent with Franco-Mauritians being just 2 per cent of the total (Ericksen 1998). The French, who ruled the island from the early eighteenth century, ceded colonial control to the British but they were allowed to retain their language, religion and sugar estates under the terms of the treaty of Paris of 1814. Upon the abolition of slavery in 1835, Creoles refused to work on the plantations after the degradation they had suffered and indentured labor from India was imported to replace them.

Despite these inequities, the aesthetic theme of Sugar Beach continues to purvey an "authentic" and nostalgic version of Mauritian colonial sugar production. Other features include ponds used by estates to breed wildfowl and fish, a plantation bar, designed in a style reminiscent of the colonial era, and a host of smaller furnishings such as lampposts and benches. The accommodation is fitted with "authentic antiques," pieces stylistically derived from Provence, France, based on items of old furniture which, relocated to second homes, would traditionally be brightly painted. Not evidently colonial in origin, these objects are thought to resonate with the atmosphere and style of the resort. Similarly, the "kids club" at the resort is hosted in a less grandiose building, a thatched "cottage" more in keeping with traditional notions of what building forms best accommodate children's play.

The most obvious omission from the design of Sugar Beach is that there are no slave quarters adjacent to the resort and indeed no representation or mention of slavery or indentured labor, the very factors that enabled such estates to prosper. This blatant disregard for the oppressions of French and British colonialisms, the grotesque brutalities based on notions of "race," is captured in a ceremony whereby newly arrived guests to the resort are welcomed as the reenactment of a colonial marriage party proceeds to take place.

This weekly themed performance takes place on the staircase of the manor house. To the strains of the recorded "colonial overture," a groom and bride in French nineteenth-century aristocratic costume descend the staircase, and are looked upon by the marquis and marquess of the plantation, clothed in their silken finery. The music continues as the sides of the staircase are lined by smiling waiters and maids in nineteenth-century outfits performing graceful, choreographed movements with serving trays and feather dusters, giving a preview of the service that guests can expect (Figure 10.2). The performance culminates in the manager of the hotel introducing the key staff of the premises via a microphone, as he too is surrounded by costumed servants. The inference is clear: that standards of service from the colonial era will be strictly adhered to in attending to the needs and desires of hotel guests. As they watch the ceremony as ersatz partygoers at the wedding, the guests are offered tropical cocktails and snacks.

Figure 10.2 Themed performance on the steps of the Manor House, Sugar Beach Resort, Mauritius. Photograph by Uma Kothari, 2002.

What is remarkable about this display is that the cast, apart from the hotel manager, a white South African, are Mauritians of Creole or Indian descent. All plantation owners and managers would inevitably have been white Franco-Mauritians, those original proprietors permitted by the British to continue their businesses after they replaced the French as colonial governors of the island. Yet as well as the serving staff, here we have the descendants of former slaves and indentured laborers garbed in expensive European robes, a strikingly dissonant image for those familiar with the inequities of Mauritian colonialism.

These incongruities clash with other, more fastidious attempts to theme Mauritian colonialism through architecture and design. A mixed approach to producing authenticity holds sway. For instance, the production of a "colonial atmosphere" is encouraged by the playing of early New Orleans jazz, perhaps because it may evoke similar French colonial architecture and fashions by association, conjoining fantasies about graceful American-Southern living and European grandeur. Indeed, the manager of the hotel said that the desired intention of combining early jazz with architectural motifs was to create a syncretic sensation he described as a *Gone with the Wind* effect, an atmosphere, he claimed, that resulted in the effect that "when you stand on the manor house staircase you feel like Rhett Butler or Scarlett O'Hara."

A similarly relaxed approach to authenticity – or at least one that focuses upon affect rather than faithfulness to historical circumstances – is found in the uniforms of waiters, bar staff and other workers. While based on those of the Raffles Hotel in Singapore they are given more vibrant, candy-colored stripes to convey a less formal appearance and to resonate with the sounds of New Orleans jazz. According to the manager, these intertextual, inter-spatial references to luxury foster a synergy between European colonialism and the culture of the American South that reinforces theming.

These staff, if they were to truly ape the deferential manner of colonial servitude in their encounters with tourists, would induce extreme discomfort amongst the guests, who expect a kind of informal interaction with staff who are required to act in a respectful but friendly way. The crucial point here is that designers of themed space aim to produce convincing historical renditions, but rely on the evocations of popular culture – of music, film and fiction – as much as on architectural verisimilitude. Rather than reproducing material and social authenticity, these references perhaps achieve an authenticity of affect – of the feelings and atmospheres of an imaginary colonialism. The play of romantic allusions and the selective excision of uncomfortable historical realities also produces a particular kind of tourist stage, as we will now discuss.

Staging, Performing and Sensing Staged Space

Tourist resorts such as Sugar Beach are enclaves (Freitag 1994; Ayala 1991; Torres 2002), devised and policed to keep the world outside at bay. In addition to the preservation of external spatial barriers, internally, the maintenance of ordered textures, smooth surfaces and manicured vegetation – ceaselessly reproduced through the toils of hotel workers – safeguards the illusion of semiotic, material and social order. There is rarely any matter out of place, whether in the form of dirt, jarring sights, smells and sounds, potentially "threatening" persons, or "inappropriate" behavior from guests or staff. "Enclavic" tourist space such as this, contrasts with "heterogeneous" tourist space, where tourism coexists within a more complex matrix of other activities, spaces, people and sensations (Edensor 1998). The desire for otherness can be satiated within heterogeneous tourist realms although tourists may experience displacement, a frightening immersion in unfamiliar sensations amongst baffling cultural practices without any familiar reference points.

In contradistinction to the apparent otherness (for Western tourists) of less purified, multipurpose forms of tourist space, single-purpose tourist enclaves must contextualize, commodify and contain the "exotic" and the different. The paradox that such themed spaces face is that these attributes of otherness must be contextualized within a context of homely familiarity and security, within the serialized codes that inform the production of enclavic tourist space. In effect, sites such as Sugar Beach could be anywhere in the world that is hot and has a beach. As such, attempts to engender a sense of place are crucial to the desires of tourists to experience "otherness," however mild such desires might be. Accordingly, the discrete placement of signs of otherness – objects, photographs and artworks, furnishings and architectural signifiers – rarely litter space but are framed and exhibited against an uncluttered, smooth background.

At a global level, the "exotic" and the different (to Western aesthetics, identities and cultural values) is increasingly channeled into tourist, retail and media networks (Appadurai 1990) where it is domesticated, made mundane and safe by its emplacement in familiar place. Yet within these networks, notions of the "exotic" persistently coagulate around several reified themes – around spicy and rich food, erotic apparel and mores, "sensuous" cultural practices and colorful fauna and flora. Such themes have been imported and exported since colonial times (Said 1978), as certain "exotic" elements have been traded whereas other aspects of "otherness" – the incomprehensible, sophisticated, and complex – have been derided and rarely feature in shop displays, media representations or tourist sites. They are not easily themed. In domestic space, otherness is commodified and displayed within a homely context. In the realm of the other, familiarity is reproduced in international hotels, retail outlets and tourist spaces that (re)present and (re)produce "otherness" through various culinary, architectural, informational and performative techniques.

Enclavic tourist spaces such as Sugar Beach are organized to maximize the amount of time – and hence money – visitors spend within their confines. Frequently the "outside world" may be portrayed as dangerous or chaotic, playing upon tourists' already existing fears about what lurks beyond the familiar. Indeed, at Sugar Beach, a majority of visitors spend the whole of their vacation within the resort, although a minority partake in guided tours around parts of Mauritius in the mobile enclave of the air-conditioned coach. Typically, the tours focus upon "single purpose" spaces (Sibley 1988) that are similarly smooth, such as museums, tropical parks and gardens and shopping centers, sites that have be created to expand the tourist product and encourage spending. Rarely do these resort tourists visit "messier," more mixed spaces such as local beaches or markets. These "smooth" sites, dwelt in and visited by tourists, thus constitute an extensive network of highly encoded and regulated spaces that tend to minimize disruption to normative ways of strolling, gazing and purchasing, entrenching a common-sense understanding about the identity and use of tourist space. The sequence of spatial similarities according to design, surveillance, service and single-purpose activity instantiates powerful common sense spatial conventions although it can never entirely eradicate the possibility of disjunctures and disruptions, for askance perspectives might reveal peculiarities and incongruities – if the codes are read differently, when masks slip and facades are peeped around.

The contextualization of the "exotic," the endless upkeep of interrelated smooth spaces, and the instantiation of relationships between outside and inside may all be conceived as part of an assemblage of techniques used to order space in accordance with the imperatives of efficiency, calculability, predictability and familiarity akin to the McDonalidization of food provision (see Ritzer and Liska 1997). In addition, we can also consider how performative norms similarly order these tourist spaces.

Themed spaces can be considered to be particular kinds of stages upon which both tourists and tourist workers perform (Edensor 2001). We have already indicated that Sugar Beach acts as a stage for the enactment of pseudo-colonial theatrical productions, in the shape of the wedding drama outlined above. In addition to this production, the resort holds themed evenings in which different ethnicities – Indian, Creole, Chinese – are performed by musicians and dancers, connoting the "exotic" ethnic mix, the "unity-in-diversity" theme that constructs Mauritius for tourists (but also for Mauritians) as an exemplary multicultural, multiethnic "rainbow nation."

The resort is more subtly dramatized by the roles adopted by bar staff, reception staff and waiters. As Phil Crang (1997) has shown, tourist workers are trained to enact appropriate roles that fit in with their institutional setting and express attributes such as deference, correct body language, eagerness to please and (kinds of) friendliness. These "cast members" are often required to wear outfits and expressions that are harmonized with themed environments. Along with these visible workers are those who are responsible for maintaining an ordered staged environment and guide visitors towards notions of "appropriate" conduct and along preferred routes. These "stage-managers," "directors" and "choreographers" typically organize and maintain spatial norms, synchronize the activities of events, assist tourists in performing dances and attaining sporting techniques, and facilitate the smooth running of equipment, routines and activities throughout the resort.

Besides the trained performances of staff, tourists themselves adopt a range of conventional roles in familiar tourist space. Tourism is often conceptualized as extraordinary, being marked against the habitual, routinized world of work and home. However, commercial strategies have fostered highly predictable tourist routines, habits and dispositions so that most forms of tourism are replete with conventions about what kinds of activities to undertake in particular kinds of space. Through practising and experiencing space as part of a wider tourist matrix, modes of walking, listening, gleaning information, relaxing and socializing reveal persistent and regular forms of bodily hexis and embodied praxes which are consistently reproduced. As an immersed practice, the accumulation of repetitive events becomes sedimented in the body to condense an unreflexive sense of being in place. Accordingly, tourist stages are organized to accommodate and perpetuate these performative conventions, and a particular sense of tourist place is consolidated through the instantiation of routine, and the ways in which individual paths and habits coincide with those of others. Reinforced by the suggestions of guide-books and guides, and the organization of activity in resorts, such norms are persistent. Desires to visit particular sites, to learn something about the culture visited, to develop the self, to pamper the body, to restore health, are all catered for by an infrastructure of familiar amenities comprising tour operators, health, sports and beauty facilities, shops, banks and information services. Similarly, a particular kind of conviviality is collectively produced by tourists and tourist workers and managers which relies upon distinct forms of social and material comfort. The fostering of a sense of intimacy and enclosure within a bounded resort enables the familiar performance of forms of sociability and bodily comportment within the context of the peculiarly temporary community that is germane to tourism.

Such tourist spaces are akin to "taskscapes" (Ingold and Kurttila 2000), usually identified as those everyday spaces that are fostered by the ways in which habits and habitation recreate local and domestic space and render it comfortable and homely. Mundane maneuvers and modes of dwelling are unreflexively carried out in such spaces, constituting a practical knowledge of what to do and how to behave. Habituated bodily dispositions emerge out of these routine practices, becoming embedded over time to produce a sort of touristic habitus (Bourdieu 1984). Yet such habits require well-ordered environments if they are to persist, and the spatial constraints and opportunities which inhere in enclavic tourist spaces facilitate the reproduction of conventional tourist performances.

To be more specific, if space is understood as "a concrete and sensuous con-catenation of material forces" (Wylie 2002: 251), performance in familiar tourist space relies upon specific materialities and the ways in which embodied subjects physically interact with space and objects. The surfaces, textures, temperatures, atmospheres, smells, sounds, contours, gradients and pathways of places encourage humans – limited and advantaged by their normative physical abilities – to follow particular courses of action, developing a practical orientation and a multisensory apprehension of place and space. Again this sensual understanding of place is not "natural" but enmeshed within learnt apprehensions and cultural techniques of discernment. Smooth tourist space is devised to accord with familiar and comfortable sensual experiences, and we can identify the serial affordances which are distributed through an organised touristic network. International tourism thus produces ways of dwelling within very similar taskscapes, producing an extended sense of place. The production of these spatial affordances is part of the architectural development of resort tourism, and increasingly informs the design of themed space (Pine and Gilmore 1999).

Tourism is part of the redistribution of sensory experience, which is distributed more widely across space. Richard Sennett (1994) has argued that, in an urban context, the reduction of diversity, disjuncture, confrontation and discomfort can lead to a reduced public realm, a dearth of social interaction and the desensitization of the body. Tourism certainly reproduces the conditions that Sennett identifies but we would argue that, too often, tourist theory has similarly proffered dystopian notions about how this inevitably leads to anomie and alienation, an impoverished and asocial experience. This dim view about tourist identity, however, neglects the predictable pleasures of order and comfort that enclavic tourist resorts are adept at providing. If smooth space were to colonize all social space then such arguments might be more resonant but we should not deny the possibility that such sites may produce utopian sentiments, comfortable sensations and wellbeing, accommodate modes of conviviality and achieve a sense of temporary community (Edensor 2003). Moreover, it is important to stress that architectural and spatial elements can never wholly condition sensuality, fantasy and affect, or enforce social conformity, which may be disrupted by those refusing to accord with normative values and roles. Such conventions may be transgressed by those who may drink to excess, behave without due seriousness during shows and themed occasions, behave rudely, speak too loudly and be improperly dressed.

Reconsidering Themed Spaces

Having identified some of the key ingredients – performative, material and archi-tectural – that constitute the themed, enclavic tourist space of Sugar Beach, we will now broaden our exploration to look critically at the theoretical depictions of themed spaces. We have already pointed out the discontinuities, contradictions and ambiguities in the presentation of the specific theme of Mauritian colonialism offered at Sugar Beach. We argue that the disjunctures highlighted above reveal more broadly that themed spaces are less effective than their critics assume in presenting a seamless, commodified environment whose sign-laden ideologies and semiotics channel visitors' understanding and practice along preferred lines, suggesting that they are helpless victims of manufactured meanings. Instead, the meanings and effects of themed spaces are replete with discordances and accom-modations with the wider spatial and cultural context within which they are situated, whether conceived as local, regional, national or global. Moreover, themed spaces, like everywhere else, are complex places that fold into their social and cultural textures multiple influences and energies from outside. They are therefore inevitably replete with a host of interspatial reference points from elsewhere. Themed spaces are always situated at the center of numerous networks comprised of flows of images, ideas, people, money and social practices that sustain them but also challenge their coherence as illusory bounded spaces, are always enmeshed within a "progressive sense of place" (Massey 1993).

Generalized accounts of themed spaces have tended to read their characteristics via conceptual apparatuses which relate to rather specific exemplars such as

A Mauritian Themed Resort

Disneyland or Las Vegas. Analysts such as Sorkin (1992), Eco (1986) and Gottdiener (1997) foreground an analysis based upon the semiotic construction of space and the ways in which usually hegemonic meanings are encoded into built forms. Such accounts suggest that users of themed spaces are largely unable to resist the ideological signs designed into places, are unable to defer, bypass, deconstruct, use and read these encodings differently irrespective of the various dispositions or cultural understandings they bring with them. Such sites may indeed be read in accordance with preferred meanings, but they may also be subject to negotiated or resistant meanings (Hall 1981), along with other potential interpretations. But equally importantly, this emphasis on semiotic fixity neglects the diverse social activities and relationships, habits and pleasures of visitors, and all the cultural baggage that visitors bring to sites. It also ignores the spatial materialities and affordances that accommodate and stimulate tourist performance. Such accounts suggest that tourists purposively read space when, conversely, interpretations of space are more commonly carried out in a distracted state.

This critique does not imply that the ideological or repressive effects of highly managed and encoded space are benign, or that the imposition of the preferred meanings of corporate planners cannot restrict spatial use and meaning. Yet the perceived threat to "democracy" alluded to by Sorkin, or the encoding of urban space in ways that reproduce that found in themed space (Zukin 1995) appear to emerge out of overdrawn critiques. By using "typical" models as points of embark-ation from which to theorize, these accounts implicitly postulate that themed spaces are inevitably signs of an expanding spatial homogeneity, a dystopian notion that radically decontextualizes space, effacing the cultural contexts under which themes are identified and materialized. And as Kelsall (2003) shows, the supposedly postmodern, sign-laden characteristics of these spaces have been a feature of pleasure gardens and carnivalesque spaces since the nineteenth century.

Themed spaces have all too often been conceived as separate, *fake* spaces detached from surrounding "real" space. Implicitly suggested in these accounts is an "authenticity" that lies elsewhere – in the past, outside the West, in the "public" sphere – an idea which preoccupies western theorists and others. The bounded characteristics of the enclave are often literally taken to mean that such sites are entirely disconnected from the world around when, like all other places, they are linked in multiple and changing ways. Themed resorts, for instance, import goods and services, are often subsidiaries of transnational corporations, and are linked through transport, power and water and other amenities and services to surround-ing locales. They are also workplaces – places to routinely commute to for local workers, which often employ managers from elsewhere. For tourists, as we have mentioned, such sites are part of a much bigger spatial matrix of hotels, attractions and transport networks and depend upon and enfold widely circulating information and communication practices (for instance, postcards and telephone calls home) into their constitution. They are thus hardly detached from the outside, but are constellations within numerous cultural and social networks and thus utterly linked to localities and other spaces.

Arjun Appadurai (1990) has sketched out the ways in which globalization can be conceived as composed of flows of money, technology, ideas, people and media. All these flows are pertinent to tourism; indeed, the flow of people across the world includes the huge movement of tourists. Here, however, we want to focus upon the particularly apposite notion of mediascapes to exemplify how places are located within spatial networks which link them with other places and times. At one level, themed spaces draw upon a range of images and narratives from other times and places in the constitution of place. They are thus inevitably intertextual and interspatial, never as enclavic as designers may wish. Themed spaces organize the past, present and future in heterodox ways, producing architectural signifiers, memories and representations as a shifting historical and geographical melange. The flows of tourist imagery and fantasy that constellate at Sugar Beach mingle the local, the national and the global, the generic and the specific, the familiar and the "exotic" (and different). So it is that colonial Mauritius can be presented as a period of grace and leisure, rather than one of severe exploitation and brutality. The resources of imagery and fiction from far and wide mean that familiar tropes of a colonialism – one not necessarily attached to place – can be repackaged to construct a benign fantasy that melds vague ideas about romance, fashion, quiescent service and luxury, ingredients that can be exquisitely mapped onto a tourist imaginary in search of tropical pleasures. As Edward Said (2003: 3) writes, this is part of a "soft-core version" of colonialism that includes "Raj revivalism, the cult of Merchant Ivory and interminable documentaries, coffee-table books, fashion accessories." This intertextual effect, composed out of numerous Western cultural forms, means that Western tourists are able to draw upon the *Gone with the Wind* allusions, resonances conjured up by the "age of jazz" and costume dramas, and these may be melded with other media memories represented in heritage films, television dramas, fashion shoots or pictures in tourist brochures and holiday programmes. Tourist space is infested with references to popular culture, deliberately or not, so it is invariably intertextual in specific ways.

The constitution of Sugar Beach and other similar sites may suggest the "non-places" described by Marc Augé (1995), which he distinguishes from "anthropological" places, which are grounded in specific common-sense histories and socialities. The infusion of images and ideas from elsewhere, seemingly irrespective of local context, apparently reflects a place that could be anywhere. Yet as Augé also insists, both modes of space invade each other, so that elements of place colonize the apparent placelessness of the themed site. As we have shown, the design specifics of Sugar Beach both refer to local architectural forms but also include features brought from elsewhere.

The multiple associations and flows that constitute place in ongoing ways can also be identified in the Mauritian-ness of Sugar Beach, which is (also) strongly shaped by its local context. It initially seems peculiar that the colonial theme could be devised, even allowed, by Mauritians but its meaning and consumption amongst Mauritians is more ambivalent than we might expect. Any celebration of colonialism seems unlikely in a country that was, until 1968, a colony of the U.K. and has witnessed horrific exploitation through slavery and indentured labour, subsequent colonial administrative domination and persistent patterns of inequality. However, if we consider that human history on Mauritius is a mere 400 years old, and has always been colonial (right from the start) other historical themes are not immediately evident – at least not those that will not disrupt the relaxation of tourists. As a Mauritian worker replied when we asked whether he felt indignant about the presentation of colonialism at Sugar Beach, "But what else can we gain pride from?."

The policy that keeps tourists away from non-tourist areas of the country for fear of "cultural problems" – and the fear of tourists towards venturing outside the enclave – means that the experience of cultural difference which tourists desire must be recreated in touristic locations. A working version of national identity is transmitted to outsiders that asserts that Mauritius is a shining example of unity in diversity, an exemplary mix of tension-free ethnicities, religions and traditions. Although this idealistic version is mirrored in attempts at nation building by a cultural elite, Mauritians are painfully aware of the underlying tension between groups, emerging out of the inter-ethnic inequalities in employment, housing and education. This tension spilled over into large-scale riots in 1999 to tarnish the reputation for harmony. Nevertheless, attempts to find "common denominators" that act to build a sense of collective national identity persist (Ericksen 1998). Colonialism here serves as one such common denominator. Like most such convergent symbols, it is constructed differently by groups who were positioned differently within the colonial project. For instance, many Creoles wanted British rule to continue, fearing that they would be dominated by the Indian majority and would lose a mooted favorite status.

In a contrary fashion, Mauritius tries hard to present itself as a modern nation that has overcome its harsh colonial legacy, pointing to its global profile in "modern" spheres such as information technology, the export processing of clothing as well as tourism (Kothari and Nababasing 1996, 2000). Yet these global aspirations have only been achieved since the demise of colonial rule, a regime which hindered development and ensured that Mauritius languished in poverty at the end of British colonial rule in 1968. Accordingly, there is undoubtedly a contradiction, a tension in the nostalgic versions of colonialism and the envisioning of a nation which has striven to overcome the colonial legacy.

However, rather than foregrounding these contradictory elements, we might consider the themed production at Sugar Beach to be a depiction of the way colonialism *might* have turned out, a reclaiming and reinterpretation of colonial history that is positive, devoid of the real inequalities. This is a fantasy colonialism that might serve as a common denominator. Here colonialism is productive of a benign, friendly atmosphere exactly akin to the kinds of service and convivialities produced by contemporary resort tourism. In postulating a different past, present and future, Sugar Beach reconfigures spaces and histories to suggest there could have been a utopian colonial society – one in which there were Creole marquises and marquesses, mutual respect between plantation owners, managers and workers, a sharing of graceful behavior and fine costumes amongst ethnic groups and classes. The moans and songs of slaves and indentured laborers are replaced by the soft thud of ball on racket, the swish of the palm trees and the strains of hotel muzak.

The construction of this faux-colonial space depends upon the telescoping of historically disparate colonial elements – besides the colonial geographies of the island's existing sugar plantations, there is a colonial style bar, ponds for fishing, a sugar mill and a host of smaller touches in décor and furnishings. This collapsing together of distinct spaces blurs the disparate periods and local contexts in which colonial plantation life was enacted and lived. Perhaps more importantly, the reconfiguring of Mauritian history at Sugar Beach exists amongst a growing number of other postcolonial sites where a reflexive reworking of national history and identity are being undertaken. In this wider context, romantic, themed colonialism does not dominate but augments and clashes with other versions articulated in exhibitions, literature, alternative histories and myths. There is a proliferation of stories about colonialism, a reappropriation of the past that allows for many versions from various perspectives. For instance, somewhat ironically, the mountainous promontory of Le Morne dominates the view from the resort to the south. As its name implies, this is one of the most tragic sites in Mauritius, for myths surround the site about how escaping slaves, familiar only with the confined space of the plantation, were surprised that their dash for freedom was thwarted by the huge cliffs that revealed that they were trapped on a small island. With slave-masters in pursuit, they are believed to have hurled themselves to their death from these cliffs.

Despite the evils of colonialism, the strands of colonial re-presentation highlight how homes, locales and nations are all configurations of a "multiplicity of histories all in the process of being made" (Massey 2000: 229). The interweaving versions of colonialism in Mauritius simultaneously evoke attempts to fix identity in time and space, and mix ideas about authenticity and nostalgia, "fact" and "fiction." This mingling of pasts and futures is a familiar trope within nation-building attempts (Bhabha 1990) but is increasingly locally and globally redistributed through popular cultural forms and practices (Edensor 2002). Sugar Beach is a definitively Mauritian space that does not conjure up a fixed, national essence but is contingently produced out of a series of assorted, often changing elements. This situatedness rebukes notions of the universal placelessness and hyperreality of themed spaces, highlighting instead how locality here may be conceived as amidst a juncture of global tourist flows, including Mauritian reconfigurations of history, domestic and foreign investment, architectural and design technologies and wider discourses and representations about colonialism.

Conclusion

We certainly do not wish to suggest that colonialism in Mauritius was in any sense benign, and we disassociate ourselves from recent revisionist notions that colonial projects should be positively conceived because they progressively modernized and ordered chaotic parts of the world (for example, see Ferguson 2003). Initially, we were horrified when we first visited Sugar Beach and wondered what other notorious historical periods might be themed. The Spanish inquisition perhaps or the Holocaust? Perhaps the revisionism that has downplayed the genocide, deprivation and racism that typified many colonial adventures is partly responsible for the seemingly uncontroversial reception of the colonial theme. Yet it was clear that neither Mauritian workers nor tourists at the resort appeared to feel much outrage at this romantic, nostalgic production.

A critical engagement with history is anathema to the tourist quest for pleasure, but we wanted to explore why this rosy-hued colonial theming seemed to ruffle so few feathers. We refute simplistic notions that tourists are unreflexive dupes under the sway of stage managers, choreographers and directors. Rather, there is a willing suspension of critical faculties and the adoption of a disposition that foregrounds specific forms of pleasure generic to the resort holiday. The most crucial way in which space is produced at Sugar Beach is the serial manufacture of affordances and surfaces, the smooth spaces and the enclavic-maintaining boundaries that render the resort a home from home, a familiar kind of habitable space. The way which tourists interpret the colonial theme is thus strongly shaped by these known spatial parameters. They are already habituated to the kinds of unreflexive performances that such spatial order facilitates and are also informed by ideas about what constitutes "appropriate" performance in specific spatial contexts. Thematic encodings are expected but not in ways that disrupt an immersion in comfort and relaxation, and encounters with otherness are similarly required to be mild. We have argued that the production of colonial Mauritius at Sugar Beach chimes with the tourist values of graceful setting, romantic allusion and high standards of service. Moreover, this romantic colonialism can never be detached from a host of other popular narratives, images and commodities that flow across the world to produce a constellation of related sentiments and affects.

We have also contended that themed and enclavic resorts are not non-places but like all other places are constituted out of the ceaseless flows that center upon and flow through them. Accordingly, we have refuted simplistic notions of themed space as purely semiotic because of their evident material affects, but also because there is an ongoing attempt to organize the multiple constituents – the conjunctions of history, economic policies and ventures, tourist and working practices, local and national identities, ideas, commodities and images – which constellate around the becoming of place. In unique ways, themed spaces bring together familiarity and difference, home and abroad, past and present, and desires for order and escape. They are far more "messy" spaces than they may first appear, depending upon much maintenance work to ensure their coherence for tourists. Yet a melange of historical references, relationships with elsewhere, and imagined states and materialities feed into the multiple constitution of place that facilitates varied and ambivalent readings.

References

Appadurai, A. (1990), "Disjuncture and Difference in the Global Cultural Economy", in Featherstone, M. (ed.), *Global Culture*, London: Sage.

Augé, M. (1995), *Non-Places: Introduction to an Anthropology of Supermodernity*, London: Verso.

Ayala, H. (1991), "Resort Hotel Landscapes as an International Megatrend", *Annals of Tourism Research*, 18: 568–87.

Bhabha, H. (ed.) (1990), *Nation and Narration*, London: Routledge.

Bourdieu, P. (1984), *Distinction*, London: Routledge.

Crang, P. (1997), "Performing the Tourist Product", in Rojek, C. and Urry, J. (eds), *Touring Cultures: Transformations of Travel and Theory*, London: Routledge.

Eco, U. (1986), *Travels in Hyper-Reality*, London: Picador.

Edensor, T. (1998), *Tourists at the Taj*, London: Routledge.

Edensor, T. (2001), "Performing Tourism, Staging Tourism: (re)producing tourist space and practice", *Tourist Studies*, 1: 59–82.

Edensor, T. (2002), *National Identity, Popular Culture and Everyday Life*, Oxford: Berg.

Edensor, T. (2003), "Sensing Tourism", in Minca, C. and Oakes, T. (eds), *Tourism and the Paradox of Modernity*, Minneapolis: University of Minnesota Press.

Eriksen, T. (1998), *Common Denominators: Ethnicity, Nation-Building and Compromise in Mauritius*, Oxford: Berg.

Ferguson, N. (2003), *Empire: How Britain Made the Modern World*, Harmondsworth: Penguin.

Freitag, T. (1994), "Enclave Tourist Development: for Whom the Benefits Roll?", *Annals of Tourism Research*, 21: 538–54.

Gottdiener, M. (1997), *The Theming of America: Dreams, Visions and Commercial Spaces,* Oxford: Westview Press.

Hall, S. (1981), "Encoding/Decoding in Television Discourse", in Hall, S. (ed.), *Culture, Media, Language*, London: Hutchinson.

Ingold, T. and Kurttila, T. (2000), "Perceiving the Environment in Finnish Lapland", *Body and Society*, 3–4: 6.

Kelsall, G. (2003), *The Development, Production and Consumption of the Theme Park as Multiple Landscape: A Case Study of Alton Towers, Staffordshire*, University of Staffordshire unpublished thesis.

Kothari, U. and Nababsing, V. (eds) (1996), *Gender and Industrialisation: Mauritius, Bangladesh and Sri Lanka,* Mauritius: Editions de L'Océan Indien.

Kothari, U. and Nababsing, V. (eds) (2000), *New Industrial Strategies: Gender, Migrant Labour and the Export Processing Zone*, Mauritius: Mauritian Research Council.

Massey, D. (1993), "Power-geometry and a Progressive Sense of Place", in Bird, J., Curtis, B., Putnam, T., Roberson, G. and Tickner, L. (eds), *Mapping the Futures*, London: Routledge.

Massey, D. (2000), "Travelling Thoughts", in Gilroy, P., Grossberg, L. and McRobbie, A. (eds), *Without Guarantees: In Honour of Stuart Hall*, London: Verso.

Naipaul, V. S. (1973), *The Overcrowded Barracoon*, Harmondsworth: Penguin.

Pine, J. and Gilmore, J. (1999), *The Experience Economy*, Boston: Harvard Business School Press.

Ritzer, G. and Liska, A. (1997), "'McDisneyization' and 'Post-tourism': Complementary Perspectives on Contemporary Tourism", in Rojek, C. and Urry, J. (eds), *Touring Cultures: Transformations of Travel and Theory*, London: Routledge.

Said, E. (1978), *Orientalism*, London: Routledge.

Said, E. (2003), "Always on top", *London Review of Books*, 25(6): 3–6.

Sennett, R. (1973), *The Uses of Disorder*, Harmondsworth: Penguin.

Sennett, R. (1994), *Flesh and Stone*, London: Faber.

Sibley, D. (1988), "Survey 13: purification of space", *Environment and Planning D: Society and Space*, 6: 409–21.

Sorkin, M. (1992), "See you in Disneyland", in Sorkin, M. (ed.), *Variations on a Theme Park*, New York: Noonday Press.

Torres, R. (2002), "Cancun's Tourism Development from a Fordist Spectrum of Analysis", *Tourist Studies*, 2(1): 87–116.

Wylie, J. (2002), "Becoming-icy: Scott and Amundsen's South Polar Voyages, 1910–1913", *Cultural Geographies*, 9: 249–65.

Zukin, S. (1995), *The Culture of Cities*, Oxford: Blackwell.

–11–

Doing it Right: Postwar Honeymoon Resorts in the Pocono Mountains

Barbara Penner

> I'm not sneering at sex. It's necessary and it doesn't have to be ugly. But it always has to be managed. Making it glamorous is a billion-dollar industry and it costs every cent of it.
>
> Chandler, *The Long Good-bye* (1953: 384)

My fascination with honeymoon hotels has been with me a long time; from childhood, in fact, as I grew up 15 minutes away from "the honeymoon capital of the world," Niagara Falls. In the 1970s the Falls were a beautiful but boring sight we visited only when relatives came to town. Far more bizarre and interesting to me were the honeymoon motels stretching for miles down a forlorn strip called Lundy's Lane, their neon signs advertising cheap room rates and heart-shaped tubs.

When I began to study architectural history, my childhood curiosity was transformed into a more serious interest, particularly upon realizing that Niagara Falls was not the only place in North America specializing in the domestic honeymoon business. Nor was it the most successful. In 1969, while 22,000 newlyweds honeymooned in Niagara, a remarkable 115,000 honeymooned in the Pocono Mountains in northeastern Pennsylvania (Shields 1991: 150; Honeymoon Havens 1969: 90). By the early 1970s, twenty-eight Pocono "love nests" drew close to 15 per cent of America's billion dollar honeymoon industry between them, handily beating out other romantic destinations like the Caribbean, Las Vegas and Miami (Seligson 1973: 243).

Honeymooning was – and continues to be – a lucrative and very visible part of America's domestic tourist industry. On this basis alone, a study of Pocono honeymoon resorts certainly seems warranted. With one recent exception, however, few academics have attempted to analyse them seriously (Bulcroft Smeins and Bulcroft 1999). To be sure, as an academic, when faced with the shag carpets and heart-shaped tubs that define Pocono honeymoon suites, it is difficult to know where and how to begin. Perhaps the one established aesthetic category we have to work with is "kitsch" or even "pornokitsch" to borrow Gilles Dorfles's phrase. What seems inadequate about this term is that, to most theorists, kitsch necessarily represents the falsification of sentiment. For example, meditating on the relationship that exists between mass tourism and kitsch, Dorfles states: "the relationship between the tourist and the environment that surrounds him is only rarely genuine, and it is this veil of falseness, imitation and admiring sentimentality that makes the world, as it appears the tourist, vomit kitsch all over itself" (Dorfles 1969: 154).

There is something odd about Dorfles' belief that genuine feeling cannot exist in the vulgarity of kitsch environment, as if emotion can only be experienced authentically in environments of good taste. Quite apart from the philosophical or sociological objections one might make to this assertion, it certainly does not tally with the way Pocono honeymoon suites were understood by the entrepreneurs who built them or the newlyweds who flocked to them. In fact, both Pocono entrepreneurs and honeymooners worked from the opposite premise: they believed that the honeymoon suites' fantastic stage-set décor would actually help newlyweds to express themselves to each other, emotionally and sexually. Through their designs and their advertising, the suites were continually positioned as being ideal settings for newlywed sex and self-revelation and held out to young couples the promise of starting marriage off "right." Although it is doubtful that they always delivered, it was largely this promise that drew honeymooners to the Poconos in increasing numbers between the 1940s and the 1970s.

You are Entering the Land of Love

The honeymoon suite has a long, if forgotten history in America. The precursors to honeymoon suites, bridal chambers, first appeared in the northern U.S. in the 1840s: by the 1850s they were a central feature of palace steamboats plying the Great Lakes and the Hudson River, and of the vast luxury hotels then springing up in northern city centers. When an English visitor to America, Charles Weld, was permitted to peek at the bridal chambers aboard the *Western World* steamboat in 1855, he was astounded by their "regal splendour." He wrote:

> The beds [in the bridal-chambers] are covered with white satin, trimmed with gold lace: painted Cupids are suspended from the ceiling; the toilet furniture is of the finest china; . . . the chairs and sofas are covered with the richest velvet; the carpets are of the softest pile; and walls display beautiful flower design. (Weld 1855: 184)

Expensive and exclusive, the bridal chamber – like the romantic honeymoon itself – remained a sign of privilege throughout the nineteenth century (Penner 2003). Its democratization really only began in the twentieth century: just as the nineteenth-century bridal chamber was enabled by the rise of the railroad, the steamship and middle-class tourism, the twentieth-century honeymoon suite was enabled by the motor car, the highway system and mass tourism.

At first glance, the Pocono Mountains is not an obvious destination for romance tourism; typically described as "scenic" with woodlands and rolling hills, it lacks the sublime natural features that have historically attracted honeymooners to rival destinations like Niagara or Yosemite. Ultimately, a key factor in the area's success was its accessibility. Located a few hours drive from New York, Washington and Philadelphia, it was an ideal getaway spot for young couples who could not afford to fly or to take a long vacation (Squeri 2002: 169–206). Canny entrepreneurs, sensing an opportunity, began to target honeymooners early on.

The first dedicated newlywed resort in the Poconos, The Farm on the Hill, started operating in the early 1940s and, spurred on by the postwar marriage boom, the region's honeymoon industry took off (The Poconos 1964: 213; Couple's Country 1970: 219, 225). By the end of the 1950s, would-be Pocono honey-mooners could choose from a wide variety of boarding houses, cottage colonies, ranches or resorts. Some of these establishments catered exclusively for newly-weds, others did not; some were folksy and homelike in character, others were glitzy and exotic. As *Bride's Magazine*, which regularly promoted the joys of a Pocono honeymoon, remarked at the end of the 1950s: "The door you're ushered through may remind you of a Victorian homestead, a mountain ranch or a near-Neapolitan Villa" (Your Honeymoon 1959: 201).

During the 1950s and first half of the 1960s, it was the "hominess" and "com-fort" of these honeymoon retreats that articles and advertisements tended to stress. Honeymoon cottages replicated the architecture of suburban homes, complete with picture windows, porches, sitting rooms and fireplaces. As such, they were pro-moted as being ideal places for the newlywed pair to practice being married, house-keeping and entertaining. Of the cottage plan, *Bride's Magazine* enthused: "One of the nicest things . . . is that it gives you the feeling of being a hostess in your own home . . ." (Your Honeymoon 1959: 201). A typical advertisement for Honeymoon Colony featured the testimony of the Clarks who told readers that they began to "feel married" in the privacy of their cottage: "Betty never remembers to turn off lights. Bob hangs clothes on every available doorknob." To signal their successful initiation married coupledom, the Clarks hosted a farewell party in their cottage at the end of their stay (advertisement for The Honeymoon Colony 1959: 238–9).

Over the course of the 1960s, however, there was a noticeable shift from hominess and companionability to hedonism and pleasure. In resorts like Pocono Gardens Lodge, Penn Hills, Honeymoon Haven, and Cove Haven, the familiar iconography of the Pocono honeymoon suite – sunken baths, round beds, and mirrors – appeared and was constantly elaborated. In addition to these features, each resort developed one or two of its own special gimmicks. At Mount Airy Lodge, the mere touch of a button would bathe the suite's massive bed in "lavender

Figure 11.1 Promotional material for Honeymoon Haven, 1967. Collection of the author.

light." At Honeymoon Haven, every time a cottage door was opened, chimes played out "Here comes the bride" (Honeymoon Havens 1969: 90).

From the outside, however, little had changed. Far from looking like places dedicated to adult love, resorts like Cove Haven or Honeymoon Haven still resembled suburban housing tracts or even summer camps, with clusters of small cottages, parking lots, a central hall, playing fields, volleyball courts, and swimming pools (Figure 11.1). The true nature of the resorts was only revealed through a series of exterior clues. Clue number one: entering the property at Cove Haven, one passed a large sign announcing, "You are Entering the Land of Love." Clue number two: the concrete pools were shaped like hearts. Revealing though these clues were, they may not necessarily have prepared guests for what lay inside. Not all Poconos honeymoon suites were the same, but their designs tended to be characterized by three main elements: decorative excess, variation in room levels, and prominent beds and baths.

Wastrel Spaces

By the mid-to-late 1960s, Pocono honeymoon suites were a riot of color, with crimsons, lavenders, blues, and pinks splashed liberally throughout. Soft surfaces abounded – wall-to-wall or wraparound carpeting, velvet curtains, and satin bedspreads – with every material appearing inches thick. Shapes were curvy, beds were round, tubs were heart shaped. For those who were overwhelmed by the profusion of color, textures and soft surfaces, there was little relief: windows were usually guarded with curtains and the gaze was continually returned into the room through a variety of reflective surfaces, floor-to-ceiling mirrors on the walls and, later, the ceiling. By these means, the suite constantly reinforced its own interiority, amplifying its Rococo effects.

The impression of abundance, I would argue, was precisely the desired effect of the later honeymoon suites. To quote the architecture critic, Mary Josephson: "[Their surface] becomes a medium for visceral and tactile fulfilment, for what might be called a 'pornography of comfort'" (Josephson 1971: 109). Indeed, as Josephson suggests, such spaces seem unabashedly infantile, appealing not to the mind, but to the body: to touch, above all, but also to the appetite. Like the famed Pocono all-inclusive meal where "seconds and thirds are encouraged," the honeymoon suite invoked the image of the unrestrained body, through its tacit invitation to feel, to stroke, to recline onto, to sink into, to grasp, to indulge, to consume.

Seeing such places in terms of an indecent, even grotesque, physicality, is the only way in which we can understand the revulsion critics feel for them. (Why else, for instance, does Dorfles refer to kitsch "vomiting all over itself?") Such comments suggest an insatiable body that does not know when to stop, gorging itself well beyond the limits of its hunger. Rather than seeing this invocation to consume as repulsive, however, we should recall that there is a long tradition that connects overindulgence to festivities. Indeed, excess defines celebrations to a large extent. As Leigh Eric Schmidt remarks in his brilliant study of American holidays: "A common feature of festivity is to overindulge, to eat, drink, or spend to excess, lavishly to use up resources otherwise diligently saved . . . In other words, festive behavior is built in large part on wastrel prodigality, on surplus and abundance, on conspicuous consumption" (Schmidt 1995: 8).

Weddings have been – and continue to be – one of the most profligate of all celebrations. The bride wears a costly white gown and guests are invited to dress up, drink, feast and dance. Afterwards, in a veil of publicly sanctioned secrecy, the newlyweds sneak off for their honeymoon, billed as a "once-in-a-lifetime" trip. Most honeymooners want to spend that trip in an environment which, like the wedding cake or bridal gown, is sumptuous and spectacular. And the Pocono honeymoon suite obliged in all respects. It was a masterpiece of wastrel prodigality, stuffed with the latest technological gadgets (televisions, hi fi, "professional" hair dryers and sun lamps), gargantuan furniture (12 ft. round beds and 9 ft. round baths), as well as design features so impractical as to be laugh-out-loud absurd (bathrooms with wall-to-wall carpeting and crystal chandeliers).

No doubt a major part of the suite's attraction was that these were features that most couples were unlikely to have had (or, in some cases, would not have been able to afford) in their own homes, thus clearly marking it out as a "special" environment. Nonetheless, recognizing the importance of excess, even of flagrant uselessness, to honeymooners does not alone explain why the suite's iconography developed in the specific way it did between the 1950s and the 1970s. To put it another way: how do we explain the shift from the Colonial bed to the "crown and veiled," or the replacement of the round sunken tub by the crimson heart-shaped one?

Setting the Stage

While, practically speaking, honeymoon suites were private (inward-looking and occasionally windowless), they were also decidedly theatrical, devoted to display and to looking. Many suites or cottages, for instance, were split-level; all moved their occupants up or down to an almost exhausting degree. As the journalist Marcia Seligson observed in the early 1970s: "Everything . . . is either sunken or raised – beds on platforms, bathtubs sunken. You step up to the toilet or down to the closet, down to the fireplace, up to the shower" (Seligson, 1973: 247). Most significant, in the particular suite that Seligson described, the living room over-looked the bed, a massive edifice she dubbed "The Shrine." In these suites, prominent features like baths or beds could be seen before they could be approached and entered, a tactic that still defines honeymoon suites today: for instance, the "world famous" Champagne Tower at Caesars Cove Haven, a 7 ft. tall perspex jacuzzi shaped like a champagne glass, visually dominates the room yet the means of entering it is discretely tucked away.

This design strategy – of moving guests up and down – was commonly used in 1950s and 1960s resort hotels to create a sense of drama and excitement. In particular, it was the signature trademark of the premiere resort architect of the day, Morris Lapidus. In his Fontainebleau Hotel, built in 1954 in Miami Beach, there was a famed staircase that went nowhere, its sole purpose being to allow guests to ascend or descend in what Lapidus called "a grand manner" (Lapidus 1996: 286). Lapidus quite consciously saw the role of his architecture to make people feel as if they were on stage. As he noted:

> People love to feel as if they are on stage when travelling or stopping at an elegant hotel. In most hotels that I designed, I have arranged the levels so that when guests enter the restaurant they find themselves at the top of a short flight of stairs in a position to see and be seen . . . In the Fontainebleau guests go up three steps to arrive at the platform, walk out onto the platform, and then go down three steps. (Lapidus 1996: 286)

Lapidus made clear that his up-platform-down strategy was influenced by the movies. He explicitly positioned himself as a "set designer" on the Fontainebleau project and cited Busby Berkeley films and early musicals as his design inspiration.

Considering the design of Pocono honeymoon suites during this period, it is evident that they too were being conceived of and constructed like Hollywood stage sets. Although some of the glitzier resorts like Mount Airy Lodge made use of the up-platform-down strategy in their public spaces, most pushed this tactic to the limit within the honeymoon suites themselves. With their multi-level viewing platforms and carefully controlled sightlines, they effectively internalized the "see and be seen" dynamic that Lapidus established in the Fontainebleau's lobby and restaurant. But, in place of the guest's body, it appeared here to be the suite's props that were being framed and that became objects of the gaze.

Although these props might have consisted of oversized and dramatically spotlit beds or bathtubs, it was the latter that were emphasized in most suites. Indeed, from the late 1950 onwards, the majority of Pocono resorts offered fancy baths of one sort or another: Strickland's Mountain Inn & Cottages featured "Hollywood tubs;" Merry Hill Lodge and Cottages, a "Mosaic-tiled ROMAN bath with sunken tub;" and Pocono Gardens Lodge, a spectacular pink Roman sunken tub. As if to further underscore the hedonism of the suites, the bathtubs in this period were over-whelming Roman in theme, although this was Rome as visualized in *Spartacus*, *Cleopatra*, and *Ben-Hur*. No doubt resort owners realized, as Lapidus himself did, that their clients' cultural references came "not from school, nor from their travels, but from the movies, the cinema . . ." (Friedman 2000: 44).

Without doubt, however, the Pocono water feature that receives the most attention today is the heart-shaped bath. Although fairly common by the 1970s, it was first invented in the mid-1960s by the co-owner of Cove Haven, the former plumbing contractor-turned-hotelier, Morris Wilkins. Discussing the lure of the heart-shaped tub, Wilkins told one interviewer: "each [bath] costs over 3,000 dollars to build, but it's worth it. Couples call us for reservations and don't even care what kind of accommodation they get, as long as they get the big bath" (Seligson 1973: 247). Wilkins attributed the popularity of baths to 1930s Holly-wood films: perhaps, like Lapidus, he was thinking of Busby Berkeley films such as *Footlight Parade* (1933) whose "By a Waterfall" made spectacular use of fountains, waterfalls, pools and female bodies.

Several recent historians have been fond of crediting Wilkins' heart-shaped tub with having single-handedly invented or defined the modern Pocono honeymoon industry (Bulcroft *et al.* 1999: 136; Squeri 2002: 217). This claim should be taken with a grain of salt. By the time Wilkins came on the scene, the Pocono honey-moon was already a well-established phenomenon and luxury bathtubs of various sorts (sunken, round, "Hollywood," "Roman") had been used to lure in business for around a decade. If anything, until the mid-1960s, Cove Haven was behind the times, the dowdy cousin of splashier resorts like Pocono Gardens Lodge and Penn Hills whose role in transforming the Poconos into a honeymoon mecca also deserves to be recognized. But Cove Haven did have an undeniable impact on the public image of the Poconos in one specific way: studying the resort's advertising, it is evident that it was the first explicitly to use the promise of great sex, as embodied in the heart-shaped tub, to sell the region to honeymooners.

Selling Sex

The shift in Cove Haven's marketing tactics around 1966 was remarkable, particularly given the dull, amateur advertisements it had used up to that point. In the February/March 1966 issue of *Bride's Magazine*, for instance, the resort was represented by a black-and-white advertisement depicting a couple breakfasting primly in their living room, along with two grainy photos of the lake and heart-shaped pool. In sharp contrast, on the facing page, was a full-page color advert for Pocono Gardens Lodge, featuring a photo of a woman reclining in her round Royal Suite pool-bath in the midst of bubbles, mirrors and Roman statuary; below were a series of smaller images of the newlyweds enjoying the Lodge's pool, nightclub, and winter sports (Figure 11.2). There was no question as to which resort seemed more alluring.

But then, literally overnight, Cove Haven changed its tack. The next issue of *Bride's Magazine* featured an eye-catching full-page color advertisement for the resort, showing a smiling woman in her heart-shaped tub, surrounded by mirrors, heavy drapery, and an ornate chandelier (Figure 11.3). The heart-shaped tub was the *only* element of Cove Haven now shown; though described in the accompanying text, no photos of any of the resort's other features – not its 53-acre lake, swimming pools, or public areas – were reproduced. And, while the photo of the tub was staged with similar props as in Pocono Gardens Lodge's – smiling woman, bubbles, potted plant, lotion and perfume bottles – its tone was subtly different.

With its pastel colors and its Doris Day look-alike model, Pocono Gardens Lodge's image seemed playful but ultimately decorous. Every element in the advertisement signified "delicious" self-indulgence, from the spaciousness of the bathroom to the superabundant foam in the bathtub, a setup that was no doubt designed to appeal to the predominantly female readership of *Bride's Magazine*. Roland Barthes; analysing the use of foam in laundry detergent advertisements, persuasively claimed it was able to represent luxury through its sheer uselessness, abundance and airiness (Barthes 1993: 36–8). Indeed, water, bubbles and cleanliness came together in the round pool to form a potent image of luxury, suggestive yet with nothing exposed, like that of a film star idling in her bath.

In contrast, due to the bold color scheme, tighter camera angle, and the model's direct gaze into the camera, Cove Haven's image was more immediate and saucier. By pointedly expunging all traces of Cove Haven's exterior, the resort effectively turned itself inside-out, directing all attention to its lush interiors: suddenly, rather than being depicted as part of a larger package of offerings, the fantastical tub became *the star* of the Cove Haven experience. (In fact, as Wilkins himself acknowledged, for years after, his advertisements never focused on any other feature – it became the symbol of the whole resort.) In this context, the tub's heart shape did become significant. For, unlike the Pocono Gardens Lodge ad where one

Figure 11.2 Pocono Gardens Lodge advertisement, *Bride's Magazine*, Spring 1965, p. 244.

could account for the woman's smile in any number of ways – was she simply enjoying the pleasure of an unusually large bathtub? – the heart-shaped tub left no room for doubt. It was not for cleansing oneself or for private relaxation but for sex of a decidedly self-conscious and theatrical sort.

The way Cove Haven dramatized the performance of conjugal sex was picked up by *Life* in 1971, which featured a photo of newlyweds kissing in a heart-shaped tub surrounded by mirrors. This photo also included one striking detail: a camera on a tripod was reflected in the wall-to-ceiling mirror behind the couple. According to *Life*, it had been provided "courtesy of the management" so the honeymooners

Figure 11.3 Cove Haven advertisement, *Bride's Magazine*, April/May 1966, p. 181.

could record their passionate bubble bath for posterity. (Interestingly, it is the bride who holds the shutter-release cord, thus controlling exactly which moments are snapped.) Contemplating the image, *Life* asked if it proved that America had entered an age of "affluent vulgarity," opining: "Apparently, just being with each other doesn't seem to be enough. We need, or think we need, some affirmation – mirrors, heart-shaped pool – to tell us we're really here at last" (View 1971: 10–11).

Figure 11.4 Honeymooners at Honeymoon Haven, 1967. Collection of the author.

Significantly, far from damaging Cove Haven's business, the charge of vulgarity served to only further boost it. Emboldened by the surge of interest which followed *Life's* article, the resort's advertising became more frank: instead of featuring a naked woman alone in a bubble bath, it began featuring a naked couple, with an open bottle of champagne, clutched in a passionate embrace. In the advertisement, the link between foaming waters, the heart-shaped bath and sexual consummation was made unambiguous. As Wilkins proclaimed in the 1970s, "We're selling one thing here and one thing only. Sex" (Seligson, 1973: 245).

Doing it "Right"

Just as earlier honeymoon cottages had been designed to enable the performance of domesticity, the later suites were unapologetically designed to enable the performance of sex. Through their orchestration of viewing platforms, mirrors and Brobdinagian props, the suites provided an environment of fantasy, removed from everyday time and space and, most significant, the space of home. In this self-contained interior world ("private as an unlisted telephone number" crowed Mount Airy Lodge), couples were encouraged to role-play: to become the directors, stars and spectators of their own sexual encounters. These spaces were legitimate, in the sense that the sex within in them was sanctioned by marriage, but they were given an extra *frisson* due to their deliberate invocation of risqué environments as seen in films or in magazines like *Playboy:* entrepreneurs appeared to have been particularly inspired by Hugh Hefner, for instance, and the round, 8 ft. vibrating bed at the Playboy Mansion (Petersen 1999: 266).

At first glance, recognizing how Cove Haven's suites encouraged a more performative form of sexual practice, blurring the visual distinction between the licit and illicit, would appear to be the key to understanding their popularity during this period. According to sex surveys, the significance married couples placed on sex was on the rise: in the same way that "frequent, pleasurable, varied and ecstatically satisfying sex" was coming to be seen as "the preeminent sign of personal happiness," so too was it coming to be regarded as an index of the health of marriage. Indeed, many married couples in the early 1970s reported "greater variety, higher levels of satisfaction, and more frequent intercourse" with their spouses (D'Emilio and Freedman 1988: 336, 340). In this heady atmosphere of liberation, it would seem appropriate to assume that newlyweds went to the Poconos fully intending to take advantage of its racy environment.

The only problem with this assumption is that newlyweds did not necessarily respond to their suites with a explosion of sexual activity. For one thing, far from attracting bohemian, swinging couples, the average Pocono honeymooner in this period was young (19–25 years old), of modest means and "not traveled" as one couple put it (Richard and Rose Pelletier, e-mail communication with author, 26 January 2003). According to both anecdotal evidence and industry insiders, many were also inexperienced sexually (Honeymoon Havens 1969: 90; Seligson 1973: 248–9). For some of them at least, the consummation of marriage was difficult and traumatic on occasion: during the late 1960s and early 1970s, for instance, the night secretary at Cove Haven was also a registered nurse who spent much of her time soothing and counseling couples (Seligson 1973: 252).

By reinserting the typical user into the scenario, we are left with a perplexing question: what was the attraction of such over-the-top *Playboy*-esque spaces to inexperienced newlyweds? Joan Didion, writing about the 1960s Las Vegas wedding industry, argued that its success was never due simply to convenience but to the fact that it offered nervous young couples the promise of "doing it 'right';" that is, getting married with the appropriate ceremony and accoutrements for a reasonable cost (Didion 1968: 70). To some extent, the same could be said of the Poconos. However much the advertisements insinuated that they encouraged impromptu experimentation, the suites were actually highly conventional, working through a finite number of sexual scenarios. They were like romantic stage sets, their props and choreography guiding couples from one fixed coital encounter (on the bed) to another (in the bath or in front of the fireplace). In other words, they showed young couples how "it" was to be done within a carefully circumscribed menu of possibilities.

To make the obvious point that these environments were conventional or choreographed, however, is absolutely not to claim, as a critic like Dorfles would, that authentic feeling or bodily pleasure could not be experienced within them. Instead of seeing love as being incompatible with or degraded by convention, I would argue that its expression is deeply bound up with it. This view is strongly supported by sociologist, Eva Ilouz, in her sensitive study of the relationship between the expression of love, material culture, and class. In this work, Illouz argues that, when it comes to experiencing love, no one truly escapes the ideal of romance as constructed by literature, films, advertising and, I would add, design. Her conclusion is that romance always "consists of a kind of 'fit' between . . . narrative frameworks and different categories of phenomenal and physical experiences" (Illouz, 1997: 171).

While Illouz's statement would not suggest that newlyweds blindly adhered to the suite's sexual "script," it does support the idea that it helped ultimately to frame or organize their physical and emotional experience. Far from being turned off by the suite's role in mediating their encounters, most Pocono newlyweds welcomed it, drawn, even reassured, by its literalness and air of regimented hedonism. They did not want surprises after all: they wanted what they paid for – a romantic environment that, despite its naughty appearance, was controlled and familiar, providing all the expected props for the right price.

The Terror of Privacy

In addition to the honeymoon suite itself, there was another level on which the newlyweds' experience was mediated in the Poconos. The honeymoon suite was just one aspect of what we might call the honeymoon resort world. After check-in, couples were not left alone to frolic in their "Garden of Eden" suites but were absorbed into the social life of the community. As Pocono ads regularly promised, "You'll be part of a gay, fun-loving group of Honeymooners, whose days and nights are filled with a 'whirl' of activities." True to their word and their appearance, honeymoon resorts were actually run more like tightly programmed summer camps than secret love getaways with social directors who organized activities and mixers for their guests. The days of visiting couples were filled with a range of scheduled activities, from boating to target shooting, while their evenings were devoted to dining (at tables of four or more) and Vegas-style shows. So successful were they at providing guests with "everything," as Cove Haven put it, most couples did not venture outside their resort during the course of their stay.

Indeed, the majority of couples appeared to participate wholeheartedly in the resorts' convivial regime. In interviews, former Pocono honeymooners claimed to have enjoyed the opportunity of mingling with others and some even cited it as being as important to them as the suite itself (Judy Medley, e-mail communication with author, 24 January, 2003) (Figure 11.4). While some newlyweds no doubt simply liked getting to know new people, journalists and resort employees were quick to suggest another reason why others appreciated the enforced sociability of resort life; the fear of being alone. Even if they had been sexually active before marriage, many newlyweds still felt awkward on their honeymoon – nervous and uncertain how to act. As an earlier article in *Good Housekeeping* bluntly warned:

> Newlyweds are bound to feel strange wherever they are. They feel strange toward each other and toward themselves. Every familiar thing takes on a new aspect in the light of marriage . . . Later, variations [in behavior] seem natural, part of the day's work; but at the beginning, each difference and difficult may seem enormous and threatening.

This article went on to claim that it was the sudden abundance of privacy that was a particular burden for newlyweds. "But very soon the premarital sense of not enough privacy," it stated, "can turn into the honeymoon terror of too much" (Eustis 1950: 102, 295). Although the writer's remedy was that couples should defer their honeymoon to a later date (preferably until they had school-age children), the honeymoon resort world provided another, more practical, solution for how to ease the pressure of the couple's first few days alone. Its programmed "whirl" of activities and events clearly aimed to head off newlywed anxiety, nerves or disappointment by prolonging the excitement of wedding celebrations and keeping guests diverted and busy (Honeymoon Havens 1969: 90–1; Seligson 1973: 249–58).

In other words, the most successful resorts like Cove Haven or Pocono Gardens Lodge did not just offer privacy for newlywed couples but also sought to bring them out in public again in appropriately managed and supervised situations, encouraging them to interact with other couples and members of staff. Though a specific analysis of all the ways in which they did this is beyond the scope of this chapter, it is worth noting that they constantly counterbalanced the couple's private and public time together. So, while resorts provided newlyweds with opportunities to be alone in their deluxe suites (and the privacy of these rooms was always stressed in advertising), they also set up a myriad of group activities so that couples would not feel trapped by the surfeit of privacy. Similarly, resort staff tended to fuss over each couple's newlywed status upon arrival to underscore their "specialness" and to extend the aura of exception generated by their marriage. But they also carefully took steps, like making newlyweds show their marriage licenses at check-in, to remind them that were participating in a larger communal experience, always validating and affirming their new married status on a social, public level.

For Honeymooners or Romantics Alike

Today Caesars Cove Haven and other Pocono "love nests" continue to flourish, although Pocono Gardens Lodge, Mount Airy and Strickland's are no more (Jacobs 2001). The remaining resorts have been modernized and updated, but it is telling that overall they have changed remarkably little since the 1960s: their iconography and the way they are run, for instance, has remained more or less unchanged, although many of the new generation of guests now prize them for their camp quality. The most striking shift is that Pocono honeymoon resorts have now mutated into "couples-only" resorts where people, whether married or not, can come for a passionate getaway. The area still claims to draw 200,000 "lovers" per year (Bulcroft *et al.* 1999: 138).

This is not to say that honeymooning as a practice is dead. According to Kris and Richard Bulcroft and Linda Smeins (1999: 154, 162–3), honeymooning is even more important to newlyweds now than it was in previous generations. Their assertion is borne out by a recent report in *Bride's Magazine* that claims that, of the $32 billion dollars spent on weddings annually in the United States, $4.5 billion dollars is still spent on honeymooning. Fully 99 per cent of *Bride's Magazine* readers claim that they intend to take honeymoons, though increasing numbers are opting for what are called "WeddingMoons," combining the wedding and the honeymoon (Ingraham 1999: 28, 59). But, as purveyors of honeymoons, Sandals Resorts, Carnival Cruises and even Disneyworld have decisively overtaken the Poconos. Niagara Falls and the Pocono Mountains are not able to complete with the pleasures of the Caribbean, Europe, or Florida.

Despite the pleasanter beaches or more refined cultural attractions, however, today's most popular honeymoon operators, Sandals and Disneyworld, still operate on the same magic formula established at the Poconos: they provide a safe and controlled setting for couples' emotional and sexual explorations; and they make couples feel individual and special while publicly affirming their participation in a larger collective practice (marriage, heterosexual coupledom). Moreover, if tourism generally has learned any other lessons from massive success of places like the Poconos, it is that heterosexual romance sells vacations. Although it is done in a less literal way than at the Pocono resorts, the promise of true love and great sex in a fantasy setting is regularly used to market Caribbean holidays and exotic tours. The modern tourist industry, in fact, is completely saturated and driven by such romantic imagery and these advertisements – showing couples taking a beach stroll at sunset, kissing in a whirlpool, enjoying a buffet heaped with food – have now become constitutive part of the dominant image of romance.

Acknowledgements

I would like to thank Medina Lasansky and Michael Hatt for their generous editorial help with this piece. I would also like to thank Judy Medley and Rose and Richard Pelletier for sharing their 1960s Poconos honeymoon experience with me. Finally, I would like to acknowledge Condé Nast in New York for access to their library, as well as Caesars Cove Haven for generously allowing me to reprint images of their resort.

References

Advertisement for Cove Haven (1966), *Bride's Magazine* (February/March): 218–9.
Advertisement for Cove Haven (1966), *Bride's Magazine* (April/May): 181.
Advertisement for Cove Haven (1972), *Bride's Magazine* (December): 127.
Advertisement for The Honeymoon Colony at Vacation Valley (1959), *Bride's Magazine* (Spring): 238–9.
Advertisement for Honeymoon Haven (1964), *Bride's Magazine* (Spring): 216.
Advertisement for Merry Hill Lodge and Cottages (1959), *Bride's Magazine* (Spring): 250a.
Advertisement for Mount Airy Lodge (1961), *Modern Bride* (Spring): 215.
Advertisement for Pocono Gardens Lodge (1966), *Bride's Magazine* (February/March): 218–9.
Advertisement for Pocono Gardens Lodge (1961), *Modern Bride* (Spring): 219.
Advertisement for Strickland's Mountain Inn and Cottages (1961), *Bride's Magazine* (Summer): 234.
Barthes, R. (1993), *Mythologies*, translated by Annette Lavers. London: Vintage.
Bulcroft, K., Smeins, L. and Bulcroft, R. (1999), *Romancing the Honeymoon: Consummating Marriage in Modern Society*, Thousand Oaks: Sage Publications.
Chandler, R. (1953), *The Long Good-bye*, London: Penguin.
"Couples Country: The Poconos," (1970), *Bride's Magazine* (February): 219, 225.
D'Emilio, J. and Freedman, E. B. (1988), *Intimate Matters: A History of Sexuality in America*, New York: Harper & Row.
Didion, J. (1968), *Marrying Absurd. Slouching Towards Bethlehem*, London: Flamingo. 68–71.
Dorfles, G. (1969), *Kitsch: The World of Bad Taste*, London: Studio Vista.
Eustis, H. (1950), "Alone at Last!" *Good Housekeeping* (April): 102, 294–5.
Friedman, A. T. (2000), "The Luxury of Lapidus," *Harvard Design Magazine* (Summer): 39–47.

"Honeymoon Havens," (1969), *Newsweek*, 23 June: 90–1.

Illouz, E. (1997), *Consuming the Romantic Utopia: Love and the Cultural Contradictions of Capitalism*, Berkeley: University of California Press.

Ingraham, C. (1999), *White Weddings: Romancing Heterosexuality in Popular Culture*, New York: Routledge.

Jacobs, A. (2001), "The Thrills are Over at Mount Airy Lodge," *The New York Times*, 2 November.

Josephson, M. (1971), "Lapidus' Pornography of Comfort," *Art in America*, (March): 108–9.

Lapidus, M. (1996), *Too Much is Never Enough*, New York: Rizzoli.

Penner, B. (2003), *Alone at Last: Honeymooning in Nineteenth Century America.*

Petersen, J. R. (1999), *The Century of Sex: Playboy's History of the Sexual Revolution, 1900–1999*, New York: Grove Press.

"Pocono Charm Blends Airy Mountain Beauty and Open-Hearted Welcome," (1961), *Bride's Magazine*, (Summer): 223, 226–9, 235, 237.

Schmidt, L. E. (1995), *Consumer Rites: The Buying and Selling of American Holidays*, Princeton: Princeton University Press.

Seligson, M. (1973), *The Eternal Bliss Machine: America's Way of Wedding*, New York: William Morrow & Company.

Shields, R. (1991), *Places on the Margin: Alternative Geographies of Modernity*, London: Routledge.

Squeri, L. (2002), *Better in the Poconos: The Story of Pennsylvania's Vacationland*, University Park PA: The Pennsylvania State University Press.

"The Poconos: Year "Round Mountain Magic," (1964), *Bride's Magazine*, (Spring): 213–18.

"View from U.S. 80," (1971), *Life* (8 January): 2–21.

Weld, C. (1855), *A Vacation Tour in The United States and Canada*, New York: London: Longman, Brown, Green & Longmans.

Wilson, B. (1959), *The Bride's School: Complete Book of Engagement and Wedding Etiquette*, New York: Hawthorn Books.

"Your Honeymoon in the Poconos," (1959), *Bride's Magazine*, (Summer): 195–202.

Part V
The Postmodern Imagination

–12–

New Politics of the Spectacle: "Bilbao" and the Global Imagination
Joan Ockman

In 1997, virtually overnight, "Bilbao" appeared on the map (Figure 12.1). Frank Gehry's dazzling design for a far-flung branch of the Guggenheim Museum was not just an extraordinarily audacious architectural achievement, nor was it merely another new destination for the art-world jet set and a global ego trip on the part of its ambitious New York director. The museum immediately became synonymous with an entire city and a symbol of regeneration for a troubled region of Spain. That a single building in a provincial locale could so capture the popular imagination – globally and locally, high brow and low – was one of the stunning architectural surprises of the *fin de siècle*. Had not postmodernism, in repudiating the hubris of modernism, consigned urban architecture to modest infill operations within the historical fabric of the city?[1] Had not the critical theorists of post-modernity written off spectacle buildings as the epiphenomena of a commodified culture and alienated social relationships? Finally, had not the digital world bypassed bricks and mortar, according built monuments the currency of dinosaur eggs?

Precisely two decades earlier, in 1977, the Centre Pompidou in Paris opened to a comparable hailstorm of public opinion. Like Bilbao, 'Beaubourg," designed by the Italian-British team of Renzo Piano and Richard Rodgers, represented a spectacular new redevelopment strategy for an obsolescent urban district. As at Bilbao, the architecture of the art museum was literally an act of exhibitionism, violating the rules of urban decorum and flaunting its own difference. It fetishized the ideologies of transparency, high technology and mass participation, dematerial-izing the brutalist "servant-served" poetics of Louis Kahn and, in the post-1968 atmosphere, hybridizing them with the populism of Cedric Price's Fun Palace. Standing in the emblematic capital of Western art and culture, it presented itself as a kind of "empty center" much like the Eiffel Tower a hundred years earlier – a function and an event more than a place, a container waiting to be filled.[2] In the exorbitant critique of Jean Baudrillard, the building was a hyperarticulated and diabolical machine designed to suck masses of hapless spectators through its exposed guts into a "black hole" signifying the end of culture. Its erector-set

Figure 12.1 Frank Gehry, Guggenheim Museum, Bilbao.

skeleton of glass, steel and color-coded ducts was destined to be so overrun by swarming tourists, Baudrillard predicted (or wished), that it would ultimately implode (Baudrillard 1982: 3–13).

In fact, like its predecessor on the Champs de Mars, the Centre Pompidou has proved to be perfectly durable (despite a recent renovation that compromised its polemical openness, turning loftlike exhibition spaces into conventional *en suite* galleries). Yet if the Beaubourg effect may be said to be the product of ambivalent historical impulses – the centrism of the French state and the ephemeralism of late-modern culture, the monument and the antimonument – it is evident that the Bilbao effect is of a different order. Arguably, it represents a new moment in the evolution of the society of spectacle and its global architectural representations.

To begin with, the Bilbao museum is centrifugal, not centripetal, with respect to the psychogeographic imaginary. Spurning the machinic rationalism of Le Corbusier's *ville radieuse*, belatedly embodied by Beaubourg, it harks back to the anarcho-expressionist visions of Bruno Taut's Glass Chain circle, in particular the grotesque fantastications of Hermann Finsterlin. Taut himself, in the aftermath of the First World War, dreamed of the dissolution of big cities; he wished to see them replaced by an astral network of spaced-out, crystalline "city-crowns." The city of Bilbao, located in the northeast corner of Spain at the mouth of the Nervión River, is remote from the main pilgrimage routes of contemporary tourism and requires an effort to get to (at least one connection from major international airports). A mercantile and industrial town, originally chartered in 1300, it reached the peak of its influence as an international port and center of ship-building and iron and steel production in the 1920s. By the mid-1970s, however, the fourth largest city in Spain had fallen victim to postindustrial economics and had little of tourist cachet to offer. The opening of the Guggenheim reversed this. Within the first year of operation, the museum attracted some 1,360,000 visitors, exceeding all expectations and infusing $160 million into the local economy. It continued to draw an average of 100,000 tourists a month to the city through the summer of 2001, over half from outside the region and the vast majority naming the museum their primary destination (Plaza 2000: 264–74).[3]

Even before Gehry's museum became the jewel in Bilbao's crown, however, the city fathers seemed to grasp the potential of a new form of tourism constructed around architecture. Starting in the late 1980s, they embarked upon an ambitious $1.5 billion revitalization program, including the refurbishment of historic older buildings as well as the planning of new culture and leisure facilities, public works and environmental infrastructures, commissioning many of these projects from international architects with "signature" reputations. The first phase of a futuristic subway by the British architect Norman Foster was completed in 1995. A design by the virtuoso Spanish architect-engineer Santiago Calatrava for an arching parabolic pedestrian bridge was inaugurated in 1997, and his soaring airport expansion opened in 2000. Another bridge by Calatrava will provide a link to a new urban zone created by the Japanese architect Arata Isozaki, featuring a pair of twenty-two-story mixed-used glass towers, residential and municipal buildings, shops and recreation space, centered around a rehabilitated customs building. Other projects by established or rising stars in the architectural firmament include an intermodal transportation hub for buses and trains by the office of James Stirling/Michael Wilford (put on hold after Stirling's death); a conference center and concert hall by the young Madrid architects Federico Soriano and Dolores Palacios, completed in 1999; and – destined to seal the gentrification of Bilbao's rundown waterfront – a million sq. ft. office mall and shopping complex masterplanned by Cesar Pelli, the architect of the World Financial Center in Manhattan, with buildings by Disney architect Robert A. M. Stern and the Mexican Ricardo Legorreta.[4] Ironically, precisely the singularity and difference that up to now have given Gehry's building its extraordinary impact may end up being eroded by the museum's absorption into the wider urban development it was intended to trigger.

This potential paradox of success aside, however, the existence of such a development in Bilbao is all the more remarkable inasmuch as it has occurred in a city that is also the capital of the Basque country. The region has long asserted its independence from the rest of Spain, aggressively insisting on the prerogatives its own culture and language. Since the repressions of the Franco era, Basque separatism has taken the form of a deadly terrorist campaign by the ETA movement

(Euskadi ta Askatasuna, or Basque Fatherland and Liberty). Indeed, the museum's opening was seriously marred by an incident in which ETA members attempted to plant a bomb at the building's entry and a security guard was killed when they tried to flee. Yet coincidentally or not, the new museum literally seemed to have a disarming effect, at least temporarily, when, in 1998, ETA announced a unilateral ceasefire. Although a year-and-a-half of peace overtures ended in early 2000 with a new escalation of violence, an unprecedented climate of optimism is galvanizing the region as it becomes associated with art and commerce rather than bombs. Who would have imagined that a building "made in the U.S.A." could provide an authentic image and a sense of hope for a place so fiercely protective of its own identity and autonomy? Indeed, prior to the building's opening, the notion that Spain's largest artistic undertaking to date should be a branch of an American museum was objectionable to many.[5] But at least for now the museum's triumph has led to a revised judgment. Possibly a building in a provincial locale can have a radical cultural effect *only* when it is cosmopolitan enough to enter into a wider conversation.[6]

Meanwhile, from the standpoint of the architect, Frank Gehry's claims during the design process to have felt an affinity with Bilbao's tough urbanscape cannot be written off as entirely disingenuous. However cloying, in light of his current stardom, are the architect's frequent references to his parents' working-class background and his status as a self-made practitioner, Gehry is in fact a Canadian transplant and a Jew. He was marginal to the American architectural mainstream for many years before making his reputation in the late 1970s at the age of fifty on chicken wire, corrugated sheet metal and jarring formal juxtapositions. Might not an architect of this extraction feel a certain empathy with a rough-and-ready place like Bilbao? While unlikely at first glance, the marriage of Bilbao regionalism and avant-garde internationalism seems to have had its own inevitable logic.

But let us return to the building itself and elaborate further on what we may call the microdynamics of centrifugal space. Whereas the see-through envelope of Pompidou remains firmly locked by its orthogonal geometry into the dense Marais district of Paris, the museum in Bilbao insouciantly unfurls its titanium-clad petals on its former shipyard site like some exotic excrescence. Extending tendrils in multiple directions along the Nervión, it appears at once noble and nonchalant, aggrandizing and informal. On the river elevation, only a single Karnakian column roots it to the bank, arresting it from being swept downstream like some shimmering lilypad as it also sweeps up city, river and bridge in a new conjuncture of landscape forces, radically refocusing the frayed milieu. Heidegger's insight that it is the bridge that makes the riverbanks appear has an unexpected confirmation in Bilbao.

On the city side the building appears almost apparitional as it looms up at the end of a street vista. From here the main approach is downward. Upon passing a giant Cerberus (artist Jeff Koons's 40 ft. high topiary *Puppy)*, one descends a flight of limestone steps vectoring sharply into the building's belly. Once again, the contrast is maximal with Beaubourg, where one passively escalates skyward, parallel to the box's glazed perimeter; this defers the moment of entry, which, once achieved by means of a right-angle turn, is never really consummated because the grand public space has already been ejected from the building container to the outdoor plateau. At Bilbao, in contrast, even the most blasé visitor cannot fail to be enthralled upon arrival in the central atrium. One is in the hall of the mountain king, in the core of a volcano, in a vortex of glass, steel and stone. Not surprisingly commentators have wallowed in a "hypertrophy of metaphors" (Ramirez 1997: 51).[7] The aura of Architecture – capital A – is total; there is no disappearing act on the part of the author. One half-expects to find him pulling strings behind a velvet curtain (or Jenny Holzer's cascading LED of words) in this towering space, orchestrating his effects like the wizard of oz. Unlike at Beaubourg, the confoundingly complicated articulations of the custom-cut steel infrastructure – which in the construction photos looks like a gigantic roller coaster – are here "magically" concealed on inside and out by the metal and limestone cladding, creating an illusion of organic totality, literally at all costs.

Yet one arrives in this hyperbole of a center only to be spun out again, as in a centrifuge, toward the museum's extremities. Gyrating off the central space are the galleries, including the extravagantly overextended limb of the principal ground-floor exhibition hall. Here Richard Serra's gravity-defying *Torqued Ellipses* received a full and privileged display shortly after the museum opened, echoing the dislocating forms and experience of Gehry's postindustrial architecture. How paradoxical – again – that the massive and warped Cor-Ten planes of this American sculptor associated with the New York avant-garde should have appeared so much at home in the Basque rustbelt! Anyone who saw them exhibited in this space at the same time as the retrospective of the sculpture of Eduardo Chillida in the second-floor galleries – Chillida, who died in 2002, was a native Basque artist whose work likewise exploits the brute materiality of oxidized steel – felt with a kind of shock the overridingly *local* nature of the Bilbao museum. In the coruscations of the building's matt-metallic scales picking up the mud-gold coloration of Bilbao's river, Los Angeles and New York receded like a far-off dream.

In short, the sleep of reason – California dreaming – succeeded in producing a most magnificent monster in this proud region of Spain. In the land of the baroque and the country of Gaudí (the ironwork for some of whose Barcelona buildings was fabricated in Bilbao), the architect, the museum impresario and the local client collectively intuited that the occasion demanded not a fetish of rationalism, as at Beaubourg, but an untrammeled flight of fantasy. The escape from functional form making resulted in a spectacular cadenza, which, against the odds, transcended the potential to be a bombastic exercise in self-expression or an expensive publicity

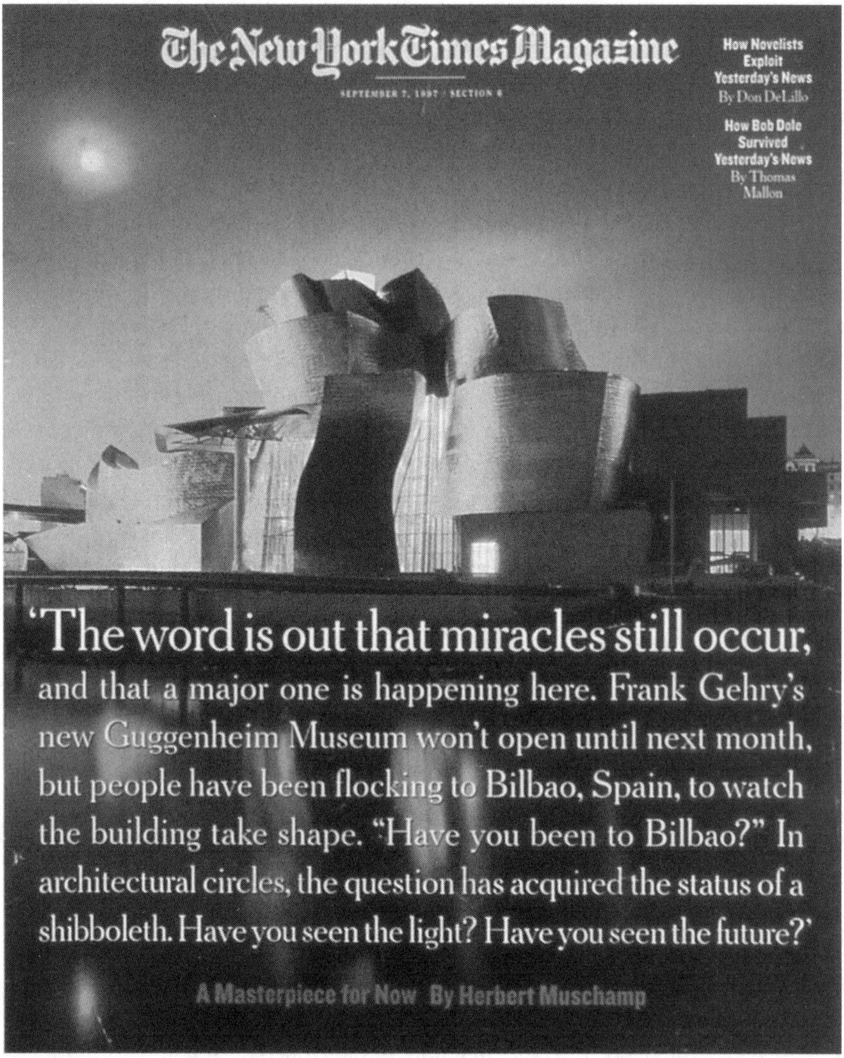

Figure 12.2 Cover, *New York Times Magazine*, with story on the Guggenheim Bilbao by Herbert Muschamp, September 7, 1997. © 1997. *The New York Times*. Reprinted by permission.

stunt. The by-now iconic images and florid descriptions of the photogenic building, endlessly circulated in tourist brochures, the popular press and the critical litera-ture, hardly convey its complex urban reality adequately, even if they have un-doubtedly mediated its reception and contributed to the general mythography (Figure 12.2).

From some of these perspectives it is interesting to compare the museum in Bilbao to two predecessors with which it shares both similarities and differences. At the Sydney Opera House, designed by the Danish architect Jørn Utzon in 1956–7 and also the outcome of an international competition, a foreign architect was likewise called to a remote city and succeeded in endowing it with an iconic image.[8] Like the Bilbao museum, the Sydney building derives much of its energy from its location on the edge of the water. This condition helps to license its formal otherness and sustains its oscillation between the ontologies of architecture and landscape. Not coincidentally, the Sydney Opera House was designed at a moment when the novelty of the glass curtain-wall building of the International Style was becoming exhausted around the world. Moreover, despite the oceanic distance between Denmark and Australia, the geocultural parallels between the two countries, both peripheral to the Europe-America axis, indubitably gave Utzon a certain "feel for the job." In this sense it made him a less far-fetched choice than Gehry in Spain. (As it turned out, though, in contrast to the relatively smooth process at Bilbao, local politics surrounding the Sydney commission turned acrimonious. The architect was forced to resign and the opera house was not completed until a decade after Utzon designed it, ultimately by a local firm.)

An edge condition also characterizes Bilbao's most explicit forebear, Frank Lloyd Wright's Guggenheim museum in New York, commissioned in 1943 and realized following a protracted period of design and construction just after the architect's death in 1959. Here the frontage on Central Park – the great green exception within Manhattan's grid – is essential to the building's display of difference, which is both poetic and political. Wright's antipathy to the International Style, to cities and to New York in particular is ostentatiously expressed in this building that repeatedly elicited (especially in the 1950s) the metaphor of an alien spacecraft. From its inception Wright's museum was also accused of hostility to its program, of subordinating the requirements of displaying art to the grand architectural gesture. The building's dynamic form not only competed with the equally dynamic paintings of Kandinsky – the core of the Guggenheim collection at the time of Wright's design – but destabilized the contemplative viewing of everything else. More recently, similar criticism has been leveled – with justice – at Daniel Libeskind's Jewish Museum in Berlin, a powerful monument and tourist draw that nonetheless, in insisting on its own singularity, remains a curatorial nightmare. Surprisingly enough, Gehry's building is quite accommodating on this score. With the exception of the atrium, which can only tolerate site-specific installations (like the Holzer sculpture), and the long gallery (which dwarfs most art other than Serra's), the rest of the exhibition spaces function fairly conventionally. At the same time, the lack of an important permanent collection in Bilbao gave Gehry a freer hand to make architecture the main event.

The "spontaneous" massing of Gehry's building – carefully unstudied – also comes off as less absolutist than that of his predecessor. Wright's upward processional (or downward, if one takes the elevator and begins at the top) is, in fact, much closer in spirit to another archetypal project for a spiraling museum, Le Corbusier's zigguratlike Mundaneum (1929). In their reverent ideology of art, the buildings by the two modern masters mark a profound historical gulf with Gehry's less pious take. At the same time, Gehry's building also eschews the irony infecting much "postmodern" architecture. Its exuberant urbanity manifests a potent sense of optimism. Indeed, like both the Sydney Opera House and the Guggenheim New York, Bilbao is the kind of building that postmodernist theorists Denise Scott Brown and Robert Venturi disparaged in their book *Learning from Las Vegas* (1972) as a "duck." A duck, according to Scott Brown and Venturi, is a building permeated with naively or gratuitously expressive values. The concept derives from a restaurant on Long Island specializing in poultry and built in the form of a duck (Venturi, Scott Brown and Izenour 1977: 130–1). From the Venturian perspective, the Beaubourg solution is preferable: a "decorated shed" (or neutral container with its symbolic or decorative content applied to the exterior) is always more "honest" by virtue of its clear and economical separation of function and meaning. In the 1990s, when computer-generated design began to make this already questionable distinction even more moot, an updated version of the duck versus decorated shed argument resurfaced in advanced architectural circles in a debate over "blobs" versus "boxes."[9] Clearly, though, something is at stake in this recurrent aesthetic argument other than honesty or even tacit stylistic preferences. Historically, these opposing tendencies tend to be mobilized in order either to stabilize or to destabilize an existing spatial order. Thus, within the context of the rationalist ethos of modernism, organic or expressionist architecture functioned as an explosive challenge to the norm, an insight the Italian architect and critic Bruno Zevi, for one, tried to mobilize after the Second World War (Zevi 1945). Likewise, the free and intuitive form of Bilbao operates as a critical gesture with respect to the museum-as-box tradition, at least for now. This presumably gives it a certain political dimension.

Of course, such a critical gesture may not matter much except within the circumscribed politics of architectural discourse, contentious as these are – and then perhaps only for a Warholian 15 minutes. Occasionally, however, aesthetic politics have broader resonance. In the case of Bilbao, precisely the convergence between the "mediascape" of global architecture – the spectacular imagery of Frank Gehry – and the "ideoscape" or "ethnoscape" of Basque regionalism – the desire for a strong, "other" form of expression – resulted, as if by spontaneous combustion, in a singular event. I borrow the terms in quotation marks from Arjun Appadurai, who in his book *Modernity at Large* (1996) has attempted to elaborate something like a typology of what we have called the psychogeographic imaginary.[10] These sometimes real and sometimes virtual fields, which also include "technoscapes" and "financescapes," are part of our quotidian experience and perception of architecture. Their interactions and tensions, conjunctions and disjunctions, are played out within historically and territorially specific contexts, and they serve to constitute the "imagined worlds" we inhabit. As Appadurai writes, "The work of the imagination through which local subjectivity is produced is a bewildering palimpsest of highly local and highly translocal considerations" (Appadurai 1996: 198).

This view of the production of built space counteracts the more monolithic narrative of homogenization, commodification and Americanization that has pervaded recent architectural theories founded on the assumption of an antagonistic relationship between globalization and regional identity. It serves as a rejoinder to the Cassandras who decry the evils of global culture, denouncing the advance of a brutal high-tech civilization and the colonization of local identities through the juggernaut of advertising and the media. "What these arguments fail to consider," Appadurai states, "is that at least as rapidly as forces from various metropolises are brought into new societies they tend to become indigenized in one or another way" (Appadurai 1996: 198). The concept of indigenization affords a more nuanced understanding of the way architectural ideas get disseminated and the experience of their varied materializations. It reminds us that the "context" of any built work encompasses not just the "authentic," pre-existing characteristics of a place. Architecture also has the capacity to embody the often conflicted feelings a place harbors about its own past and future, its insecurities about being provincial, its fantasies and desires for a reality that is alternative to the present. The assimilation of foreign tendencies within a local situation is in this sense not just, or not necessarily, a hegemonic process, but sometimes, as at Bilbao, one of voluntary adaptation and a consciously or unconsciously acknowledged need for change.

As such, we may suggest that the museum in Bilbao raises the possibility of a new kind of *politics of appearance*. By this I mean a way to confront and reverse some of the forces that have historically produced the obsolescence and marginality of certain cities. Architecture is inherently a positive form of enunciation; it allows something that was previously latent to become visible. If this strategy was mainly the client's at Bilbao, and if the architect and the museum director had their own, different agendas, nonetheless the success of the museum is attributable to a convergence of the interests of all three. Nor do we take anything away from Gehry's creative accomplishment in insisting that the force fields that determine the context and reception of any built work go well beyond the individual architect and his or her talents as a form maker.

I should stress that by a politics of appearance I mean something altogether different from an *aestheticization of politics*, an approach that employs techniques of architectural seduction to mask or sublimate a repressive reality. I also mean to counterpose the politics of appearance to what certain commentators have characterized with regard to the contemporary situation as an *aesthetics of disappearance*. The latter is an effete response to the ephemerality and depthlessness of "postmodern" experience; it is exemplified by Baudrillard's interpretation of Beaubourg, as well as by recent theories that see the "virtual" as superseding the "real" in a false dichotomy (Virilio 1991).[11] In contrast to these approaches, it may be useful to begin to reconceptualize the contemporary architectural spectacle in less negative terms. Guy Debord was correct in prophesying that the spectacle would become a fact of life in late-capitalist society; certainly the spectacularization of the art museum by means of architecture for purposes of urban gentrification – a strategy that proliferated internationally in the 1990s – epitomizes this phenomenon.[12] But to condemn it out of hand today, in an age when the media competes for our attention – and distraction – in ever more demanding ways, is ultimately less an act of resistance than of irrelevance.

For the moment at least, a rethinking of the spectacle along these lines seems to be a requisite cultural strategy. We are admittedly dealing with a perspectival concept. What appears positive and unique in Bilbao risks looking crassly sensationalistic in, say, New York or Los Angeles, where the politics of appearance have different dynamics and novelty tends to be consumed as quickly as it is produced. Nor should this argument be construed as implying a preference for a particular aesthetic style – i.e., "organic" over "rationalist" – inasmuch as the very qualities that make Bilbao the phenomenon that it is will become *de rigueur* once they are mindlessly and formulaically replicated. Indeed, the prospect of Bilbao-like clones cropping up in cities around the globe is not a happy one – and Gehry's own scheme for a downtown Guggenheim museum in New York already resembles an act of self-plagiarism.

Yet when the director of a new art museum in Cincinnati, Ohio, hired another "starchitect," Zaha Hadid, to "do another Bilbao," he was not seeking a building that looked like Bilbao so much as a metonym for his own city: a tourist attraction whose unabashed visibility might radically transform a shabby urban image, a catalyst for renewal through the apparently still potent vehicle of built architecture.[13]

Acknowledgements

An earlier version of this chapter appeared in French in the catalogue *Architecture Instantanée: Nouvelles Acquisitions*, edited by Alain Guilheux (Paris: Editions du Centre Pompidou, 2000), pp. 57–63, and in the Turkish magazine *domus m,* special issue on "Other Geographies under Globalization" (February–March 2001), pp. 71–4. I am grateful to John Rajchman for some initial insights informing this paper (Rajchman, 1999: 10–11).

Notes

1. Compare, for example, the epigraph of one of Aldo Rossi's books: "To what, then, could I have aspired in my craft? Certainly to small things, having seen that the possibility of great ones was historically precluded" (Rossi, 1981: 23).

2. For Roland Barthes, the Eiffel Tower was a "pure – virtually empty – sign," "a kind of zero degree of the monument." Its polyvalent meaning derived precisely from its lack of programmatic specificity, allowing viewers to project their own fantasies onto it (Barthes, 1982: 236–50).

3. "9/11" had an adverse impact on tourism in Bilbao as everywhere else. Nonetheless, the museum still attracted some 850,000 visitors in 2002 and brought in 162 million euros.

4. For a list of projects built or currently under way in Bilbao, consult the elaborate interactive Web site sponsored by the city, http://www.bilbao-city.net. The original redevelopment plan was put together by the city of Bilbao in concert with two private-public partnerships, Bilbao Ría 2000 and Bilbao Metrópoli 30, as part of the "Strategic Plan for the Revitalization of the Bilbao Metropolitan Region," initiated in 1987, which envisioned a museum of modern art as a central component of the redevelopment of the city's old industrial core.

5. Nor, of course, were the costs of becoming a Guggenheim franchise only symbolic. Although the full details of the secretly negotiated deal have not been published because of a clause in the agreement forbidding public disclosure, it is clear that the Guggenheim – cash-starved at the time – succeeded in driving a hard bargain. The Basque government and the city of Bilbao paid a hefty $20 million for the franchise, plus were required to spend $20 million on related urban improvements and $50 million on art acquisitions. The building itself cost $100 million, of which the initial contract specified an architectural fee of $10.3 million to Gehry's firm. The local and provincial authorities are also committed to subsidizing the museum's capital and operating costs for at least thirty years. In return the Guggenheim is required to operate the museum and provide 80 per cent of its exhibitions.

6. This is the thesis of Gilles Deleuze and Félix Guattari with respect to the effect of Franz Kafka's decision to write in high German rather than his native Czech; see Deleuze and Guattari (1986: 16–27).

7. See as well as other contributions in the same issue of *Arquitectura Viva*, devoted to the museum upon its opening, especially those by Luis Fernández-Galiano and Joseba Zulaika. Two other excellent articles by Zulaika, which I came upon after writing this chapter, are Zulaika 2000: 262–74; and 2001: 1–17; see also Zulaika's book (1997). For the most over-the-top example of the metaphoric genre of writing, see Herbert Muschamp's cover story in the *New York Times Magazine* (Muschamp, 1997: 54–9, 72, 82), where *The Times*

architecture critic compares the building to both the pilgrimage cathedral of Lourdes and the seductive curves of Marilyn Monroe. Muschamp has taken credit for instigating the "Bilbao effect" with this review.

8. The Sydney competition had 230 submissions. Its four-man jury included Eero Saarinen, who had just embarked on an expressionistic design of his own for the T.W.A. Terminal in New York and reputedly picked Utzon's project out of a pile of rejects. The Bilbao commission was the result of a limited competition in 1991 that included, besides Gehry, Coop Himmelblau of Vienna and Arata Isozaki of Tokyo. It was decided by a selection committee composed of Basque and Guggenheim Foundation representatives. The Centre Pompidou competition was the largest. Held in 1971, it elicited 681 entries from fifty countries including France, and had an international jury that included Oscar Niemeyer and Philip Johnson among others.

9. Most polemically in the context of the "Light Construction" show at the Museum of Modern Art in New York in 1995.

10. The concept of psychogeography is not Appadurai's but goes back to the Situationists.

11. A similar critique of present-day experience as evanescent and unreal is implicit in Guy Debord's *Society of the Spectacle* (Debord 1995) and throughout Baudrillard's writings. On the aestheticization of politics, see the well-known concluding passage of Walter Benjamin's "The Work of Art in the Age of Mechanical Reproduction" (Benjamin 1969: 242), where Benjamin coins the concept to characterize the fascist deployment of spectacle as a strategy for solidifying the loyalty of the masses.

12. For a book emblematic of this phenomenon, and taking the Guggenheim Bilbao as its quintessence, see (Newhouse 1998).

13. It is perhaps worth underscoring that in focusing this chapter on a novel phenomenon of recent years, namely the potential of the single and singular work of architecture effectively to embody the aspirations of a locale. I have dwelled less on the more familiar arguments about the way spectacle buildings also advance the interests of gentrification. As mentioned, however, the Guggenheim Bilbao is the centerpiece of an extensive and ongoing redevelopment program. It is difficult to say how the relationship between the museum and the context from which it currently draws its energy will change once Bilbao's industrial character is preserved only in memory or pastiche.

References

Appadurai, Arjun (1996), *Modernity at Large: Cultural Dimensions of Globalization*, Minneapolis: University of Minnesota Press.

Barthes, Roland (1982), "The Eiffel Tower", in Sontag, Susan (ed.), *A Barthes Reader*, New York: Hill & Wang.

Baudrillard, Jean (1982), "The Beaubourg Effect: Implosion and Deterrence", *October*, 20 (Spring): 3–13.

Benjamin, Walter (1969), "The Work of Art in the Age of Mechanical Reproduction", in *Illuminations*, New York: Schocken Books.

Debord, Guy (1995), *The Society of the Spectacle*, New York: Zone Books.

Deleuze, Gilles and Guattari, Félix (1975, 1986), "What Is a Minor Literature?" in *Kafka: Toward a Minor Literature*, Minneapolis: University of Minnesota Press, pp. 16–27.

Heidegger, Martin (1975), "Building Dwelling Thinking", in Martin Heidegger, *Poetry, Language, Thought*, New York: Harper & Row, pp. 143–62.

Muschamp, Herbert (1997), "The Miracle in Bilbao", *New York Times Magazine* (7 September): 54–9, 72, 82.

Newhouse, Victoria (1998), *Towards a New Museum*, New York: Monacelli Press.

Ockman, Joan (2001), "Applause and Effect", *Artforum*, (Summer): 140–9.

Plaza, Beatriz (2000), "Evaluating the Influence of a Large Cultural Artifact in the Attraction of Tourism: The Guggenheim Museum Bilbao Case", *Urban Affairs Review*, 36(2): 264–74.

Rajchman, John (1999–2000), "The Bilbao Effect", in Adams, Nicholas and Ockman, Joan (eds), *Architecture USA: Forms of Spectacle,* special issue of *Casabella*, 673/674 (December–January): 10–11.

Ramírez, Juan Antonio (1997), "La explosion congelada: Bilbao-Babel, metáforas del Guggenheim", *Arquitectura Viva*, 55 July–August: 51.

Rossi, Aldo (1981), *A Scientific Autobiography*, Cambridge MA: MIT Press.

Sitz-Gento, Cristina and Betancourt-Salazar, Carlos (2003), *Facing Globalism: Bilbao and the Guggenheim Museum, Close Encounters in the Culture of Spectacle*, M.A. thesis, Columbia University Teachers College.

Venturi, R., Scott Brown, D. and Izenour, S. (1977), *Learning from Las Vegas*, Cambridge MA: MIT Press.

Virilio, Paul (1980, 1991), *The Aesthetics of Disappearance*, New York: Semiotexte.

Zevi, Bruno (1945), *Verso un'architettura organica: saggio sullo sviluppo del pensiero architettonico negli ultimi cinquant'anni*, Turin: Einaudi.

Zulaika, Joseba (1997), *Crónica de una seducción*, Madrid: Nerea.

—— (2000), "'Miracle in Bilbao': Basques in the Casino of Globalism", in Douglass, W. A., Urza, C., White, L. and Zulaika, J. (eds), *Basque Cultural Studies*, Reno: University of Nevada, 262–74.

—— (2001), "Tough Beauty: Bilbao as Ruin, Architecture, and Allegory", in Resina, J.R. (ed.), *Iberian Cities*, New York and London: Routledge, pp. 1–17.

Egypt on Steroids: Luxor Las Vegas and Postmodern Orientalism
Jeffrey Cass

Luxor Las Vegas and Postmodern Orientalism

At the end of Martin Scorsese's film *Casino*, Robert De Niro's character, Ace Rothstein, muses over the recent social, political, and economic forces that have transformed casino management practices in Las Vegas from a crude, seedy, if flashy gangsterism to a slick, controlled, chilly corporatism. He reluctantly concedes that hotels like the Tangiers, the glitzy casino whose operations he oversaw in his wiseguy heyday, have given way to multimedia, virtual reality theme parks. More and more, the new money lies in the affluent who flock to a reconstructed, family-friendly environment that nonetheless retains Las Vegas's otherness, its campy and commodified difference. Driven less and less by volatile gambling, substance abuse, and sex addictions, the local economy depends upon a burgeoning industry in mementos and keepsakes, metonymies of the tourists' own experiences as travelers in search of the exotic. Ace Rothstein recognizes that the day of a precorporatist style of management, up to and including overt (and violent) criminality, has passed. As if to underscore the emergence of new bureaucratic regimes, the camera pans over the Luxor Las Vegas and the Sphinx that lies in wait in front of it – a new kind of casino with a new kind of guardian (Figure 13.1). The Sphinx's eyes eventually fade into Ace Rothstein's. A living caveat against the dangers of unexamined experience, Rothstein can only observe the action of Las Vegas; he can no longer be a principal player. Brooding from the margins, he survives as a bookie in San Diego taking bets for mafioso friends, clearly Scorsese's version of gambling hell.

More importantly, the film subtly replaces one version of Orientalism for another. The Tangiers, much like other older Oriental-themed hotels such as the Aladdin and the Sahara, depend upon campy reifications of the Oriental Other to draw customers into their spaces. The bogus mysticism of the now razed Sands, its nearly forgotten, kitschy Buddhist garden in the center of the Shangri-la Café, or the peculiar conventionality of the new Aladdin with its 500,000 sq. ft. shopping mecca "Desert Passage," or the cultural banality of the Sahara's Caravan Coffee

Figure 13.1 Luxor Las Vegas, 1996. Courtesy of Luxor Las Vegas.

Shop or Sahara Steakhouse all retain glittery but superficial Orientalist signatures. Their eclectic and exotic references are adornments to the more functional spaces of the casino, rather like what Venturi once called the "decorated shed." But the billion dollar Luxor is no decorated shed. Its management intends much more than merely tantalizing tourists with its easily identifiable architecture and iconography. In fact, Luxor Las Vegas has been designed to direct and channel consumer desire to socialize tourists and bury them within its Orientalist landscapes. Like many of the recent megahotels, the Luxor stands as a Disneyesque theme park in which "the careful structure of entertainment and social relations supersedes the routinized contours of everyday life" (Sorkin 1992: 226). But Luxor Las Vegas also testifies to a newer form of Orientalist inscription that bears a different ideological intent.

One clue to the nature of what may be termed the "postmodern Orientalism" of the Luxor Las Vegas lies in the starkly segregated use of enclosed architectural landscapes and the ways in which tourists interact with their environment. Unlike previous usages of Orientalism in older Vegas hotels, the Luxor deploys its Orientalized art, iconography and architecture in order to coerce surreptitiously its visitors into internalizing their experience of cultural others. As geographer Michael J. Dear (2000: 204) has noted in his book, *The Postmodern Urban Condition*, "The Luxor makes no pretense at attracting casual passers-by off the street; its physical arrangement actually discourages this." Its undecorated exteriors disguise its "physical" immensity (the hotel covers 47 acres), but even a cursory glance at its interior spaces confirms this: a 100,000 sq. ft. casino, 20,000 sq. ft. of meeting space, and 4,474 rooms on thirty floors. At first, the stark nature of the Luxor's architecture – its eerily opaque acres of glass, its lack of neon lights, its darkly tinted interior design – seem to contradict the managerial desire to facilitate greater family access to (and enjoyment of) the hotel's interiors. The fact, however, that travelers must be intrepid in their quest for the delights the Luxor promises is a further inducement to the archeological adventures that await them inside. That is to say, because the tourists' pleasure depends upon discovery and conquest of the very spaces they have paid to inhabit, they participate in a process of othering. The Luxor's management gives the tourists/consumers the illusion that they are hearty outsiders who have arrived both to enjoy and assess Egypt and its massive monumentality and archeological treasures. But it is a process of representational "othering" that feeds into and is, in turn, fed by a prior and collective understanding of a version of Egypt that favors metonymic indices such as entombed pharaohs and exotic treasures, rather than those that merely denote the mundane rituals and cultural practices of everyday life. To be sure, in this Orientalized version of ancient Egypt, even mundane objects become rife with mystery. Predictably, visitors regard this Orientalized version of ancient Egypt as culturally "authentic" even though it has its actual genesis in the eighteenth and nineteenth centuries, a time when European archeology and tourism were inextricably linked to the activities of imperialism. A cultural critic and one of the original exponents of the theory of Orientalism, Edward Said (2000: 156) argues that during this period of archeological rediscovery, Egypt was:

> . . . available as a place to be ransacked for treasures and imposing ruins, a great many of which found their way into the major European museums . . . Egypt was in everything but name a European annex, traveled and raided – scientifically and enterprisingly at will.

Not coincidentally, the Luxor's management "ransacks" Egypt for the simulated "treasures and imposing ruins" that undergird this tourist attraction, even as it convinces tourists that their archeological experiences – their discoveries – do not implicate them in discomfiting imperialist logics. In a very real sense, the Luxor becomes a playful postmodern museum, in which Egypt takes its place as an "annex" of American venture capitalism. And just as archaeologists of the eighteenth and nineteenth centuries were not necessarily interested in artifacts from all periods of Egyptian history, so the Luxor seems indifferent to the presentation of an evolving or contemporary Egypt.

Even the imagineers of the Luxor's Virtual Reality ride, "In Search of the Obelisk," create a corporate technofuture rooted in the iconography of ancient Egypt. They posit an ancient archeological site that lies directly beneath the hotel, a site presumably discovered by developers while building the hotel. Within the Luxor Las Vegas, Egypt truly remains a civilization mummified, frozen in perpetual, ever-renewing ancientness, whose fascination and authenticity lie in consumers discovering and rediscovering its idealized and simulated ruins. Tourists wait in line to see the excavation site and while they wait they can see a news show (also fabricated) that features the principal characters of the virtual reality ride. They include: Kurt "Mac" McPherson, action hero and land developer of the Luxor properties; Colonel Oliver Claggart, military bogeyman who wishes to exploit the Luxor's archeological treasures; Carina Wolinski, linguist who can translate hieroglyphs, including those from unknown civilizations (she is also Mac's love interest); and the evil Dr. Osiris, who steals the crystal obelisk – the Luxor's most powerful treasure – in order to achieve world domination. Though the story plays out in utterly unsurprising fashion (Osiris kidnaps Carina; Mac saves her and the obelisk and the world), it coincides neatly with tourists' static understanding of ancient Egypt and its history, as well as their internalized expectations about capitalism and its relationship to empire. The virtuosity of the ride and the exorbitantly expensive iterations of Egyptian art, myth, and culture that inform its VR content reinforce an Orientalized version of ancient Egypt that tourists bring with them and actually prevent the evolution of a more accurate, less ideologically charged picture of Egyptian history and civilization. Further, because "Mac" appeals to the tourists' desire for adventure and risk, "Mac" reifies a capitalist ethos that sees no contradiction between the aggressive acquisition of wealth and the aggressive protection of heroic, selfless virtue. Nor do they discern that the capitalist exploitation of the Oriental Other can in itself become an adventure in imperialism.

To accomplish the task of molding tourists into "Mac" MacPherson explorers, the management erects its culturally "authentic" Egypt within the now familiar language of Disney attractions. Unquestionably, the Luxor's management has clearly learned several lessons from the Disney Corporation, at the same time that they wish to rival and surpass it. First, they derive the paradigm of simultaneously educating and entertaining their audience. At Disney World, for example, the Epcot Center, attempts to teach the history of communications through narrated rides and interactive video and machine displays. Its dimpled tower is a testament to the educational power of fun and games, although its animated dioramas in its principal ride now seem hopelessly outdated and unintentionally retro. Second, Disney blurs the boundaries between authentic and inauthentic cultural experiences. Their food pavilions, for instance, amount to a fusion of imported cuisines and Americanized standards of taste. Third, and perhaps most relevant, Disney succeeds at the construction of an efficient tourist experience – an environment constantly under surveillance, in which the tourist/consumer learns about cultural Others under safe and predictable conditions. Finally, depending upon the logic of the framed space, the management will also profit from either blurring the distinctions between historical reality and historical recreation or making such distinctions so exaggerated and glaring that they become campy entertainments.

Whenever the Luxor management prefers the porous boundaries between Egyptian antiquities and realistic simulations, it does so because this ambiguity forces tourists into the role of amateur archaeologists, sifting and sleuthing through the hotel's many contested spaces. Maps of the property site illustrate two principal levels – the Casino Level and the Attractions Level. The Attractions Level includes virtual rides, an IMAX theater, a museum devoted to the life of King Tutankhamen, a two-story video arcade, a number of gift shops, a food court with recognizable corporate franchises, and a number of kiosks whose services range from selling pearls to sizing pictures. At the Casino Level, there are more adult entertainments, such as a spacious cocktail lounge (Nefertiti's), the Luxor Theater that showcases the Blue Man Group, the Ra Night Club, and the hotel's most expensive restaurants. Bracketed by the East and West Towers, and toward the North Entry to the Luxor, tourists enter the uncompromisingly forbidding lobby (buttressed by figures that replicate those of the temple of Abu Simbel), as well as a vast indoor atrium. The floor plans, however, sound far more rational and gridded than the actual experience of walking the floors. There is a confusing array of ramps, escalators, and stairs that principally serve to imprison tourists within the confines of the pyramid. This control of tourist traffic is, as Hal Rothman (2002: 256) writes in *Neon Metropolis*, one of "Las Vegas's oldest strategies: keep them in the hotel." With Luxor Las Vegas, however, the use of architecture is not merely practical or profitable, it is ideological.

Like many of the newest hotels on the Strip – Paris, the Venetian, the Bellagio, and Mandalay Bay – the management's ability to simulate famous forms of architecture and their environments, often at great expense, renders all forms of "real" travel superfluous. Tourists need no longer be aliens in culturally "other" environments. Instead, like Anne Tyler's "accidental" tourists, consumers may vicariously enjoy their archeological excavations in predictable comfort and dull safety, which in an age of homeland security and terrorist threats makes the protected experience of the Cultural Other even more attractive. While previous versions of the Oriental Other made no pretense at cultural authenticity, in the case of the Luxor, the appearance of authenticity, however sanitized and safe, is both a key selling point and crucial element of this shift toward postmodern Orientalism. Even the traditional Las Vegas of Fremont Street, geographically and temperamentally at some remove from the corporatism of the Strip, employed architect Jon Jerde to revamp "Glitter Gulch" in order to alter fundamentally the tourist experience of the downtown. At the Luxor, the management totalizes tourists' experience of ancient Egypt by immersing them, sometimes in the minutest of detail, in all of its iconography. But its historical past has also been refashioned to suit Las Vegas's new corporate style – a lucrative, technologically planned future that ensures that the histories of cultural others are mediated and shaped by capitalist processes.

Because postmodern Orientalism intersects so strongly with a corporatist philosophy, the architecture and iconography of the Luxor appear less about the creation and celebration of shared public space, than they do about the maintenance and channeling of consumerist desire. Stanley Matthews (1993: 3) argues in his essay, "Architecture in the Age of Hyperreality:"

> The bottom line is that what we think of as "authentic" architectural experience is increasingly subordinated to the production of mediated meaning for and within the mass culture of the consumer marketplace . . . [architects] are increasingly pressed into service as imagineers for the production of architectural commodity; the production of space is directed into the generation of new images for consumer culture.

In other words, the "imagineers" create architectural commodities that consumers need not interpret for themselves because "the mass culture of the consumer marketplace" has already dictated their semiotic significance and cultural meaning. In essence, architectural spaces take shape through commodified images. Now "pressed into service," architects of the postmodern have unwittingly become complicit with corporatist capitalism. Veldon Simpson, the Luxor's architect, says as much. In the slickly packaged, *The Making of the Luxor* (1993), he openly confirms this new relationship between architecture and corporate money: "I think we've reached the point where architecture now becomes a very important element in casino-hotel work." This pragmatic connection also explains his work on the Excalibur, another megahotel that links "casino-hotel work" to architectural; design, in this case a dreamy castle that cleverly commodifies Camelot. This brazen complicity, which maximizes profits even as it exploits the integrity of architecture, might not surprise Robert Venturi, the great theorist of Las Vegas architecture and Pritzker Architecture Prize Laureate, yet his own critique of modernism still theorizes the hope for revolutionary change. Venturi believes that in an age of decreasing public funding for architectural forms, the architect must "find formal languages suited to our times" in order to address and shape social concerns. The use of symbols, particularly the symbols within popular culture, becomes for Venturi intimately associated with the "revitalization" of architecture and, by extension, of revolutionary social change (Taylor 1992: 190). For them to be effective, architectural symbology must be overt, immediately recognizable and not obscure or intellectually abstract. This view assumes, however, that the commonplace is not also fraught with ideological problems that may also obscure "revitalization" or social change. Thus, while Veldon Simpson's architectural vision of the Luxor remains firmly rooted in a popular version of ancient Egypt, replete with easily recognizable images and symbols, his vision does not ultimately engender a public reflectiveness or call to arms that Venturi's populist aesthetics implicitly demands. Instead of goading the public to new "sensibilities," which permit the confrontation with the contradictions within contemporary society, the "symbols" of hotels like the Luxor primarily act as a spur to further consumption.

Venturi certainly felt that modernist architecture had lost its ethical and social dimension, but he overestimated the social ethos evoked by the production of postmodern spectacle. The new corporatism, which Ace Rothstein instinctively loathes, makes use of figural eclecticism – an ideal foil for all forms of Orientalism that assist tourists in the navigation of their own consumer desire. But desire is not reflection, and postmodern Orientalist figures deliberately blunt a thoughtful consumerism, which might resist casual or manic consumption. The profusion of Egyptian icons and other Orientalist signs located and distributed throughout the Luxor undercores Veldon Simpson's understated connection between the utilitarian "work" of the casino and the physical forms that give expression to those interests. The managers of the Luxor seek to inculcate an ideology of public play, although beneath that "play" lurk the corporate logics of monitoring and control. Inasmuch as tourist playfulness, in and of itself, remains unpredictable and fickle, corporate planning seeks to minimize such variability, and the pyramid and its accompanying signs reify expected management practices.

But they do a great deal more than that. They represent, as Robert Mugurauer (1995: 31) suggests, a colonizing displacement of "'timeless' presence and identity." For the tourist who fancies a dependable and secure, archeological adventure into the Oriental Other, the Luxor displaces its Giza counterpart, even as it relies upon the sacredness of that very recognizable Egyptian monument. In fact, the Luxor's management appropriates Egyptian monumentality to create the illusion of sacred timelessness and changelessness, at the same time pandering shamelessly to the consumers' desire for novelty and change. The new corporate pharaohs profit from the "fictive basis" of the Luxor, which stresses the exotic mysteriousness of Egypt and its artifacts, yet, if financially necessary, these same corporate heads will not hesitate to remap the Luxor's interiors to buoy their balance sheets. Hence, the management scrapped its unprofitable Nile ride with its slow-moving barges, as well as its ecologically insensitive use of water resources, in favor of the much trendier (and "spendier") Pharaoh's Pheast. The chic buffet not only made the running of the Luxor more cost effective, it also assisted the management in the tourists' experience of archeological recovery and conquest. The buffet quite literally iterates the acquisition and consumption that the management of Luxor Las Vegas encourages and promotes – an undying hunger, an insatiable appetite. Far from embodying an architecture that affirms the serenity and stasis of afterlife, surely the intention of pharaohs who constructed their own funerary pyramids (or the intention of those who entombed the pharaoh), the Luxor becomes a marker of worldliness and profitability. Though not intended as a description for the Luxor, Mugurauer's phrase "presence and identity" seems especially apt, for the Luxor's "presence" along the Strip, its "identity" among the city's megahotels becomes that of capitalist expansion and colonization, rather than spiritual or physical rebirth. Eating their way to archeological glory, tourists gleefully (if imaginativly) become accomplices to cultural grave robbing, "exhuming icons from the mythical detritus of a culture that is easily recognized, mined, and profitably commodified" (Cass and Dennis 1996: 3).

"Egypt on Steroids:" Proliferating Orientalist Icons

In 1996, the Mandalay Resort Group (the new name for Circus Circus Enterprises), under the leadership of Mike Ensign, chief executive and father of Nevada's junior U.S. Senator John Ensign, began to reconceive and restructure the pyramid's interiors, in particular rescaling and remodeling its many public venues in order to attract more upscale tourists. Billy Richardson, the General Manager of the adult night club Ra, and son of the second largest stockholder in the Mandalay Resort Group, has indicated his personal intention to present the Luxor to consumers as "Egypt on steroids" (interview with Clydean O'Conner). Attracted to the Luxor's expensive and ubiquitous reproductions of Egyptian motifs, upscale consumers could afford to enjoy Orientalist alienness, mass-produced yet quite stylish. Indeed, even more than when it opened in 1993 under the aegis of Circus Circus Enterprises, the Luxor's profusion of Orientalist figures, icons, replicas, and artwork underscores what Frances Anderton has entitled Las Vegas's "success of excess" – a gorgeous and profitable "muddle that resonates with an eclectic group of cultural images." In short, the Luxor reveals itself to be an iconographic pastiche, an assemblage that is nonetheless, as Edward Said might have predicted in *Orientalism*, consistent with itself. In other words, while managers wish to evoke the exoticism of the "Orient," they do not necessarily wish to remind tourists of Asian cultures and their "real" cultural differences, preferring instead to assault them with more easily digestible, commodified simulacra. Like the older style Orientalist hotels, establishments such as the Luxor relies on reassuring iconographic stereotypes. Unlike these hotels, however, the Luxor does not simply

Figure 13.2 Talking camels at entrance to Giza Galleria, Luxor Las Vegas, 2002. Photograph by author.

evoke the Oriental. Rather, its management has made a studied, prolific, and consistent use of that imagery, occasioning assemblages of coherent metafictions, drawing upon and expanding the tourists' prior knowledge of the Oriental Other, specifically of Egypt and Egyptians. Not coincidentally, in the Luxor's interior and exterior spaces, both those in 1993 and those remodeled in 1996 and after, Egyptian simulacra are everywhere – hieroglyphs adorn ATM machines; friezes cover the back walls of elevators; murals depicting Egyptian rites and ceremonies decorate the walls of most paid attractions, as well as the large walls behind the registration desks; statues of pharaohs and queens and ancient gods such as Anubis and Bastet preside over other public spaces, ranging from the casino to the health spa to Sobek's sundry store.

By far the most interesting commodification of this profusion of Egyptomania occurs in the Luxor's principal shopping arcade, which is cleverly situated near the registration desk by the North Entry but removed from the enormous traffic of the casino. Known as the Giza Galleria, this "bazaar" at once alludes alliteratively to the ancient tradition of an Egyptian open market and to the modern convenience and luxury of a Southern California upscale mall. Gracing the entrance to the Giza Galleria are the hotel's two animatronic talking camels, which charm tourists with a cloying, almost pre-technological simplicity (Figure 13.2). Their cuteness dissipates the immensity of the pyramid's interiors, the challenging process of navigating through them, and the strangeness of consistently encountering prolife-rating Egyptian icons. From the tourist perspective, the camels' very familiarity as Oriental symbols minimizes the Luxor as unbreachable behemoth and sparks the illusion of patron comfort and manageability through the promise of comfortable (if high-priced) shopping. What actually happens, however, is a form of Althus-serian interpellation – consumers are literally "hailed" by the camels, recruited into the corporatist logics of the Giza Galleria marketplace. Moreover, the various shops depend upon each other for an Orientalist ambiguity between the real and the fictional, between the authentic and the simulated. This confusion becomes espe-cially evident because consumers can acquire legitimate Egyptian antiquities in the same shopping arcade in which they may purchase the kitschy clones of such relics. In the Treasure Chamber, the Luxor's designated shop for antiquities, a serious treasure hunter might purchase a small bronze oil lamp (fourth or fifth century AD) for $850 or a faience fragment from the Ptolemaic Period (747–332 BC) for $550. Yet at a kiosk from the other side of the wall, hoarders of cheaper souvenirs might acquire similar objects for under $50. In effect, the Egypt govern-ment permits the Luxor to vend authenticated artifacts, at the same time that it also exports fabricated ceramic fakes of those same artifacts, consequently blurring the boundaries of authenticity and simulacrum even further. Ironic in a very real sense, legitimate "objects of cultural importance" and their simulacra may both be said to have been truly "made in Egypt".[1]

Fictive Archeology and Utilitarian Pleasure

Taking his cue from British historians Eric Hobsbawm and Terence Ranger, Edward Said writes in his essay, "Invention, Memory, and Place" that "The invention of tradition is a method for using collective memory selectively by manipulating certain bits of the national past, suppressing others, elevating still others in an entirely functional way. Thus memory is not necessarily authentic, but rather useful" (Said 2002: 245). By incarnating an "Egypt on steroids," the Luxor is no mere avatar of a recuperated and meticulously reconstructed Egyptian past. Rather, it plays upon and "manipulates" tourists' memory and knowledge of the Luxor's archeological origins by calling forth "certain bits" of Egypt's architectural and iconographic traditions, tantalizing consumers with a "selectively" chosen past and, at the same time, serving the utilitarian purposes of the Mandalay Bay Resort Group. The management can even claim that, despite its corporate interests, it sincerely wishes to educate patrons about Egyptian history and culture, however packaged and commodified and expensive that education becomes. Memory's "functionality" for the upscale tourist effectively transforms the sheer indulgence of the vacation into intellectual usefulness. Perhaps this newly emergent ideology helps explain why David Brooks (2000: 205), senior editor of *The Weekly Standard*, believes that the new upper class (whom he labels "bobos" or bourgeois bohemians) feasts on "useful" rather than "wanton" pleasures. "The code of utilitarian pleasure," he muses, "means we have to evaluate our vacation time by what we accomplished – what did we learn, what spiritual or emotional break-throughs were achieved, what new sensations were experienced?"

The desire to vindicate the time spent on one's vacation explains, in part, the recent development in Strip megahotels of incorporating famous art in their interiors; they have become, in essence, museum sites for tourists who crave "useful" as well as "wanton" pleasures. But the sheer evocation of a powerful artistic and cultural past in these spaces, in all of their lavish richness, far exceeds the "edu-tainment" that underlies exhibits at places such as Disney's Epcot Center, which cater basely to the thoroughly democratized tastes of the *hoi polloi*. The Guggenheim has two museum spaces in the Venetian, one of which has displayed pieces from modernists such as Picasso and Kandinsky, and both of which were designed by the Dutch architect Rem Koolhaas. The Bellagio has gathered works from the Phillips collection, the Private Collection of Steve Martin, as well as an impressive assortment of mobiles from its Calder exhibition. Allocating a portion of casino space as a refuge for culture junkies and art hipsters reinforces David Brooks' insight into the bourgeois tourist's search for more utilitarian pleasure, but his insight also demonstrates the desire of the new Vegas to redefine itself – reimagine itself for a new type of consumer. It is hard to picture Ace Rothstein enjoying the Impressionists. As a result, this unexpected transformation does a great deal more than rationalize tourist pleasure; it indicates that this new use of space manifests another version of corporate logics. Recognizably unique art legitimates recognizably unique (if obscenely expensive) megahotels and their meticulously "real" simulacra because the new Las Vegas on steroids is one of heightened distinctions. In a supremely droll case of the utilitarian tail wagging the venture capitalist dog, the hotel can now be constructed around the art it houses, and all so that tourists spending exorbitant amounts of vacation money will not feel guilty about such expenditures.

Since the Luxor management cannot purchase or transport actual obelisks, sphinxes, shabti, temple columns, faiences, or sarcophagi for the pyramid's interiors, its task of turning at least a portion of Luxor Las Vegas into a credible museum for Egyptian relics and, at the same time, sustaining the tourists' desire for "edu-tourism" is considerably more difficult than that faced by corporate managers at the Bellagio or the Venetian. The Luxor makes use of a fictive archeology, which provides both the illusion of the cultural and historical preservation of ancient Egypt, as tourists interact with and imaginatively excavate the Luxor for its profusion of images of an Oriental Other they already know and expect. These expectations help to explain why Luxor Las Vegas has given over an enormous amount of space to a museum devoted to King Tutankhamen. Firmly entrenched within the popular mind, perhaps because of the blockbuster exhibitions at the National Gallery in Washington, DC in 1976 and the Metropolitan in New York in 1978, the Luxor's iterations of King Tutankhamen and the treasures entombed with him provide the most utilitarian pleasures for the Luxor's ever-guilty bourgeois bohemians. Strangely, however, it is a museum without authentic artifacts. Hampered by laws against (and costs of) importing genuine artifacts, the builders of the Luxor can only erect a museum of simulacra.[1] The only legitimately "ancient" relic of Egypt lies encased in hard plastic. "Donated by the Tourism Sector of Egypt," a piece of the Great Pyramid at Giza not only validates the copies of Egyptian art in the museum itself, it also directs the cultural authenticity of the commodified fakes on sale outside the museum in the gift shop. Moreover, like the great art on exhibition in the other megahotels, the piece of the Great Pyramid also symbolizes the educational value to tourists of the Luxor's many cultural fictions. Lying as it does in the vestibule to the recreation of King Tut's burial chamber, the piece of the Giza Pyramid slyly promises an experience free of corporate management and control since museum space should ideally be unfettered space in which various populations and social classes may mingle and learn, where bureaucratic regimes do not as readily control patron conduct. Ironically, however, museums may be the most regulated and controlled of architectural spaces, in particular museums whose spatial context lies within the arcades of megahotels. As urban theorist Mike Davis (1992: 226) has noted: "The valorized spaces of the new megastructures and super-malls are concentrated in the center, street frontage is denuded, public activity is sorted into strictly functional compartments, and circulation is internalized in corridors under the gaze of private police." The museum becomes another of the Luxor's "functional compartments," an essential component for "a new Pan-opticon" (Cass and Dennis 1996: 4) that prevents the free "circulation" of the inhabitants who remain under the gaze and scrutiny of its corporate managers. And the latter persistently manipulate tourists' experiences within the Luxor. In effect, the museum becomes another profitable space, which clandestinely supports the utility of pleasure.

In addition to a fragment from the Great Pyramid at Giza, the vestibule to the museum holds a large number of replicated Egyptian artifacts, whose descriptions deliberately obfuscate and evade their artificial origins. As the following label of one such exhibit notes: "These necklaces are made from a variety of stones chosen for their rich colors. Quartz, lapis lazuli, and amethyst are among the semiprecious stones that adorned the King's neck." Such a circumlocution decorously avoids the fact that none of these artifacts is genuine. But the museum's corporate "curators" still want tourists to accept their legitimacy. In the above example, the writer states that "these necklaces are made from a variety of stones chosen for their rich colors." He does not say, however, that "these necklaces" were not found with

King Tutankhamen, nor does he ever state that the stones in "these necklaces" are not "semiprecious," such as the ones that were found with the boy pharaoh – merely that they are colorful. In the other examples, and elsewhere in the museum, phrases such as "like this one" or "such as this one" serve to make all statements literally true, but they also draw the museum patrons further into yet another fictive archeological expedition for utterly convincing simulacra.

After a perusal of the exhibits and a five-minute BBC clip about the discoverer of King Tut's tomb, Howard Carter, tourists may move on to the next stage: entry into the recreated burial chamber. First, though, they will observe a historical timeline that decorates the hallway, a timeline that records the inexorable movement of Egyptian history from Rameses and other epochs in "ancient" Egyptian history forward to the creation of the Aswan dam and finally to the establishment of the Luxor Las Vegas. The Luxor Las Vegas thus inaugurates a new period in *Egyptian* history. To commemorate this momentous occasion, the Luxor's management has framed Governor Bob Miller's proclamation on the 1993 opening of the Luxor, in which he mandates "Egyptian Day." This public declaration establishing the corporate and governmental intent to recreate in Las Vegas perhaps the most important (certainly the most famous) archeological find in Egypt signals a postmodern, post-Egyptian Egypt that can be transported to "other" geographic and cultural landscapes, morphed into commodified formats, and sold to would-be "Egyptian" tourists. Even King Tutankhamen, the progenitor of these fabled treasures, has been popularized and truncated to "Tut" – the eponym for a plethora of memento mori, ranging from cheap children's toys like Teddy Tuts and Tiny Tut Trolls to expensive recreations of Tut's funeral mask, retailing for $10,000. The CowParade Holdings Corporation even makes cow kitsch reproductions, the most pertinent of which is Tutan*cow*mon, an Orientalized cow adorned with Tut's funeral mask. King Tutankhamen, in this instance, is not merely the grist for the corporate vending mill. He has been feminized, for Tutancowmon's very prominent udders attest to the malleability of King Tut, hammering him, gender notwithstanding, into any of a number of profitable shapes and sizes.

The Egyptian invitees who witnessed the "momentous event" of the raising of Luxor Las Vegas did not recognize that they were unintentionally presiding over their own cultural death. "Egyptian Day" signals the doom of Egyptian authenticity and the birth of the postmodern Oriental, transforming important cultural and historical icons that epitomized rarefied Egyptian relics into debased, exploited iterations. As architectural form, Luxor Las Vegas embodies the corporate drive for market domination. As "metropolitan space," the Luxor is "a metaphor for global power" (MacKenzie 1995: 35). But while managers certainly seek high profits in the selling of "Egyptian" memorabilia, these "artifacts" signify a great deal more than the acquisition of wealth. As Said (1993: 10) argues in *Culture and Imperialism*, there is also a "commitment" to the "constant circulation and recirculation" of imperial signs, ensuring that these Orientalized simulacra of King Tutankhamen insidiously remind tourists of their obligations to capitalist enterprises, not only of their ideological commitment to the transnational corporate logics that underwrite the Luxor, but to their personal responsibility to "circulate and recirculate" these images of imperial commodification. While Governor Miller's "proclamation" celebrates the spectacular "recreation" of Egypt in the architecture and iconography of the Luxor Las Vegas, the ironic consequence has been the utter displacement of a heterogeneous, "real" Egypt. Tourists in the market for an Egyptian adventure, but who have no desire to travel, need no longer go halfway around the world to enjoy one. Tourists goaded by intellectual interest into a "real" Egyptian adventure, men and women who eagerly crave a journey to Egypt and its actual ruins, will still be guided by their Orientalist preconceptions about that version of Egypt that they wish to experience. And the Egyptians themselves are complicit in this displacement, although their presence at the Luxor's gala opening might at first only appear to be taking pride in one's national identity and cultural difference. Nonetheless, the supportive actions of "Egyptian officials' are, as Gayatri Chakravorty Spivak (1999: 319), a prominent postcolonial theorist, denounces in a *Critique of Postcolonial Reason*, "the benign rusing face of what allows the United States to "export democracy" to "older cultures" even as the globetrotting self-ethnicizers dine out on difference."

The slippage between the real and the simulated in King Tut's museum, which allows for this "dining out on difference," culminates in the tape-recorded tour of King Tut's burial chamber. Perhaps the most fascinating oddity of the tour is that its narrator is the simulated voice of none other than Howard Carter. Although a widely respected and well-trained scientist, financial exigency eventually forced Carter to abandon the study of archeology in favor of its commercial interests and questionable business practices. Lord Carnarvon eventually employed him, and Carter eagerly assisted Lord Carnarvon in the acquisition of an enormous collection of expensive Egyptian antiquities. Subsequent to Carnarvon's death and the cataloging of the artifacts of Tutankhamen, Carter himself became a "collector" of artifacts. He later died in the Winter Palace Hotel at the "real" Luxor.[2] Reborn at the Luxor Las Vegas, and free of treacherous historical facts, the resurrected (if disembodied) Howard Carter narrates the story of archeological triumphs to tourists who crave the spicy entertainment of 1920s tomb raider archaeologists. Because of his connections to British imperialism in Luxor and the Valley of the Kings, and because of the inevitable associations with "Tutankhamen's Curse," the simulated figure of Howard Carter Orientalizes Egypt and Egyptians. He becomes a useful historical construct that both educates his audience on the niceties of archeology and impresses upon them a colonialist ethos that transforms the immorality of imperial theft into the necessity of historical preservation, something of which indigenous inhabitants are not, in this view, capable.

Protected by the Western cultural supremacy guaranteed by their own Orientalist preconceptions, tourists of the Luxor Las Vegas can thus thrill to the vague
menace of exotic Egyptian representations – Hathur, Guide to the Underworld; the
vulture god, Nekhbet, and his supremacy over Upper Egypt; the jackal god Anubis,
Lord of Embalming; or the rebirth symbology of the twelve baboons that represent
the first twelve hours of night. Whether casual patrons or museum aficionados,
however, all tourists will be able to identify with the unexamined but tacitly
understood story of British imperial possession, of artifact ownership and control.
Feeding this illusion even more cravenly, the management of Luxor Las Vegas
displays Dover reprints of Howard Carter's key archeological work, *The Discovery of the Tomb of Tutankhamen.* Tourists logically covet what Carter uncovered
in Tut's tomb, which explains why one step beyond the tour lies the ubiquitous
museum gift shop. They can assume the role of Lord Carnarvon, commemorating
Carter's ghostly museum tour by acquiring a treasury of tasteless souvenirs
stamped with the Luxor name, including ashtrays, shot glasses, mugs, soap dishes,
soap dispensers, salt and pepper shakers, beer glasses, bells, trivets, children's forks
and spoons, teething rings, bibs, cups, plates, water bottles, change purses, key
chains, and back scratchers. The gift shop succeeds in recodifying the utilitarian
pleasures of imperial excavation into easily marketed things of everyday use, a
contemporary equivalent of Carter's own treasure seeking. In this context, Luxor
Las Vegas most nakedly realizes an Americanized, corporatized iteration of the
once British-dominated Luxor. What was a bone of contention between imperialist
London and nationalist Cairo has become, 80 years later, an international complicity to fuse truth with myth. The landscapes and tourist artifacts inscribed by the
Luxor's management substitute the actual history and culture of Egypt with a
"hieroglyphic culture" (Said's term) whose architectural and iconographic signs
interpellate tourist-archaeologists into the market logics of the postmodern Oriental
Other, at once enticingly alien and comfortingly pre-Islamic. As Edward Said
contends in his essay "Egyptian Rites," "Underlying the contemporary American
interest in ancient Egypt is . . . a persistent desire to bypass Egypt's Arab identity,
to reach back to a period when things were assumed to be both simple and amen-
able to the always well-intentioned American will" (Said 2000: 160). "Egyptian
officials" have effectively allowed Egyptian cultural difference to be commodified
within American consumer culture, even as they have traded their richly dense
"real" history for a highly commodified and constructed one.

In a rather humorous vein, the Luxor's corporate manipulations regarding the
experience of archeology include eating – literal consumption – since their massive
buffet – Pharaoh's Pheast – is intended (according to Clydean O'Conner,
Advertising and Publicity manager for the Luxor) as an experience in
archeological recovery. As tourists enter Pharaoh's Pheast, they encounter what
appear to be half-buried Egyptian artifacts, whose seemingly "natural" condition

Figure 13.3 Series of columns at Pharaoh's Pheast Buffet, Luxor Las Vegas. Photograph by author.

in the fake sand invites would-be explorers to excavate these artifacts and restore them to pure condition. Interestingly, on one side of the buffet space, there is a series of columns that progresses from a battered condition to a restored one, the flutes on the unsullied column more pronounced, with its capitol pristinely refashioned (Figure 13.3). This parade of columns embodies the spirit of archeological reconstruction, perhaps, but this progression from ruined artifact to perfected recreation also persuades tourists of the power of capitalism, not only to outfit archeological digs, but to employ the finds to the ends of consumerism. The art and the science of archeology now rightfully serve the interests of monied and discriminating consumers. After all, their buffet line must be both intellectually stimulating and aesthetically interesting. But this affiliation between archeology and food also diminishes the guilt of patrons who, surrounded by ever-proliferating Egyptian simulacra, gorge on delicacies that many Egyptians themselves could not afford. The "edu-tainment" provided by this space justifies the expense of the "pheast" because such an experience is both useful and pleasurable. As tourists exit Pharaoh's Pheast, they can adoringly gaze on an enormous golden pharaoh's head; its presumed pricelessness is only made possible by a commodified archeological knowledge, the importance of which patrons have been socialized into accepting. But the golden head is also a metonymy for the riches that lie in wait for qualified diggers. Lying directly beneath the casino proper, the buffet launches tourists into the gaming areas. Like many of the European colonialists who first stole artifacts for profit in Egypt (and throughout Africa and Asia), overstuffed tourists sally forth into the Luxor's casino, comb it for buried treasure, and greedily excavate it.

Postmortem Luxor: Raising the Homoerotic Dead

While the Luxor management trumpets its meticulously crafted "blockbuster corporate architecture" (to use Michael Dear's term) in an attempt to recreate a pyramid that even time "fears" (according to the press release), it also ballyhoos its "architectural team" that conceived the Luxor's many iconographic details, including "murals depicting daily life in Ancient Egypt." In other words, tourists need not only gawk at the grand simulations that reproduce the majesty and the marvel enjoyed by pharaohs and queens but at the artwork that more neatly squares with the lives of lower caste Egyptians. But the three murals that adorn walls behind the registration desks are not realistic representations but rather, Oriental-ized depictions of events that only further exoticize "Ancient Egypt" by highlight-ing arcane rites and eroticized male bodies. In one example, perhaps the most tantalizing of the lobby murals, a very muscular Egyptian guard, arms crossed, directly stares across the mural at another scantily clad and virile guard, whose sexy and slightly feminized nonchalance strangely resembles the erotically half-dressed men of Calvin Klein advertisements, in which the boundaries between the heterosexual and homosexual male collapse (Figure 13.4). At the center of the mural, two cowled Egyptian priests pore over the forbidden knowledge offered by a burning brazier, smoke wafting upwards. They confirm the rites of maleness, the secrecy and the public taboo; they become disguised doubles of the two half-naked Egyptian guards, metonymies for the fleshly code of conduct that flashes right under the public's jaundiced eye. Outside the temple, another group of bare-chested Egyptian boy-men gather in the hot Egyptian sun.

In performing a sexual postmortem on the archeology of ancient Egyptians, the creators of Luxor Las Vegas effectively produce an architecture of capitalist seduction, a temple of homosocial relations. The guards and the priests of the lobby mural suggest a corporate economy of desire, recapitulating the greedy intent of the Luxor's cabalistic corporatocracy. Resonating strongly with the shape of this desire is the commodified profusion of images of King Tutankhamen, the glamor-ized and commodified boy-king, whose ghost haunts much of the Luxor. Ironic-ally, "Tutankhamun" iterates provocative versions of steroidal maleness and male power because historically he does little except order the construction of his own burial chamber. Indeed, just like the figures in the lobby murals, "Tutan-khamun" embodies the capricious and whimsical exercise of royal power and male privilege.

Figure 13.4 Lobby mural behind registration desk, Luxor Las Vegas, 2002, photograph by author.

At the Luxor's attractions level, perhaps the most striking iconographic parallels to the lobby mural are two important wall paintings in the *Games of the Gods* video arcade. The first, a pharaoh, morphed into a Rameses or Tutankhamen "on steroids," whose fiercely chiseled face and overdeveloped musculature are drawn directly from the aggressive imagery of the World Wrestling Federation, legitimates competition within the arcade. His rough spirit oversees the gaming drives of children and adolescents – too young to gamble for money, but certainly not too old to compete for prizes. The style of the painting, however, contrasts strikingly with the lobby mural paintings, whose grandiose realism seems almost reminiscent of eighteenth- and nineteenth-century American and European portrait painting. In the arcade, the paintings recall the coloration and *jouissance* of graffiti art. The Luxor's management recognizes that the children of upwardly mobile, suburban parents identify with the art and iconography produced by the inner city (at least as conceived and constructed by and in popular culture), just as they do with studio-produced hip-hop and canned rap music. Indeed, the "gangsta" glyphs convulse the youngest bourgeois bohemians (baby bobos) to consume video games rather rapaciously, and they do so within a hypermasculine environment that remains, amazingly enough, relatively insulated, secure, and navigable. Perhaps more importantly, these refurbished icons, even in "gangsta" format, reinforce a capitalist ethos that young boy-men may emotionally and intellectually internalize.

Corporate managers perhaps envision these embryonic pharaohs as the strongmen of new cohorts of consumers who learn the value of competition within the safe arena of virtual combat.

The cheesiness of the video arcade – its emphasis on cheap prizes and glitzy VR thrills – points, however, to a far more sinister purpose than mere socialization within a capitalist ethos. As Annalee Newitz, culture editor of the *San Francisco Bay Guardian*, contends in her provocative essay, "What Makes Things Cheesy?," any form of mediated cheesiness "recirculate[s] the identities made possible by global imperialism and enjoying them without guilt. Cheese keeps the iconography of imperialism alive, yet mediates it with satire . . . and with a perverse pleasure in situations that only seem funny if the humans in them are treated like commodities" (Newitz 2000: 79). The hilarity of the arcade games separates both adult and adolescent consumers from the darker, more serious underpinnings of their consumption and the capitalist processes that produce the Luxor's "cheesy" artifacts. Like the casino itself, the video arcade makes the safe. As a microcosm of the Luxor Pyramid as a whole, the video arcade unintentionally represents the comforting reinvention of the postmodern Oriental Other who cannot hurt us, an exhumation of the already dead Egyptian safely moored to a highly visible and public archeological past. In a post-9/11 world, where the perceived Oriental Other may indeed menace us, this reinvention suppresses the gravity of the "terrifying revolutions, repressive nationalist regimes, imperial invasion, and wartime destruction" that comprise our preconceived mental geography and cultural history of the Middle East and Asia (Newitz 2000: 79).

The iconographic cheesiness of the arcade, therefore, disguises the moral and ethical complicity of a transnational corporatism that profits from tourists' deepest fears of social and cultural Others, even as it also erects a homosocial training ground in the art of virtual war, which appears, even with the oldest and least technologically advanced of video games, to harmlessly destroy one's enemies and transfer them to digitized casualty lists. In fact, the arcade reproduces what Benjamin has identified in *The Arcades Project* as "the idea of eternal recurrence," the doctrine that "attempt[s] to reconcile the mutually contradictory tendencies of desire; that of repetition and that of eternity" (Benjamin 1999: 116–17). On the one hand, the arcade demands that its boy "soldiers" repeat their "combat" skills over and over again, for there is no end to the imperialist logics of domination and control. More is always better. On the other, combat offers eternity, the glimmering intoxication of endless praise and privilege, the luxurious fruits of martial power that overshadow the shameful and inglorious by-products of war that conceal its repetitiveness and futility. Submerged within the cheesily consumed, often homoerotic landscapes and gangsta glyphs of *The Games of the Gods* arcade is an economic colonialism that disguises itself within the contours and iconographic signatures of the VR arcade, and it is a colonialism that trades in racial and cultural identities, encouraging tourists to culturally cross dress, assume the glamorous shape of the appropriated Other, and then easily dispatch of its used husk. It is a colonialism in which racial Others "can be bought, sold, and traded . . . [and] thrown away whenever one wishes . . ." (Newitz 2000: 79). In the final analysis, an excavation of the Luxor and its interior spaces uncovers a hermeneutics of ethnic disposability, perhaps the darkest if most utilitarian secret for a rising generation of global capitalists to decipher.

Reified in the architecture and iconography of the Luxor, the managers of the Mandalay Resort Group have arrogated to themselves a territorial, colonizing expansion of their power that requires no public discussion or justification because such theorizing contravenes tourist self-gratification and puts into stark relief corporate motives. Mike Davis believes that the "crucial point about contemporary capitalist structures" is that "they are symptoms of global crisis, not signs of the triumph of capitalism's irresistible drive to expand" (as quoted in Willis, 1989: 64). Davis assumes, however, that "global crisis" and the "triumph" behind capitalism's "drive to expand" are necessarily exclusive arrangements. On the contrary, a tourist economy driven by the rising tides of transnational capital requires a concomitant expansion in territory and territorial control. And the Luxor Las Vegas is merely a microcosm of the changing managerial configurations of Las Vegas as a whole, configurations to which Ace Rothstein clearly falls prey in *Casino*. As national and international economies destabilize, the assertion of corporate control becomes even more paramount for diehard, venture capitalists. Nevertheless, for optimal profit-taking in this new environment, management must remove itself from overt public display, receding into a faceless bureaucracy that mysteriously and effort-lessly pulls the levers and switches of its entertainment industry, controlling the workings of its own operations and the experiences of the clients who voraciously consume them. Luxor Las Vegas thus simulates and *dis*simulates at the same time, for its questionable socializing practices lurk behind any perceived civic utilitarian-ism or virtue. The Luxor pyramid is emblematic of what Baudrillard (1988: 173), following Bourdieu, calls a legitimating "moral superstructure," for it employs aptly Orientalist signatures in its architecture and iconography in order to disguise management's "unscrupulous" push for capital (Baudrillard 1988: 173). The more pyramidal its hierarchies, the more the Luxor management rationalizes its intent. Managed, socialized, troped into a consumerist feeding frenzy, tourists prefer the hyped hope of a virtual technofuture to the humdrum and platitudinous present, to which, they believe, they are forever bound. Pretending to the status of miraculous, self-fashioned artifact, Luxor Las Vegas hypostasizes itself as continual industrial movement and endless aesthetic exchange. The hyperbolic Orientalism that underlies its architecture and constitutes its postmodern spectacle tautologically conjures the Luxor as both the originary object of its own Orientalized, steroidal gaze and the originary subject of its own imperious consumerism. It is not a lesson to be taken lightly. And yet even if the Luxor's upscale tourists did reflect upon the frenetic nature of their own conspicuously excessive consumer sprees, even if they actually perceived that they had become replicants of an entrenched corporat-acracy, they probably would not care. And that, too, is part of the sadness of Ace Rothstein's sphinxlike eyes.

Notes

1. In the Treasure Chamber, the Luxor's store that sells authenticated Egyptian antiques, one sign reads in a glass display case: "All of the objects exhibited here have been acquired legally in the United States and Europe and with full consideration of all international treaties governing objects of cultural impor-tance." On some of the objects, a particular Egyptologist has certified specific objects for their historical and cultural authenticity.
2. For an excellent discussion of Carter and his tense relationship with the Egyp-tian government following the death of Carnarvon, see Christina El Mahdy, *Tutankhamen. The Life and Death of the Boy King*.

References

Althusser, Louis (1971), "Ideology and Ideological State Apparatuses", *Lenin and Philosophy*, New York: Monthly Review Press, pp. 127–86.

Anderton, Frances (1997), *The Success of Excess*, London: Ellipsis.

Baudrillard, Jean (1983), "The Orders of Simulacra", *Simulations*, translated by Foss, P., Patton, P. and Beitchman, P., New York: Semiotext[e].

—— (1988), "Simulacra and Simulations", in Poster, Mark (ed.), *Jean Baudril-lard. Selected Writings*, Stanford, CA: Stanford University Press, pp. 166–84.

—— (1989), *America*, translated by Turner, C., London: Verso.

Benjamin, Walter (1999), *The Arcades Project*, translated by Howard, E. and McLaughlin, K., Cambridge MA: The Belknap Press of Harvard University Press.

Brooks, David (2000), *Bobos in Paradise. The New Upper Class and How They Got There*, New York: Simon & Schuster.

Bruny, Tom and O'Conner, Clydean (2002), "Man Fears Time, Time Fears the Pyramids", Press Release.

Carter, Howard and Mace, A. C. (1977), *The Discovery of the Tomb of Tutan-khamen*. New York: Dover Publications.

Cass, Jeffrey and Dennis, Dion (1996), "Ground Zero: Las Vegas Luxor. An Imagined Archaeology of American Post-Civilization", *CTheory*, Event-Scenes (E062), November 6 (http://www.ctheory.net).

Davis, Mike (1992), *City of Quartz*, New York: Vintage Books.

Dear, Michael (2000), *The Postmodern Urban Condition*, Oxford: Blackwell.

El Mahdy, Christine (1999), *Tutankhamen. The Life and Death of the Boy King*, New York: St. Martin's Press.

MacKenzie, John (1995), *Orientalism. History, Theory and the Arts*, Manchester and New York: Manchester University Press.

Matthews, Stanley (1993), "Architecture in the Age of Hyperreality", *Architronic*: 1–7.

Mugurauer, Robert (1995), *Interpreting Environments. Tradition. Deconstruction. Hermeneutics*, Austin, TX: University of Texas Press.

Newitz, Annalee (2000), "What Makes Things Cheesy? Satire, Multinationalism and B-Movies", *Social Text*, 18(2): 59–82.

O'Conner, Clydean (2002), Interview by author, Las Vegas NV, 5 August.

Rothman, Hal (2002), *Neon Metropolis. How Las Vegas Started the 21st Century*, New York, London: Routledge.

Said, Edward (1979), *Orientalism*, New York: Vintage Books.

—— (1993), *Culture and Imperialism*, New York: Alfred Knopf.

—— (1999), *Out of Place*, New York: Alfred Knopf.

—— (2000), "Egyptian Rites", *Reflections on Exile and Other Essays*, Cambridge, MA: Harvard University Press.

—— (2002), "Invention, Memory, and Place", in Mitchell, W. J. T. (ed.), *Landscape and Power*, 2nd edition, Chicago and London: University of Chicago Press, pp. 241–59.

Sedgewick, Eve Kosofsky (1985), *Between Men. English Literature and Homosocial Desire*, New York: Columbia University Press.

Sorkin, Michael (1992), "See You in Disneyland", in Sorkin, Michael (ed.), *Variations on a Theme Park. The New American City and the End of Public Space*, New York: Hill & Wang, pp. 204–32.

Spivak, Gayatri Chakravorty (1999), *A Critique of Postcolonial Reason. Toward a History of the Vanishing Present*, Cambridge MA: Harvard University Press.

Taylor, Mark C. (1992), *Disfiguring. Art, Architecture, Religion*, Chicago and London: University of Chicago Press.

The Making of the Luxor, (1994), Scott Morris Productions.

Venturi, R., Scott Brown, D. and Izenour, S. (1994, 1972), *Learning from Las Vegas: The Forgotten Symbolism of Architectural Form*, Cambridge MA: MIT Press.

Willis, Sharon (1989, 1988), "Spectacular Topographies: Amerique's Post Modern Spaces", in Diani, Marco and Ingraham, Catherine (eds), *Restructuring Architectural Theory*, Evanston IL: Northwestern University Press, pp. 60–66.

Index

About, Edmond, *King of the Mountain*, 39
academic study, Greece, 44–5
Adler, Judith, 2, 24, 53–4
agency, 3
Aguilar, M., 135
Alcázar of Toledo, Spain, 93, 94 (Figures 5.1, 5.2), 104–5
    declaration as national monument, 96–7
    publications, 97–9, 101
    religious conventions, 95, 98–101
    representations, 101–4
    siege, 93–5
    site of memory, 96
    tourist destination, 95–8
    see also Toledo, Spain
Alfonso VI, King of Spain, 93, 102
Alfonso XIII, King of Spain, 131, 139, 141
Alhambra, Granada, Spain, 141
Alsace, France, 151
    pavilion, Regional Center, Paris, 153, 154 (Figure 8.3), 156
    see also fairs and exhibitions, Regional Center, Paris
Althusser, Louis, 250
Andalusia, Spain, 129, 141–2
Angelou, Maya, 113
Annals of Tourism Research, xv
antiquities, Greece, 37
Apollo Belvedere, 21, 24
Appadurai, Arjun, 195
    globalization, 200
    indigenization, 235
    Modernity at Large, 234–5
Arab Café, Tripoli, Libya, 81, 82 (Figure 4.2)
Arch of Constantine, Rome, 55
architectural and design practice, xvi
architectural collage, 134
architectural history, 4, 5
architourism, 10
Armstrong, Isabel, 41–2

Ashworth, Gregory and J. E. Tunbridge, 2, 8
Athens, Greece, 39
Aubert, O. L., 158
Augé, Marc, 3
    "non-places," 200
authenticity, xviii, 9, 19–20, 24, 81, 89
    actions, 111, 121–3, 122 (Figure 6.3), 125n8
    individual, 111, 118–21
    performance, 137–8
    see also MacCannell, Dean
automobile *raid*, 75, 80
    see also transportation, Libya
Ávila, Spain, 97, 129, 141
Ayala, Mariano López de, 96

Badoglio, Pietro, 83
Baedeker guides, 23, 59
Balbo, Italo, 77, 79, 83
Barcelona, Spain, 131
Barnett, Canon, 66
Barthes, Roland, 214, 237n2
Baudrillard, Jean, 227–8, 236, 260
Beaux-Arts architects, 44–5
Beckford, William, *Italy*, 58
Bell, Claudia and John Lyall, 2
Belloc, Hilaire, 67
Belvedere Antinous, 21
Belvedere Torso, 21, 29
Benghazi, Libya, 77, 79
Benjamin, Walter, 19, 259
Berbers, 83, 84, 87, 89
    see also indigenous culture, Libya
Berkeley, Busby, 213
Bhabha, Homi, 202
Bilbao, Spain
    Basque separatism, 229–30
    development, 228–9, 237n4
    see also museums – Guggenheim Museum, Bilbao
Birchall, Emily, 61

Blache, Paul Vidal de la, 150
Black Arts, 114
Black Power Movement, 114
Blue Guide, 25
Boone, Sylvia Ardyn, 113
Bourdieu, Pierre, 54, 260
    habitus, 197
Bracci, Pietro, cameo casts, 21, 22 (Figure 1.3),
    30–1
Brach, Libya, 80
Breton, France, 160
bridal chambers, 208–9
Bride's Magazine, 209, 214, 221
British Society of the Dilettanti, 40
British tourists, Italy, 53
    see also tourism
bronze replicas, 18
Brooks, David, 251
Brunete, Spain, 97
Buchon, Jean-Alexandre, 45–6
Bueno, Guzmán el, 102
Buïgas, Carles, 140
Bulcroft, Kris and Richard, and Linda Smeins,
    221
Byron, Lord, 54
Byzantine architecture, 41–8 passim

Café del Pueblo Español, Barcelona, Spain,
    135
    see also fairs and exhibitions, Poble
        Espanyol, Barcelona
Calatrava, Santiago, 229
calzada del Cerro, Habana, Cuba, 179
Calzini, Raffaele, *Da Leptis Magna a
    Gadames*, 80
Camillo, Giulio, 33
Cancúnization, 170, 172
Carcassone, France, 153
Carlos, Don, 96
Carnarvon, Lord, 254
Carpenter, Edmund, xviii
Carpentier, Alejo, 183
Carreras y Candi, Francisco, 134
Carter, Howard, 253–5
    The Discovery of the Tomb of Tutankhamen,
        255
cartes de visite, 65
Castile, Spain, 129, 131, 135

castles and forts
    Cape Coast, Ghana, 109, 110, 112 (Figure
        6.1), 113–15 passim, 116, 118–23
        passim
    Christianborg castle, Osu, Ghana, 109
    Elmina, Ghana, 109, 110, 113–15 passim,
        116, 117 (Figure 6.2), 118–22 passim
    Ghana, 109–10
Castro, Fidel, 178
Castro regime, Cuba
    development policies, 167–8, 174, 181
Catalonia, Spain, 132, 135
Catholic Monarchs, Spain, 95, 101–2
Catholicism, 56
Centre Pompidou, Paris, 227–8, 230–1
Champs-de-Mars, Paris, 147
Chandler, Richard, *Ionian Antiquities*, 40
Charles V, King of Spain, 93, 95, 101, 102
Charles-Brun, Jean, 150
Chillida, Eduardo, 231
Christianity
    conquest of Spain, 98
Chronicle of the Morea, 45–6
Cicero, 32
cinematic space, 130, 135
Cipriani, Lidio, 80, 89
Clémentel, Etienne, 150
Clifton, James, xviii
Coleman, Simon and Mike Crang, 4
collage, 7
collection
    body of knowledge, 30
    pastime, 29–30
    print and cast, 29
collective memory, 16, 139
Colombier, Pierre du, 160
colonial politics
    Libya, 79
    Mauritius, 201
Colosseum, Rome, 15, 55
comfort, 197
commodification, 1
    environment, 198
    place, xvii
Communism, Spain, 95
composition, *Beaux-Arts*, 153, 156
Congress of Colonial Studies, Italy, 83
consumption, 10

Cook, Thomas, 40, 63
  see also tourist industry
Coppola, Francis Ford, *Godfather II*, 173
Corinth, Greece, 43
Cortez, Hernán, 172
Côte d'Azur, France, 151
Couchaud, André, *Choix d'églises byzantines en Grèce*, 44, 45 (Figure 2.1)
Coyula, Mario, 171
Crang, Phil, 196
Crouch, David and Nina Lübbren, 4
crusades
  nineteenth century legacy, 45–6
Cuba
  General Assembly, 171
  Ministry of Tourism, 181
  Spanish colonial rule, 167
cultural exchange, 1
cultural production, 10
cultural productivity, xviii

Dauphiné, France, 151
Davis, Mike, 252, 260
De Bono, Emilio, 83
Dear, Michael J., *The Postmodern Urban Condition*, 243, 257
Debord, Guy, 236, 238n11
Del Castillo, Orestes, 170
Deleuze, Gilles and Félix Guattari, 237n6
Dent, J.M., 66
desire, image of, 9
Di Fausto, Florestano, 78, 84–9 passim
Didion, Joan, 218
difference, 130
diorama, 135
Disney Corporation, 251
Disney World, 221, 242, 244–5
Disneyland, 199
"Door of No Return," 116, 123
Dorée, Gustave, 39
Dorfles, Gilles, 207–8, 211, 219
  see also kitsch environments
Dörpfeld, Wilhelm, 41–2 passim
Douglas, James, 68
Doyle, Richard, *The Foreign Tour*, 61, 62 (Figure 3.2)
Du Bois, W.E.B., 113, 124n5
Duban, Félix-Jacques, 44

Duc, Louis, 44
Dufrène, Maurice, 152

early travelers, Greece, 38–9
  representations, 42–4
Eco, Umberto, 199
Edensor, Tim, 2–3, 53, 194, 198, 202
edutainment, 256
Egypt, ancient, static interpretation, 244
Eiffel Tower, Paris, 147
Eisner, Robert, 39
El Cid (Rodrigo Díaz de Vivar), 102
El Escorial, Spain, 97
Eliot, George, *Romola*, 63
ETA movement (Euskadi ta Askatasuna), 229–30
Etruscan she-wolf, 15
Evelyn, John, 32
exotic, 194
  themes, 195
Extremadura, Spain, 129
Eyewitness Travel Guides, 25

fairs and exhibitions
  Exhibition of the War Trophies Taken from the Enemy, San Sebastián, Spain, 97
  Exposition internationale des arts et des techniques dans la vie moderne (1937), Paris, 147
  Ibero-American Exposition, Seville, 139, 141
  International Exposition, Barcelona (1888), 139
  International Exposition, Barcelona (1929), 129, 132, 139–40 passim
  Poble Espanyol, Barcelona, 129–30, 130 (Figure 7.1)
    design, 133–4, 137 (Figure 7.3)
    National representation, 141–3
    planning and design, 133–7
    regional festivals, 137, 138 (Figure 7.4)
    site of collective memory, 138–9
    see also Café del Pueblo Español, Barcelona
  Regional Center, Paris, 147–9
    building type, 153–4
    centralization, 150
    goals, 147–9
    mapping of France, 150–1

master plan, 148 (Figure 8.1), 151–2, 152
    (Figure 8.2)
materials, 154–6
modernism, 149, 151, 159
publicity and representations, 157
results, 158–9, 161
style, 152–3
see also Alsace, France; Flandre-Artois,
    France; France, history of regions;
    regionalism
World Exposition, Paris (1878), 167
Falangist Party, Spain, 95, 96
Farnese Hercules, 21
Feelings, Tom, 113
Felini, Pietro Martire, 23–4, 25, 26 (Figure 1.4)
Ferdinand and Isabelle of Spain, 95
Ferguson, James, 47
film, 1, 3, 111
    authenticating actions, 122–3
Finsterlin, Hermann, 228
Flamenco, 141, 144
Flandre-Artois, France
    pavilion, 153, 155 (Figure 8.4), 156
    see also fairs and exhibitions, Regional
        Center, Paris
Florence, Italy, 55, 57–9, 61, 63, 65–6
Folgera, Francesc and Ramón Reventós, 132–5
    passim
Forestier, J.C. Nicolas, 167
Forster, E.M., *A Room with a View*, 23, 59, 68
Foster, Norman, 229
Foucault, Michel, 33
Foxá, Augustín de, 100
France
    history of regions, 150
    see also fairs and exhibitions, Regional
        Center, Paris
Franco, General Francisco, 93, 95–105 passim
Fratelli Alinari, 66
French Historical Monuments Service, 40
French Regionalist Federation (FRF), 148, 150
Furner, Mary, xv
Fusco, Coco, 2

Galicia, Spain, 129
Garian, Libya, 77
Gaudí, Antonio, 231
Gehry, Frank, 227, 229–30 passim, 233–4

Genoa, Italy, 55, 58
German Archeological Institute, 40
Germina, Haile, *Sankofa*, 122–3
Ghadames, Libya, 75, 77, 82–4, 87–9
Ghana
    Museum and Monuments Board, 109, 119
    see also castles and forts
Gillis, John, 138
global tourism, 111, 113
globalization and regional identity, 235
Godbarge, Henri, 159–60
Goethe, Johann Wofgang von, 18, 37, 57, 59
    Faust, 46
Golan, Romy, 155
Goldberger, Paul, 171–2
Gone With the Wind, 193–4, 200
Good Housekeeping, 220
Goodman, Nelson, 54
Gothic, origins, 44–8 passim
Gottdiener, Mark, 199
Government Office of Indigenous Applied Arts,
    Libya, 81
    see also indigenous culture, Libya
Grand Tour, 17, 23, 24, 37–8, 54–5, 58
Graziani, Rodolfo, 75
Greber, Jacques, 149
Greene, Graham, *Our Man in Havana*, 173
Greenhill, Hooper, 29
Greenwood, Davydd J., xv, xviii
Guevara, Ché, 178, 183
Guggenheim Museum, Bilbao
    see museums, Guggenheim Museum, Bilbao
guidebooks, 98

Habana Vieja, Cuba, 167, 168–9
    colonial heritage, 168, 171–3
    Habaguanex company hotels, 174–6, 175
        (Figure 9.2), 179
    heritage sites, 172
    master plan, 169
    North American domination, 173–4
    Plaza Vieja, 180 (Figure 9.3)
    tourist appropriation, 179–81
    tourist destination, 176–7
    tourist system, 166
    tourists and *Habaneros*, 177–80
    see also Habana Vieja, Miramar
        neighborhood; Vedado neighborhood

Index

Hadid, Zaha, 236
Haley, Alex, 114
Hansen, Christian, 43
  and Theophilus Hansen, 44
Hare, Augustus, *Walks in Rome*, 59
Hefner, Hugh, 218
Heideck, Karl Wilhelm von, 43
Heidegger, Martin, 33–4, 230
Hemingway, Ernest, 174
Herculaneum, Italy, 40, 55
heritage tourism, 7, 166
  see also tourism
Hermant, Paul, 157
Hernandez, Angel Llorente, 96
Hersey, George, *High Renaissance Art in St. Peter's and the Vatican*, 25–7
Hess, Peter Von, 43
Hetherington, Kevin, 53
Higuero Bazaga, Francisco, 142
Hints to Lady Travelers, 65
Hispanidad, 95
historic preservation, 81, 88–90, 119–20
historical reenactment, 111
history, Fascist retelling of, 6
Hitchcock, Henry Russell, and Philip Johnson, 161n2
Hobsbawm, Eric and Terrence Ranger, xviii
Hogarth, William, 21–3, 28, 31
holy relic, 18
Holzer, Jenny, 231
honeymoon resorts, Poconos, PA, 208–10
  advertisement, 210 (Figure 11.1), 214–17, 215 (Figure 11.2), 216 (Figure 11.3), 217 (Figure 11.4)
  cinematic themes, 213
  Cove Haven, 209, 212–13, 221
    advertisement, 214–15, 216 (Figure 11.3)
  design strategies, 212–13
  Honeymoon Haven, 209–10, 210 (Figure 11.1)
  modern tourist industry, 221
  Mount Airy Lodge, 209–10, 212
  Pocono Gardens Lodge, 209, 213
    advertisement, 214, 215 (Figure 11.2)
  programmed activities, 219–20
  Rococo effects, 210–11
  sexual performance, 217–19
  see also hotels; resorts; *Life Magazine*

honeymooning, 207–8, 211, 221
hotels
  Fontainebleu Hotel, Miami Beach, FL, 212–13
  Hostal Conde de Villanueva, Habana Vieja, Cuba, 176
  Hostal del Tejadillo, Habana Vieja, Cuba, 176
  Hostal el Comendador, Habana Vieja, Cuba, 176
  Hotel Ain el-Fras, Ghadames, Libya, 87–9, 88 (Figure 4.5)
  Hotel Florida, Habana Vieja, Cuba, 176
  Hotel Nalut, Libya, 85–7, 86 (Figure 4.4)
  Hotel Rumia, Jefren, Libya, 84–5, 85 (Figure 4.3)
  Hotel Santa Isabel, Habana Vieja, Cuba, 176
  Hotel Telégrafo, Habana Vieja, Cuba, 176
  Libya, 79, 84–9
  Luxor Las Vegas, NV, xviii, 242 (Figure 13.1), 243, 245
    Attractions Level, 245
    capitalist seduction, 257–61, 258 (Figure 13.4)
    Casino Level, 245
    consumerism, 255–7
    Games of the Gods video arcade, 258–9
    Giza Galleria, 249–50, 249 (Figure 13.2)
    images of Egypt, 248–50
    invented traditions, 250–5
    Pharoah's Pheast, 247–8, 255–7, 256 (Figure 13.3)
    postmodern Orientalism, 243–8
    souvenirs, 255
    Treasure Chamber, 250, 261n1
    Virtual Reality ride, 244
  Uaddan Hotel and Casino, Tripoli, Libya, 77
  see also honeymoon resorts; Lapidus, Morris; Mandalay Resort Group; resorts
Hugo, Victor, 40
human geography movement, 150

identity construction, 7
Illustración Ibero-Americana, 140, 143
Ilouz, Eva, 219
indigenous architecture, Libya, 84–9 passim
  see also troglodyte houses, Libya
indigenous culture, Libya, 75, 80, 90
  see also Berbers; Tuareghs

indigenous politics, Libya, 76
industrialization and urbanization, 64
Ingold, Tim and Terhi Kurttila, "taskscapes,"
  197
International Commission on Monuments
  (ICOM), 110
Islam, 44
Isozaki, Arata, 229
Italian Touring Club (TCI), 77, 80
Italy, modern, 54
Italy, nineteenth century tourism, 54–5
Itinerario Tripoli-Gadames, 84, 86

Jackson, J.B., 10
Jackson, Zig, 2
Jefren, Libya, 77, 83, 84–5
Josephson, Mary, 211
journal writing, 56
Judd, Dennis R., "tourist bubble," 2, 178–9

Kahn, Louis, 227
Kakum National Park, Ghana, 110
Kandinsky, Wassily, 233
Kardomyle, Greece, 46
Kelsall, G., 199
Kemble, Fanny, 57
Kirschenblatt-Gimblett, Barbara, 115
kitsch environments, 207–8
  see also Dorfles, Gillo
Koolhaas, Rem, 251
Koons, Jeff, 231
Kothari, Uma and Vidula Nababsing, 201
Krazeisen, Karl, 43
Kyparissia, Greece, 46–7, 47 (Figure 2.2)

Labbé, Edmond, 147–9 passim, 151–2 passim
Labrouste, Henri, 44
Lafréry, Antoine, 18, 19
Lagarde, Eduardo, 96
Lam, Wilfredo, 183
Landau, David and Peter Parshall, 29
Languedoc, France, 151, 153
Lansky, Meyer, 173
Laocoön group, 21, 24
Lapidus, Morris, Fontainebleu hotel, 212–13
Las Vegas, Nevada, 199
  "Egyptian Day," 253
Le Bas, Philippe, 43

Le Corbusier, Mundaneum Project, 234
Le Corbusier, *ville radieuse*, 228
Leal Spengler, Eusebio, 169–74 passim,
  177–84 passim
Lee, Vernon, 66, 67
Lefebvre, Henri, 8
Legoretta, Ricardo, 229
Lennon, John and Malcolm Foley, 113
Leoni, Leone, *Charles V and the Fury*, 101
Letrosne, Charles, 159
Lever, Charles, 63
Lewis, Norman, 174
Libeskind, Daniel, 233
Libya, 79
Libyan Tourism and Hotel Association (ETAL),
  77, 81, 83, 86
  see also tourism – system, Libya
Life Magazine, honeymoon suites, 215–16
  see also honeymoon resorts
Lippard, Lucy, 2
literary discourse, 83
local materials, 153
Lynch, Kevin, 69n2

Machimbarrena, Vincente, 100–1
Madrid, Spain, 97, 104, 139
Maigrot, Emile, 157
Mandalay Resort Group, 248, 250, 260
  see also hotels – Luxor, Las Vegas, NV
Marineau, Harriet, *How to Observe*, 56
Marseilles Cathedral, France, 44
Marzuq, Libya, 80
mass spectacle, 134–5
Massey, Doreen, 189, 198, 202
Matthews, Stanley, "Architecture in the Age of
  Hyperreality," 246
Maubourg, Michel, 157–8
Mauritius, 189–90
  colonial representation, 201–2
  Creole colonial style, 190, 191 (Figure 10.1)
  economy, 191–2
  mobile enclaves, 195
  modern nation, 201
  plantations, 191
  racial demographics, 192
  slaves and indentured workers, 191–2
Mayne, Thom, 167
MacCannell, Dean

front and back regions, 115
modern ethnography, 33
staged authenticity, xv, xviii, , 1–2, 76, 111
see also authenticity
McKim, Mead & White, 173
Meade, L.T., 67
mediation, 3
mass, 166
medieval buildings and sites, Greece, 38, 40–1
memory
art of, 32
performance, 111, 114
Mexias, Juan Francés y, 104
Michelangelo
Moses, 18, 25–8, 26 (Figure 1.4)
Pietà, 15
Mies van der Rohe, Ludwig, 129
Mihura, Jules, 149
Millet, Gabriel, *Greek School of Byzantine Architecture*, 39, 47–8
travel to Greece, 48, 49 (Figure 2.3)
Miramar neighborhood, Habana, Cuba, 168
see also Habana Vieja, Cuba
modernity
elimination of, 140
modernization
Libya, 76, 79
Mont Blanc, France, 154
monuments
Rome, 15, 17, 19, 25
Mordini, Antonio, 80
Morton, Patricia, 76
Moscardó, Colonel José, 93–5, 97, 102–5 passim
Moscardó, Luís, 93, 95
Mugerauer, Robert, 247–8
Muguruza, Pedro, 100
Murray, John, *Handbooks*, 58–61 passim
Muschamp, Herbert, 10, 237n7
museums
Casa de la Obra Pía, Habana Vieja, Cuba, 176
Guggenheim Museum, Bilbao, Spain, xviii, 227–8 passim, 228 (Figure 12.1), 232 (Figure 12.2)
exterior, 234
interior and galleries, 231–2

politics of appearance, 235–6
site relationships, 230–1
Museum of Colonial Art, Habana Vieja, Cuba, 176
Museum of Contemporary Art, Habana Vieja, Cuba, 174
Museum of Mementos of Toledo's Alcazar, Spain, 96
Museum of Rum, Habana Vieja, Cuba, 174
Museum of the Maqueta, Habana Vieja, Cuba, 176
Museum of the National Revolution, Spain, proposal, 96
Mussolini, Benito, 75
Mystras, Greece, 43, 46, 48

Naipaul, V.S., 189
Nalut, Libya, 77, 83, 85–7
Naples, 55, 58
Napoleon III, 39
national heritage, 132
negotiated meanings, 199
neo-grèc architects, 44, 47
Neumann, Mark, 2–3
New Orleans Jazz, 193–4, 200
Newitz, Annalee, 259
Niagara Falls, 207
Niquet, Stephane, 44
Nkrumah, Kwame, 113, 124n5
Nogués, Xavier, 132–3, 135, 143
Nora, Pierre, *lieux des memoire*, 114–15, 122
Normandy, France, 151

Ockman, Joan, 4
Office of the Historian, Cuba, activities, 169–71, 185n2
publications, 181–3
restoration practices, 170
Okey, Thomas, *The Story of Venice*, 66
Olympia, Greece, 40–2 passim
opera sarcinesca, 41
Opus Habana, 182–3
organized travel, Greece, 40
Orientalism, postmodern, 241–2, 246, 259
originaires, 150
orthodox religious buildings, Greece, 43–4
Otamendi, Miner, 98–9

Otto, King of Greece, 39
Ottoman Empire, 41

Padua, Italy, 55
Paestum, Italy, 55
Palgrave, Francis, 58
Pan African Festival of Performing Arts, 111,
  121
Pantheon, Rome, Italy, 55
Parr, Martin, 2
Passarell, Jaume, 142
patriotic tourism, 96
Patronato Nacional de Turismo, 140
Payne, Edith, 41
Pelli, Cesar, 229
Peloponnese, 39, 45
Pennell, Elizabeth Robins, 67
Philip II, King of Spain, 93, 95, 101, 172
photography, xvii, 1, 3, 7, 111
  authenticating action, 121–3
  authenticity, 131–2, 133–4, 143–4
  fragmentation, 134, 143–4
Piano, Renzo and Richard Rodgers, 227
Piccioli, Angelo, *La Porta Magica del Sahara*,
  83
pilgrimage, 17
Piranesi, Giovanni Battista
  Antichità Romane, 28, 31
  representational conventions and techniques,
    20–1
  Veduta della vasta Fontana di Trevi, 19–21,
    20 (Figure 1.2)
  views of Rome, 19–20, 28
Pisa, Italy, 55
Plandiura, Lluís, 132–3
plaster casts, 18
Playboy, 218
Plaza de Armas, Habana Vieja, 176–7
Pocono Mountains, 207
  description, 209
Polevitzky, Igor B., and Verner Johnson, 173
politics, cultural and economic, xvi
politics of appearance, 235–6
Polynesian themes, 190
Pompeii, Italy, 40, 55
Ponte Fabricio, Rome, Italy, 28
Pope Julius II, 25
Popular Front Party, 157

popular imagery, 3
postcards, 60 (Figure 3.1), 67, 68 (Figure 3.3),
  98, 137–8
preservation, 7
  indigenous culture, 81–2
  see also urban preservation
Presidential Palace, Havana, now Museum of
  the Revolution, 168
Price, Cecric, 227
Primo de Rivera, General Miguel, 131, 139–40
printing workshops, 17
propaganda, Spain, 93–6
Provence, France, 151, 153
Pugin, Augustus Charles, 44
Pyrénées, France, 151, 153, 160

Queen, 56
Quicchelberg, Samuel van, 30, 32
Quintilian, *Institutio Oratoria*, 32–3

regionalism, 8, 150
  centralized, 150
  architecture, France, 159–60
  see also fairs and exhibitions, Regional
    Center, Paris
Regionalist Commission, 147
reification, xvii
representations of antiquities, Greece, 40
resorts
  Sugar Beach Resort, Mauritius, 190–1
    aesthetic theme, 192
    tourist enclave, 194–6, 198, 203–4
    Colonial space, 200–3
    mixed authenticity, 193–4
    themed performance, 192–4, 193 (Figure
      10.2)
    tourist stages, 196–7
  see also honeymoon resorts, hotels
Ricci, Matteo, 33
Rogers, Samuel, 54
Romanesque, 44
Romantic Historicism, 42, 43, 48
Rome, 55, 57, 61, 64–5, 67
  early modern, 16–17
  pensionnaires, 40
roots tourism, 110, 113–14, 118, 119, 121, 123
Ross, Dorothy, xv
Rossi, Aldo, 3, 237n1

Index

Rothman, Hal, *Neon Metropolis*, 245
Ruskin, John, 44, 55, 64, 66
   Stones of Venice, 58

Sabha, Libya, 80
Said, Edward, 195, 200
   Culture and Imperialism, 253–4
   "Egyptian Rites," 243, 255
   "Invention, Memory and Place," 250
   Orientalism, 248
Saint Andrew, Patras, Greece, 42
San Francisco de Paula, Havana, Cuba, 174
Santiago-Irizarry, Vilma, xviii
Santomeri, Greece, 43
Savoie, France, 151
   pavilion, Regional Center, Paris, 154
   see also Regional Center, Paris
Scarin, Emilio, *L'Insediamento umano nella*
   Libia occidentale, 83
Schiller, Friedrich, 43
Schmidt, Leigh Eric, 211
School for Advanced Study in Hotel
   Administration and Tourism, Habana, 181
Schultze & Weaver, 173
Scorsese, Martin, *Casino*, 241, 260–1
Segovia, Spain, 97
Segre, Roberto, 173
Seligson, Marcia, 212
Sennett, Richard, 197–8
Serlio, Sebastiano, 18
Serra, Richard, 231
Sert, José Maria, *El Diario Vasco*, 100
Servicio de Recuperación del Patrimonio
   Artistico (SERPAN), 100
Sharah al-Shatt, Libya, 77
sightseeing, 58
Simpson, Veldon, 246–7
Sims, G.R., 67–8
simulacrum, 147, 150, 157
Sin Novedad en el Alcázar/L'assedio
   dell'Alcazar, 101
Slave Routes Project, 110
slave trade, 109, 111
Smith, Valene, xv
smooth tourist space, 8, 195–8 passim
   see also Edensor, Tim
Soriano, Federico and Dolores Palacios, 229
Sorkin, Michael, 199, 242

Sotomayor, Fernando Álvarez de, 102, 103
   (Figure 5.3)
souvenirs, xvii, 1, 3, 5, 16 (Figure 1.1), 137–8,
   166 (Figure 9.1)
   authenticity, 24–5
   cabinet of curiosities, 31, 32 (Figure 1.5)
   definition, 15–16, 34n1
   early industry, 17–19, 24
   format, 21
   fragmentation, and reconstruction, 27–8
   logics, 34
   mass produced, 18, 23
   medieval, 18
   memory, 32–3
   reproducibility, 18–19
   social implications, 21–3
   tourist vision, 24
Soviet Union, 168
Spain
   see Alcázar of Toledo, Spain; fairs and
     exhibitions, Poble Espanyol, Barcelona
Spanish Civil War, 93, 95
spectacle, 236
   postmodern, 9
   see also Debord, Guy
Spivak, Gayatri Chakravorty, *Critique of*
   Postcolonial Reason, 254
staged tourist environments, xvii–xviii
Starke, Marianna, *Letters*, 58
Stern, Robert A.M., 229
Stirling, James and Michael Wilford, 229
Stuart, James and Nicholas Revett, *Antiquities*
   of Athens, 40
Sudan, 82
Suknah, Libya, 80
Suñer, Ramón Serrano, 97
Switzerland, 55
Symons, Arthur, *Cities of Italy*, 65, 67

Taut, Bruno, Glass Chain circle, 228
Taylor, Catherine, *Letters*, 55–7, 64
Thackeray, William, 61
themed space, 8, 189, 196
   authenticity, 199
   reconsidering, 198–200, 203–4
   see also Edensor, Tim
Tischbein, Heinrich Wilhelm, 37
Tivoli, Italy, 55

Toledo, Spain, 93, 97, 104
  see Alcázar of Toledo, Spain
Touring Club of France, 148
Tourism Pavilion, Regional Center, Paris, 161
  see also Regional Center, Paris
tourism
  activities, Libya, 77–8
  amenities, Ghana, 109–10
  architecture, Libya, 79, 84–9 passim
  authenticity, 115–18, 120–1
    Alcázar of Toledo, 100–1
    Mauritius, 192–4
  built environment, xviii–xix, 1
  colonialism, xvi
  consumption, 42
  craft industries in Libya, 81
  cultural importance, xvii–xix, 53
  development, 6
  environments, xvii–xviii
    Libya, 81–2
  experience, 131
    Libya, 75, 81
  historic preservation, 119–20
  industry, xvi, 1, 41
    Spain, 140
  itineraries, 1
  memory, 114
  modernity, 140–1
  modernization, 64–5
  moral judgements, xix
  narratives, 54
  nationalism, Spain, 95–8, 141
  performance, 53–4, 189
  popular imagery, 3–4
  practices, xv, xvii, 4–6 passim
    British middle class, 55–6, 65–6
    British middle class, criticism, 61–4
    historical genesis, xvi
    photography, 65–6
  propaganda, Spain, 95–6, 98–9, 101–5
  publications, Italy, guidebooks, 58–61
  race, 90, 118–19
  regenerative force, 166
  regionalism, 160
  religious devotion, 98
  representations
    caricatures of early travelers, 39
    literary, 67–8
    stereotypical, 56–8

Rome, 17
scientific research, 80, 83
simulation, xvi
sites, meaning, 3
social class, xix–xx, 20, 23
Socialist politics in Cuba, 183–4
system, Libya, 76, 77–9, 78 (Figure 4.1),
  83–4
types, xix
workers, 196
  see also British tourists; heritage tourism;
    Libyan Tourism and Hotel Association;
    photography
tourists
  archaeologists, 245
  student, 66
tradition and modernity, 156
Traficante, Santo Jr., 173
transportation, Libya, motor coaches, 79, 83
  see also automobile *raid*
transportation, railway, 40
travel
  history, Greece, 37
  industry, 54
  letters, 56
  publications, Greece, 38–9
  to Italy, nineteenth century, 54–5
  writing, 5
  nineteenth century, 37–8
Tripoli, Libya, 77, 79
Tripolitania, Libya, 75, 76
troglodyte houses, Libya, 84
  see also indigenous architecture, Libya
Trollope, Frances, 62
Tuareghs, 80
  see also indigenous culture, Libya
Tuckett, Elizabeth, 63–4
Tung, Anthony, 184
Turkey, travel publications, 38
Tutankhamen, King, museum, 252–3
Tyler, Anne, 245

UNESCO, 110
  designation of Cape Coast and Elmina, 113
  designation of Habana Vieja, 171
urban preservation, 8
  see also preservation
Urrutia, Federico de, 96
Urry, John, 2

Index

Utebo Bell Tower, Zaragoza, 134, 136 (Figure 7.2)
  see also fairs and exhibitions, Poble Espanyol, Barcelona
Utrillo, Miguel, 132–3
Utzon, Jørn, 233, 237n8

Vaillat, Léandre, 151
Vatican Museum, 30–1
Vaudoyer, Léon, Marseilles Cathedral, 44
Vedado neighborhood, Habana, Cuba, 171
  see also Habana Vieja, Cuba
Venetian Gates of Nauplion, Greece, 42
Venice, Italy, 55, 56, 61
Venturi, Robert, Denise Scott Brown and Steven Izenour, 9–10, 246–7
  "decorated shed," 242
  Learning from Las Vegas, 234
Venus de' Medici, 21
Verneihl, Félix de, 44
Verona, Italy, 55, 61
Vesalius, Andreas, *De humani corporis fabrica*, 28–9
Vie d'Italia, 77, 80

Villadomat, Domingo, *Laureados de España*, 102
Viollet-le-Duc, Eugène-Emmanuel, 44
Volpi, Giuseppe, 75, 76, 82–3

Walsh, Kevin, 115
War Routes, Spain, 96–7
Weems, Carrie Mae, *Slave Coast Series*, 122
Weld, Charles, 208
Wharton, Annabel Jane, 4
Wharton, Edith, 58–9
Wilkins, Morris, 213–14, 217
Winckelmann, Johann, 30, 37
women travelers, 65
Wood, Robert, 40
Woods, Joseph, 42
Wright, Frank Lloyd, 233–4
Wright, Richard, 109
  Black Power, 113
Wylie, John, 197

Zamora, Spain, 135
Zevi, Bruno, 234
Zukin, S., 199